The Companion to Richard Berengarten

Norman Jope has published four books of poems: *For The Wedding-Guest* (Stride Publications, 1997); *The Book of Bells and Candles* (Waterloo Press, 2009), *Dreams of the Caucasus* (Shearsman Books, 2010) and *Aphinar* (Waterloo Press, 2012). With the late Ian Robinson, he co-edited the anthology *In the Presence of Sharks: New Poetry from Plymouth* (Phlebas, 2006) and has edited the literary/cultural magazine *Memes*. His poetry and criticism have appeared in many magazines, webzines and anthologies, including *Tears in the Fence*, *Poetry Salzburg Review* and *Terrible Work*, and his poems are currently being translated into Romanian. Born in Plymouth, Norman Jope has lived in other UK cities, most recently Swindon and Bristol, and in Budapest. He currently works as an administrator at University College Plymouth St Mark & St John.

Paul Scott Derrick is a Senior Lecturer in American literature at the University of Valencia. His main fields of interest are Romanticism and American Trans-cendentalism and their manifestations in subsequent American literature and art. He has published two collections of essays in English and has co-authored a number of bilingual, critical editions of works by Ralph Waldo Emerson, Emily Dickinson and Henry Adams. He is co-editor of *Modernism Revisited: Transgressing Boundaries and Strategies of Renewal in American Poetry* (Rodopi, 2007). His most recent book-length publication is *La tierra de los abetos punti-agudos* (Biblioteca Javier Coy, 2008), a translation and critical study of Sarah Orne Jewett's *The Country of the Pointed Firs*. He has published translations into English of poems by Jorge Luis Borges, Luis Cernuda and Pablo Neruda, and co-translations of Richard Berengarten's poems into Spanish.

Catherine E. Byfield is a graduate of Lucy Cavendish College, Cambridge, where she read Anglo-Saxon, Norse and Celtic. Her main scholarly interest is Medieval Welsh dialogue literature. Her publications include a study of the *Pedeir Keinc y Mabinogi*, and Welsh translations of the *Ioca Monachorum* (co-authored and co-edited with M. J. Bayless), in journals such as the *Bulletin of the Board of Celtic Studies* and *Studia Celtica*. She is currently preparing editions and translations of four more Medieval Welsh texts, with critical commentaries, while working on her first novel. Born in Ohio, she moved permanently to the UK in 1978.

The Companion to Richard Berengarten

Edited by
Norman Jope,
Paul Scott Derrick
and
Catherine E. Byfield

Shearsman Books

Published in the United Kingdom in 2016 by
Shearsman Books Ltd
50 Westons Hill Drive
Emersons Green
BRISTOL
BS16 7DF

Shearsman Books Ltd Registered Office
30-31 St. James Place, Mangotsfield, Bristol BS16 9JB
(this address not for correspondence)

www.shearsman.com

ISBN 978-1-84861-447-5
Second Edition

*First published in 2011 by Salt Publishing, Cambridge,
as The Salt Companion to Richard Berengarten.*

Contents

Acknowledgements

Several essays in this volume have been published, some of them in variant forms, as follows:

Paul Scott Derrick (2010), 'A Poet for a Time of Need', *Jacket* (March) http://jacketmagazine.com/40/index.shtml

Maria Filippakopoulou (2009), 'Foreign in Our Own Country', *International Literary Quarterly* 9 (November) http://interlitq.org/issue9/filippakopoulou/job.php

Andrew Frisardi (2008), 'Black Suns on the Scales', *Contemporary Poetry Review: Archive* http://www.cprw.com/archive-plugnpay

philip kuhn (2010), '"'Tis Death is dead, not he" *or* Reading Richard Reading Richard Reading', *Jacket* (March) http://jacketmagazine.com/40/index.shtml

Andrija Matić (2007), 'Do vidjenja Danitsé': the beauty of complexity', *Sibila* http://www.sibila.com.br/index.php/sibila-english/362-goodbye-balkan-belle

Neli Moody (2010), 'A Syntax of Stones: Pre-Text, Edifice, and the Sacred Space in Richard Berengarten's "Avebury"', *Jacket* (March) http://jacketmagazine.com/40/index.shtml

Paschalis Nikolaou (2010), 'In Light of Hellas: Experiences of Greekness, Versions of Memory and Roles for Translation in Richard Berengarten's Poetry', *Jacket* (March) http://jacketmagazine.com/40/index.shtml

Aleksandar Petrov (2009), 'The Blue Butterfly Effect' (translated by Vera V. Radojević), *International Literary Quarterly* 7 (May) http://www.interlitq.org/issue7/aleksandar_petrov/job.php

Mark Pirie (2010), 'A Reading of *Book With No Back Cover*', *Jacket* (March) http://jacketmagazine.com/40/index.shtml

Simon Jenner (2010), 'Janus Masks: on the Many Facets of Richard Berengarten's Work', *Jacket* (March) http://jacketmagazine.com/40/index.shtml

Chee-Lay Tan (2010), 'Cross-cultural Numerology and Translingual Poetics: Chinese Influences on the Poetry of Richard Berengarten', *Jacket* (March) http://jacketmagazine.com/40/index.shtml

—. (2010). 'Cross-cultural Numerology and Translingual Poetics: Chinese Influences on the Poetry of Poet Richard Burns', C. L. Tan, *A Delicate Touch: Essays on Chinese Influences and Chinese Genres.* McGraw Hill Education (Asia): Singapore, pp. 1–17.

Stephen Wilson (2009), 'Hath Not a Jew Hands?', *International Literary Quarterly* 8 (August) http://www.interlitq.org/issue8/stephen_wilson/job.php

Two essays first appeared as follows:

Svetozar Ignjačević (2000), 'U znaku plavog leptira' ['At the sign of the Blue Butterfly'], *Zemlja čuda u izlomjenjom pogledalu – ponovo* [*Wonderland Through A Cracked Mirror – Again*]. Belgrade: Filološki Fakultet i Narodna Knjiga (171–186).

Slobodan Rakitić (2007), 'Pesnik u vlasti leptira' ['Poet in the power of a butterfly'], in RB, *Plavi Leptir* [*The Blue Butterfly*], Plava tačka, Belgrade and Kragujevčki oktobar, Kragujevac (pp. 151–156).

The editors would also like to thank the following translators: Vera V. Radojević for the three essays from Serbian, by Svetozar Ignjačević (pp. 302–314), Aleksandar Petrov (pp. 347–356) and Slobodan Rakitić (pp. 315–324); Michael Eleftheriou, for the essay by Nasos Vayenas from Greek (pp. 175–180); and Gabriele Poole and Vladimir Scott, for the essay by Mario Nicolao, from Italian (pp. 43–47).

Finally, the editors wish to express their thanks to Richard Berengarten who, from the beginning of this project, has been unstinting with advice, encouragement and friendship. We hope this book does justice to him and to his work.

NJ, PSD & CEB
February 2011

Abbreviations

General

AAE	*Academic American Encyclopedia* (1980)
Corr.	correspondence
NDQ	*North Dakota Quarterly*. See also *OOY* below
OED	*The Oxford English Dictionary*
RB	Richard Burns / Richard Berengarten
TES	*Times Educational Supplement*

Titles of works

For the following titles, the authorial name under which the work was published is shown in parentheses. Full publication details of each title are provided in the *Bibliography*, pp. 404–419.

ALF	'A little further? Twelve propositions'. http://www.berengarten.com/site/A-little-further.html (Berengarten, 2005)
ALF1	'A little further? Twelve propositions', *Serta* 9: 7–12 (Burns, 2006–2007)
AP	*Against Perfection* (Burns, 1999)
AVE	*Avebury* (Burns, first edition, 1972)
AVI	*Avebury* (Italian version, tr. Roberto Sanesi) (Burns, 1976)
BB	*The Blue Butterfly* (Berengarten, second edition, 2008)
BB1	*The Blue Butterfly* (Burns, first edition, 2005)
BL	*Black Light: Poems in Memory of George Seferis* (Burns, first edition, 1983)
BWNBC	*Book With No Back Cover* (Burns, 2003)
CRDT	Ceri Richards (1980), *Drawings to Poems by Dylan Thomas* (Burns, ed. 1980)
DF	*Double Flute* (Burns, 1972)
DVD	'Do vidjenja Danitsé' (in *UBL* below).
EVW	'Elegy for Vernon Watkins', poem by Roberto Sanesi, in *Poetry Wales* 17(2): 52–53 (Burns, tr. 1981)

FL   *For the Living* (Berengarten, second edition, 2008)

FL1   *For the Living* (Burns, first edition, 2004)

GTGS 'A Grove of Trees and a Grove of Stones' *Tel Aviv Review* (Burns, 1989–90) and in *OOY/NDQ* See also: http://www.berengarten.com/site/Grove-of-trees.html

GTGS1 'A Grove of Trees and a Grove of Stones' (Jadrana Veličković, Serbian tr., 'Gaj kamena i gaj drveča'). (Bernz, 1988)

IMW *Address to the Plenary Session of the 36th International Meeting of Writers* (Burns, 1999)

INR   'Is NATO Right to Bomb Yugoslavia?' http://www.yurope.com/kosovo/articles/Richard_Burns.htm (Burns, 1999)

ITD   *In a Time of Drought* (Berengarten, second edition, 2008)

ITD1 *In a Time of Drought* (Burns, first edition, 2006)

IVI   *In Visible Ink: Selected Shorter Poems* by Roberto Sanesi, *Aquila* 13 (Burns, ed. and tr. 1982)

JL   Limburg, Joanne. 1992. 'Human above all: Richard Burns's *The Manager*'. *The Jewish Quarterly* 185 (Spring): 17–23.

JLI   'Interview with Joanne Limburg' (Burns, 2001, unpublished typescript)

KT   *Keys to Transformation: Ceri Richards and Dylan Thomas* (Burns, 1981)

LT   *Learning to Talk* (Burns, 1980)

MAF '"My" Anne Frank, a memoir', unpublished typescript (Burns, 2007)

MTA Richard Berengarten and Joanne Limburg (2016), 'Managing the Art', *International Literary Quarterly: English Writers 3*. Online at: http://www.interlitq.org/englishwriters3/joanne-limburg/job.php

MF   *Mavro Fos* (Nasos Vayenas and Ilias Lagios, trs., Greek version of *Black Light: Poems in Memory of George Seferis*, 2005)

MN   *Menadžer* (Vladimir Sekulić and Jasna B. Mišić, trs.) (Serbian version of *The Manager*, Bernz, 1990)

NA   'Notes on Avebury', Unpublished typescript (Berengarten, 2008)

OOY *Out of Yugoslavia*. Special issue of the *North Dakota Quarterly* (*NDQ*) 61(1). (Burns and Stephen Markovich, guest eds., 1993)

OP   'A Poet in Cambridge', *Times Educational Supplement*, January 1, 1971.

PIIN *Richard Berengaraten: A Portrait In Inter-Views* (eds. Paschalis Nikolaou and John Z. Dillon) (Berengarten, forthcoming 2017)

PL   *Plavi leptir* (Serbian version of *The Blue Butterfly*, tr. Vera V. Radojević) (Burns, 2007)

PRV 'With Peter Russell in Venice, 1965–66' (Burns, 1996, 1997)

PS   'Poems from *Book With No Back Cover*'. Bilingual text, with Chinese translation by Chee Lay Tan, *Poetry Sky: Blue Sky Quarterly* (Burns) http://www.poetrysky.com/quarterly/quarterly-5-richardburns.html

RB online	Richard Berengarten's website: http://www.berengarten.com/site/
RL	*The Return of Lazarus* (Burns, 1971)
RR	*Roots/Routes* (Burns, 1982)
RS	'Roberto Sanesi: An Italian Among Welshmen', *Poetry Wales* 17(2): 42–51 (Burns, 1981)
RSI	'Introduction' to Roberto Sanesi, *In Visible Ink: Selected Shorter Poems, 1955–1979* (Burns, 1982)
SLJ	'Statement for *Love and Justice*' (Unpublished typescript, Burns, 2002–2003)
TDP	'Ten Drachmas for a Pound' (Unpublished typescript, Berengarten, 2008)
TM	*The Manager* (Berengarten, second edition, 2008)
TM1	*The Manager* (Burns, first edition, 2001)
UBL	*Under Balkan Light* (Berengarten, 2008)
UVS	*U vreme suše* (Vera V. Radojević, tr., Serbian version of *In a Time of Drought*, Burns, 2004)

Introduction: Everywhere Centre

Norman Jope

This *Companion* aims to guide readers through the many-faceted poetic output of Richard Berengarten (formerly Burns[1]): an output that has appeared, over the past five decades, in a wide variety of places and contexts but which nonetheless is perhaps only now achieving the degree of attention it deserves in the UK. The fact that thirty-three contributors can each approach that work from a slightly different angle is in itself a testimony to the breadth of Berengarten's output. And since more than a third of these contributors have a first language other than English, and with over a dozen nationalities represented in this volume, it is also a testimony to the recognition of his work by fellow writers and critics across cultural, linguistic and geographical boundaries and frontiers. The sheer range of poetic canons to which Berengarten's *oeuvre* responds – and whose influence, as I shall discuss later in this introduction, has enabled him to put down 'multiple roots' in a number of literary traditions – may even have served to hamper his reception in the UK as a poet of stature. However, the collections recently re-published in the *Selected Writings* series will surely help to redress this state of affairs. For some readers, this *Companion* will accompany those editions, although its target readership also includes those who might not have encountered Berengarten's work at all or have done so in snatches and fragments. None of the essays in it, therefore, assumes a detailed knowledge of Berengarten's poems and extensive quotation seeks to encourage readers to delve further.

---

[1] In June 2008 Richard Burns changed his name to Richard Berengarten. This change was announced in notes in the first five volumes of his *Selected Writings* (Cambridge: Salt Publishing 2008; reissued by Shearsman Books, 2011): "Richard Berengarten used to be known as Richard Burns… [H]e now repossesses the family name of his father, the cellist and saxophonist Alexander Berengarten" (e.g. *FL* inside back cover). Henceforward, all references to the poet himself will use the name Berengarten.

Like Berengarten's work itself, this *Companion* also seeks to be readable – indeed, *hospitable* – to anyone with a working knowledge of literary issues and concepts. Hospitality is a key poetic virtue for Berengarten: he writes:

> Ancient laws of reciprocity, hospitality and magnanimity are necessary to the poetry of this time and this place too. Anything else or less is not good enough and will not serve adequately. A poet without such qualities can only be second-rate, however clever, skilled and cunning (*ALF*, RB online[2]).

How do these virtues translate into poetry, and Berengarten's poetry in particular? They relate above all to his openness to past and present poetic practice across cultural, linguistic and geographical boundaries. That openness is traceable not only in Berengarten's poems, but in his related activities as translator, pedagogue, cultural ambassador and poetry activist. He is the least confined of writers and this in itself sets him apart from the constructors and aficionados of cliques and coteries.

Berengarten has lived and worked outside the UK (mainly in Italy, Greece, former Yugoslavia and the USA) for much of his adult life: distanced, literally, from the rifts and schisms of the contemporary British poetry scene. Moreover, if the common British distinction between the two competing camps of the 'mainstream' and the 'avant-garde' can be applied, it is certainly hard to fit Berengarten into either one. Although his openness to modernist poetries in other European languages is arguably more often associated in the UK with the oppositional avant-garde (in opposition, that is, to the 'little-England' tendencies of The Movement and its successors), his use of traditional form and rhetoric, often derived from pre-20th century sources in English literature, makes it equally difficult to relate his work to that of so-called 'linguistically innovative' writers. Rather, Berengarten's most characteristic work almost always involves an engagement with the manifold legacies of the past, as if from an intention to produce something that might turn out (who knows?) to be of value to succeeding generations. This process of hosting-and-guesting is defined by Berengarten, as follows:

> Whenever the guest arrives, the host is reciprocally hosted. The particular interior that encompasses both guest and host is the

---

[2] Editors' note: 'RB online' will be used throughout this volume to refer to RB's website at www.berengarten.com. *ALF* refers to RB's essay 'A Little Further?', on his website.

anterior timespace that itself first gave welcome to the host. Poetry, being itself a gift, flourishes in that generous presence of arrivals, meetings and gift-givings (*ALF*, RB online).

Since the range of accessible canons has become, potentially, international, the traditions of English and North American literature are no longer hegemonic for any adventurous writer. This widening of options can help such a writer to avoid the tropes of the 'received' canon in his or her language of expression and to encourage fresh and distinctive blends. The newness in Berengarten's work, therefore, derives not from disjuncture but from *synthesis*.

∓

As already indicated, the number and range of contributions in this volume reflect not only the breadth of Berengarten's output and his appeal, but the multiplicity of critical approaches that his work sustains. Furthermore, it has been impossible to arrange these contributions into tidy, self-contained sections. Essays about particular pieces inevitably cover wider themes; essays on wider themes draw their evidence, as they must, from particular pieces; and coverage of Berengarten's ancillary activities sheds light upon the core of his work. As he puts it himself, in the final section of 'Avebury': *'now every / where centre'* (*FL* 50); and this is eminently true of this volume. Clearly, a collection such as this requires a running order, even if readers are, as ever, at liberty to wander back and forth as if each essay existed in parallel to the others. However, chronological patterning has also informed its arrangement and, in particular, readers who approach the essays in the second section in sequence will acquire some sense of Berengarten's development.

Whether considered separately or together, the first eight essays offer an overview by ranging across the entire span of Berengarten's published *oeuvre* to date. They cover such diverse themes as Berengarten's Jewish heritage and influences (Moses and kuhn); his Mediterranean affinities (Nicolao and Voncu); his deep and long-lasting interest in symbol, myth and Jungian psychology (Hooker and Ransford); the multiplicity of voices he adopts and masters (Jenner); and the relationship that exists, in his work, between mortality and the poetic impulse (Derrick). But this is to simplify matters almost to vanishing point. Each of these essays ranges widely in its own right, drawing together sources and influences and suggesting points of departure for further reading and scholarship.

3

Taken as a whole, they present a sophisticated analysis of where this poet has come from, what he has accomplished so far and the comparative measure of his achievement. Here, in particular, one also gets a sense of the *empowerment* (rather than Bloomian anxiety) of influence in Berengarten's *oeuvre*. These pieces reveal him as a poet who has always been willing to tap into multiple canons and diverse heritages; who is open, in the words of Octavio Paz, to the "wind from all compass points" (Paz 1991: 258–269) that is available to refresh and inspire all writers of ambition and curiosity. This first group of essays, then, throws down a challenge to all notions of exclusivity and the closure of borders, in the spheres of both poetry and life as a whole.

The second group of essays covers specific works and is arranged in the chronological order of those works' completion. With the exception of Berengarten's 'The Balkan Trilogy', they cover Berengarten's major poetic achievements. Of the fourteen pieces in this section, three consider 'Black Light' (Filippakopoulou, Nikolaou and Vayenas) and three, *The Manager* (Calder, Gelashvili and Kobakhidze, and Query). In the view of the editors, this emphasis happens to mirror the comparative importance of these sequences. The other works discussed in this section are 'Avebury' (Moody); 'The Rose of Sharon' (Sri); 'Angels' (Gery); 'Tree' (Casella); 'Against The Day' (Llorens Cubedo); 'Croft Woods' (Woelfel); and *Book With No Back Cover* (Pirie and Tan).

The three pieces on 'Black Light' are all written by Greeks, including Nasos Vayenas, one of Greece's most respected contemporary poets. Taken together, these essays present an informed examination of the Hellenic influence on Berengarten, in particular that of the poetry of George Seferis. Indeed, these critics locate 'Black Light' within a living context, constructed both out of life-experience in Greece and from Greek literary models, that is in large part recognisable 'as being Greek' to Greeks themselves. This parallels the readings of four Serbian critics later in the volume (Matić, Rakitić, Petrov and Ignjačević), which not only locate 'The Balkan Trilogy' within the geopolitical zone of former Yugoslavia, but confirm it as an accurate depiction of Balkan life-experience and culture. Such responses not only embed Berengarten's work in literary traditions other than that of English: they also suggest a wider, 'European' importance for his work, as well as the establishment of literary canons that transcend geographical, linguistic and cultural boundaries.

Most of the pieces in the second section are concerned with issues of form and subject their texts to close analysis. Among other things, this highlights the fact that Berengarten's *oeuvre* contains some startlingly 'traditional' poems – startling, that is, to anyone who believes that the old forms are discredited. However, these pieces also indicate clearly that Berengarten makes these forms work, because he has the sophistication and skill required to do so – and that, in skilled hands such as his, their resonance remains undiminished. And, no less, these contributions show that it would be inaccurate to portray his approach to form, in its entirety, as solely concerned with salvage and renewal. Formal innovation is at the heart of his poetry and expresses itself in a multiplicity of ways, from the tight rhyme-schemes of 'The Rose of Sharon' (*FL* 91–96) and the villanelles that form 'The Death of Children' (*BB* 17–25) through to the jagged open forms of 'Avebury' (*FL* 23–50), the verse-paragraphs of *The Manager*, and the expansive long lines of 'Flight of the Imago' (*BB* 73–101). Other key themes are explored in this part of the book too, such as myth and spirituality (Moody, Sri, Casella and Woelfel); Chinese cultural traditions, particularly the *I Ching* (Tan); visual art (Llorens Cubedo and Woelfel); typography and book design (Pirie); the influence of 'Sarf-Eastern' colloquial parlance (Calder); postmodernism (Query); and Berengarten's relationships with Pound and Eliot (Gery, and Gelashvili and Kobakhidze). Once more, however, it might be argued that a summary of this kind risks simplifying and even trivialising the complex concerns with which these essays engage.

The third section consists of eight essays which focus entirely on 'The Balkan Trilogy': *The Blue Butterfly, In a Time of Drought* and *Under Balkan Light*. Although placing these essays together does not necessarily amount to a claim, on our part, that this trilogy represents the apex of Berengarten's poetic achievement to date, it certainly reflects the comparative enthusiasm that contributors have displayed for it (bearing in mind, also, the extensive references to the trilogy contained in the first section). Readers will also note that there is a considerable degree of overlap within this section, particularly among three of the four Serbian writers (Rakitić, Petrov and Ignjačević). However, the angles and areas of concurrence this uncovers lead, in our view, to a deeper reading of the trilogy. The other pieces in this third section are written by Anglophone critics (Jones, Lucas, Frisardi and Wilson), all of whom approach the trilogy from unique perspectives. Jones draws upon his own extensive knowledge of the languages, history, culture and literature of the former

Yugoslavia; Lucas focuses on the political and historical dimensions of the work; Frisardi highlights the influence of the post-Jungian writer and thinker, James Hillman; and Wilson, by approaching *The Blue Butterfly* from Jewish perspectives, complements the earlier contributions of Moses and kuhn by emphasising specifically Jewish currents and associations within Berengarten's work. Finally, this section also contains an in-depth study of a particular piece, 'Do vidjenja Danitsé', by the fourth Serbian writer (Matić), which, in its close textual attention, relates to some of the essays in the second section. Together, these pieces not only build up a composite picture of this particular area of Berengarten's work, but also illustrate how a poetry of ambition and risk can elicit different, yet complementary responses from critical readers.

The final section, containing three essays, hints at the range of Berengarten's ancillary roles: as literary activist (Gowar), TEFL/TESOL teacher / entrepreneur (Křivský) and teacher of poetry to children (Setchell). This section, regrettably, is incomplete in coverage despite our best efforts to expand it; for example, there is nothing about Berengarten's work as a translator (although the bibliography at the end of this volume includes some basic information), or about his literary and art criticism and other prose writing, or his role as a teacher to adults. However, in highlighting some of the other 'hats' that Berengarten has worn (to allude to the 'Hatman' persona that he has adopted, at times, in his pedagogical activities with children), this section suggests the range and consistency of his concerns. Around the inner core of his life's work – the poems themselves – there is an outer ring of diverse, yet compatible concerns and activities, and a record of achievement in all of them. These activities have also influenced much of the writing; after all, if Berengarten had not gone to Serbia to earn a living, then his 'The Balkan Trilogy' would have either not existed at all or taken a very different form.

✁

I have sought, in surveying the contents of this *Companion*, to touch upon the multiple themes of Berengarten's work. However, I would argue that what distinguishes him most, and marks him out as a writer of importance, is his courage in engaging with the subject of mortality. Indeed, Berengarten writes under the gaze of death to a remarkable extent, playing for high stakes by comparison with some more favoured writers. Whereas a great deal of writing about death, particularly

6

in the contemporary 'mainstream', is actually about bereavement – the experience of separation and loss, in which one's own survival is (almost as if) taken for granted – Berengarten takes the fact of his own mortality to heart, beats poetry out of himself with it, works through to a realisation of what is worth the living, precisely because he has displayed the requisite courage. By deliberately placing his writing under the shade of that threat, Berengarten is able to write more deeply and vividly. And the way in which death haunts and deepens his writing suggests the works of other artists and musicians as well as writers: Mahler is one such comparison that springs to mind, not least for the role that erotic love also plays in much of Berengarten's work.

Moreover, Berengarten is also prepared to confront death's agents: the killers of love, who are not only the agents of entropy but traitors and deserters in the face of our common enemy as human beings. From the first poem in *For the Living*, 'The Easter Rising 1967' (*FL* 1–14), to the recent work on twentieth-century conflicts collected in *The Blue Butterfly* and *Under Balkan Light*, Berengarten conducts a many-faceted dialogue with 'Master Death' – whether by way of an interrogation of His foot-soldiers and their works, or by arraigning the Adversary himself. In this, his mindset is reminiscent of the Knight in Bergman's *The Seventh Seal*: both the Knight/Bergman and Berengarten, in their own ways, explore a psychic space in which they are able, for just long enough, to stave off Death and its intractable demands. As Berengarten puts it:

> Poetry is a challenge to mortality and a criticism of Death. Crossing deaths, poems are spacetime-travellers: they encapsulate a non-self-defeating irony, the only defeat Death might admit, if Death had words. (*ALF*, RB online).

"Crossing deaths, poems are spacetime-travellers" brings us back to the idea of gift-giving encapsulated in one of the earlier quotations from 'A Little Further' and the hope that, in writing poetry, one might be handing on something of value, not only to one's contemporaries but to generations to come. This is not, perhaps, a fashionable approach to take. In the face of a media-driven culture of instant gratification, of the erosion of historical context from contemporary discourse and of the overwhelming ecological threats we confront, it is safer to hope, at best, for the pleasure of a task well done and the respect of our immediate peers. However, Berengarten's self-imposed challenge is to write *as if a legacy remained possible*; not from megalomania, because posthumous reputations are of no use at all to the dead, but from love towards those as yet unborn.

Whether or not this legacy is accepted remains to be seen – as in the case of any other living writer – but Berengarten's courage, in daring to address the deepest aspects of the human condition, is exemplary. We hope very much that this courage comes through in what follows, and that the importance of his work – as well as the extent to which it invites further dialogue, rather than seeks hierarchical closure – is conveyed to this *Companion*'s readers.

REFERENCES

Jope, Norman. 2005. 'Range and Resonance: review of *For the Living* and *Book With No Back Cover*', *Tears In The Fence* 42: 116–120.

Paz, Octavio. 1991. *Collected Poems 1957–1987* (ed. Eliot Weinberger). London: Paladin.

PART I

A Poet for a Time of Need

PAUL SCOTT DERRICK

Remember the one who said, What's the use of poets in a mean-spirited age? – that's him, sitting there. He was already here long before I arrived, and here he will stay, like me. No doubt his memory will long outlast mine…(Richard Berengarten, 'Ambassador' (*FL* 175))

I

It isn't easy to give an accurate assessment of the work of a living poet. Nor is it, perhaps, advisable to try. So many trees in the woods seem overwhelming when we're standing right beside them. We need to have the benefit of distance to judge how tall they really are. But how does one credibly criticise poetry anyway? In other words, how can we most effectively talk about it? A much better writer (and thinker) than I has put the matter succinctly: "The experience of poetry, like any other experience, is only partially translatable into words." And if this utterance is a patent truth that all of us are – or should be – aware of, he further reflected on how this truth impinges on the performance of the critic:

> some people who are inarticulate, and cannot say why they like a poem, may have deeper and more discriminating sensibility than some others who can talk glibly about it. … Even the most accomplished of critics can, in the end, only point to the poetry which seems to him to be the real thing (Eliot 1980 [1933]: 17, 18).

Having stood under one or two trees by now, I feel that I can point to the one named Richard Berengarten, and say, "This tree seems to me to be the real thing. If our children's children are permitted to look back at the forest of what we were, this distinct form will stand out above the fuss and flutter of the surrounding foliage."

But then, Berengarten has a propensity for trees. Several of his most significant poems take place in their proximity. It's almost as though poems like 'The Voice in the Garden', 'May', 'In the parks and among the flowering gardens', 'Croft Woods' and of course, 'Tree', were written under their tutelage. Because, importantly, Berengarten is a poet who listens before he speaks:

> Say, isn't every secret worth its keeping
> as open-hearted, generous and full-throated
> an outpouring, as the choir of these dumb trees
> you walk among here, hearing, overhearing,
> their aweful and tremendous joys and sadnesses (*UBL* 72)

A secret that is kept by being expressed through silence: how seriously can we take an idea like this? A tree, or a chorus of trees, or anything else in the outside world, whispers without words into the poet's ear, and the secrets they tell form the muted burden of the poem. We should in fact take it very seriously. Walt Whitman did. That whole fabulous, loquacious, contradictory, astounding, sensual and entertaining message that is 'Song of Myself' allegedly emerged from his intent contemplation of a "spear of summer grass", in which he heard the wordless thrumming of the soul:

> Loafe with me on the grass, loose the stop from your throat
> Not words, not music or rhyme I want, not custom or lecture,
>   not even the best,
> Only the lull I like, the hum of your valvèd voice.
>   (Baym, 1989 v. I: 1977)

We need to take this idea seriously because, as Whitman already knew in 1855, doing so directly affects the way we understand our relationship with the so-called outside world.[1] And this, in turn, leads us to a deeper

---

[1] Or, to provide another example, think about the first six lines of 'Mowing', one of Robert Frost's earliest published poems:
> There was never a sound beside the wood but one,
> And that was my long scythe whispering to the ground.
> What was it it whispered? I knew not well myself;
> Perhaps it was something about the heat of the sun,
> Something, perhaps, about the lack of sound –
> And that was why it whispered and did not speak. (Baym, 1989; v. II: 1083)

The rest of this modified sonnet is devoted to fathoming, and expressing, the wordless message whispered by the speaker's scythe.

question, one that addresses perhaps the most essential quality of human being: where does authentic language – speech that reflects most deeply on what we are and tells us what we need most desperately to know about ourselves – come from?

Berengarten has given his own response to questions such as these in an unpublished interview with Joanne Limburg. Talking about the lyrical voice, and the rich variety of formal patterns it assumes in his work, he describes what might best be called a receptive, open attitude. It could be termed a 'listening':

> I think the voices of poems emerge according to rules, laws, volitions, directions of their own. I think the poet participates with them but doesn't direct them … If the Heraclitan and Hermetic dictum carries – and I think it does – then perhaps one might be entitled to invert the Jungian spatial metaphor, so that one could equally well say that a poem's voices come from layers higher than the conscious mind. (*JL1*)[2]

This statement conjures up echoes of both Whitman and of the Emersonian 'Oversoul'. Not many contemporary poets would wish to be thought of as 'Romantics', but a profession such as this places Berengarten directly in the central stream of the modern (and postmodern) Romantic tradition.

More than 160 years have passed since Ralph Waldo Emerson, the great synthesiser of Romantic thought for the culture of the United States, wrote that

> …what is called Imagination, is a very high sort of seeing, which does not come by study, but by the intellect being where and what it sees; by sharing the path or circuit of things through forms, and so making them translucid to others. The path of things is silent. Will they suffer a speaker to go with them? A spy they will not suffer; a lover, a poet, is the transcendency of their own nature, – him they will suffer. The condition of true naming, on the poet's part, is his resigning himself to the divine aura which breathes through forms, and accompanying that. (Emerson 1989 [1844]: 993)

The message may sound outmoded, but we would still do well to attend to what he says. The path of things is silent. The poet though – unlike the scientific spy – communes with what is there and then responds.

[2] Interview on *The Manager*, with Joanne Limburg, December 2001 (text provided by RB) (hereafter *JL1*). For the feature written from this interview, see *JL*.

Through the poet, nature transcends itself. He, or she, speaks its heart (which is also the poet's own), and essences (secrets) flower into words:

> The sea, the mountain-ridge, Niagara, and every flower-bed, pre-exist, or super-exist, in pre-cantations, which sail like odors in the air, and when any man goes by with an ear sufficiently fine, he overhears them and endeavors to write down the notes without diluting or depraving them. (Emerson 1989 [1844]: 992)

Aren't these "pre-cantations" another name for what Berengarten refers to as "layers higher than the conscious mind"?

I hardly mean to suggest, though, that Berengarten is an antiquated throwback to the nineteenth century. The issue is more complex than that. I might just as well argue that Emerson was a 'conceptual sling-shot' into the twenty-first century (which would, in fact, be closer to my intentions). What I do want to say, and to illustrate with Berengarten's poetry, is that even though most of us refuse to acknowledge it, we are still in our time dealing with the core issues raised by our Romantic predecessors.

One of those issues is how we are related to the world. The contemporary philosopher Stanley Cavell, who has spent much of his professional life attending to Emerson's words, agrees that we have yet to understand correctly the dynamics of that relation. For example, discussing Emerson's essay 'Experience', he writes:

> The universe is as separate from me, but as intimately part of me, as one on whose behalf I contest, and who therefore wears my colors. We are in a state of 'romance' with the universe…; we do not possess it, but our life is to return to it, in ever-widening circles. (Cavell 1933: 193)

The principal point of Cavell's reading of Emerson is that this constantly expanding return to the universe is carried out through a particular and careful use of the mind. He describes it as a respectful, reverential and responsive form of thinking. And since one of Cavell's purposes is to bring to light an underlying continuity between the thought of Emerson and that of Martin Heidegger, it should be no surprise that his description of Emerson's more passive, receptive use of the mind closely corresponds with what Heidegger, at mid-twentieth century, delicately interpreted as 'reflection'.[3]

---

[3] In the essay 'Wissenschaft und Besinnung' ('Science and Reflection', originally published in 1954), he writes: "We do not yet have reflection when we have only consciousness.

II

> [T]he responding in which man authentically listens to the
> appeal of language is that which speaks in the element of poetry.
> The more poetic a poet is – the freer (that is, the more open
> and ready for the unforeseen) his saying – the greater is the
> purity with which he submits what he says to an ever more
> painstaking listening, and the further what he says is from the
> mere propositional statement that is dealt with solely in regard
> to its correctness or incorrectness. (Heidegger 1975: 216)

This is what I hear in Richard Berengarten's poetic speech: an affectionate, marvelling, reverential response to the world that we inhabit and have no choice but to learn how to love. And this is why it seems to me that 'The Voice in the Garden', that celebration of self-possessed surrender, could be read as a defining statement for entry into Berengarten's work. As Emerson wrote in 1844: "I know not how it is that we need an interpreter, but the great majority of men seem to be minors, who have not yet come into possession of their own, or mutes, who cannot report the conversation they have had with nature" (Emerson 1989 [1844]: 985). This poem makes such a report. It traces original language back to its sources in the abiding silence of Being, and it lets the world pronounce itself through the poet's voice.

Here we have a double, or embedded, response. Berengarten has listened to the voice of Yugoslav poet Ivan V. Lalić, who has reported his own disturbing conversation with nature. The pertinent line by Lalić forms the epigraph to an entire section of *Under Balkan Light* that is also entitled 'The Voice in the Garden', and is the starting-point for this circular revelation: "Who can I ask about the voice in the gardens?" (*UBL* 67).[4] This poem offers a reply to Lalić's haunted question. But in order to interpret the voice that Lalić has heard, Berengarten must also hear it himself. Due to its complex syntax, the first stanza, which is one complete sentence, needs to be quoted entire:

Reflection is more. It is calm, self-possessed surrender to that which is worthy of questioning" (Heidegger 1977: 180).

[4] The poem 'The Voice in the Garden' was published in the first edition of *For the Living* (2004, p. 133), where the following further lines by Lalić appear as part of its epigraph: "As for the dead, whom I am afraid/To ask in case they know too much, too much, /…they are outside the gardens anyway."

Did you ask for apotheosis, or transcendence,
or something else, not either, yet still higher,
when that curious voice assailed you in the garden
with song, unearthly, that you could not fully
comprehend in origin or depth, but knew
and recognised for what it was – a miracle
woven out of the silences, the pauses,
gaps and gulfs between perfumes, colours, movements,
or grace abundant, superimposed on grace –
realising the voice inside your head,
wired into time, earthed, forking out through space,
was the living call to the unborn from the dead? (*UBL* 71)

What is moving in Lalić's complaint is his fear that the voice in his mind may come from the dead, which is a feeling we can sympathise with. Most of us in this culture are afraid of ghosts, afraid of whatever death may have to reveal, afraid of death itself. But the speaker of Berengarten's poem has listened more keenly. There seems to be a paradox here. The song is "unearthly", yet it also emerges from the garden: "woven out of the silences, the pauses / gaps and gulfs between perfumes, colours, movements". What, then, are these 'empty spaces' in the texture of the world? The suggestion, I believe, is that Being contains non-Being, that the All contains the Nothing, or that the living world is pervaded with death.

Here we come close to Heidegger's concept of 'nihilation' [*Vernichtung*]. In the essay 'What Is Metaphysics?'[5] he deploys this term to explore what he considers the most essential quality of Being: the fact that everything-that-is is constantly disappearing. The ceaseless flow of nature, of which we form a part, can be thought of as a process of 'de-becoming'. In Heidegger's understanding, a sudden recognition that everything, including ourselves, is forever pulling away into nothingness, induces an unsettling sense of alienation from the world, that is, a sense of the world's essential 'otherness', which causes the emotion of dread [*Angst*].

I suggest that this is one way to appreciate the feeling that Lalić so strongly expresses.

However, thinking through the emotion of dread offers the opportunity to comprehend Being in its wholeness. That irrevocable process of disappearance can also be understood as the source of language, since we use our words and the concepts they express both to 'lift' the multiform

---

[5] 'Was Ist Metaphysik?', originally published in 1929.

constituents of the world out of the amorphous flow of Being and also to prevent the totality of what-is from sinking into oblivion. Language is what 'delivers' the world, all that we can know, from the flux of Being into *ex*-istence.

We therefore need to use our language carefully. This kind of careful, thoughtful speech is what Heidegger refers to with his well-known concept of 'letting-be'. Our gravest responsibility is not to impose our will and thereby transform Being into what we want it to be. Instead, by listening responsively, we should free ourselves from the will, and so permit the world to open itself, as it already is, through what we say and how we say it.[6]

> Spilling out from itself, all singing is
> what cannot be contained, the singular glory
> of being, itself, its own apotheosis
> which needs ask nothing, nothing being all it holds (*UBL* 73)

This response to Lalić's mood of dread is a reassurance. The texture of Being includes non-Being; but that non-Being is a component of what we are. The dead are not "outside the garden", somewhere beyond and thus alien to the world. Death is an integral part of the process of life, as integral as the flowing movement of thought. 'The Voice in the Garden' therefore reinterprets dread, corrects it:

> do not be mistaken:
> the dead have not gone elsewhere. They are here
> inside us, in the song. This is its sense.
> We are their audience and the instruments
> they play on... (*UBL* 73)

If art is our ultimate access to truth, then the ultimate truth may be 'engendered' in the 'womb' of death.

This is one of those core issues of Romantic thinking. Once science had made Christian beliefs about the afterlife untenable, the Romantics gradually came to realise that they needed to reformulate the concept

---

[6] In this context, it is interesting to consider another passage from RB's interview with Limburg: "[S]urely it isn't inconceivable that the craft itself may well have its own purpose in working its way through the artist – not so much in order to 'enable that artist to achieve', but to enable the artist to become the channel (tunnel, tube, pipe for the delivery [deliverance, appearance, birth]) of the created 'object'. Rumi's hollow reed; the Aeolian Harp; the gong in the oaks at Dodona ... Childbirth? Prophecies? Oracles?" (*JL*).

of death in Western culture. Consequently, one of the fundamental elements of the Romantic (re)turn to nature was the effort to re-conceive both life and death as aspects of a single, larger phenomenon, that is, as intimately related facets of an endless, flowing process.

This is what we nowadays call a 'holistic paradigm'. Emerson was aware that the Romantic vision was holistic. The poet, he wrote, "re-attaches things to nature and the Whole" (Emerson 1989 [1844]: 990). We can find one of the first, somewhat faltering efforts to do so in American poetry as early as 1779. In *The House of Night*, Philip Freneau's strained attempt to imagine the deathbed scene of death itself, the speaker suddenly interjects:

> What is this Death, ye deep read sophists, say,—
> Death is no more than one unceasing change;
> New forms arise, while other forms decay,
> Yet all is LIFE throughout creation's range. (Baym 1989: v. I: 718)

Freneau was a victim of his own time, caught between the Age of Reason and the rising tide of Romanticism. Both his thinking and his poetry suffered as a result of the competing pulls of these two very different ways of thinking the world.

By the middle of the nineteenth century, though, Walt Whitman was able to formulate the same idea in a much more powerful form:

> What do you think has become of the young and old men?
> And what do you think has become of the women and children?
> They are alive and well somewhere,
> The smallest sprout shows there is really no death,
> And if ever there was it led forward life, and does not wait at the
> end to arrest it,
> And ceas'd the moment life appeared. (Baym 1989: v. I: 1978)

Reattaching things to nature and 'the Whole' entails a re-conceiving of logical dualities. The ultimate logical opposites are our ideas of life and death. This is why it is so hard for us in the West to accommodate a holistic paradigm. Yet that is the final burden of 'The Voice in the Garden'. As we have seen, the song in the poet's head, which also becomes and is the poem, is both unearthly and earthly. It comes into language out of silence. It carries a message to the living from the dead, and will speak through the living to the not-yet-born. One of the points, if not the main point, that the poem communicates is precisely the need to bridge this kind of logical paradox. 'The Voice in the Garden' speaks in words that propagate the wholeness of Being.

ɛ৲ৎ

Where does language come from? How do we assimilate the phenomenon of death into a post-Christian system of thought? I propose that we are still involved in the long and complicated process of resolving these two problems that the Romantic thinkers only began to articulate for Western culture. 'The Voice in the Garden' elegantly addresses them both, and therefore takes us one step further along this alternative – or recessive – line of Western thinking, or, as Heidegger often described it, this particular "pathway" through thought.

Heidegger's later essays mark a high point on this pathway and offer a profound elucidation of those questions the Romantics were struggling to formulate. Clearly, we can find the proper answers only when our questions are properly framed.[7] This is why, for Heidegger, the thinker and the poet are kindred travellers on this path, closely related through their mutual task of listening. He called this receptive use of the mind *ein eindenkendes Denken*, a thinking that memorialises and responds (Heidegger 1975: ix). In 'Science and Reflection', he proposes this more contemplative approach to the world as a possible antidote for the dangerous spiritual impoverishment of modern man. Heidegger's argument is also a twentieth-century metamorphosis of Emerson's concept of 'Reason' (an intuitive response to nature) as opposed to 'Understanding' (an analytical grasp of nature). As already noted, Emerson says that "the condition of true naming, on the poet's part, is his resigning himself to the divine aura which breathes through forms, and accompanying that" (Emerson 1893 [1844]: 993). Heidegger writes:

> *Language speaks as the peal of stillness* ... the very nature, the presencing of language needs and uses the speaking of mortals in order to sound as the peal of stillness for the hearing of mortals. Only as men belong within the peal of stillness are mortals able to speak in their own way in sounds (Heidegger 1975: 207, 208).

What better explication of 'The Voice in the Garden' – and of the

---

[7] Or, according to Thomas Pynchon's third Proverb for Paranoids: "If they can get you asking the wrong questions, they won't have to worry about answers" (Pynchon 1973: 251).

19

poet's voice – could we ask for? "The thinker utters Being. The poet names what is holy" (Heidegger 1970: 360). This kind of loving response to experience not only restores us to a healthier, more harmonious relationship with the world, it also breaks down our culture's pre-conceived barriers between life and death.

☙

Berengarten deals with the same theme, on a much more personal and emotional level, in 'May' (*FL* 177–184). Responding to the exuberant, intoxicating life-force of spring, and in the company of his two young children, he feels the urge to burst into speech himself, and to make a poem for his son and daughter 'out of' the powerful scent of lilac in the garden. But, "borne on the lilac's perfume, whispering through my mind", he hears the voices, and music, of "ghosts" (*FL* 182) – the presences that Lalić seemed to be so afraid of in that other garden.

In the midst of life, there is death. In the midst of all this joy, there is sorrow. The poem itself can be released only by expressing that muted "litany of sadnesses" (*FL* 182).

It is no coincidence that the trigger that releases this expression is his daughter's first efforts at speech:

> *Fthah*, says Lara, pointing. Does she mean *There*
> or *Flower*? And the whole garden opens around her,
> you can see it in her wide eyes, as, two years old,
> cheeks burning, she toddles on the brink of speech. (*FL* 179)

Berengarten may be playing somewhat coy here; for "*Fthah*", the key that turns the lock in the door of memory, may well indicate neither "*There*" nor "*Flower*", but 'Father'. The child's first, imperfect word points the poet back toward the waiting ghosts of his own childhood, at once opening him to them and permitting them to speak through him, just as through his daughter's eyes the garden itself now 'opens up' for them both.

"*Fthah*": the father's presence waits to be unfolded from this word and to 'flower' through the poet into speech. What is calling through the joyful power of spring, and what the poem gradually uncovers, is the memory of Berengarten's younger sister, Sarah, born deaf and dumb and blind. The effect of this on his father, Alexander Berengarten, a cellist, was devastating, and apparently led to his untimely death.

Thus, the poet first discovers that what he has been trying so long

20

not to hear was Alexander's "first concert", performed night after night in their home, as he played again and again 'The Swan of Tuonela' into his daughter's unhearing ears, pouring all of his love through a song that seemed to be lost forever, to disappear into absence and nothingness. The sorrow may have caused Alexander's heart to stop, but neither the love nor the music were really lost. His son has heard them both; and

> Now, walking in this garden, among blossoms falling,
> with my own daughter Lara and son Alexander,
> I hear my father's music call me from his grave,
> and the Swan of Tuonela rises from the lake
> to beat its white wings against my shuffled heart. (*FL* 182)

This poem, written in the mid-1980s, meticulously and lovingly executes the knowledge that 'The Voice in the Garden', written in 1988, will also reveal:

> [T]he dead have not gone elsewhere. They are here
> inside us, in the song. This is its sense.
> We are the audience and the instruments
> they play on, who conduct all living things
> as willing pipe and horn and shimmering strings. (*UBL* 73)

A transitory moment in the garden, a moment's powerful emotion, is miraculously unfolded into speech and suspended out of time. Alexander's cello plays from the grave through Richard's voice, and its message of love and pain reaches Richard's children, Lara and Alexander. This is the 'meaning' of Richard's father's art – and the poet's own. This is what Richard, as a son, has to learn to accept, and then pass on to his own children: love, pain and death are all a part of the miracle of life. As 'The Voice in the Garden' tells us, "[e]verything, even suffering, is a gift" (*UBL* 74).

III

> People always ask: For whom does the poet write? He needs only to answer, For whom do you do good? Are you kind to your daughter because in the end someone will pay you for being? … The poet writes his poem for its own sake, for the sake of the order of things in which the poem takes the place that has awaited it. (Jarrell 1980: 26)

As Berengarten explains in the 'Postscript' to *The Blue Butterfly*, there was a specific – and very terrible – 'order of things' waiting to be dealt with by this extraordinary collection of poems: the massacre at Kragujevac, in central Serbia, in October, 1941. An odd occurrence inspired him during a visit to Kragujevac with his daughter on May 25, 1985. He describes that experience in the Postscript: "While we were queuing to enter the museum [that commemorates the massacre], a blue butterfly suddenly came to rest on the forefinger of my left hand – that is, my writing hand. Lara and I each had just enough time to take a photograph of the creature" (*BB* 123).

Was this occurrence a miracle, or a coincidence? What might have been no more than a moment's amusement or mild surprise for anyone else, turns out for the poet to be a portentous visitation. This uncanny junction of two living beings in time and space is reminiscent of Emerson's chance encounter with the Rhodora and of Robert Frost stumbling unawares on a dimpled white spider that was holding up a dead moth on a white heal-all. All three encounters led to poems.[8] And in Berengarten's case, more than one poem. The touch of that blue butterfly set off a process of composition that stretched over twenty years and finally produced this book. Berengarten reports that first small nudge, as well as his response to it, in 'Nada: hope or nothing':

> like a silent song sung by the ghost of nobody
> to an unknown, sweet and melodious instrument
> buried ages in the deepest cave of being,
>
> like a word only half heard, half remembered,
> not yet fully learned, from a stranger's language,
> the sad heart longs for, to unlock its deepest cells,

---

[8] In Emerson's case, 'The Rhodora'; in Frost's, 'Design'.

a blue butterfly takes my hand and writes
in invisible ink across its page of air
Nada, Elpidha, Nadezhda, Esperanza, Hoffnung. (*BB* 9)

The Blue Butterfly accomplishes on a larger scale what has already
been sketched out in 'May' and 'The Voice in the Garden'. By dowsing
and fathoming the "faintest sounds / that hatch through cracks of
timelessness in time" (*UBL* 74), in a place made sacred as a memorial
to human injustice and human suffering, the poet once again becomes a
channel through which the voices of the dead can speak both to the living
and to the not-yet-born.

If we can think of *The Blue Butterfly* as a culmination of this central
line of development in Berengarten's work, then I would also suggest that
it might be considered as a culmination of a similar line of development
in the 'recessive' Romantic component of Western culture, in which I
locate Berengarten's work.

The book's tightly-controlled structure and technical complexity plot
out a maze-like design (akin, perhaps, to the design on the wing of a
butterfly) whose intricacies might be explored and unravelled for years.
The Blue Butterfly is much more than either a poetic condemnation of all-
too-human inhumanity or a moving commemoration of the suffering and
nobility of the almost 3,000 victims of the Kragujevac massacre. When
that blue butterfly settled on Berengarten's writing hand, it called him to
an even deeper task: to work his way into and through the labyrinth of
horrors enacted in that place, to bring death back into the texture of life,
and to try to restore the 'wholeness' of Being.

☙

In 'What Are Poets For?',[9] one of his most compelling discussions of the
function of language within Being, Heidegger writes: "In the age of the
world's night, the abyss must be experienced and endured. But for this it
is necessary that there be those who reach into the abyss" (1975: 92). In
this essay, Heidegger is responding to the poetry of Rainer Maria Rilke.
But everything he says in it might equally apply to *The Blue Butterfly.*

Berengarten also reaches deeply into the abyss of the impoverished
human spirit in our destitute time. As did Rilke and Heidegger, he
understands the need to change our approach to death, to stop resisting

---

[9] 'Wozu Dichter?', originally published in 1950.

it (or to learn to resist it in a different way), and to acknowledge that death is the most intimate aspect of what we are. Heidegger suggests that this is the ultimate existential lesson that we are still on the difficult way to learning (or re-learning):

> The time remains destitute not only because God is dead, but because mortals are hardly aware and capable even of their own mortality. Mortals have not yet come into ownership of their own nature. Death withdraws into the enigmatic. The mystery of pain remains veiled. Love has not been learned. (Heidegger 1975: 96)

Love, pain, and the relationship between the living and the dead are also Berengarten's central concerns. Would it be too far-fetched, then, to propose that Berengarten's poetry takes us one more step toward assuming the ownership of our own nature?

When Berengarten incorporates the blue butterfly into the body of his poetry, it also becomes a symbolic link between the living and the dead.[10] The 'real' creature introduced him to his subject; but the symbolic one carries his awareness, across the frontier of life, into what Eliot called "death's dream kingdom".[11] It hovers in the poems above both life and death. Therefore, in the extended Romantic context to which I am appealing, it should be no surprise to discover that the figure of the blue butterfly fulfils the same function in Berengarten's sequence as Rilke's 'Angel' in *The Duino Elegies*. On 3 November 1925, Rilke wrote to Witold Hulewiez:

> The angel of the Elegies is that creature in whom the transformation of the visible into the invisible, which we are accomplishing, already appears in its completion...; that being who guarantees the recognition of a higher level of reality in the invisible (Rilke 1987: 317).

The butterfly and the Angel converge in this way because both Rilke and Berengarten are following the same "pathway" of thinking-towards-death that was initiated in Western culture by the Romantic revolution, and that Heidegger devoted so much of his own thought to illuminating.

---

[10] The butterfly flits in and out of the book, just as we might imagine it flying back and forth between this world and the next, appearing not only in the title poem, 'The Blue Butterfly', but also in 'Nada: hope or nothing', 'The telling', 'Seventh Wreath', 'Conversation Between a Butterfly and a Murdered Man at One of the Gates of the Underworld', 'Signet Ring' and 'Grace'.

[11] In 'The Hollow Men', l. 20.

And this is why Rilke's explanation of his intentions, in that same letter, tells us more about *The Blue Butterfly*, and more effectively, than anything else I could say at this point:

> IN THE "ELEGIES" AFFIRMATION OF LIFE AND AFFIRMATION OF DEATH RE-VEAL THEMSELVES AS ONE … Death is our reverted, our unilluminated, SIDE OF LIFE: we must try to achieve the greatest possible conscious-ness of our existence, which is at home in BOTH OF THESE UNLIMITED PROVINCES, which is INEXHAUSTIBLY NOURISHED OUT OF BOTH … The true form of life extends through BOTH regions, the blood of the mightiest circulation pulses through BOTH: THERE IS NEITHER A HERE NOR A BEYOND, BUT ONLY THE GREAT UNITY, in which the "Angels," those beings that surpass us, are at home (Rilke 1963: 93).

The seven sections, or movements, of *The Blue Butterfly*, each consisting of seven poems, constitute a gradual penetration of the labyrinth of Being that moves the lyric consciousness – and, it is to be hoped, the readers' consciousness – into the "reverted, unilluminated side of life." At the end of section 4, for example, in 'Unmarked Voices from a Mass Grave', we are poised, in awe and apprehension, on the brink of the immovable mystery where knowable experience ends and comprehensible language is nourished by silence:

> You have come to a place, not a place, where no-one can remember
> any words they may have heard, or ways out of the maze,
> or steps once learned in dancing, or their subtle variations,
> and time is a catacomb, a grove of bones, a permanence,
> a station and a destiny, but not a destination,
> where all contours of yesterdays are stratified in a fault
> and tomorrow is an abyss, and the trains of space-time halt. (*BB* 49)

This is the same frontier between language and silence, rational knowledge and mystical revelation, life and death, that American Romantics such as Poe, Whitman and Dickinson often felt compelled to explore, and attempt to report on, in the nineteenth century. However, like Rilke, Berengarten goes even further in the attempt to reclaim a place for the abiding unknown within the human edifice of knowledge.

The speaker is ushered across this final frontier in the seventh poem of section 5, 'Diagonal' (*BB* 70–72). Here, "in the shade of early evening / in a place I did not know, and yet recalled", he encounters a mysterious female figure under whose spell of beauty he is drawn toward a kind of revelation "…in the core of darkness / among the deepest terrors, you must face …. alone, devoid of help from other men". But this passage into the night must be made, as the final words of the poem reveal, in order to discover there "the secret source of day" (*BB* 70–72).

The climax of this journey occurs in section 6, 'The Flight of the Imago', which also rings with distant echoes of the journey of Orpheus into the underworld. In the book's longest poem, 'Conversation Between a Butterfly and a Murdered Man at One of the Gates of the Underworld', human thought and language go as far as they can possibly reach toward the impassive mystery that is the other side of life. This is a region that Emily Dickinson visited quite often in her masterful poems on the epistemological quandary of death.[12] The whole of this 'Conversation' takes place in the amorphous interval between the moment of death and the dissolution of the individual consciousness, which I have elsewhere described as "the locus of the Romantic imagination" (Derrick 2003: 92).[13] "Blow on this Dandelion", the butterfly begins,

> Spread its seeds on
> the wind. I'll rest in your hand while you're dying.
> […]
> Your time of times has come. Now is the last
> of your moments. Now you must pass for ever
> out of time. (*BB* 89)

This extended moment of juncture between all that the mind can know and something else, which we name death, can be read as one more step in a continuing process of inquiry that our Romantic predecessors began for us. The 'Conversation' itself consists of a series of variations on the problem of how to think the unthinkable, how to say what we cannot know, and which is therefore unsayable; and it transports us into the same uncanny 'place-that-is-no-place' that Rilke expresses so powerfully in his 'First Elegy':

---

[12] See, for example, 'I felt a Funeral in my Brain' (J280), 'I died for Beauty' (J449), 'I heard a Fly buzz – when I died –' (J465), 'Because I could not stop for Death' (J712) and 'This Consciousness that is aware' (J822).

[13] 'Ballad of the seagull' occupies the identical intermediate zone between life and death (*BB* 42–44).

True, it is strange to inhabit the earth no longer,
to use no longer customs scarcely acquired,
not to interpret roses, and other things
that promise so much, in terms of a human future;
to be no longer all that one used to be
in endlessly anxious hands, and to lay aside
even one's proper name like a broken toy.
Strange, not to go on wishing one's wishes. Strange,
to see all that was once relation so loosely fluttering
hither and thither in space. And it's hard, being dead,
and full of retrieving before one begins to espy
a trace of eternity. (Rilke 1963: 25)

From a sense of estrangement to the first faint glimmer of the light of home: this is precisely the process that long conversation between the butterfly and the murdered man encompasses. Rilke ends this passage with the following reflection:

Angels (they say) are often unable to tell
whether they move among living or dead. The eternal
torrent whirls all the ages through either realm
for ever, and sounds above their voices in both. (Rilke 1963: 25)

It is more than a simple coincidence that, at the end of Berengarten's poem, after the butterfly has calmed the man's fears and prepared his mind to accept an infinite mindlessness, the speaker addresses it as:

Angel of life or death, my butterfly, no matter. You
Blue speckler and flecker of wind, handsomest airborne drifter,
Master lightfoot, with your club-tipped antennae, go, shimmering.
(BB 98)

IV

Ours is a culture that is threatened with many serious crises. This Romantic pathway back toward a different conceptual framework for death may offer us a viable way forward, a way to save ourselves from ourselves. Heidegger clearly believed that it did. What he found in both Rilke and Hölderlin only confirmed his own conviction that the gift of thought should be used to find our way through the confusion that we sponsor toward a harmonious and healthy relationship with the world of which our sponsorship forms a decisive part. Perhaps, Heidegger suggests, the ultimate implication of the initial Romantic impulse toward a holistic paradigm is that an acceptance of death is the key to wholeness. "Death", he writes, "is what touches mortals in their nature, and so sets them on their way to the other side of life … Death thus gathers into the whole of what is already posited" (Heidegger 1975: 126).

The health of Being (which embraces the health of us all) depends on our accommodating mystery, the secret waiting in "the core of darkness" (*BB* 72). And that secret, precisely because it extends beyond our reach, beyond what we are, can be thought of as 'holy'. This, suggests Heidegger, is what poets are for in a time of need. The rationalistic, materialistic culture of the West has banished any serious concept of 'spirit' from our frameworks of explanation. Poets though, follow the trace of the disappearing gods, and sing to heal a world that is falling into pieces. Heidegger reminds us that in German, as in English, such words as health, haleness, wholeness and holiness are cognate. Etymologically, each implies all the others:

> Holiness can appear only within the widest orbit of the whole-some. Poets who are the most venturesome kind are under way on the track of the holy because they experience the unholy as such. Their song over the land hallows. Their singing hails the integrity of the globe of Being. (Heidegger 1975: 141)

Berengarten's poetry witnesses, commemorates, laments, affirms and blesses. The final poem of *The Blue Butterfly*, 'Grace', is a simple hymn, to 'hallow' the land and to confirm the hope for our long and difficult journey back to 'wholeness':

> Under the hills, quiet
> fire. From their graves
> the dead awaken.
>
> Blessing on you
> who live, they call
> through our own voices,
>
> as in their places
> we too shall call
> our own unborn.

Under hills, this
grace flows
through everything.

Chestnut and oak
bud, green
earth's carpet.

Red tulip petals
scatter. A blue
butterfly hovers. (*BB* 111)

If there is indeed "a Hand to turn the time", as Thomas Pynchon ambiguously suggests at the end of *Gravity's Rainbow* (1973: 760), it just might be the hand of a poet like Richard Berengarten, that can draw a blue butterfly out of the sky, and write its silent, life-giving 'message of death' for all of us to hear.

REFERENCES

Baym, Nina *et al.* (eds). 1989. *The Norton Anthology of American Literature* (2 vols). New York, NY, and London: W. W. Norton and Company.

Buell, Lawrence (ed.). 1993. *Ralph Waldo Emerson: A Collection of Critical Essays*. Upper Saddle River, NJ: Prentice Hall.

Cavell, Stanley. 1993. 'Thinking of Emerson' in Buell: 191–198.

Derrick, Paul Scott. 2003. *"We Stand Before the Secret of the World": Traces along the Pathway of American Romanticism*. Valencia: Biblioteca Javier Coy d'estudis nord-americans.

Eliot. T. S. 1980 [1933]. *The Use of Poetry and the Use of Criticism*. London and Boston, MA: Faber and Faber.

Emerson, Ralph Waldo. 1989 [1844]. 'The poet' in Baym et al 1989: 984–997.

Heidegger, Martin. 1970 [1949]. *Existence and Being* (ed. Werner Brock) Chicago, IL: Gateway.

______. 1975. *Poetry, Language, Thought* (trans. Albert Hofstadter). New York, NY: Harper Colophon Books.

______. 1977. *The Question Concerning Technology and Other Essays* (trans. William Lovitt). New York, NY: Harper Colophon Books.

Jarrell, Randall. 1980 [1953]. *Poetry and the Age*. New York, NY: The Ecco Press.

Johnson, Thomas H. (ed.). 1979 [1955]. *The Poems of Emily Dickinson*, (3 vols) Cambridge, MA: The Belknap Press of Harvard University.

Limburg, Joanne. 2002. 'Human above all: Richard Burns's *The Manager*'. *The Jewish Quarterly* 185 (Spring): 17–23.

Pynchon, Thomas. 1973. *Gravity's Rainbow*. New York, NY: The Viking Press.

Rilke, Rainer Maria. 1963 [1939]. *The Duino Elegies*. (trans. J. B. Leishman and Stephen Spender). New York, NY: W. W. Norton & Company.

______. 1987 [1980]. *The Selected Poetry of Rainer Maria Rilke*. (trans. Stephen Mitchell). London: Picador.

Janus Masks:
On the Many Facets of Richard Berengarten's Work

Simon Jenner

Peter Sellers once famously imitated a senior BBC mandarin, phoning the Head of Variety, to engage this 'Sellers character'. Richard Berengarten shares with Peter Sellers this ability to spring a good hoax. Berengarten sent his poem 'The Easter Rising 1967' via courier to England, where it was published in the January 1968 edition of the *London Magazine*; the necessary pseudonym, Agnostos Nomolos ('Solomon' spelt backwards) was readily accepted by the editor, Alan Ross. For a long time the alleged authorship seemed secure, despite suspicions that must have lurked in some Anglo-Greek minds (*FL* 219).

'The Easter Rising 1967' is the opening poem in Berengarten's first retrospective, *For the Living: Selected Longer Poems 1965–2000*. Here is the first of its nine sections:

> I am sick of the twittering of swallows' voices,
> My Lord, I have come down from the North
> To find only You, but sitting by the well
> I was assaulted by perfumes
> And the babbling of a thousand animals
> Performing the rites of Spring. I am sick to death
> Of them all, My Lord.
> You do not walk among them. (*FL* 3)

This is like nothing else being written in English then or later. Perfumes reminiscent of Cavafy's 'Ithaca' (Cavafy 1961: 29) might have been dreamed up by someone with a sense of pastiche, but a wider reading is also suggested by the hinted underlying presence of Seferis and Elytis –

in the starkly tinctured landscape, drypoint tragedy and epic sweep. But what Berengarten has most evidently achieved here is to invoke his own gods, his visionary company, in a way that in late 1960s Britain most reviewers and critics would hardly have found welcome. In this early pseudo-translation, therefore, the lineaments of the poet are already fully formed. Later, with his power and self-positioning in a tradition of his own choosing, he elicited a similar bafflement in the early 1970s with his long poem 'Angels' (*FL* 51–56).

These two features of ventriloquism and symbolism – the first not uncommon on a smaller scale, the second not common at all – distinguish Berengarten from his British contemporaries. They configure him, rather, in a modern European tradition – though one that is nonetheless rooted in English poetry, as is suggested by his invoking of Keats and Mandelstam together in 'Croft Woods' (*FL* 197–209). Indeed, given the range of Berengarten's influences, it would certainly be possible to consider his work in terms of Harold Bloom's 'anxiety of influence'. However, Berengarten is a sufficiently accomplished writer to be wide open to influences without risking the disappearance of his own voice. In an almost bewildering display of both traditional and modernist techniques, Berengarten's own tone is unmistakable.

By turns visionary, sardonic, elegiac and – when the dead speak – hallucinatory, his work exhibits a strong kinship with that of Blake and, indeed, the name of the little press Berengarten started in Cambridge, Los Poetry Press, is based on the character in Blake's *Prophetic Books* who symbolises the creative imagination. However, unlike such post-war poets as Allen Ginsberg and Michael Horovitz, Berengarten has no need to echo Blake's poetic devices or imitate his stylistic trappings. Rather, he is most akin to Blake in never allowing himself to be undermined by that almost universal British fear of taking oneself too seriously. If you don't risk accusations of over-seriousness, Berengarten implies, why bother?

Moreover, Berengarten appears to have considerably closer affinities with Yeats and Pessoa than with most of his English contemporaries – both of whom happen to share Berengarten's astrological sun sign, although there is no evidence in his work of any sympathy with, let alone belief in, astrology. In this connection, whilst the opening section of *The Manager* is entitled 'Gemini' (*TM* 7), this short piece, in fact, is something of a firecracker: rather than consider Berengarten's sun sign, it sends up those lunatic glossy magazine horoscopes. Beginning with measured cliché, the language explodes in the two-word phrase "Particularly Friday", where finally the reader is warned away from 'voices' – "Lest untamed angels in disguise … smother you in sorrow", and "sudden breakdown or memory lapse tumble and flood you in darkness". The reader's impression here is of a mind wandering over cliché to find itself hanging over a cliff-edge of insanity; as the banality of sentiment triggers its own dislocated misreading, the presentiment of breakdown is voiced. However, Berengarten is subtle enough not to colour his drama with implausible excesses of either character or confession.

In its overall structure and patterning, *The Manager* recalls some of Beddoes' dramatic fragments in their mordancy, their wit and their nightmarish quality. Indeed, in the context of another poem by Berengarten, Act III, Scene III of Beddoes' *The Brides' Tragedy* comes specifically to mind: in this passage, the last shipwrecked sailor is watching sea monsters "For his dead messmates warring all, save one / That leers upon him with a ravenous gaze" (Beddoes 1950: 15–16) – which is about to eat him. This extinction of one's own kind, ending with the doomed witness anticipating his own extinction, strangely prefigures Berengarten's extraordinary 'Angels'. Beddoes, of course, also wandered over Europe for much of his life. Berengarten's ludic wit turns to deadly purpose, again making him decisively a European rather than an insular British poet. Geoffrey Hill, despite his Miltonic protestations, is of a similar cast of mind.

℀

Norman Jope has suggested that Berengarten is one of those poets, modernist in scope and reach, whose focus on both the visionary and the act of translation locates him in a zone excluded by either modernist or mainstream.

> Richard Berengarten (Burns) is just one obvious example among other writers I particularly admire, who fall foul of a kind of schism … I'm not sure if one can identify a unified 'third stream' but would suggest two zones of exclusion, to start with – writers who deal with issues of spirituality and personal transformation, and writers whose influences are strongly or mainly from other literatures in translation. Both the mainstream and the *avant-garde* are set, on the whole, against both of these tendencies (quoted in Jenner 2008: 16).

Jope's eclecticism clearly embraces many of the most interesting poets, wary of schools, who are determined to continue to absorb and learn from 'foreign' poetry. However, from the point of view of getting published, at least until recently, living abroad hasn't generally proved to be a particularly good tactical move for a British poet either: too many interests, too much politics, too much garish colour.

❧

'Actaeon' (1965–1966) and 'Avebury' (1971) with its dedication to Octavio Paz – both of which are ambitious and experimental in their approach to poetic form – honed the poet's imagistic precision in splintered stanzas. 'Avebury' is in twenty-four sections, and moves far from considerations of that flint-strewn place. Section VIII is particularly rich:

> and at Samothraki
> striding out   came dancing
>   Nike
>   the daughter
>
>   headless
> in the wind   and taking wings
>   her robe a river of hair
> over the jutting curve of her
>   incredible arrogant breasts
>
>   and the breakers
>   confluent
>   under the belly
>   forming   like an unseen hand
> protecting her cave   the mouth of her (*FL* 32)

Berengarten merges the standing stones of Avebury with images 'set in stone' from elsewhere, in order to depict a disturbed and eroticised topography. The spacings and patterning of words on the pages mean that each section actually 'reads' like fractured and piled stone. What whistles through these gaps is worth capturing: a sonority of barrow-wraiths. 'Avebury' is perhaps an interrogation of myth and history, a prising of rock, by tapping it at the right angle.

'Angels' (1974–1976), on the other hand, is presciently ecological, and almost anticipates Lowell's dolphin poems – themselves often hailed as prescient – which were published in the year before 'Angels'. But Berengarten's poem is, both metaphorically and literally, a deeper sounding altogether. First published as one of his poster poems, 'Angels' explores the extinction of a large mammal hunted on land, whose last survivors manage to reach the ocean. By changing habitat, the species is reprieved, and under water it breeds, evolves and thrives. However, resultant complacency dooms the whale-like though never explicitly identified angels to a second, now permanent extinction:

> Then we were few: three, perhaps, four.
> To zones unhaunted, by no fish followed,
> where water's weight and sheer blackness
> pressed till we shrank and merged with shadows,
> down we dived, deeper than terror.
> Then we were two, and we sang each other
> of Tiphareth, of the Throne, of the Glory.
> Indescribable our lamentations,
> we the uncounted, the unaccountables,
> sons and daughters of the starry heavens
> become a lost calling without a name
> drifting among unfathomed valleys,
> until I called, recalled, and heard
> no answering song. Then quietly I climbed
> and on a still sea trumpeted, took air
> and dived for ever. And you'll not find me
> nor you nor you, till the almond tree flowers
> on the mountain, and there is no more sea. (*FL* 55–56)

Berengarten's variations on Kabbalistic, liturgical and Biblical images and references, such as "Tiphareth", "the Throne", "the Glory", "almond tree" and "no more sea" – and his homophonic variations like "uncounted" and "unaccountables" (a neologism too) – contribute to the single huge *breath* of the poem. The steady sway of the phrasing and the accusatory interruptions of repeated key phrases ("nor you nor you") reinforce the poem's trance-like ambience, which persists even when its rhythms thrash, plunge and dive most forcefully through the watery heights and depths. One of Berengarten's most moving poems, 'Angels' far transcends its principal constituent metaphor; it is almost as if the terrible beauty of its final Biblical invocation involves the inhalation of searing lungfuls, not of air, but of fire.

'Ode on the End of the Third Exile' (1976–1978) proves that Berengarten's early immersion in Greece and in the work of Seferis (as the homage in *Black Light* makes explicit) was hardly an ephemeral accident. It is almost as if Berengarten relocated to Greece because that was where his poetry needed to be – in the same way as happened again, years later, in Yugoslavia. This 'Ode' is playfully Ovidian, in its exilic slant and in the metamorphoses of both protagonist and his sometime siren, who is sexily described in Section II. From the outset, "resin and thyme" clearly evoke the Mediterranean and perhaps also the background hum of Seferis. Inlaid description vies with a diction that is demotic and casual ('going barmy') to fill out the Berengarten landscape:

> Bearer of the double flute among those hill walled cities,
> through villages hive crowned, smelling of resin and thyme
> and the swallows going barmy in their ivy hung eaves,
> in wood stacked fishing hamlets precarious on estuaries,
> breezing into valleys of silvering olive trees (*FL* 57)

All too typical of legendary sea voyages that involve a poet, the sequence of five sections climaxes with the crew demanding that the "fat Hebrew" sing them out of a storm. Refusing that particular office, the protagonist lets himself be thrown overboard; he's then borne aloft, fantastically, by a female apparition: "Son of earth, sky breather, / Enough of sea and weeping. Now it is time to return." (*FL* 63). And so he returns, on the green-eyed siren's back, as if riding a dolphin – to "work for love and justice". It's a remarkable fable, even though the end owns a 1968ish, flatly delivered expression of reforming zeal.

Other poems like 'Tree' illustrate (very literally) Berengarten's virtuosity when it is placed in the service of the natural order, both poetically and botanically. The reader's focus is kept on the breathless movement of the poem's narrow ribbon of text. 'Tree' maintains an extraordinary resource of metaphor, never flagging in its arboreal reach or apposite growing-points.

℘

'Black Light' (1982/1986) is subtitled 'In Memory of George Seferis, 1900–71', and in its explicit homage this sequence shows Berengarten at his most ambitious and achieved (*FL* 147–176). He often *names* the poets he's invoking, because his voice is powerful enough to confront them, pay homage, and render something different. Here, each poem in the sequence is prefaced by an epigraph from Seferis. Berengarten's ability to base his own work on the resource of a *cantus firmus*, whether from the near or distant past, is one that any poet born before 1800 would have taken for granted as a basic tenet of the Art. In 'Black Light',

36

Berengarten's range extends from the two strict villanelles that structurally and thematically frame the beginning and end of the sequence – a form to which he later returns with overwhelming force and point in 'The Death of Children' (*BB* 17–25) – to intimations of friendship and mortality, couched in a variety of other forms, that seem all the more masterful for being delivered so casually. In 'Soulmonger' (*FL* 155–156), the theme is broached in loosely-knit hexameters:

> And my guide said, 'Do not probe too deeply in darkness
> but construct your world out of daylight. As for dreams,
> you should listen to them carefully, for their voices
> may often be prophetic, pointing the true way (*FL* 155)

Another poem, 'Cicadas I', evokes an intimacy at the meal table, strongly inflected by the Greek language (*FL* 159). But the fullest strength is felt in poems like 'Volta':

> Porous city, her name is *Eleftheria*,
> and though your scars are grey flecks in her eyes
> still, at this hour when light and light's inflections
> play subtly in her face as speech or song,
> hers is the ancient right to walk this quayside
> as instrument and guardian of your light
> collecting it in the wells of her deep pupils,
> and hers, the darling freedom, to tread you like a dancer.
>
> Darling evening, light thousands of years old,
> clear throated singer, lovely as this woman,
> how can I not adore the grace you cast
> this city and its people in, a mould
> that sculptures all it touches, the whole world?
> I have become your slave, if not your citizen.
> And thirsting to drink you wholly, I would fill
> every pore with your radiance, her freedom. (*FL* 158)

The variegated patterning of "light" in the sequence is concentrated, by a single flashing feminine glance, in full Mediterranean intensity. This light also provides a kind of release from the almost tangibly 'lived-in' aspects of the sequence, replete with all its local words, colours and coffee smells. At the time he was writing 'Black Light', Berengarten had virtually no peer in English in his exploration of the post-romantic use of language – that is, in the visionary, wryly fabulous scope he was making his own.

With such an intimate evocation in mid-career as this, I would argue that here Berengarten came of age as a poet: this elegiac and metaphysically searching meditation announces his reach as one who, among other things, is able, as William Empson put it, to "argufy" in verse with other poets.

એ૦

Several masterpieces of Berengarten's maturity demand full treatment, notably *The Blue Butterfly*. But 'Croft Woods' (1998–1999), which combines a dense surface reminiscent of Keats' 'Ode to a Nightingale' with a Shelleyan sweep of lyrical argument, offers a more manageable example from his mature period. This, incidentally, is a manner that Hart Crane would have recognised; and, as has already been mentioned, Keats and Mandelstam are explicitly invoked in the poem itself. 'Croft Woods' displays Berengarten at the height of his transcendent powers:

> The light here hangs diagonally down,
> an alphabet of traceries and shadows
> I have not learned, but only half intuit.
> Illiterate, I stumble like a foreigner
> who cannot read the simplest of its messages.
> But still it daunts me, calls me deep into it.
>
> Blue moss, moonwort, fronded maidenhair,
> dusty spores of buckler and hart's-tongue nestling
> under cow-grass and nettles, where I tread,
> cry for release: *Go soft now and in peace.*
> I wish I were a ghost, not to disturb
> their roots planted more deeply than our dead. (*FL* 199)

The formal quality here is Shelleyan in its intellectual power, while the sensuous detail and texturing in the second of these stanzas are, more precisely, Keatsian. Exhortative measures such as *"Go soft now"* are recognisable as pure Berengarten: he has carried these keys with him from a time before even the writing of 'Black Light' (where, like the light itself, they solidified). The movement in 'Croft Woods' is a journey towards voices through "a slanted source of sunlight" (*FL* 143); and this visual aspect bears direct comparison with the setting of another poem, 'Diagonal' (*BB* 70–72), in which the protagonist is visited by a fleeting, Beatrice-like guide. Such figures, voices and musical sounds often flit in and out of Berengarten's poems; and although these are sometimes

38

capable of flirting, like Ondine, to lead the protagonist astray, they are usually benign – more like Odysseus' goddesses. In 'Croft Woods', lute sounds invoking "Dowland, Wyatt's, Shakespeare's" give way to an overhearing of oneself:

> I am a shell without a listening child
> to hear the sea in. I'm the sea itself
> solidified, without a moon to pull
> a wind or raise a cloud or comb a wave.
> Where have I gone – where has my own self gone
> out of this everlasting-seeming pause? (*FL* 200)

The forest of other voices is so dense that it "hollows one out" by comparison. This dark wood itself is both a translation of listening and a negation of it. More than individuality is threatened; the humanity of speech, of listening and of silence is overwhelmed by the half scrubbed-out palimpsest of anti-voices. Primordial, certainly kin to the savage gods of depression and the blackness plunging one into silence, these also threaten all individual voicing:

> And these translucent symphonies of sap
> print negatives of speech, gaps, absences,
> unstitching and unweaving human voices
> to dim inverted echoes of our origins,
> as shimmering escarpments, cliffs and peaks
> reflect in lakes through which the abyss speaks.
> [...]
> Unbearable polyphonies! I'm hemmed
> on all sides by a shadow-orchestra
> playing not sound, but mirrorings of sound,
> an anti-music, music's twin and opposite,
> fluid in meanings, filled with coded messages
> of bodiless bodies, dry dews, airless airs. (*FL* 202–203)

Not only are 'Avebury' and 'Angels' echoed in this unusually denotative language; they are also challenged, as the next stanza affirms, in "punning alien non-calls". Thus Berengarten's language, even at its most richly orchestrated, switches back to the vernacular and checks itself against 'common sense' in a constantly critical, criss-cross deconstruction of the very elaborate trajectory of the poem which, all the while, is proceeding in almost regally measured stanzas.

Inevitably, perhaps, the muse that haunts so much of Berengarten's best work italicises his text in a whisper so that, after ambivalent exhortations ("*come and be sentry to these catacombs, / the minotaur of labyrinthine caves*"), the poem turns:

> and listening to this music is descending
> a ladder dangling in an endless void,
> to reach its end, let go, and still to tumble
> throughout one's self until all self is blown
> like breath from dying lungs or a balloon,
> and further fall, a meteoric stone.
>
> Deeper than self entirely, made transparent,
> the dreamer enters unsleep, a new zone,
> and in so doing, *climbs*! If this is falling,
> it is a falling upwards, a dawn breaking
> a dream undreamed, redressed, a double-waking,
> and through fear so far gone, fear is unknown. (*FL* 204–205)

In this "climb", the speaker identifies strata of artists and their artistry, ("I touch a world inside the veins of rock / which Michelangelo knew before he chiselled …/ I'm Goethe's Faust …/ I am at one with Keats and Mandelstam / I am the bloodless blood inside the rose." [*FL* 205]). The poet who, like Orpheus, Aeneas or Dante – not to mention Lazarus – began his descent in 'negative' mode, is now able to "print out" his 'positive' affirmation: "And now, I have the key – of songs perpetual…". His penetrating meditation on the roots of the theme of 'Welcome joy, and welcome sorrow' is reminiscent of this gloss by Keats on his own melancholy, in his eponymous 'Ode' (Keats 1895: 352). Berengarten, however, is more explicit and takes more envisioned risks, extraordinary in any period but particularly unusual in a climate of post-modern irony and scepticism:

> These boughs and trunks are valves the underworld
> allows the dead we tread on underfoot
> to breathe a little through from atmospheres
> funnelled from earthly moistures. Each porous
> bulb, root, tuber is a well sprung door
> hinged between death and life and keyed by dream.
>
> Withstanding stresses higher than our hopes,
> through hollowed pipes which subtly coil and bend
> on stems stretched taut, to analyse and parse

galactic grammars without start or end,
blossoms and flowers, like astral telescopes,
in petalled bowls snatch impulses from stars. (*FL* 207)

The only passage I can compare to this "string theory" vision of the connectedness of vegetable and stellar worlds is Crane's *The Bridge*, in particular its final section, 'Atlantis'. Very few poems since then can begin to match Crane's rhapsodic parabola of hymned steel. However, 'Croft Woods' runs it close. 'Croft Woods' is a considerably longer piece than 'Atlantis', but it contains several passages that possess a ringing authority, coupled with an imagistic precision – or *incision*, almost akin to the visual and tactile effect of drypoint. This makes Berengarten's lines tremulously alive to the ways in which

[c]hords brushed from nothing, plaited lacy stuff,
chains out of nowhere, cables combed from void,
join death to us across their bridge of hair. (*FL* 208)

℘

I have suggested some of the ways in which Berengarten has proceeded from his glued-in poem of revolt, hanging like a chrysalis from inside the back cover of *The London Magazine*, to the epic sweep of his later work. And, as 'Croft Woods' spells darkly, a genuine loss involving the 'Janusing' or negativing of self – like that of 'Solomon' into 'Nomolos'– is a prerequisite for entering the self's striated darkness and returning to the world of language with poetry of lasting impact. Beyond a very few contemporaries such as Mario Petrucci, with his marvellous *Heavy Water*, and of course Geoffrey Hill, there are few who dare to claim this Shelleyan, vatic inheritance for poetry – even when such claims are vital for its continuance. And fewer who can.

REFERENCES

Beddoes, Thomas Lowell. 1950. *Plays and Poems* (ed. H. W. Donner).London: Routledge and Kegan Paul.

Blake, William. 1956. *Poetry and Prose* (ed. Geoffrey Keynes). London: The Nonesuch Library.

Cavafy, Constantine. 1961. *Complete Poems*, expanded (trans. Rae Dalven). New York, NY: Harvest.

Crane, Hart. 1999. *Complete Poems, Centennial Edition* (ed. Marc Simon). New York, NY: Liveright.

Empson, William. 1987. *Argufying: Essays on Literature and Culture*. Iowa City, IA: University of Iowa Press.

Jenner, Simon. 2008. 'Introduction' to *Orphans of Albion* (ed. Barry Tebb). London: Survivors' Press: 7–17.

Keats, John. 1895. *The Poetical Works* (ed. Harry Buxton Forman). London: Reeves & Turner.

Lowell, Robert. 1973. *The Dolphin*. New York, NY: Farrar, Straus.

The Ghost of the Mediterranean

Mario Nicolao

Translated from Italian by Gabriele Poole and Vladimir Scott

A Homage to Agnostos Nomolos

And I hear my secret sea flood in, my hushed inner sea
('Cicadas', FL 171)

The Mediterranean contains many ghosts under the ceaseless to-ing and fro-ing of its green-blue waves. The ghost of Jaufré Rudel who crossed it to reach Tripoli and die. The ghost of Percy Bysshe Shelley who drowned off the coast of Lerici; the sea gave back his body but not his soul, which perhaps still screams during storms, or warbles sweetly, like a skylark, among the olive groves of Liguria.

The Mediterranean itself is a ghost, the ghost of a god that wiped out a civilisation by calling up the fury of the volcano of Santorini, even though I believe, with Pierre Vidal-Naquet, that Atlantis was 'just' an Athenian myth. But it was the Mediterranean that swallowed the bodies of the Persians at Salamis and later those of Turks and Christians alike at Lepanto.

The Mediterranean, moreover, is the ghost of many of the civilisations born out of its briny coitus. It is the sea of the Phoenicians and the Greeks. It is the purple sea of Odysseus and of Rubaldo Merello. It is the crescent moon-tipped green sea of the pirate Admiral Khaireddin, who defeated Andrea Doria at Preveza (and of the Syrian-Lebanese poet Adonis, our contemporary), and it is the almost stagnating sea of the Venetian lagoon, where Richard Berengarten wrote 'Actaeon'.

And how many people have been killed, gutted and slaughtered, and tossed into the huge cleansing bowl that all seas are, but especially this sea, so vast, yet at the same time so closed in on itself? A sea that continues to hone down and eventually scatter millions of skulls and bones, century after century.

Yes, the Mediterranean is the ghost of a god, a god more powerful than Pan or Dionysos, a god who swallows and shuts up, and who shudders and quakes the lands that he himself has fathered and nourished: the lands of Greece, the lands of Italy, and also the lands on the other side, to the east.

ↁ

Richard Berengarten is the latest in a long line of English poets who have ardently sung the Mediterranean and its *terra* par excellence, Greece: the Hellas that Shelley dreamed against the 'Persians'. But while other English nomads, Forster and Durrell, have sung it through the Alexandrian poet Cavafy, Berengarten has sung it with the Ionian poet George Seferis who wrote in demotic Greek, just as did the bard of Alexandria.

As we read Berengarten's poems, they interweave with those of Seferis. It is as though they echo Seferis, like "waves / expanding, re-echoing" ('Avebury', *FL* 50). Berengarten was living in Greece at the time when a military junta (the Colonels) ousted the legitimate government in the *coup d'état* of April 1967. Berengarten's poem 'The Easter Rising' (*FL* 1–14), written in Thebes that year, had to be smuggled out of Greece and published under the pseudonym of Agnostos Nomolos, to whom I have dedicated this brief statement. George Seferis died four years later, in 1971. Three years after that, in 1974, the military dictatorship was overthrown.

The poems which I have chosen to comment on first span the years 1965 to 2000 and are included in *For the Living, Selected Writings 1*. And I shall speak of only one facet of Berengarten's poetic opus: his connection with Mediterranean culture, a connection that much great English poetry has maintained.

ↁ

There are poets of the sea and poets of the land. Sea poets love waves and clouds, whatever is constantly changing yet perennial. Land poets love what is stable but subject to ruin. Berengarten is a land poet. His heraldic symbol is the tree, that which roots itself into the ground and reaches for the sky, that which dares the lightning:

44

survivor tree
    skeletal
under storm clouds
    budding slow
through despair
    thrusting hopes
of high skies
    cirrus strewn
milky ways
    and birds returning (*FL* 119–120)

Berengarten's Greece is not only the Greece of the sea, but also that of the land-dwellers: he often sings Greece with his back towards the sea and his eyes toward the land, while in his ears the constant *basso* of the waves rumbles on "in the sea's secret speech" ('Shell', *FL* 170). So too the "blue island" in 'Song, for Petro' (*FL* 168) is seen as a land risen from the sea. Berengarten observes people, their toil, their songs and their laughter. In the evening, he walks along the shore, where the night fishermen are preparing their boats, with "motors chugging, paraffin lamps in the bows", and the lovers stroll, arm in arm ('Volta', *FL* 157). He listens to the summer landscape, thick with cicadas:

> where, in high pitched voices, they argue my destiny
> till their whole assembly has reached its decision
> and I can smell them, out there in the darkness. (*FL* 171)

And he recounts combatants in the modern-day Greek struggle: Theodorakis, Papandreou, Kanellopoulos, Glezos ('The Easter Rising', *FL* 8).

Like a wandering singer, he gathers their voices, their joy and their desperation. And we sense that Richard Berengarten, who now lives in Cambridge, is one of us: a child of our fateful sea, the Mediterranean.

❧

Further up the coast of Greece, past the Strait of Otranto, the Mediterranean narrows into a deep, long gulf, the Adriatic. Here, as one sails north towards Trieste, one finds on the left the coastlines of Italy, which are almost always low and sandy, while on the right the shore is rocky and battered by high waves, suddenly announcing the mountains of Albania – and then those of Montenegro, Croatia and Slovenia, and Serbia and Bosnia inland: countries that all, until a few years ago, went under the name of Yugoslavia. A rugged, tormented land, repeatedly invaded and bathed in blood. How right Berengarten was when he wrote in 1991, "Watch where you walk. You think you tread on stones? / You're wrong, my friend. It is your brother's bones." (*BB* 16).

Berengarten belongs to all of us: he is Greek, Italian, Yugoslav; in short he is Mediterranean. The blue butterfly that rests for a moment on the hand of the English poet in Šumarice (*BB* 8) reminds him of the blood that was spilled, the mass murders perpetrated by the soldiers of the *Wehrmacht* and the SS in the Balkans (and after 1943 in Italy, just as all over Europe). This blue butterfly, blue and sad at once, both in its colour and in its double meaning, is the seal that the spirit of the age has stamped on the poet: but with the lightest, slightest touch, that awakens him to the horror of human history, because sometimes a caress can affect one more than a punch or a blow.

> The glimpse, the graze, the grasp,
> the only true synchronicities, of the inner and outer combining.
> To know them, to know one knows, and then to let go
> of knowing, like this blue butterfly's flight
> here in Šumarice, over these hills, this Maytime:
> dance of the imago (*BB* 101)

Beauty and goodness express themselves quietly, in an undertone, as Berengarten does in these lines, which are more often than not played *pianissimo*. I would almost go so far as to say that 'blue' is the colour of his tone and of his memory: the colour of his verse, of these lines.

Berengarten is not a politicised poet, but he is a poet of the *polis*, a *poeta civilis*, as was Primo Levi, who appears in one of the book's epigraphs, along with Rebecca West and Zhuang Zhou, the latter in the celebrated fable of the butterfly much loved by Borges. Berengarten's poetry immediately and naturally takes the path of denunciation and defence: denunciation of the crime and defence of the oppressed, of the humiliated, of the victimised. Yet there is no overstatement. Berengarten enters the mind of the victim; his voice becomes the victim's voice:

> Straining to gaze upwards, I heard another burst
> Of gunfire wash over me, as from some distant hill.
> [...]
> So my world ended. My eyes rolled open, still. (*BB* 44)

And you'll not find me
nor you nor you, till the almond tree flowers
on the mountain, and there is no more sea. (*FL* 56)

I can understand why Berengarten has translated Cesare Pavese (1969) and Umberto Saba (in Lopez 1971), Italian authors who spoke quietly and whose work echoes more loudly for precisely this reason.

Sometimes it is enough to list numbers, as Berengarten does in 'Two documents': 19,545 Serbs imprisoned in the camp at Šabac, 405 hostages killed in Belgrade, and so on (*BB* 5). Stark facts for stark verse-in-prose. Or to report messages, as in the words: "*Tell the comrades to fight till they crush the enemy*" ('Don't send bread tomorrow', *BB* 6). Words of hope, words that the butterfly writes "in invisible ink across its page of air", where the word *nada*, which in Spanish means 'nothing', means and will always mean, no more and no less: 'hope' (*BB* 9).

References

Lopez, Guido. 1971. 'Trieste's Umberto Saba' (trans. RB), *European Judaism* 5(2): 28–37

Pavese, Cesare 1969. 'Three poems' (trans. RB), *Southern Review* 5(1): 98–103.

Love's Integument:
The Poetry of Richard Berengarten

Tessa Ransford

"We knew. We were not fools." This half-line from Richard Berengarten's poem 'In the Room Suddenly' (*AP* 41), a complex lyric capturing the essence of a moment, provides an apt place to begin considering his work as it affects me, a near contemporary, writing in the same language and also connecting to a European tradition. The poem appeared on the first page of the first issue that I edited of the poetry magazine *Lines Review*, in December 1988. In my introduction, I wrote that I was looking, as editor, "not just for quality *per se*, but for a particular quality: a poetry that is happening now and is itself part of that happening" (Ransford 1988: 4). Seeking to present a poetry "searching momentarily for its own presence in order to move on to another threshold of understanding", I quoted Kierkegaard's definition of faith as "an objective uncertainty held with passionate inwardness" (in Cruikshank 1984: 5).

"She is the song she plays, and what it's saying" is a line in Berengarten's intricately interwoven poem 'Against the Day' (*FL* 194), a poem sequence inspired by Vermeer's painting *The Guitar Player*. Here, not only do we have the singer and the song, but also the picture and the painter who makes the picture and, enveloping these, the poet making the poem partaking in the painting, the picture, the girl and the singing – reaching out also to an invisible potential audience for the girl, for the picture and of course for the poem, whose readers embrace the folds within folds of the creative process as it interacts with life. There is an echo of Yeats' question, "How can we tell the dancer from the dance?" in the attempt to express the mutual "coinherence" (a word coined by Charles Williams in *The Descent of the Dove*) of maker and the made in *poeisis*. The last verse of 'In the Room Suddenly' asks: "But who will mend the lovely broken chain / …unless by metamorphosis we grow / seeds from that moment's core back in the brain?" (*AP* 42).

I had heard of Richard Berengarten through Joy Hendry and Walter Perrie, founding editors of *Chapman* magazine, and I knew that he had helped to introduce Sorley Maclean and other Scottish poets to a readership south of the border through the 1975 Cambridge Poetry Festival, which he had founded and organised. He visited the Scottish Poetry Library in its early years and took an informed interest in our work in Scotland, as both poets and as cultural activists. This has been typical of his approach to life: taking trouble to listen to the inside story of what is happening, the particular details, in the specific locality, and also to understand how these relate to each other and to the whole. He spells out this kind of attentiveness in his credal poem 'Nothing is lost always', revolving on his chosen icon that had apparently chosen him, the blue butterfly: "What, then, is love but quality / of attention to details, to surfaces, and to tracing / in them the depths you may call understanding…?" (*BB* 76).

In a working energised organism, it is not enough for each part to perform its function in relation to the whole; each part also needs to relate in as 'conscious' a manner as possible to the other parts, or the necessary balance, vital to life, will be lost. Patrick Geddes, the Scottish philosopher, environmentalist and city planner (died 1932), adopted the motto (from the French philosopher Laplace): *folk, work, place*, as a key to the understanding of interactive functioning. Poetry cannot be expected to exist and be valued in isolation from folk, work and place. I used this motto as a touchstone for the operations of the Scottish Poetry Library, where I also consulted the *I Ching* before important meetings and decisions. Berengarten understands such dimensions as these, for he knows that poetry is transformative, working by metamorphosis in and out of life, in and out of the material.

It is in this sense that I respond to his line "We knew. We were not fools." The "we" has to mean poets who realise that poetry is drawn from an energy field larger than their own and that it demands from them their skilled work and craft, in continuing mutuality. Such an approach is in the tradition of Yeats and Graves and, in Scotland, of Sorley Maclean, George Mackay Brown and Edwin Muir. And George Steiner, who taught Berengarten at Cambridge, claims that "the magnetic fields around 'creation' are exceptionally charged and manifold" (2001: 14).

Berengarten wrote a detailed, illustrated monograph on the Welsh painter Ceri Richards and his drawings and paintings based on the poems of Dylan Thomas. It is entitled *Keys to Transformation* (1981) (*KT*). In it he traces the layers of symbol and myth behind particular images in poetry, drawing and painting. I link this approach with that of Kathleen Raine's *Temenos* magazine, where she brought together, in interpretative manner, painting, poetry and what she called "the perennial philosophy". In *Temenos* I discovered and was inspired by the painter Cecil Collins, with his themes of fools and angels. In the courts of the world, poets may indeed appear as 'fools', because of their unconventional ways of seeing things. But they may also be thought of as 'angels', in that they reveal and manifest the truth within natural phenomena: their 'glory'. Berengarten deploys this word to indicate the invisible within the visible, transfiguration, the Jewish concept of the *Shekhinah*: that which conceals in order to reveal (for full revelation would destroy) when the doors of perception are open. 'The Rose of Sharon' (*FL* 91–96) is also based on this understanding; and Berengarten's ephemeral, transformative blue butterfly itself belongs to this mode of discourse. In a poem specifically addressing this theme of transfiguration, he writes: "I plead with glory, greet me at your door, / … But you come always partially concealed…" (*BB* 109).

Charles Williams' Fool, in *The Greater Trumps*, who appears useless yet enables change to happen, provides a further example of this motif: "By the slightest vibration of the light in which she saw the world she saw it all differently…. Nothing was certain but everything was safe – that was part of the mystery of Love" (1975: 168). Small wonder then that in the following issue of *Lines Review* appeared Berengarten's poem-sequence 'Transformations', inspired by Frances Richards' lithographs for Rimbaud's 'Les Illuminations'. "Her work is spiritual / and belongs to the world" is the ending of his poem entitled 'In Memory of Frances Richards' (*FL* 106–107). Transformation, the deep interrelation of literature and art, and translation in its several meanings, all of which are present within the 'ground of being', are conjoined in this web of creativity.

At about this time, 1988, we invited the Italian poet Roberto Sanesi, whose work straddled poetry, translation and painting, to visit Edinburgh and read at the Edinburgh Festival for the Scottish Poetry Library with Edwin Morgan and other translators. We did not know before then that Sanesi and Berengarten were friends who had influenced and translated each other's work. At that time, I was also attending lectures and classes on Traditional Cosmology, organised by Emily Lyle of the School of

Scottish Studies, where we were initiated into the mysteries of the often mathematical, astronomical and practical exactitude of mythologies and legends.

Berengarten explores and deeply researches some of these primal connections as found in the rainmaking and St. George's Day ceremonies in South-Eastern Europe, distilling them in his long incantatory poem *In a Time of Drought*. His clarification that St. George in the Balkans is represented as a 'green man' is a helpful revelation, which provides another example of fertility myths and practices distorted later by the pagan-fearing church (*ITD* 97–100). That poem, however, points to the dust and ashes on which water must be poured in the spring rites, as well as to the historic and contemporary slaughter in the Balkans, while allowing the Flora-like village girls to be pushed on swings through the night: "Yes, fix my swing to a tree where the dead / Lie sleeping under the ground we tread" (*ITD* 28).

Berengarten has lived in several European countries, among them Greece and Italy in the 1960s, and in former Yugoslavia in the late 1980s, immediately prior to the outbreak of the conflict in the Balkans. When in 1967 the coup of the Colonels happened in Greece, he wrote a poem while living in Thebes and sent it back to *The London Magazine* under the pseudonym of a Greek poet, supposedly in translation. The title 'The Easter Rising 1967' echoed Yeats: sardonic yet lyrical, it was a young man's poem, full of derision, disgust and fury, yet a well-crafted piece of poetry rather than a diatribe. This is not a poet of innocent rhymes, but of measures that do not flinch from the blood, sweat, flesh, desperation, self-hate and historic revengeful evils that inhabit us as humans. He is in this sense a 'witness', a term used at the May 2006 International PEN Congress in Berlin, on 'Writing in a World Without Peace', where the witness was seen as linking past to future in daring to imagine the present.

Later Berengarten wrote a sequence called *Black Light* (1983) in memory of George Seferis, focusing on his theme of darkness at the heart of light (cf. Henry Vaughan's "deep but dazzling darkness", quoted in this sequence, as well as in a translation Berengarten made of Sanesi's 'Elegy for Vernon Watkins' [*EVW*], in 1981). In the Celtic year the dark precedes the light. Samain is the New Year on 1 November, followed by Beltain on 1 May to herald the light half of the year. In a similar way "it was evening and it was morning on the first day" in the book of Genesis; and the eve of Christmas and New Year is when the 'day' of celebration begins: thus night precedes day. Logically, following on from this, death must precede life. Death not only precedes but underlies, indeed encircles life, as it does for the bird that flies through the lighted feasting hall from darkness to darkness. But is that darkness, that death, void? Our objective uncertainty hints that there is no nothingness and that at the heart of the void is creation itself.

Berengarten has edited a book of Sanesi's poetry in translation and contributed several translations himself. The title of the book of trans-lations is *In Visible Ink* (1982). He translates the poem 'Letter VII' with the lines, 'I follow attentively the black / silent scrabbling of words' (*IVI* 50). *In Visible Ink* is a clever pun, but also an image that links us with Seferis' 'black light'. Berengarten explains in his introduction

> "the ways in which the written poem connects with the world (itself a larger 'written text') which surrounds and receives it; for the poem not only comments upon the world, but also enters it, and by entering it, is entered – subtly changing it, but also being changed by it" (*ibid.* 11–12).

We are "in the room suddenly" again, but here the poem rather than the poet has the effect of Charles Williams' archetypal Fool – who is no fool. Berengarten later refers to "the invisible ink of the universal text". He does not specifically refer to Rilke, who found inspiration in "the winds and the birds" and "the great great nights" (Rilke 1954: 106) but he is certainly in touch with Rilke's identification of turbulent creativity within cosmos, nature and poet (maker). As he makes clear, these identifications and understandings are a constant theme "coming from a common source in the Gnostic traditions of all the major Western religions" (*IVI* 11), restoring the infinite and eternal from within the finite and temporal. The tree of this spiritual aesthetic is a deep-rooted one with many branches and leaves. Any poet who shares in this aesthetic is at one with others, past and present. This sense of archetypal belonging, while remaining individual in our interpretation and experience, in our style and emphases, makes Berengarten's *oeuvre* into a 'locus' where many of us can meet. Such interweavings reach to the core of what we might call 'elemental life', life that finds its ongoing meaning in this manner through language, which is itself, as George Steiner expresses it, "embedded in its cumulative past and in a manifold present" (2001: 128).

Berengarten's long poem 'Tree' (1980) is a *tour de force*, a sequence of metaphors and evocations in as many lines as the days in a calendar year, whose number exceeds the height in feet of the tallest redwood tree in the world. The symbolism of the tree rooted in the underworld, manifesting in the middle world and reaching into the 'overworld', makes it iconic for the earth itself turning on its axis in a cosmic field. We can choose our favourite metaphor from this poem, which is as packed with them as George Herbert's 'Prayer': "runged ladder / for the soul's fingers" is one of my choices, as well as "pain tree / evergreen" and "unpruned / untameable / immortal tree" (*FL* 124, 126, 130). Again we have claims made for identification between the material here-and-now and the immortal or everlasting, only 'touchable' by love that risks all – as in Seferis' poem 'The Thrush': "I'm not speaking to you about things past; I'm speaking about love" (*FL* 165). Berengarten's villanelle 'There is Scant Hope' is an example of Kierkegaard's 'objective uncertainty held with passionate inwardness'; as he writes: "there is scant hope, yet courage still there is, // and there's no choice but love. There never is…" (*BB* 24). In *The Manager* Berengarten tries to enter 'Hope Street' again and again, and manages it only when death is accepted and even 'cradled': "Now blessèd I backwalk up Hope Street, alive. My cup runneth over" (*TM* 149).

I'm glad that courage is brought in here in connection with love. Robert Louis Stevenson, in his essay 'The Morality of the Profession of Letters', claims that "the first duty of any man who is to write is intellectual," and that "[i]n all works of art it is first of all the author's attitude that is narrated, though in the attitude there be implied a whole experience and a theory of life" (1910: 64). Stevenson expects an intellectual courage in the writer, who should not be afraid to be impartial – in that sense a 'witness': he expects that we should not be afraid to be as honest as we can with ourselves and the material, with the pattern and the argument.

Although, as I have indicated, deep-rooted unities make us feel at home in Berengarten's work, its strength also lies in always being able to surprise and move us, for instance with his use of long lines, prose poems with insistent cadences, marvellous words like "soulmonger" (*FL* 157) and echoic lines such as "Let in the wind that's hammering at the door" (*BB* 25) and "The sun's dark horses call your heart away" (*FL* 153). In *Learning to Talk* (1980) we have some poems reflecting on the miracle of children learning to talk and one about a "wounded stone": "its gigantic stone body all / core, so radiant / through time it can only scatter / its dust on the quick invisible / air, unendingly // reckless, transparent" (*LT* 14). And in another powerful poem entitled 'The Core', we have the frustrated, almost sinister sense of the core being forever unattainable, due to the transience of our experience, however fiercely we attempt to "bite the day to the core" (*AP* 23). Indeed, this driving persistence is a characteristic feature of his poems, in their artistic, intellectual and mystical 'integument' – "love's integument / Against the day" (*FL* 193), as in the Vermeer painting which is the subject of his poem 'Against the Day'.

In 'What the Photograph Said' Berengarten writes: "You don't know where / to go after this seeing into and through / things, not at them, this knowing / finding isn't keeping…" (*LT* 29). Here again, Rilke comes to mind, along with Lawrence and Hopkins. But there may be an echo of MacDiarmid here as well, from his extraordinary long poem 'On a Raised Beach' – "The arduus [*sic*] furor [*sic*] of the stones –" and "No visitor comes from the stars / But is the same as they are" (1993: 423, 435). Teilhard de Chardin in his *The Phenomenon of Man* expresses the understanding that spirit must indwell the lithosphere from the beginning if it is to evolve in a process of complexity-consciousness to manifest in the noosphere; and Scotland's John Muir told how he listened to the rocks on Yosemite crags. To quote MacDiarmid again: "Every energumen an Endymion yet?" (*ibid.* 422).

Berengarten's technical wizardry with a variety of poetic forms, measures and rhyme-schemes is as seemingly effortless as is nature or music in manifesting its perfections of form and measure, its variations on a theme. Yet perfection is deadly, as is reflected in his book title *Against Perfection* (1999). For Berengarten, as for all true poets, the forms are an orchestrated counterpoint to the dance of the words and are not for virtuoso display; rather they are integral to what is happening in and through the poem. For instance in 'Building a Snowman' – that most ephemeral of works of art – we find, "it is easy to impose / a pattern / less easy to make it / stick / less still / to discover one there" (*LT* 27). With few exceptions, he doesn't impose a pattern but finds "one there", whether sinuously in a traditional form or more like Ronald Duncan in his epic poem *Man* (1970: 108), where he declares, "I am not trying to write poetry. / Poetry is what I write."

Not only a poet but also (sometimes despite himself) a shaman, Berengarten does not avoid the darkness within his own and all creativity. Nor does he resist the deep, intuitive, even incomprehensible interconnections he can discover when he has set out to do some serious 'objective' research. 'Croft Woods' (1999) in particular describes, in a beautifully musical poem, a shamanistic experience of *at-one-ment* with nature. He was three years old when his father, who was a professional cellist, died. The music of Berengarten's poetry pays honour to that father, and that early encounter with death speaks through almost every line of this poem, where it is embraced as integral to the wholeness of the human experience of life:

> Our speech is built on spirals spun of air,
> voice-pillars that support whole architectures
> of meanings on their shoulders, caryatids
> without whose weight the topless roofs of thought
> would crumble and cave in, as mountains might
> be one with valleys, on the Day of Judgement. (*FL* 201)

Here in a single stanza – built in one sentence, itself a spiral spun of air and a whole architecture of meaning that takes in the *Kore*, the sculpted caryatids which grace the Parthenon, Handel's *Messiah* where "every valley shall be exalted" and Mozart's *Dies Irae* – we have a manifestation almost of Daniel Barenboim's 2006 Reith lectures. There, talking of music, Barenboim said: "Music does not communicate: it is the communication. Notes are bound to each other; they are physical as well as invisible; they are becoming rather than being; the sound ultimately dies. In these ways they constitute life" (2006).

In 'Croft Woods', in a deep descent into the earth's own essences – "like sap in winter – all I was has vanished" (*FL* 200) – losing self-conscious awareness, that bane of humanity separating us from our life as part of nature, the poet Berengarten describes himself as "a shell without a listening child" (*FL* 200); and yet, out of this experience of utter nothingness and surrender comes a trust "in the heights *and* depths of things. / Love cannot grow, die, be reborn. *It is*" (*FL* 208).

How then, does someone as instinctual, as musical, as steeped in archetypal images and primal lore as Berengarten come to write *The Manager* (2001)? He gave me a copy in February 2003 on a visit to Edinburgh and wrote in it: "to Tessa, fellow-poet, friend, fellow-traveller on the road". I share this because the wording is typical of his generosity of spirit towards others, and particularly towards other poets: he realises that we need to support one another in the particular kind of courage that our task demands. When I went to boarding school from India at the age of ten, in a strange country (Scotland), my mother wrote for me a text from Joshua 1.9: "Be strong and of a good courage; be not afraid, neither be thou dismayed: for the Lord thy God is with thee whithersoever thou goest." Reading Berengarten's poems reminds me of this, and that the belief that some destiny for good was with me may have helped in those dark days. To encourage one another in our daily life is, I think, surely our priority as humans, whatever our circumstances. *To manage* is also to cope, to get by, to keep passionate faith with life even in objective uncertainty.

In *The Manager*, Berengarten has achieved an epic poem for our times. That in itself is remarkable. It is amusing, satirical, deadly sarcastic, confessional, both mirroring and pitying society with an almost Shakespearean richness of vernaculars, characters and images. To read the poem straight through is unsettling, as reading all good poetry should be, even when we find comfort in it. I'm reminded of the anonymous dirge, set to music by Benjamin Britten, and the abyss into which we can fall every night: "This ae nighte, this ae nighte, / Every night and alle…" (Op. 31, 1943). The rhythms in *The Manager* are driving and desperate, the despair of frustration as much as of fear: frustration at not being in control, not able to do anything about oneself, one's life, one's children and family and society, about human life on earth. There is an Endymion-like quality to the poem too: "I have clung / To nothing, loved a nothing" might be said of its search for true love in the presence of those who "lord it o'er their fellow-men / With most prevailing tinsel". Berengarten's image of looking for the missing jigsaw piece of joy and his diatribe in the language of excuses – "All the people I need to talk to seem to be unavailable" (*TM* 135) – are masterly. The poem, while portraying the behaviour of a certain type of upwardly mobile, meaningless existence in England in the latter decades of the 20th century, also reflects the pain in the accompanying loss of purpose and meaning. Throughout, it is as if underneath the surface we are hearing that "singular quiet voice / speaking out of the darker side of cliché" from the earlier poem 'Jordan: for Veronica Forrest-Thomson' (*LT* 34). That "no person", that "fourth person singular" seems to become, as it were, an alchemised Endymion.

One of my favourite poems in Berengarten's prolific *oeuvre*, among many I treasure, is 'Traces we cannot name: fifth statement of a survivor' (*BB* 63–65). Nothing can really be added to or taken away from the lines:

> Though all we desire consists
> of impossibilities,
> and though the dream persists
> and without hope this is
> a mad, unholy feast
> for liar, fool or priest,

and though no dream alone
built Ithaca or Zion
on the pillow of a stone,
it's still desire we lie on. (*BB* 65)

To conclude, I can say that I am grateful, and that our literary community can be grateful, for Berengarten's corpus of work as he has pursued his poetic path through the last four to five decades without regard to fashion or fame, academic or financial reward, or literary trendiness. The inconsequentiality of some modern poetry may well be what makes it impossible to 'market'; yet we also suffer under a control and limit mentality which cannot allow anything that espouses the search for meaning to be 'marketed'. However, fidelity to the calling which is language itself, and which calls us to answer, seeks and deserves a readership rather than just a market – given that, whereas a market is manufactured and disposable, a readership is renewable and can keep on growing far beyond our lifetimes. I hope that Berengarten's readership will increase, and that those who discover the wealth his poems have to offer will find themselves enriched in the deep interwoven way that is sustaining for us in our own journey. Those readers, with me, can repeat: "We knew, we were not fools."

REFERENCES

Barenboim, Daniel. 2006. *In the Beginning Was Sound (the Reith Lectures)*.
    Online at: http://www.bbc.co.uk/programmes/b00729d9/episodes/guide.
    Consulted, 2 February 2016.

Cruikshank, Andrew. 1984. *After the Wager, the Dice and the Games*.
    Edinburgh: Macdonald Publishers.

de Chardin, Teilhard. 1959. *The Phenomenon of Man*. London; Collins.

Duncan, Ronald. 1970. *Man*. London, The Rebel Press.

MacDiarmid, Hugh. 1993. *Collected Poems* (Vol. 1). Manchester: Carcanet
    Press.

Ransford, Tessa. 1988. 'Introduction', *Lines Review* 107 (December): 4.

Rilke, Rainer Maria. 1954. *Letters to a Young Poet* (trans. M. D. Herter
    Norton). New York, NY, and London: W.W. Norton and Company.

Sanesi, Roberto. 1981. 'Elegy for Vernon Watkins' (trans. RB), *Poetry Wales*
    17(2): 52–53.

______. 1982. *In Visible Ink: Selected Shorter Poems, 1955–1979* (ed. RB). *Prospice* 13 (special issue). Skye: Aquila Publishing Company.

Steiner, George. 2001. *Grammars of Creation*, London, Faber and Faber.

Stevenson, Robert Louis. 1910. *The Art of Writing*. London, Chatto & Windus.

Williams, Charles. 1963. *The Descent of the Dove*. London and Glasgow: Collins Fontana.

______. 1975. *The Greater Trumps*. London: Sphere Books Ltd.

A Poet Like a Tree:
Some Comments on the Poetry of Richard Berengarten

Răzvan Voncu

Translated from Romanian by Simona Drăgan

Among the critical responses to Richard Berengarten's poetry to date, there has been a common thread: an almost unanimous agreement on the singularity of the poet's experiences and artistic strategies. This singularity is evident from quite early on in his career, as one might well expect from the opening pages of a poetic *oeuvre* that has been built up scrupulously over a long period of time. For this is a poet who writes not only differently (most genuine poets do that) but also on different issues from those to be found in most contemporary poetry written in English – and not only in English for that matter.

The period when Berengarten's work began to emerge was full of literary movements and manifestos.[1] Starting out from Cambridge, and with no affiliation to any fashionable *-ism*, he set about rediscovering and reinterpreting his individual self and the world through poetry. This process is all the more noteworthy as Berengarten is not a poet who is exclusively 'inspiration-oriented', but one whose breadth of cultural reference is as striking as any to be found in contemporary poetry. This fusion of natural talent and bookish spirit is so subtle in Berengarten's poetry, and these two elements are so profoundly woven into it, that they have practically become one, like inseparable halves.

---

[1] His first published book was *The Easter Rising 1967* (1969).

Here, for instance, is what John Burnside – a writer who has paid careful attention to Berengarten's poetic development – says about the experience embedded in the unusual volume *In a Time of Drought*:

> What Richard Berengarten is doing is vital. *In a Time of Drought* marks him as someone who stands in a unique place in current British writing, a brave and inventive poet who is able to take risks, not for the sake of mere 'experimentation', but in order to stay attuned to a wider European tradition. (*ITD1* back cover).

Frank Kermode, in turn, describes Berengarten's long poem *The Manager* with the laconic yet no less explicit qualification: "A strange and impressive work" (*TM1* back cover). Last but not least, Alan Sillitoe offers the comment that this huge poem is "[a] wonderful and very special piece of work, something new, deep and not beyond anybody's comprehension" (*TM1* back cover). I think these three examples should confirm that this poet's originality, breadth and artistic courage have been recognised accurately enough by critics. Furthermore, they show that Berengarten's work has been interpreted and valued not only from the point of view of subjective intention and within a context of literary experiment, but also in terms of its overall achievement: that is, as a combination of particular and general issues.

So what are the sources of Richard Berengarten's originality? I will begin with the most obvious source, that is, *his cultural background.*

❧

In modern poetry, ever since the Symbolists (and most certainly since Valéry), a strong emphasis has been placed on the need to intellectualise emotion, to evade both the 'moral' injunctions underpinning Classicism and the imperative to express 'natural feeling' in Romanticism. Even earlier than the Symbolists, Edgar Allan Poe had dismantled his own poem *The Raven*[2] allegedly to prove the importance of reason and of lucid construction in poetry, thus reversing the ancient myth that inspiration issues directly from "a heavenly god", as Phemios, the suitor-bard in *The Odyssey*, put it much earlier.[3] Valéry in his *Cahiers*, in turn, also asserted

---

[2] In his essay 'The Philosophy of Composition', first published in 1846.

[3] *Editors' note*: In *The Odyssey*, Book 21, the bard Phemios (or Phemius), one of Penelope's suitors, pleads with Odysseus to let him live, on the grounds that he has composed all

60

– no less defiantly than Poe – that, during composition, by comparison with the proportion due to conscious application, the percentage of value attributable to inspiration is actually insignificant, making the poet a "geometer of spiritual states" (Valéry 1989: 567). In Valéry's time, the exponents of modernist poetry seemed to be experiencing a sort of shame due, it is likely, to the stigma of sharing values they deemed obsolete, such as old-fashioned inspiration, emotion – even lyricism itself. The de-lyricisation of poetry, which is a historical fact, found wide and various modes of expression: it nourished not only the mainstream (for example, in France, the cognitive poetry of writers such as Saint-John Perse, and Jacques Prévert's prosaic embroidery of everyday life), but also more 'extreme' literary phenomena, such as the socialist realism of the 1950s in Eastern European literatures, as well as the politically-committed poetry of 1968 in the West (represented by poets such as Hans-Magnus Enzensberger). This explains why John Barth defined literary modernity in terms of its prevailing concern for language and form, to the detriment of content and subjectivity (Barth 1986: 119).

In his debut volume in 1967, Berengarten turns his back on such directions. Even if Greece, as a modern myth designed in the light of Seferis' poetry, would emerge later in his career,[4] it is certain that by this point the poet was already a believer in the ancient myth of Orpheus – the creator who tamed not only the gods in human beings but sometimes the beasts in them too. Nor, apparently, did the story of the gifted Amphion, who built walls by singing his own songs, leave him entirely indifferent.[5] Yet, even in this first book, poetry is scarcely deemed to be the verbal expression of 'intellectual emotion' – or, indeed, of 'cultural emotion' – whether as an echo of human alienation or, still less, as an instrument of propaganda. In its capacity to represent ideal beauty through material

his songs himself and his inspiration comes directly from heaven. Odysseus spares him. Chapman's translation is as follows: "It will here after grieve thee to have slain / A poet, that doth sing to Gods and men. / I of myself am taught, for God alone / All sorts of song hath in my bosom sown / And I, as to a God, will sing to thee."

[4] In *Black Light*, first published in 1983.

[5] *Editors' note*: Amphion and his brother Zethus were the mythical co-founders of the city of Thebes. Amphion became a singer and musician after Hermes taught him to play and gave him a golden lyre. While the two brothers were building their walls around the citadel, Zethus struggled to carry his stones. But Amphion played his lyre, and his stones followed after him and gently glided into place (Ovid, *Metamorphoses* 6: 152). RB spent a year living in Thebes in 1967–8, where he wrote 'The Easter Rising 1967'. Curiously, no stones moved of their own accord.

means, poetry not only heals and unifies but also clarifies understanding and quickens the positive resources of humanity.

The core layer of Berengarten's cultural experience is obviously English. One would expect English-language poetry to hold a fascination for most poets, and not only those who write in English; and I doubt that Berengarten would ever be perverse enough to reject anything of value from this precious tradition. While he is by no means a traditionalist – as can be seen both from *Book With No Back Cover* and, again, from his magnum opus, *The Manager* – tradition, from pre-Shakespeare to post-Romanticism, is in no sense alien to him. Nor is he a modernist, although he pays great attention to the formal and technical aspects of poetry, which in his poems share an importance equal to that of textual meaning. Paradoxically, in Berengarten's work the recycling of obsolete forms and the turning of the poetic act into a kind of stylistic archaeology count as *innovations*, since how the poet relates to these strata in English poetry is strictly personal and original. Without being either mimetic or appealing to pastiche or parody, and without ever seriously cultivating desuetude or anachronism, Berengarten still succeeds in staking out his personal poetic territory and in establishing a type of discourse, a poetic mythology and an imagery which are to the greatest extent particular to him, as I have already suggested. The rhetoric of his lines may sometimes seem almost Shakespearian, although this may well be no more than a surface effect, an outcome of the loosened connections with tradition which we all experience nowadays. In fact, what is under discussion here is Berengarten's courage in revisiting territories that were once the preserve of 'the Classics', which he has now brought back to life. This, then, is not just a question of archaeology, but, also and equally, of restoration.

The second stratum is that of Jewish spirituality. Born in 1943, into a Jewish family which had emigrated from Eastern Europe and settled in London at the end of the nineteenth century and the beginning of the twentieth, Berengarten writes a poetry infused with the warm humanism, and even what might be called the gentleness, that characterise Jewish thought. He is certainly sensitive, and probably more exposed to anguish than others. But the denunciation of human pain is intermixed with compensatory elation at the beauty of nature, particularly of nature's simple patterings, foundations and formations. The result is a unified, complex and comprehensive vision of human nature and history, which takes in extremes of both good and evil, as in the book *The Blue Butterfly*. The title poem of this collection concentrates and encapsulates the poetics of the entire volume.[6] Its optimism and its passion for perennial and insoluble themes of art, not to mention its visionary and sometimes prophetic spirit, might well derive from the treasures of the Jewish cultural heritage.

Furthermore, this treasure accords well with the Mediterranean, particularly if the Mediterranean is conceived of as a *spiritual space*: for this is one that includes Jews, both those of ancient Israel and Palestine, and those who were exiled from Spain, many of whom passed the Balearic Islands and Italy to settle in the Balkans and other areas of the Ottoman Empire. And it is in the Balkans, above all, where Berengarten finds 'space' to admire, not the over-used Romantic myths of ancient Hellas, but the mixture of light and darkness, of the tragic and the risible, that together make up the identity of modern Greece. The title 'Black Light' is intriguing, especially if one considers that Greece, in stereotypical representation at least, is flooded by a burning, violent sun. That sequence shapes a Hellenic area both natural and bookish, in a unique and strange dialogue with the work of one of the great poets of the world, George Seferis. But in contrast to those poets who might 'use nature' in order to invent a mythology, Berengarten behaves completely atypically. He starts out, rather, from a ready-made and universally known mythology, and then reconstructs a 'nature' – which turns out to be none other than Greece itself. This poetic reconstruction of Greece by literary means, starting from poetry itself and its most commonly used myths, helps Berengarten to avoid all the 'obstacles' to originality created by centuries of intense literary propagation of the Greek *topos*. Thus, with this 'black light', the pantheon of poetry has been extended to include a modern myth which is bookish in origin but has been 'given back' to nature; and in this return resides an achievement that may be read as both a supreme act of humility and a statement of deep pride. The poem 'Volta' eloquently expresses the power of this rhetorical trope. It develops from an epigraph from Seferis, and builds towards the gloriously vivid image of *drinking* the light, "like wine, like music":

> King sun, rosy cheeked, day's sovereign coin,
> you touch me, and my skin becomes a cornea,
> my spine an optic nerve, and my body trembles
> half dazzled by the pool of gold you pour
> over this sea and city, and I'm blinded.

[6] *Editors' note*: 'The Blue Butterfly' is quoted fully on pp. 357-358.

Here once stood rows – and still I know they stand –
of houses and streets, belonging to another city,
not this one you have utterly transformed.
[…]
Sweet evening skyglow, spread on hills and bay,
your arm grazes mine now, as if by accident,
like the touch of this young woman who walks beside me
with heavy hips, small steps and swinging gait,
jet hair swept back, delicate throat and shoulders
deep summer bronzed, and her olive brown eyes laughing.
I drink you, shimmering light, like wine, like music,
as her ancestors have drunk you thousands of years. (*FL* 157)

&

Close to Greece lies the cultural zone inhabited by the south Slavs, and this is one that Berengarten knows particularly well, since he lived in Belgrade for several years prior to the political dismemberment of Yugoslavia. During his travels at that time, he met some of the outstanding cultural personalities of a geographic space that, unfortunately, over recent years has acquired an unfair reputation for violence and barbarism. A friend of Ivan V. Lalić and of other great contemporary Serbian writers, Berengarten undertook a fabulous expedition into the universe of Balkan culture, popular as well as literary. For throughout this region the myth of Orpheus is still very much alive: it is given voice and expression by the traditional popular singers still to be found all over Serbia, Macedonia and Bosnia, as well as in Romania and Bulgaria.

And it is in the Balkans that Berengarten has put into practice, restored and re-invented yet another of the traditional roles possessed by the poet: that of the popular, anonymous "singer of tales".[7] This set of attributes involves a magical ritual the roots of which go back to prehistoric times, even though its effectiveness has long since been transformed into pure 'aesthetics'. But *In a Time of Drought* is more than a modern reconstruction in English of the folklore related to the tradition of *dodole*.[8] And despite being a contemporary English poet, Berengarten

---

[7] *Translator's note*: the reference is to the traditional analphabetic oral poets of the Balkans. See the classic study by Lord, 1960.

[8] Known to the Balkan people under various names, the custom that the Slavs call *dodole* is a ritual performed in rainless summers (times of drought) by a group of girls dressed in clothes made from dry vegetation, who enact various ritual dances and sing specific songs in order to invoke rain.

succeeds in forgetting about 'himself' and plunging into the depths of the material itself,[9] to forge lines rich in magical connotations, to which he nevertheless gives an entirely modern content. For the 'drought' of which he writes is not only the climatic one provoked by, let us say, global warming. To a larger extent what concerns the poet is the spiritual drought of the world we live in, which poetry can scarcely avoid hoping, somehow, 'to cure'.

In this book, the deities Richard Berengarten conjures up and appeals to are the old fertility gods and goddesses who are so richly in evidence in Bulgarian, Serbian and Romanian folklore, since it is the 'modern gods' – such as productivity, money, individualism and political correctness – that have brought people to this terrible drought. Yet inside this spiritual desert lie forgotten values which, when brought back to life by poetry, seem to be the only ones capable of saving us. This volume suggests a culmination of sorts in Berengarten's ongoing dialogue with archaic spirituality.

Mention should also be made of the fact that Berengarten is a moving tragic poet and a gifted composer of elegies. However, it is not only this sense of the tragic, originating in the rivers of blood that have flowed through the past century (probably the most violent in the history of mankind), that is of central concern to Richard Berengarten, but also the other sense of the modern, that Jean-Marie Domenach has defined as "a tragic sense of triviality, kitsch and pornography" (1995: 36). This is the tragedy of the pointless, humdrum mechanisms of everyday life in the computerised, post-industrial society in which we live.

This kind of tragic sense forms the substance of *The Manager*, a richly conceived poem that is truly a contemporary *Odyssey*, in which Ulysses becomes the common, contemporary man, embodied by 'the Manager' himself (here ironically scarcely able to remember his ancestor, Adam Kadmon). As a poor creature lost in the nightmare and routine of a de-spiritualised experience centred on alienating toil rather than on any form of inward life, and as a complete slave to the machines and democratic standardisation that together are indispensable for 'success', this new Ulysses doesn't even know that Ithaca exists. He may have inklings here and there, but these come from nowhere and have nowhere to go.

With remarkable artistic intuition, the poet has developed a stanzaic form, the *verse-paragraph*, that articulates and embodies this confusion

---

[9] See 'Arijana's Thread' (*ITD* 73–77).

perfectly. Endowed with incantatory value and resembling the verse forms of religious texts, in prosodic terms the verse-paragraph has no beginning or end and extends from the left to the right margin of the page, in just the same way that the Manager himself lives a life with no target – in an aimlessness that can be read between the lines of the clichéd language Berengarten employs:

> Well this Adam Kadmon mate what's the name of his group.
> Don't you come yobboing me Charlie. You're the wrong side
> of town for that stuff. We can't have the likes of you

> Talking to people like that. Disturbing all the neighbours. Of-
> fending bystanders and suchlike. You just ask Joe here. You
> could get yourself arrested. Using provocative language.

> What's that you never. Look mate I heard what you said. Really
> Charles old boy really. I really am surprised at you. You want
> to be more careful. Watch your manners a bit.

> Hey take a butchers at his trousers Joe ain't they revolting. What
> you got inside them darling. A Curly-Wurly and two Creme
> Eggs. Bet you he's got a long one in there Joe. (*TM* 76)

In an alien, mechanical world, this decomposed language translates a state of general dismemberment of human values into poetic terms.

ဆ

It can be seen that Berengarten's poetic work resembles the structure of a tree. It has had a slow, gradual growth into its present breadth and maturity. Its trunk has grown, in concentric circles, around fundamental themes and motifs, and the strata of multicultural influences have only increased its universal depth and intelligibility. Like a tree, its roots reach deep into the communal past of Europe. And like a tree, Berengarten's work needs air, light and the sky to aspire towards. A tree-like poet can give shade to the land, and make (contemporary) heat more bearable, but can also draw attention to the intensity and splendours of light. And like a tree, the poet suggests to humankind a firm 'upright' line, and does so unobtrusively, perfectly regulating the ways in which 'art' is achieved. For these reasons, I am in full agreement with George Szirtes' view that "Richard Berengarten is one of the major half-hidden poets of England"

(*ITD1* back cover) and, even more so, with that of Anthony Rudolf, who states that "Richard Burns [Berengarten] will be one of the major poets writing in English in the early years of the next millennium. There is no other voice like his" (*AP* back cover). To me, Richard Berengarten is one of the most important contemporary European poets, whose work incorporates practically all the cultural assets of the Old Continent, in a synthesis illuminated by genuine humanism and by hope and faith in humankind.

REFERENCES

Barth, John. 1986. 'Literatura Reînnoirii: Ficţiunea postmodernistă' [The Renewal of Literature: Postmodern Fiction] in *Caiete critice* [Scholar Review] 1–2: 167–185.

Domenach, Jean-Marie. 1995 [1967]. *Întoarcerea tragicului* (*Le retour du tragique*, Romanian trans. Alexandru Baciu), with preface by George Banu. Bucharest: Editura Meridiane.

Homer. 2000. *The Odyssey* (trans. George Chapman). Hertfordshire: Wordsworth Classics of World Literature. (Quoted from the Romanian edition of Homer.)

Lord, A. B. 1960. *The Singer of Tales*. Cambridge, MA: Harvard University Press.

Ovid. 1959: *Metamorfoze* (*Metamorphoses*, Romanian trans. Ion Florescu). Bucharest: Editura Academiei.

Valéry, Paul. 1989. *Poezii. Dialoguri. Poeticăşi estetică* [*Poems. Talks. Poetics and Aesthetics*] (Romanian trans. Ştefan Aug. Doinaş *et al*). Bucharest: Editura Univers.

Richard Berengarten's Art of Transformation

Jeremy Hooker

As a note on the back cover of the first edition of *The Manager* claims, Richard Berengarten's "perspectives combine English, Mediterranean, Jewish, Slavic and American influences". This suggests a rich cosmopolitan mixture. If we ask how the influences are combined, however, we find the answer lies more in a deep fusion than a mixing of surface features. Berengarten in his poetry speaks the language of symbolism, which is not confined to any one language group. In 'Avebury', for example, we find the symbol of "the cave, tomb / and temple" (*FL* 35), an ancient symbol connecting the cosmic act of generation and death, and associated with the figures of man and woman under the form of the earth mother ("little mother / of Willendorf'", "breasts / like hills" [*FL* 30]), and the primordial man:

> in my throat
> the man rises
>   from the cave he was immured in (*FL* 46).

'The Rose of Sharon' uses a different poetic language to explore the same theme:

> Now a cock in Hades crows
> and the sleepy hooded owls
> sicken as night's foetus grows:
> Adam Kadmon, in their bowels.
>
> Listen for the fire falling
> from his breath in searing rain.
> Ages thick with ghosts are wailing,
> pour your fire through us again!

Jar of nights and jar of days,
cracked in time from end to end,
gather up these broken rays,
yoke and seal them, heal and mend! (*FL* 96)

Form and language here pay tribute to the influence of William Blake and W. B. Yeats, placing Berengarten in the tradition of Romantic poetry with its roots in ancient wisdom, and its theme of contraries, or the conjunction of opposites. Adam Kadmon is a recurring figure in Berengarten's poetry, described in a note to *The Manager* as "Kabbalistic title for the first man, conceived as a representation or microcosm of the power of the entire universe" (*TM* 165). His female counterpart, the Rose of Sharon, is "the *Shekhinah*, the feminine aspect of the divine presence in the Kabbalah" (*FL* 221). The theme of the poem is thus the "*hieros gamos*, the holy union of male and female powers" (Scholem 1969: 104). This is perceived, in terms of Lurianic Kabbalah, as the union that would mend the breach in creation caused by "the breaking of the vessels" when the opposites, especially the masculine and the feminine aspects of the divine, were split apart. The imagery of cracked jars and "broken rays" derives from this myth of cosmic catastrophe. It is thus a quest to restore a state of original harmony – "yoke and seal them, heal and mend!" – that emerges from Berengarten's early poetry. This may also be described as a quest for wholeness, a quest operating at all levels, from the personal to the cultural and the cosmic.

"There is order in being" (*TM* 146). The words of the speaker in *The Manager* refer to an original condition, known both in childhood and in the divine creation. Berengarten's thinking, strongly influenced by Lurianic Kabbalah, as I have indicated, relates to a catastrophic fragmentation of original order, which joined man and woman to God and the world. Faced with a condition of brokenness affecting all aspects of life, the object of human creativity is restorative. For Berengarten, from a family of musicians, music is the primary form of making order, and his poetry is strong in forms analogous to musical composition. The seventh of 'Nine Codas' to 'Sketches with Voice-Overs' (in *Book With No Back Cover*) reflects on the experience of hearing music and on its maker:

And he or she no angel but human to the core. Who made it for
you, for me, that we

> Might see clear through it, build our own work upon it, and by
> our willing love, also transform our world. That through us,
> matter be known, transparent and resplendent
>
> As music. (*BWNBC* 46)

The poet shares with the musician the aim of creative transformation, to reveal "matter" in its true glory. Experiencing fragmentation in his own life and culture, he seeks to make whole.

Berengarten's quest develops through the growth of his language of symbolism. His symbols, including cave, fire, water, tree, "black light", and culminating in the blue butterfly of his poems set in the Balkans, are thus ways of approaching the great themes of love and death, and addressing his understanding of 'the waste land' of our culture. An underlying erotic mysticism in this poetry not only draws upon Lurianic Kabbalah and the psychology of C. G. Jung but also places Berengarten in a poetic tradition that runs as a deep current through different languages and cultures. In this sense his perspectives can be said to "combine English, Mediterranean, Jewish, Slavic and American influences". A fine example of the way in which his mind works may be seen in his research into the roots of Indo-European myths underlying the Balkan rain-maiden, "a symbol of the whole of the green world" (*ITD* 101) – research which operates together with poetic instinct.

'Black Light', Berengarten's poem-sequence in memory of George Seferis, shows the originality with which he uses tradition, turning debt into gift. Berengarten is responding here to Seferis's "drama of blood", "apparent to whoever perceives that behind the grey and golden weft of the Attic summer exists a frightful black". A major achievement of 'Black Light' is Berengarten's own rendering of Greek land and sea. Here, he develops the poetry of embodiment, seen in 'Avebury', in which the elemental universe is identified with male and female archetypes. In 'Salt', men perceive sea and Greek island as:

> that other woman
> who lies above us, invulnerable, regal in her indolence, her long
> legs enclosing an arc of the bay,
> as she dozes on her right side, colossal in the sun, swathed in her
> own smell of orchards, goats and resin (*FL* 163)

In 'Neolithic' the old man merges with the land:

And he released your arm, turned, and strode through the rub-
    ble, gigantic,
and his dog whimpered, sniffed the air, and followed him up
    the hillside,
and you stood and watched them climb, till their shapes, like
    crumbling statues,
blurred into the rock-face, and thunder rang from the mountain
    and rain poured on hills and plain,
and you took the road back to the harbour, drenched in the
    summer storm. (*FL* 167)

Berengarten is at his most powerful in this poetry of embodiment and encounter, in which the poet is taken out of himself, and both world and human figure are enlarged to disclose the lineaments of the divine.

Rain in the mountains in this passage brings *The Waste Land* to mind. Echoes of T. S. Eliot recur in Berengarten's poetry. The old man in 'Neolithic' is also a liminal figure, and his message to the poet is central to the vision of Berengarten's poetry:

stone, clay, brine are particles of radiance. Light is mirrored in
    blood,
and those who love light as I do, know dark and light are one.
(FL 167)

The voice of the liminal figure, speaking as from between, or beyond, life and death, recalls Eliot's "ghost", as do voices of the dead in Hades in Seferis' 'The Thrush' (Seferis 1982: 333). But if Berengarten and Seferis both owe a debt to Eliot, Eliot himself was imitating Dante, and behind Dante, in Virgil and Homer and the mythical Orpheus, voices from the underworld echo through European poetry. Berengarten calls up the voices because for him too the most urgent question is the question of death.

The voices of the cicadas in 'Cicadas (II)', in 'Black Light', reinforce the message of the old man and recall Berengarten's main source for the symbol he shares with Seferis:

Write, write, they wail. *Sing with us*, they hum.
Do not forget your origin. The gold sun, they shriek
is a black apple buried under the lake of darkness
and we its pips, the black seeds of the sun. (*FL* 172)

Berengarten's principal work of exposition, *Ceri Richards and Dylan Thomas: Keys to Transformation*, explores Ceri Richards's *Afal du Brogŵyr* [*Black Apple of Gower*] paintings. He quotes a letter C. G. Jung wrote to Ceri Richards after a friend had given him a study for the painting. In the letter Jung describes "the round thing" in the painting:

> It is astonishingly filled with compressed corruption, abomination and explosiveness. It is pure black substance, which the old alchemists called *nigredo*, that is: blackness, and understood as night, chaos, evil and the essence of corruption, yet the *prima material* of gold, sun, and eternal incorruptibility. I understand your picture as a confession of the secret of our time. (*KT* 61)

Berengarten's exploration of the meaning of the painting and of the visionary tradition Dylan Thomas shared with Ceri Richards is central to the meaning of Berengarten's own poetry. This may be seen especially in the idea that Ceri Richards' symbol, "the 'black sun' or 'apple' is the core of transformation itself, the very zone in which life in all its myriad forms confronts death and grows out of it" (*KT* 75). The relevance of the idea to Berengarten's own poetry becomes clearer still when, in his Introduction to Ceri Richards' *Drawings to Poems by Dylan Thomas*, he says that in the drawings

> death is seen not as a final end or goal but as a *rite de passage*… that is to say, as a necessary and inevitable part of the life-cycle, and of the processes of transformation and creativity which occur constantly throughout the phenomenal world and are celebrated as spiritual transformations in the work of every great poet and artist (xii).

Integral to Berengarten's study of the deep affinities – virtually the shared vision – of Ceri Richards' paintings and Dylan Thomas' poetry is his exploration of the "strong connection between images of death and femininity" (*KT* 44).

According to Berengarten, the "central impetus" in Ceri Richards is "celebration of female sexuality and exploration of this as a metaphor for the liberation of qualities of behaviour in our society which are traditionally regarded as feminine" (*KT* 97). The following passage has a special bearing on Berengarten's own work:

> [I]n a patriarchal society like our own, the free expression of female love – and with it, its transformative, creative power on spiritual as

well as physical levels – is regarded as a grave threat to the established order [of] things, and so has to be forced by all the prevailing social and mental pressures that can be mustered into the darkness of the subconscious whenever it threatens to raise its head into the light. And in the repressed zone it assumes nightmarish, destructive and devouring forms to both men and women alike. (*KT* 88)

Berengarten's erotic mysticism – his preoccupation with 'the holy union of male and female powers' – links liberation of "female love" to his treatment of modern sexual behaviour. Thus *The Manager*, which on a superficial reading can seem obsessively concerned with sexual experience, may be seen, in one of its aspects, as a dramatisation of the destructive results of men trying to 'manage' women. While Berengarten (or, rather, his Manager) depicts sexual consummation, he also handles a range of negative experiences such as lust, jealousy, betrayal, loss, longing, and humiliation in the relationship between a man and a woman. The poem has a good line in sexual insult, and can show a woman managing a man with wit and invective. Its range, in fact, includes bitter humour, as in this passage:

> I don't know which is worse, she said,
>
> Knowing you're pretending and pretending you don't know. Or
>   believing you're not really pretending really. Unless
>
> You believe you're pretending to be a Bastard. And really think
>   you're not one underneath the Act. I did suspect
>
> You were quite bright really, she said. In a stupid sort of way.
>   But you couldn't be that bright. Could you. Eh, stupid.
>
> (*TM* 43)

Cutting sexual comedy occurs in the poem in tension with an underlying desire for harmony between the 'male and female powers', with the male figure, a projection of Adam Kadmon, yearning for woman in all her aspects: "Oh my cousin, my sister, my unregistered beloved" (*TM* 143). Berengarten's perception of the relationship between poetry and femininity draws on the world of 'Celtic' myth, to which he is attuned.

If transformation is the key to the paintings of Ceri Richards and the poetry of Dylan Thomas, it is also the key to Berengarten's poetry, and to its form as well as its content. More than the work of any of his British contemporaries, Berengarten's poetry is distinguished by its formal variety and versatility. 'Tree', for instance, from its beginning ("Tree planted / in my core") to its conclusion ("human rainbow / blossoming") (*FL* 119–130) sustains its breath for 365 lines, and, from 'planting' to 'blossoming', incorporates the annual cycle. The idea of the tree of life, whose 'eternal round' contains all things, is the subject of a number of Berengarten's poems, for which he composes different symbolic forms. *The Blue Butterfly* contains, among much else, a series of villanelles and a series of sonnets. *The Manager* skilfully handles a form of verse-paragraph. *Book With No Back Cover* is perhaps the most original of his formal compositions. Like the other books, its formal patterning reflects the patterns that are its subject. This is true of the whole book and of the individual poems composing it, as we see in 'For Natalie, dying':

> As mist on morning's
> Horizon, and layers
> That hover on fields
>
> And droplets combed
> Minutely from foam
> On the curling waves
>
> Evaporate in wind
> And are lifted higher
> Than mountains
>
> So cloud will return
> To sea, as sea
> Will return to sky
>
> And sunlight dissolve them
> And clarify all tumbling
> And rising shadows.
>
> Come, then
> Natalie, pass
> Through gently (*BWNBC* 34)

The poem itself has a gentleness in its personal address and in its depiction of process becoming pattern – mist and water evaporating, cloud returning to sea, sea to sky, sunlight dissolving clouds, clarifying shadow: all passing through the cycle. It is not only what it says that makes 'For Natalie, dying' moving, but what it does, with a light touch, committing the spirit to the mystery from which life emerges, and to which it returns.

Berengarten's delight in his skilful composition is palpable. Like a musician, he has a gift perfected by practice, and offered as a gift – "To Whom It May Concern", as the dedications inside the two front covers of *Book With No Back Cover* say. But this does not mean, of course, that his work is not a struggle. He is a celebratory poet, but his celebrations come at a cost. This can be seen in the personal pain expressed in 'May', for example. But this poem is more than autobiographical – a fact summed up in the line: "Genealogy and mourning: the language of the Jews" (*FL* 182). Berengarten's struggle, however, is not to write exclusively of and for one people. 'For the New Year 1976' expresses his consistent aim "to earn and become the name Human" (*LT* 17). In drawing upon particular traditions, Greek in 'Black Light' and Serbian in *The Blue Butterfly* and *In a Time of Drought*, for example, he also speaks across boundaries, in a voice that is universally human. His summary of the themes which Richards and Thomas celebrate applies to his own work:

> the eternal round of birth, growth, fertilisation and death, the unitary quality of all these taken together, and the inevitability of struggle within this process – since, as Blake said, "Without contraries is no progression." For only by confrontation of death can "death have no dominion". (*CRDT* xiii)

Berengarten's 'waste land' theme, his sense not only of modern fragmentation, but of a break in the order of the universe which human creativity can help to mend, which draws on the symbolism of Lurianic Kabbalah, emphasises 'struggle within this process'. The responsibility of the artist is a healing one. As he says in *Book With No Back Cover*: "I am / responsible for this seed landed here called Human // To root it through and through me till every pore breathes". The poem acknowledges the difficulty:

> For blood, sweat, salt are particles of radiance. And shall be
> known by their true names
>
> And for what they really are. But how perfection leaks from cracks
> in the bowl of now. And how time

> Drips constant through the porous jar of presence. And how you
> and I may waste, trying to fit shards together. (*BWNBC* 43)

"Yet I will speak," he says. And the speaking, or making, involves struggle, and necessitates confrontation with death.

While this confrontation takes numerous forms, it often involves symbols or images of blackness. This, obviously, dominates 'Black Light'. Another instance occurs in *The Manager*, in which "an old man", whose "eyes gleam pitchblack light", hands the speaker a skull:

> In his red toothless laugh

> I glimpse a huge blaze. He slams the door in my face. Cradling
> death upturned in my arms, I stand on the doorstep, shiver-
> ing. And know this vessel my Grail, my singing immortal
> head. Now blessèd I backwalk up Hope Street, alive. My
> cup runneth over. (*TM* 149)

Here, the link between skull and Grail recalls Jean Markale's treatment of the subject in *Women of the Celts*, which Berengarten discusses in *Keys to Transformation*, where he notes that Markale, "through detailed examination of many Celtic stories … traces *the origin of the Graal vessel itself to a skull*, which was used as a kind of 'chalice' in pre-Christian Celtic ceremonies" (*KT* 54). Thus, in this passage from *The Manager*, symbolism of the Lurianic Kabbalah ("blaze" and "vessel") is linked to Celtic symbolism ("Grail" and "singing immortal head") and to the language of the Psalms. This is characteristic of Berengarten's layering of symbols – an imaginative process that might also be described as 'delving', to uncover a symbolic language of universals. It should also be observed that the encounters with an 'old man', or similar guardian figure, which occur on a number of occasions in Berengarten's poetry, are among the means by which he conveys traditional wisdom.

"Hope Street" is the speaker's destination, as it was also his starting point, in *The Manager*. Hope is also what Berengarten seeks in his poetry about Balkan history, in both *The Blue Butterfly*, which centres upon the massacre at Kragujevac in October 1941, and *In a Time of Drought*, which responds "to the events between 1989 and 2001 in Yugoslavia" (*ITD* 73). These subjects cannot be treated with the same gothic wit demonstrated in the Hope Street episode. Viewed superficially the blue butterfly, which landed on the poet's writing hand while he was waiting to enter the museum that commemorates the massacre, might be seen as quite inappropriate to the subject of historical tragedy and its evil causes. It could be questioned not only for its fragility as an image, but also for lending itself to poetry of Romantic gesture. As suggested earlier, however, it is the depth at which Berengarten realises the blue butterfly through his researches into Indo-European myth that makes it his most comprehensive symbol. One consequence of this is that the poems of *In a Time of Drought*, in which 'butterfly' is a name for the Balkan rain-maiden, have a profoundly ceremonial quality, and are, in effect, parts of a healing religious rite.

> And who will protect the heron and stork
> Kestrel and sparrow   finch   sparrow hawk
>
> Wagtail   marsh warbler   woodpecker   wren
> Cuckoo and curlew   crane and moorhen
>
> Swan in the rushes   gull on the shale
> Blackbird and songthrush   lark   nightingale
>
> Chittering swallow and swift in the eaves
> If not you   Dodola   girl dressed in leaves?
>
> *Call at my house   count nought and one*
> *In rain fire and storm the world was begun*   (*ITD* 63)

This portion of the poem is '*In memory of Ned Goy*', and each of the other parts of the seven-part sequence either commemorates or is dedicated to a named person. Here, too, names – the names of birds – make the poem a 'speaking for'. Rhythm and rhyme, together with the naming and the commemorative function, work with the rain-maiden symbolism to establish *In a Time of Drought* as a healing poem-sequence. But what also makes it a work capable of confronting death is that it is largely composed of questions.

The same is true of *The Blue Butterfly*, and it is this fact that makes it a fitting commemoration. Nowhere has Berengarten raised the question of death more powerfully than in *The Blue Butterfly*, and especially in part 6, 'Flight of the Imago'. Always a poet capable of sustained fluency, Berengarten is at his most eloquent here. It is not possible to do the work justice by quotation; but with this proviso: some lines from the end of 'Conversation Between a Butterfly and a Murdered Man' may be given as an example. Here, the man's words are in italics:

> Though I rise over deaths like the blue core
> in living flames, though I step light on what
> I touch, though I make future and past disappear,
> my function is not discovery, still
> less speech. I prefer easy paths on air
> across fields and meadows, where it is good
> to settle and nestle inside heads of flowers.
> You pass through these gates. I protect and watch them.

> *Angel of life or death, my butterfly, no matter. You*
> *blue speckler and flecker of wind, handsomest airborne drifter,*
> *master lightfoot, with your club-tipped antennae, go, shimmering.*
>
> (*BB* 98)

While the symbol of the butterfly is allowed its full symbolic power ("blue core / in living flames"), the dialectical nature of this conversation prevents any easy suggestion of transcendence. At the last, there is a sense of release, as at the end of 'For Natalie, Dying': "go, shimmering."

It is easy to see why Berengarten should think of himself as "a European poet who writes in English". This does not mean, however, that he stands completely outside any English-language tradition. His work, generally, is rich in intertextuality. *The Manager*, for example, contains allusions to Eliot, Pound, Empson, Shelley, and Blake, among others. For Berengarten, it is as if 'the Movement', which has had such a strong influence on post-war English poetry, never happened. Everything about his work differs from Movement-influenced poetry: its ambition, its formal variety and linguistic richness, its interest in myth and foreign poetries, its spirituality. This last feature is also what distinguishes it from the kind of postmodern *avant-garde* work that foregrounds language as constitutive of 'reality'. In ignoring the Movement, however, Berengarten has retained connections with a poetic tradition which poets such as Philip Larkin reacted against, and rejected. This is obvious from Berengarten's admiration for Dylan Thomas. But while his formal ingenuity and his symbolism for 'the eternal round' recall Thomas, the clarity of his work avoids Thomas' more obscure excesses. Nowhere in his published work does Berengarten appear as an imitator of Dylan Thomas. His affinities are rather with the tradition on which Thomas drew than with Thomas' actual writing.

It will not do to exaggerate Berengarten's affinities with 'Celtic' poets, especially if it is at the expense of the importance of his Jewishness or of the influence of Slavic and Mediterranean poetries; but it would be equally a mistake to overlook it. Indeed, Berengarten's sense of himself as a Jewish poet, a poet who speaks for a people, resembles that of Welsh poets. In both cases, however, the original link to a specific people is a means of identifying with the universally human. His interest in myth, and especially Celtic myth, also links him to Welsh poets. Myth is both akin to religion and charges landscapes with a sense of otherworldly presences and power, as we see in the imaginative world of Dylan Thomas and Ceri Richards, and the poetry of George Seferis. The landscapes of myth are liminal: borderlands between life and death. The Gower landscapes of Dylan Thomas' friend, Vernon Watkins, and especially the landscape of *Ballad of Mari Lwyd, and other poems*, are where the dead confront the living, and the living remember and question the dead. It is an ancient theme of poetry, and one that will always be among its most pressing. The Welsh soldier-poet Alun Lewis was speaking for himself, from his own desperate need, when, in a letter to his wife in April 1943, he spoke of being "more and more engrossed with the *single* poetic theme of Life and Death, for there doesn't seem to be any question more directly relevant than this one of what survives of all the beloved" (1989: 326). But Lewis was also voicing a question that poetry has always existed to ask.

Berengarten is effectively addressing the same theme when he describes the "central concern" of Ceri Richards and Dylan Thomas: "celebration of life, the wheel, the eternal round, eros and mortality: love defeating death defeating love defeating death" (*KT* 27). The affinities Berengarten has with poets such as Thomas and Watkins and a painter such as Richards are also affinities that define the kinship they all bear to Orpheus. Orpheus has incarnations in other lands than Europe, and is but one figure in what is surely the universally human drama of the underworld journey, which expresses the preoccupation of the living with the mystery and the question of death. The note on the back cover of the first edition of *Avebury* describes the book as "a series of lyrical meditations, in which man's roots are rediscovered in the modes of perception of earlier cultures". This is true; but it is also true to say that "love defeating death" is a universal theme. Richard Berengarten's art of transformation combines perspectives from a wide range of influences, but the perspectives are not of this world only. Berengarten is a poet who undertakes the underworld journey, and hears voices from Hades, as poets concerned with fundamental issues of love and death always have, and always will.

REFERENCES

Blake, William. 1961. *Complete Poetry and Prose* (ed. Geoffrey Keynes). London: The Nonesuch Library.

Eliot, T. S. 1965. *To Criticize the Critic*. London: Faber and Faber.

Lewis, Alun. 1989. *Letters to My Wife* (ed. Gweno Lewis). Bridgend: Seren.

Markale, Jean. (1975). *Women of the Celts* (trans. A. Mygind *et al.*) London: Gordon Cremonesi.

Richards, Ceri. 1980. *Drawings to Poems by Dylan Thomas* (ed. RB). London: Enitharmon Press.

Scholem, Gershom G. 1961. *Major Trends in Jewish Mysticism*. New York, NY: Schocken Books.

______. 1969. *On the Kabbalah and Its Symbolism*. New York, NY: Schocken Books.

Seferis, George. 1974. *A Poet's Journal: Days of 1945–1951* (trans. Athan Anagnostopoulos). Cambridge, MA: Belknap Press of Harvard University.

______. 1982. *Collected Poems* (trans. Edmund Keeley and Philip Sherrard). London: Anvil Press Poetry.

Watkins, Vernon. (1941). *The Ballad of the Mari Lwyd, and other poems*. London: Faber and Faber.

From Silence to Song –
Richard Berengarten: Speaking for the Dead

Antoinette Moses

It might be argued that it is perverse to write an essay about the work of Richard Berengarten which includes the word *silence* in its title. There are few living English poets, it could be claimed, who engage more strongly with so many writers living and dead, and whose words form a continuum of poetic conversation across the centuries. Moreover, years of friendship with Richard fill the store of memory with conversations, discussions, argument, words and more words. I have no recollection of any time spent with him in silence. Nor is there any other writer that I know of who responds to the texts of other writers with more vigour, honesty and generosity.

Yet this is not perversity. In my reading of Berengarten's work, I find a strong sense of words forged in the face of silence, both the silence of those who died and whose voices were cut off and that which surrounds the gestation of language:

> To make a poem, a poet needs to travel through them [languages] into silence and to return through them from silence back into language: to test (tear) the boundaries between language and silence. This two-way movement between language and silence means that every poetic journey is a Heracleitan return, not a one-way flight. (*ALF*, RB online)

In this essay, I would like to examine the silences, both actual and metaphorical, which surround and empower Berengarten's work. Reading his poetry, one is struck by the energy of words challenging silence, and his sense that the duty of the poet is to forge words in defiance of any form of restraint:

> I will speak. Yes I will. I will not, cannot be silenced. I am re-
> sponsible for this seed landed here called Human (*BWNBC* 43)

The urgency and compulsion here are, I believe, significant and suggest more than the usual poetic reflection on human consciousness; there is a moral imperative in these words. For Berengarten, poetry is an ethical act, as it is for Neruda and Elytis: the former calls it "a deep inner calling in man" (1977: 266), while the latter describes the duty of the poet "to cast drops of light into the darkness" (1974: 44). Moreover, Berengarten's imperative comes from our sense of humanity and our awareness of the past, from our need to communicate with the dead and to pass on their messages. "For the first time in our history we are contemporaries of all mankind" writes Octavio Paz, quoted by Berengarten first as the epigraph to 'Avebury' (1972) and, then, more than thirty years later, in a statement on poetics (*ALF*).

In the biographical notes which accompany Berengarten's poems, two factors stand out: he is descended from a family of Jewish musicians and he considers himself "a European poet who writes in English" (*AP* inside back cover). These are the traditions which inform his writing; and the familial, Jewish, musical voice, "born out of ghettos and shtetls, / raised from unmarked graves of my obliterated people / in Germany, Latvia, Lithuania, Poland, Russia" (*BB* 8) is central to his work. The unmarked graves of an obliterated people contain the voices of the silenced; and it is their song that Berengarten has endeavoured to recall and recapture in much of his work.

It would be simplistic and unwise to read all of Berengarten's work as an attempt to hear and speak with the voices of those killed in the Holocaust. I hesitate, therefore, to impose a political framework on Berengarten's writing, bearing in mind his own response to such an approach to the poetry of Elaine Feinstein by Peter Lawson. Berengarten comments:

> [Lawson] writes: "I approach [Feinstein's] work relating to English insularity and delimited Jewish families with such *socio-political* concerns in mind." (My italics) Yet we read poems for inspiration, consolation and illumination, not as sociological tracts or quasi-history. What is more, linguistic play, musical texturings, symbolic patternings and mystical resonances are inalienable from our Jewish poetic tradition. ('What makes a poem Jewish?', RB online)

Nevertheless, Berengarten's work honours not only the memory of the Holocaust dead but also the need to find an artistic means of expression that can allow their voices to be heard.

> Can you hear me? Are you there? There's somebody else on the
> line.

> It is the dead. Who will not lie down and rest. (*TM* 42)

Berengarten's introduction to Holocaust writing came at the age of thirteen, through *The Diary of Anne Frank*, which he first saw dramatised at the Golders Green Hippodrome in 1956. Berengarten disagrees with me when I suggest that in the period immediately following the Second World War, very little was spoken about the Holocaust; but I would argue that this absence of discourse continued through the determined, forward-looking, rebuilding decades of the late forties and fifties. "My generation," writes the Israeli author David Grossman, "the children of the early 1950s in Israel, lived in a thick and densely populated silence" (2007: online), and I would contend that the same silence generally blanketed England. If the Holocaust had been debated and written about during the early fifties as it is today (with a wealth of writing about it, even in children's literature), it would have been at a much younger age than thirteen that Berengarten "…first really 'found out' about the Holocaust or, at least, had [his] first full and shocking emotional realisation of what the Holocaust meant or should mean to everyone, and above all to Jews" (*MAF*). This is not to say that the Holocaust was taboo, but that as a young child, Berengarten (rightly, one might think) was protected, just as others were, from the full implication of the horror of the events. Thus his introduction to the Holocaust was delayed until his critical coming-of-age (he notes that this followed "very soon" after his barmitzvah), when his mother took him to see the dramatisation of *The Diary of Anne Frank*. What is interesting, however, is how his first 'real' exposure to the Holocaust prompted a literary response in an unpublished essay entitled '"My" Anne Frank':

> [O]nly now that I begin to mull this over does it occur to me that, while of course I knew very well even when I was just thirteen that these events had really happened, this very first huge impact of the Holocaust on me, through *The Diary of Anne Frank*, was not just that of documented facts, crude horror, unfiltrated pain. What I was experiencing from this dramatisation, in the heart of

safe, stolid, stable, suburban Golders Green, only eleven years after
the end of the Second World War, was already history-interpreted-
and-selected-as-story, was already suffering-dignified-and-distilled-
into-art. Already, fact had been transformed into drama. Already,
history had been heightened into living myth. Raw emotion, horror
and pain had been refined, reclaimed, reframed, even perhaps
redeemed, as tragedy. … *Tragedy, story, drama, art, poetry.* I can't help
wondering now if the main key that I took away from all this, even
then, was the conviction that the transformation of unimaginable
pain and suffering into art was what the human imagination was
designed for. (*MAF* 2007)

Berengarten's subsequent reading of *The Diary of Anne Frank* made an
equally strong impression. He notes seven separate aspects of his response
to the work, including the sensation that Anne Frank was addressing him
personally, the fact that she was addressing him at the crucial moment of
coming of age, and the idea that:

…she was speaking, from behind or from the other side of her own
death, as a timeless immortal, through her words which were still
alive even though she was not, so that her death was no more than a
screen that words crossed and could always cross with ease, at least
in one direction, that is, from the dead to the living, even if not
both ways, even if never both, as though death involved filtration
of some essence through a one-way valve or semi-permeable mem-
brane. (*ibid.*)

The seventh, final response was that "she as a writer, and as a highly
accomplished writer, was writing to me, not just as a reader, but as a reader
who was also implicitly, or who (it was somehow taken for granted) was
also *going-to-be – a writer*" (Berengarten's emphasis). And he continues:

I do have to confess now that I am not sure whether the seventh
and last of these elements was truly yet in place during that first
reading of the *Diary.* But it soon would be. And if this phrase 'It
soon would be' means that I now talk about all this in a teleological
way, as if all these factors were (?) tributaries, or contributories, all
leading up to a particular point, I think there is at least some degree
of truth and authenticity in doing so, because that is precisely how
I configure these events in my own mind, and have done ever since
that time, perhaps even since *before* it. In the process of 'becoming a
poet', it's now clear to me that this was all preparation, even though
I don't think I could possibly have known that at the time. (*ibid.*)

Furthermore, it is possible to read in Berengarten's poetry a continued attempt not only to find words but to explore whether language itself can accommodate such acts. Berel Lang notes: "We became aware that our language lacks words to express this offence, the demolition of man" (1988: 186). Berengarten himself echoes this very question: "Is it *language itself* won't do here?" (*BB* 14). In the face of this silence, how can a song be found? U. A. Fanthorpe, discussing the number of years it took for her to write about the war, quotes Anna Akhmatova:

> A woman with blue lips standing behind me… suddenly woke out of the benumbed condition in which we all found ourselves at that time and whispered in my ear (in those days we all spoke in a whisper):
> – Can you put this into words?
> And I said:
> – I can. (quoted in Herbert and Hollis 2000: 210)

For Berengarten, the equivalent moment was when a blue butterfly landed on his hand as he queued to go into the museum at Šumarice, the site of the Kragujevac massacre. It led to his book *The Blue Butterfly*.

> Can one tell, or even utter, what was utterly
> simple, wonderful, terrifying, total
> and wordless? I want to tell – an errant blue butterfly
> sat on my finger and weightlessly pressed
> two thousand eight hundred souls laid to rest
> in one thrust through me, and that wound was fatal. (*BB* 14)

'The Blue Butterfly' was not Berengarten's first poem to address the legacy of the Holocaust, though until this point his response had been distilled into a more oblique artistic representation. The search to find a voice that could transform pain and suffering into art is evident in his earlier works, in many of which he sought to engage with the past:

> There are no dead. They walk
> the air we sing.
> It's not the hills we have to move
> but domes of ashes in the mouth. (*AP* 52)

In *The Blue Butterfly*, however, his response to the Holocaust becomes explicit:

What hand, against the odds, pulled the Warsavian
musician out of the queue from ghetto to gas chamber,
denied Death his murder, and saved this man to play
for thirty more years of audiences? Why was he chosen?
Why him and not another? (*BB* 85)

Berengarten's first major work before this date to respond to the
Holocaust is 'Angels', one of his most powerful poems. Yet although
Berengarten states that this poem deals directly with the Holocaust, it is
also a poem with a wider sphere of reference. As Steve Spence notes, it
is "a powerful encapsulation of the history of human conflict presented
within a framework of evolution and adaptability, a feature which gives
the poem its sense of redemptive hope" (2003). This is evident in its final
lines:

> Then quietly I climbed
> and on a still sea trumpeted, took air
> and dived for ever. And you'll not find me
> nor you nor you, till the almond tree flowers
> on the mountain, and there is no more sea. (*FL* 55–56)

Addressing the dead has always been one of Berengarten's rhetorical
devices. In *Avebury* (1972), a work that recalls Pascal's epigraph, "If
these (the people) keep silence, the stones will speak", Berengarten places
himself within the continuum of the memory of the prehistoric stones:

> and can the stone know
> me   I wonder
>   does the stone
>   wonder
>
> even here   among the absences
> and wreckage (*FL* 27)

In Berengarten's poems the dead can lead us to an understanding which
is itself silent. He explores an aspect of this kind of silence through the
Charon-like images of 'Past Coppice Island':

> The poem-boat…
> takes us slow and steady
> Together to the point where

It comes to rest in
A final space called
Silence because I will it. (*BWNBC* 39)

It appears to me that in these poems, Berengarten is aiming for what Czesław Miłosz describes as a "borderline" that is similar, and even perhaps identical, to the one that, according to Miłosz, Polish poetry seeks: "a search for the line beyond which only a line of silence exists" (Miłosz 1983: 94). That such a place can be found amongst the dead is made explicit in the poem 'The Dead Do Not Hear Us':

But all I want is impossible. To hear and understand
whatever the dead may be saying, whatever it is they want (*BB* 81)

Since his early childhood, the dead for Berengarten have included his own father. He was three when his father died: "To disappear, like parents, from presence," he writes in *The Manager* (*TM* 147). His father's memory is recalled in many poems:

There goes my father underneath the hill. Among the shadow boxers. Consumed by memory and desire and that special sort of longing worn only by the dead. You can see it in their eyes. For love and for justice and for a better world.

There goes my father underneath the dew. A good Jew.

(RB 2006 online)

Here, the humanity investing Berengarten's work and motivating him as a poet, and the desire "for love and justice and for a better world", are given to the dead. Listening to dead poets can also be described as following a poetic tradition, and in more senses than one. More than any other living English poet I know, Berengarten belongs to a European tradition of poets, and his work demonstrates his sense of being a part of that community, with its obligation to listen to those who came before. In discussing his influences, he comments that he is "a member of a *living* poetic community"; but this community is made up of both the living *and* the dead, and there are times when one has the impression that for Berengarten the dead speak more loudly and clearly. Several lines from Seferis' poem 'Stratis Thalassinos Among the Agapanthi' come to mind here:

It's painful and difficult, the living are not enough for me
First because they do not speak, and then
Because I have to ask the dead
in order to go on farther. (1969: 279)

છ

Although Berengarten has lived in Italy and former Yugoslavia, and has been influenced by the poets and artists of both these countries, I sense (though this may well be because we share a knowledge and love of the country and its poets) that he has found his greatest influence in Greece, especially in the work of George Seferis. And Seferis is a writer for whom the "physical remnants of antiquity" speak directly of "fragments of a life which was once complete, disturbing" (Seferis 1969: vii). Berengarten has written of his close relationship with Seferis, most notably in an imagined, dream-like meeting between himself and the poet in the prose poem, 'Ambassador: An Old Man in the Harbour':

> And then, perhaps, I'll stammer, 'Although, you know, we never met, before, I've walked your favourite streets – Syngróu, Panepistimíou – and even though you were long gone, I've visited the house you lived in when you were a guest in my own country. And now at last I've found you, here in your own place…' (*FL* 175)

This is a conversation on tradition and also a tribute to those who came before. The Seferis persona tells the first person narratorial figure: "Of all the names, of all the dead I loved, / too many are forgotten who made the same journey". Norman Jope rightly observes that Berengarten is not "possessed by a desire to escape the 'clutches of the past'" (Jope 2005: 119); and I would go further and suggest that it is the past which informs his present. Berengarten listens to and reinterprets its voices. He has himself commented on how he forged his own poetic tradition while a student in Cambridge:

> …I'd decided, simply, to spend my time learning as much about how to write poems as I could … I was of course 'serious about literature', but my interests and attitudes were clearly never destined to fit into the Cambridge critical mould, or for that matter into academic orthodoxy of any kind. I was mad about Jung, the *I Ching*, Blake, Yeats, Eliot, Shelley, Keats, Milton, the Metaphysicals, Marlowe, Shakespeare, Dylan Thomas, the Beat Poets, Rilke, Seferis, Cavafy, Borges, Modern Jazz – and everything and anything to do with Italy

from Dante, Botticelli and Michelangelo to De Sica, Antonioni and Fellini. (*PRV* 108)

Even while rejecting the narrowness of the canon as taught at Cambridge, Berengarten was forging his own links to the past, his own tradition. As T. S. Eliot points out:

> The historical sense compels a man to write not merely with his own generation in his bones, but with a feeling that the whole of the literature of Europe from Homer and within it the whole of the literature of his own country has a simultaneous existence and composes a simultaneous order. This historical sense is what makes a writer traditional. (1951: 14)

Tradition and legacy are inextricably united in Berengarten's work in a sense both familial and artistic: "to name each plant… / here in memory's garden, and to forget not one, / is my task and possession, I want to explain / to my children", he writes in 'May' (*FL* 182); and *The Manager* ends with the image of the poet patching the torn aeons with love for the "Child of all our futures. Parent of all our pasts" (*TM* 157). "I'm trying to talk about love", he says (*TM* 156); "the common miracle" as he writes elsewhere (*FL* 160). "I don't believe in originality," writes Neruda. It is "a modern invention" (1977: 266). Berengarten, having found the song, the voice, hands it on:

> This voice, no longer mine, is yours now. Take it. Use it. Give it
> your own, far finer sound. (*BWNBC* 48)

And in the context of this thought, Berengarten's influence as an inspirational teacher should be mentioned. When creating the character of a poet for a recent play (2007), I drew on the memory of one of Richard's workshops for a speech in which a character, Hilary, justifies her line of work. I will quote it in full as I feel that it represents the humanity and generosity of Richard Berengarten, the 'Hatman' as he calls himself in his school work, and the way in which he has influenced generations of children:

> HILARY: Remember those workshops you used to give? I went to one – must be 20 years ago – on the Isle of Dogs. The kids were about ten or eleven and they didn't give a shit about poetry. But somehow you created a spell, you made them laugh … You got them catching

a football and told them that they had to grab words in the same way. Then you did a few basic exercises, got them writing a few lines of their own and then, when each of them read, you put that big hat on them, your poet's hat. And even though they disappeared underneath it, you could see they felt good wearing it. There was one little bugger who'd talked the whole way through. Dead small, really hard, the ring-leader, just wanted to be disruptive. I thought you'd get furious and chuck him out, but you didn't. You got him to write about someone or something dying. I mean, death is the last taboo. No one goes around in schools talking about death. But this kid wrote a poem about his Nan dying. And he read it under that great stupid hat of yours and when he stopped, you looked straight at him and said, 'Do you hear that? Do you hear that?' (*Long pause*) It was absolutely silent. 'You did that,' you told him. 'That's the power of what you wrote. You created that silence.'

Berengarten has himself created many moments of silence and great poems that confront death and confusion and celebrate humanity. The first quotation that he inscribed in his first writing diary was from *The Diary of Anne Frank*:

> Yet I simply can't build up my hopes on a foundation consisting of confusion, misery and death. I see the world gradually being turned into a wilderness, I hear the ever-approaching thunder, which will destroy us too, I can feel the sufferings of millions and yet, if I look up into the heavens, I think that it will all come right, that this cruelty will end, and that peace and tranquillity will return again. (*MAF* 2007)

David Grossman writes:

> In the Jewish tradition, there is a legend, or a belief, that every person has a small bone in his body called the *luz*, located at the tip of the spine, which enfolds the essence of a person's soul. This bone cannot be destroyed. Even if the entire human body is shattered, crushed or burned, the *luz* bone does not perish. It stores a person's spark of uniqueness, the core of his selfhood. According to the belief, this bone will be the source of man's resurrection.
>
> Once in a while, I ask people close to me what they believe their *luz* is, and I have heard many varied answers. Several writers, and artists in general, have told me that their *luz* is creativity, the passion to create and the urge to produce. Religious people, believers, have often said that their *luz* is the divine spark they feel inside. One friend answered, after much thought: parenthood, fatherhood. (Grossman 2007)

In Berengarten's poetry, as in his life, the light of his personal *luz* shines through in his humanity, in his seeking for and his celebration of being a man, a lover and a father. His is the song that comes out of the silence, a song that links with the past and that will be carried forward into the future.

REFERENCES

Eliot, T.S. 1951 [1917]. 'Tradition and the Individual Talent' in *Selected Essays*. London: Faber and Faber.

Elytis, Odysseus. 1974. *The Sovereign Sun* (trans. Kimon Friar). Philadelphia, PA: The Temple Press.

Grossman, David. 2007. 'Confronting the Beast', *The Guardian* (September 15). Online at: http://www.theguardian.com/books/2007/sep/15/featuresreviews.guardianreview2. Consulted, 1 February, 2016.

Herbert, W. N. and Hollis, Matthew (eds). 2000. *Strong Words*. Newcastle-upon-Tyne: Bloodaxe Books.

Hogg, James (ed.). 1996. *The Road to Parnassus, Homage to Peter Russell on his Seventy Fifth Birthday*. Salzburg: University of Salzburg Press.

Jope, Norman. 2005. 'Range and Resonance', review of RB, *For the Living* and *Book With No Back Cover*, *Tears in the Fence* 42: 116–120.

Lang, Berel. 1988. *Writing and the Holocaust*. Teaneck, NJ: Holmes & Meier Publishers.

Lawson, Peter. 2006. *Anglo-Jewish Poetry from Isaac Rosenberg to Elaine Feinstein*. Middlesex: Vallentine Mitchell.

Miłosz, Czesław. 1983. *The Witness of Poetry*. Cambridge, MA: Harvard University Press.

Moses, Antoinette. 2007. *Break Out*. Unpublished play, performed in 'Summer Shorts', New Wolsey Theatre, Ipswich, 2007.

Neruda, Pablo. 1977 [1974]. *Memoirs* (trans. Hardie St. Martin). London: Souvenir Press.

Seferis, George. 1969. *Collected Poems 1924–1955* (trans. Edmund Keeley and Philip Sherrard). London: Anvil Press Poetry.

Spence, Steve. 2003. '*Book With No Back Cover* by Richard Burns', *Terrible Work*. Online publication, consulted 16 August 2007. No longer available.

"'Tis Death is dead, not he"
or Reading Richard Reading Richard Reading

PHILIP KUHN

ר

The soothsayers who found out from time what it had in store certainly did not experience time as either homogeneous or empty. Anyone who keeps this in mind will perhaps get an idea of how past times were experienced in *remembrance* – namely, in just the same way. We know that the Jews were prohibited from investigating the future. The Torah and the prayers instruct them in *remembrance*, however. This stripped the future of its magic, to which all those succumb who turn to the soothsayers for enlightenment. This does not imply, however, that for the Jews the future turned into homogeneous, empty time. For every second of time was *the straight gate* through which the Messiah might enter. (Benjamin 1999a: 255 *italics added*)

ר

When Zeno the sceptic asked the oracle at Delphi what he should do to attain the best life the answer he received was: "Take on the complexion of the dead." (quoted in Nietzsche 2006: ix)

ר

FROM DEATH, it is from the fear of death that all cognition of the All begins. Philosophy has the audacity to cast off the fear of the earthly, to remove from death its poisonous sting, from Hades his pestilential breath. (Rosenzweig 2005: 9)

ר

Death is a possibility that is absolutely certain. It is the possibility that makes all possibility possible. (Levinas 2000: 49)

ר

Or I negate the sentence: the rose is a rose, when I say: the rose is not a rose; and what do I get if I then negate the negation and say: but after all the rose is a rose? (Engels 1947: 172)

ר

&

the dead rose

&

the dead rose

rose

with the dead

&

the rose

&

the rose

of the dead

rose

with the dead

&

the rose of the dead

&

the dying & the dead

rose

with the dead

when the rose

of the dead

rose with the dead.

(kuhn, 'Diptych for Richard 1')

My peregrinations begin with my reading the illustration on the front cover of *For the Living*, the first volume of your selected writings. It is a coloured reproduction of a detail from Ceri Richards' *Memorial to Dylan Thomas* – a pen and ink drawing gifted to you by Frances Richards. It shows an upturned skull resting upon the cover of a book. The skull has been hollowed out either by hand or by time: gashed out holes where the eyes and nose should have been. Although the teeth on the upper jaw are still more or less intact, the lower jaw – the mandible – looks as if it is missing. Or maybe it is concealed by what stands in front of it because inside the skull there is an arrangement of freshly-cut flowers or, to be more precise, five flowers with six and seven petals. These flowers, the genus of which I cannot identify, are interspersed with sprigs of leaves. The juxtaposition between the skull and the freshly-cut flowers suggests that the skull, which is after all still only a skull, is also a vase.

Does this uncanny arrangement of flowers, set in an upturned skull, suggest something other than what it might seem? Contraries? Paradoxes? Disjunctions? A Harmony and An Equipoise? A Fiercesome Beauty to behold? (Blake 1971: 172)

And does my reading of the picture change if I see these flowers not as freshly cut but as dried? And what if this arrangement were a bouquet? Or a wreath? "Rooted in death, but death's antithesis, / what is this wreath, if not hope's chrysalis?" (*BB* 35)

If I contract my vision I could almost believe that the skull is not a skull but a vase with flowers and this spectacle produces a modernist painting of *nature morte*.

But the teeth insist that this is a skull and not a vase. It is those mordant teeth that keep biting at my illusion(s): those teeth that make this still life. A *memento mori* for the living from the dead.

Now I turn the illustration through 180 degrees and the skull blossoms forth out of the flowers. Life thrusting into death / death thrusting out of life. Are these negations of negations?

ד

Do you remember when I first started researching your writings I asked you to tell me something about the Ceri Richards picture? In the course of your reply you remarked: "Incidentally, you may already have noticed that the skull upturned appears in *The Manager*, page 147" (see *TM1* 147). I had forgotten this, or overlooked it, or simply not noticed the significance of the reference. Here then is the passage in question: the Manager has been driving around for hours until, eventually, he finds the house that he is looking for. A strange old man opens the door. "His eyes gleam pitch-black light." He grabs the package the Manager has come to deliver and in that same instant thrusts a skull, instead, into the Manager's hands. Then the old man closes the door and the Manager is left "[c]radling death up-turned in my arms, I stand on the doorstep, shivering. And know this vessel my Grail, my singing immortal head. Now blessèd I backwalk up Hope Street, alive. My cup runneth over" (*TM1* 147).

The skull that "squats" in the old man's right arm becomes transfigured at the very moment he thrusts it into the arms of the Manager. Thus it becomes a skull that metamorphs from a "burden" into "death upturned", from "death upturned" into a "vessel", from a vessel into "my Grail", and from "my Grail" into "my singing immortal head". Or have I made too many leaps of imagination? And what of that phrase – "My cup runneth over"? I do not think it matters whether or not this was a conscious borrowing from Psalm 23, because that Psalm, let alone the phrase you have used, is so deeply engrained into our linguistic fibres. "The Lord is my shepherd; I shall not want" – "Yea, though I walk through the valley of the shadow of death" – "thou anointest my head with oil; my cup runneth over". (Cohen 1992: 67–68) But I am perhaps running away with myself.

ר

If there were only two references in your work to an upturned skull then, I suppose, they might be considered at best coincidental and not worth more than a few remarks in a footnote. But … Here are some lines from 'Avebury':

> down in the pit I have seen your face mother
>   your skull in the rockface
>
>   and who is that other
>   face in shadow
>   the cloud that lurks just behind you? (*FL* 40)

And these lines are from 'Tree':

> Tree planted
>   in my core
> spreading growing
>   tree of songs
> many branched
>   flame tree
> *rooted in death* (*FL* 119, *italics added*)

And these lines:

>   earth drinking
> sky swallowing
>   bowelled living
> *grave tree* (*FL* 120, *italics added*)

And these:

> tree of creation
>   tree of destruction
> *temple planted*
>   *in an upturned skull*
> worming woody
>   fibres through
> eye socket
>   and *mandible* (*FL* 123–124, *italics added*)

And these

> Kali's tree
>   dancing on skulls (*FL* 129)

You may recall that I smuggled a short passage from the Talmud into one of my long poems: "once at kefer saba / they found a skull stuck in the root of a sycamore tree" (kuhn 2009: 59). That skull stuck in the root and not – as in 'Tree' – "planted / in an upturned skull". Death in Life / Life thrusting out of Death.

ר

You will, of course, recall how the Manager (in *The Manager*) recalls that it was the "Shape of those roofs" and "[t]hat oak tree" which served him as a marker for "Hope Street" – the "One street on my citymap [which] always eludes me" (*TM1* 146). But isn't the Manager's remark somewhat disingenuous, for surely he should have known that those markers of orientation were also *mementos* for those long-forgotten streets on which he played as a child? And is it not strange that it was an *oak* tree that helped him find his way to the house in the newly-named Hope Street; that street to which there was no entry and from which he was to "back-walk" with an upturned skull? And what of this oak in Hope Street? Is it, perhaps, resonant with "the oldest oak in Europe" (*BB* 8)? Or perhaps with the oak of the Valla?

> Art thou, O ruin, the once glorious heaven? are these thy rocks
> Where joy sang in the trees & pleasure sported on the rivers,
> And laughter sat beneath the Oaks & innocence sported round
> Upon the green plains, & sweet friendship met in palaces,
> [...]
> Where are they, whelmed beneath these ruins in horrible
> destruction! (Blake 1971: 317)

Or is it possible that the "virginal / leaf new sprung on the oldest oak in Europe" (*BB* 8) is also a mirror of the oak tree that has shed a leaf into the lower right-hand margin of Blake's second 'Holy Thursday'? That upturned leaf which cradles a dead baby. (Blake 2000: 75)

ר

What strange threads connect your remembering Psalm 23 and 'Tree'? What clews bind *The Manager* with the illustration which you chose for *For the Living*? And how do I read these various images of death overturned now that I have confirmed (for myself at least) that somewhere in the matrix of your imaginations lurk symbols, metaphors and conceits of *upturned skulls* which issue forth out of "the valley of the shadow of death"? Skulls which beckon me into those arcane worlds of libation vessels, Holy Grails, Singing immortal heads, and – following the logic of Psalm 23 – bring me to the eternal Mansions of God.

ר

Vienna, 12 July 1892. In a letter written shortly after the death of one of his old teachers, Sigmund Freud tells his friend Wilhelm Fliess: "Last week brought me a rare human pleasure: the opportunity to select from Meynert's library what suited me – somehow like a savage drinking mead from his enemy's skull" (Freud 1985: 32).

Newstead Abbey, 1808. Lord Byron, "[o]bserving [a skull] to be of giant size, and in a perfect state of preservation", was "seized" by "a strange fancy". So he had the skull "set and mounted as a drinking cup", and then "sent it to town, and it returned with a very high polish, and of a mottled colour like tortoiseshell".

> Why not? since through life's little day
> Our heads such sad effects produce;
> Redeem'd from worms and wasting clay,
> This chance is theirs, to be of use. (1905: 80–81 and n)

Somewhere in India, sometime in 1065 (CE), there was a performance of the play *Prabodha Chandrodaya*, written by Krishnamishra (a *sannyasi*). One of the characters says: "My necklace and ornaments are of human bones; I dwell among the ashes of the dead and eat my food in human skulls. ... We drink liquor out of the skulls of Brahmans". According to Mircea Eliade (1969: online) this character may have been inspired by that "class of Shivaist ascetics, the *Aghoris* or *Aghorapanthis*, who follow[ed] the path (or the cult) of Shiva, [ate] from human skulls, haunt[ed] cemeteries, and still practiced cannibalism" well into the late nineteenth century. Eliade also believed that "These Aghoris are only the successors to a much older ... ascetic order, the *Kapalikas*, or 'wearers of skulls'." Furthermore, he also points out that there is "an inscription from the first half of the seventh century [which] names the god *Kapaleshvara* and his ascetics" and that *The Maitrāyana Upanisad* (VII, 8) also "already mentions a kapalin". Here is the relevant passage which appears under the heading *Polemic against Heretics*: "Again, there are such people who without being entitled to them, claim pretensions to wear red clothes, the ear-rings and skull ornaments (of certain ascetics)" (Deussen 1980: 382).

Some time in the eighth century (CE), the Sage Padma Sambhava (Guru Rinpoche) brought Buddhism from India into Tibet. It is worth noting that the skull-cup becomes an important symbol in the liturgy and art of Tibetan Buddhism. The skull-cup (not cap) is known in Sanskrit as the *kapala* and is fashioned from the oval upper section of the human cranium. In this tradition the *kapala* should be made from the skull of somebody who has died a violent death and, ideally, should be filled with a human heart and with human blood. In its liturgical form the *kapala* serves as a libation vessel and therefore as a constant reminder of death and impermanence. In Buddhist sacred art the *kapala* is frequently depicted in the *left hand* of Padma Sambhava (Zaharack 1998: online).

The Abbey of Monte Cassino, some time towards the end of the eighth century (CE). In his *Historia Gentis Langobardorum* Paul the Deacon makes a specific reference to a skull-cup when he records how Albion, having killed and decapitated Cunimundus, the King of the Gepide, then fashioned a drinking cup from the skull of his defeated enemy. He then offered it to his wife, Cunimundus' daughter, to drink from (Halsall: online 37).

ר

At the beginning of 'Avebury' you offer this quotation from Heraclitus: "*To rise up and become wakeful guardians of the living and of the dead*" (*FL* 18). This is, of course, fragment 63 according to the Diels-Kranz reference system (Barnes 1987: 34, 104). But let me quote from the translation that I prefer: "[Heraclitus says that] in his (its) presence they rise and become wakeful guardians of living (people) and corpses" (Heraclitus 1987: 43). T. M. Robinson glosses this fragment by assuming that Heraclitus was following Hesiod's *Works and Days* and might therefore be referring to the thirty thousand members of the golden race who were made divinities (*daemones*) by Zeus upon their death and then appointed "guardians of mortal men". Robinson goes on to suggest how this notion of the guardian could also refer to the heroes' *psyché* which, in Hesiod's view, was constituted as air that rises up "(from the earth to the realm of the gods) and thereby achieves its destiny". "After "dying, *as if overcome by sleep*", the heroes are, as guardians, "awake" once more, to protect "living people and corpses". But why should corpses need protection? Robinson's answer, which I find rather prosaic, is that those who died in battle were vulnerable to being robbed or mutilated and the Greeks found this particularly unpalatable. What is more, Robinson appears to offer no obvious suggestion as to how we might understand "in his (its) presence" (Heraclitus 1987: 125). But perhaps when all is said and done, only the dead can truly know how to take care of the dead.

ר

I want to continue these speculations by turning to a lecture course on the Pre-Platonic Philosophers which Nietzsche delivered at the University of Basel, probably during the winter semester of 1869–1870. In it he says the following:

> If everything is in Becoming, then, accordingly, predicates cannot adhere to a thing but rather likewise must be in the flow of Becoming. Well, Heraclitus perceived that contrary predicates imply each other, something like what Plato says about the pleasant and the unpleasant in the *Phaedo*: they are intertwined like a knot.

Then paraphrasing a passage from *Phaedo* (70e–72e), Nietzsche continues:

> In every human being the power of death works, like that of life, at every moment of his existence. *The entrance of life and death*, and of waking and sleeping, is only predominance becoming visible that one force has won over its opposite and momentarily begins to lose again to it. Both forces are continuously efficacious at the same time, since their eternal strife allows neither victory nor domination over time. It is one and the same thing to be living and dead, awake or asleep, young or old. Honey is both bitter and sweet. The world is a *mixing cup* that must remain undisturbed to avoid upsetting it. From the same source flow the sunny light of life and the darkness of death. (Nietzsche 2006: 65, *italics added*)

ר

Nietzsche's reading of Heraclitus leads me to that gentle soul who was Hölderlin. Let me remind you of the seventh stanza of Hölderlin's elegy 'Brod und Wein' [Bread and Wine], as offered through Michael Hamburger's translation:

> But, my friend, we have come too late. Though the gods are living,
>   Over our heads they live, up in a different world.
> Endlessly there they act and, such is their kind wish to spare us,
>   Little they seem to care whether we live or do not.
> For not always a frail, a delicate vessel can hold them,
>   Only at times can our kind bear the full impact of gods.
> Ever after our life is dream about them. But frenzy,
>   Wandering, helps, like sleep; Night and distress make us strong
> Till in that cradle of steel heroes enough have been fostered,
>   Hearts in strength can match heavenly strength as before.
> Thundering then they come. But meanwhile too often I think it's

Better to sleep than to be friendless as we are, alone,
Always waiting, and what to do or to say in the meantime
I don't know, and who wants poets at all in lean years?
But they are, you say, like those holy ones, priests of the wine-god
Who in holy Night *roamed from one place to the next.*
(Hölderlin 1994: 269–271, *italics added*)

Albert Hofstadter, in his translation of Heidegger's 1946 essay, 'What are Poets For?', renders Hölderlin's phrase (1994: 269–271) "und wozu Dichter in *dürftiger* Zeit?" as: "…and what are poets for in a destitute time?" (Heidegger 1975: 91). Julian Young and Kenneth Haynes translate it as: "and why poets in a desolate time?" (Heidegger 2002: 200). But it can perhaps also be translated as "and why poets in *wretched / miserable* times?" And do we live in wretched times? And if so, why poets?

ר

In your strangely haunting (*unheimlich*) prose poem, 'Ambassador (An Old Man in the Harbour)', you adopt the *persona* of a poet who imagines, after many years of longing and wandering, he will finally meet up with George Seferis (the poet) in whose footsteps he and (is it also you?) have been walking. And in that meeting, 'perhaps' you, and maybe also the poet in the poem [the Poet], will "stammer" these words:

"Although, you know, we never met, before, I've walked your favourite streets … and even though you were long gone, I've visited the house you lived in when you were a guest in my own country. And now at last I've found you, here in *your own place.*" (*FL* 175)

This is the harbour-town in which Seferis has finally settled because, as you or the Poet have Seferis say: he "knew" it "*for home,* only when this mongrel [dog] yapped at me" (*FL* 175, *italics added*).

In this poem which twists through strange disjunctures of time and space, you, and/or the Poet, imagine an event, which you are now describing, as occurring in some half-distant future which is also contained within a half-imagined place. For this meeting will happen simply because it is taking place. And while Seferis is already dead there is no question, in your mind, that you and/or the Poet, will eventually meet with him. The only problem – which of course you have resolved through the writing of this poem – is the difficulty you will have in finding Seferis: because *the name* of the Harbour where he lives is "*absent from maps in my language*" (*FL* 174–176, *italics added*).

Did you catch an uncanny mirror-echo as it bounced back and forth between 'Ambassador' and the ninety-fourth section of *The Manager*? Remember the Manager's journey to deliver that package to an old man who thrusts him that upturned skull. A strange encounter on the *threshold* of a house the Manager had great difficulty finding, notwithstanding that it was in a zone he knew well and in which he had spent his childhood. How he drove "back and forth hours", unable to locate Hope Street – the "*One street* on my citymap [that] always eludes me" (*TM* 148–149, *italics added*).

But back to The Harbour which not only eludes you but perhaps also alludes to you: this Harbour which is also a place of meeting: this time not with some anonymous "old man, half shadowed" who "threatens to throttle and gag" you (*TM* 148–149) but with a kind and gentle man who (as if in a mirror image of that other old man) will "shake [your] hand warmly, spread [his] palm on [your] back, and guide [you] safely across the wide avenue" where you will share a meal and "clink glasses together, toasting life, and memory, and each thinking of those we love" (*FL* 174–175).

ד

During a recent conversation you suggested that the Harbour, in 'Ambassador', could be read for Ithaca and Seferis for Odysseus. Of course the mangy dog is a reference back not only to the "half-dead from neglect, / … Argos" (Homer 1997: 300-301) but also to Seferis' own reference to Odysseus' homecoming (1973: 281). And of course behind your figure of Seferis stands "Stratis Thalassinos" (literally "Stratis the Mariner"), Seferis' own figure for Odysseus. And were I to follow your reading even further I could suggest that where Seferis is read for Odysseus and the Harbour for Ithaca then surely Ithaca must also be read for Home [*Heimat*]? For 'Ambassador' conjures up a profound sense of the already familiar (*heimisch*): the shared meal, the generosity of Seferis who is a host at ease in "the wooden chair" (*FL* 174). And if the Harbour could be read for Home then what if I were to identify that Harbour as Hope Harbour? For its resonance with Hope Street seems unmistakable. The Manager who arrives and is returning, if not exactly home, then at least to the place of his childhood. And even if he does not recall a yapping dog at least he remembers "wolves and jackals" (*TM* 148).

But this reading will only take me so far because I am not convinced that 'Ambassador' is ultimately about your relationship with Seferis. Rather I believe it to be about your (self) reflection upon your self being "the Poet". And if this is so then the Harbour (which may well be Ithaca / Home for Seferis) cannot be Home for you, or the Poet. And if the Harbour is not your Home then neither is it "Ithaca" the "ultimate goal" that might still give you "the beautiful voyage" (Cavafy 1976: 36). And because this Harbour is not your Home it is only a resting-place, and being a resting-place it must become, by virtue of *mitosis*, the crossed-road on the Poet's own long journey Home: a journey which, you hope, will eventually take you/him to that "place in the hills… which still today, as then, is an occupied city" (*FL* 175). And should that city be Jerusalem, as you have suggested, then my question is this: "Ithaca or Zion" (*BB* 65)?

ר

But I still want to linger in this Harbour for there you will have Seferis "point out a very old man at another table, intent over a book, a glass of wine before him". And you, or the Poet, will have Seferis say: "*Remember the one who said, 'What's the use of poets in a mean-spirited age? – that's him, sitting there. He was already here long before I arrived, and here he will stay, like me. No doubt his memory will long out-last mine…'*" (*FL* 175, *italics added*). Of course that very old man at another table, with his glass of wine before him, is Hölderlin.

Now Hölderlin probably composed 'Andenken' [Remembrance] in the spring of 1803 (1984: 265). In a draft, which does not appear in the poem, he wrote: "So God's weather wanders above / But you holy song / And you, poor mariner, seek the inhabited / look toward the stars." Heidegger (2000: 111), who quotes and glosses this fragment, suggests that for Hölderlin "the name *mariners* [was] the essential word for *poets*" because mariners must "know the heavenly bodies and be masters in reading the quarters of the sky." Furthermore the reference to the northeast wind, which appears in the first line of the published poem (and which blows *from* the poet's native Germany), is also significant because it "'calls' the poets to find themselves in the destiny of their historical being." Richard Sieburth extends this point in his note to the fourth strophe of the poem when he suggests that the sailors (mentioned in the first strophe) now hesitate "to go or return to the source". From here he concludes that these sailors

are like rivers whose course leads seaward, *away from their origin*. Yet
it is only in the sea, in the solitary and arduous process of voyaging,
far from the familiar, that the source may be recalled: oblivion is
integral to memory. (Hölderlin 1984: 266, *italics added*)

ר

When I asked you recently about your relationship with Seferis, you said
something like: *his Collected Works are never far from reach*. I begin to see,
now, how his presence and absence hover over your writings: a constant
companion, a fellow wanderer, a wakeful guardian, and a priest of the
wine-god. And I have suddenly remembered these haunting lines from
'In Lieblicher Bläue' ['In Lovely Blueness'], a late Hölderlin prose poem,

> …may a man look up and say: I too would like to resemble these?
> Yes. As long as kindliness, which is pure, remains in his heart not
> unhappily a man may compare himself with the divinity. Is God
> unknown? Is He manifest as the sky? This rather I believe. It is the
> measure of man. Full of acquirements, but poetically, man dwells
> on this earth. But the darkness of night with all the stars is not
> purer, if I could put it like that, than man, who is called the image
> of God. (1994: 715)

During that same conversation you also reminded me that the epigraph
for 'Ambassador' – "The first thing God made is the long journey" (*FL*
174) – was taken from 'Stratis Thalassinos Among the Agapanthi'. Here
is part of the final stanza of that remarkable poem:

> The first thing God made is love
> then comes blood
> and the thirst for blood
> roused by
> the body's sperm as by salt.
> The first thing God made is the long journey;
> that house there is waiting
> with its blue smoke
> with its aged dog
> waiting for the homecoming so that it can die.
> But the dead must guide me;
> it is the agapanthi that keep them from speaking,
> like the depths of the sea or the water in a glass.
> (Seferis 1973: 281)

Stratis Thalassinos who will finally return home, perhaps to die? Or perhaps, like Odysseus and those other poets in 'Ambassador', he has returned home from the dead. But why do the flowers of love, the *Agapanthi* (*agape* 'love' / *anthos* 'flower') "order silence" whenever Stratis calls out? Let me quote some lines from the third stanza:

> It is painful and difficult, the living are not enough for me
> first because they do not speak, and then
> because I have to ask the dead
> in order to go on further.
> There's no other way: the moment I fall asleep
> the companions cut the silver strings
> and the flask of the winds empties.
> I fill it and it empties, I fill it and it empties:
> I wake
> like a goldfish swimming
> in the lightning's crevices (Seferis 1973: 279)

And why do the flowers keep the dead from speaking? Is it perhaps because the dead can speak only when they are no longer dead? And does all of this suggest that Hölderlin and Seferis have become "wakeful guardians" of the living *and* the dead? And what about you, Richard? Are you, like Hölderlin and Seferis, another one of "those holy ones, priests of the wine-god / Who in holy Night *roam* ... from one place to the next" (*italics added*)? I am not at all surprised that you should have chosen the first three lines from this stanza as one of the epigraphs to the fourth section of *Under Balkan Light* (67), that final book in your *Balkan Trilogy*.

ר

But perhaps now it is time to begin to remember Yugoslavia.

The date was 25 May 1985. It was shortly before you would write 'Ambassador'. You and your first daughter Lara were visiting the memorial museum of Šumarice on the outskirts of Kragujevac. While you "were queuing to enter the museum, a blue butterfly suddenly came to rest on the forefinger of [your] left hand – that is, [your] writing hand" (*BB* 123). You have remarked on the significance of this moment on several occasions but perhaps nowhere more explicitly than in 'Arijana's Thread', that short and poignant essay which serves as a Postscript to *In a Time of Drought* (73–77). In that essay you relate how, in the course of

105

researching that book, you suddenly discovered that 'Peperuda', one of the names given to the Bulgarian rain-maiden, could also mean *butterfly*. This discovery confirmed your "sense that [you were] somehow being 'called'" to write *that* poem; and, at the same time, you "realised in a flash" that here "was the 'ending' to *The Blue Butterfly* which [you] had been searching for" (*ITD* 76).

I want to dwell, for a moment, on that moment, by suggesting that just as important as the coming of the blue butterfly was the manner of its manifestation – that it landed on the forefinger of your writing hand. I understood its significance only subsequently when I read the quotation from Slobodan Rakitić which you use as one of the epigraphs to section 6 of *Under Balkan Light*.

> In some beliefs, the pointing (index) finger is … the finger of life, while the middle finger is the finger of death. In another belief, the pointing finger is that of the Lord of Words … In [this] context, the pointing finger embeds both symbolisms: the finger of life is the finger of the word itself, that is, *of the poem itself.* (*UBL* 119, *italics added*)[1]

ר

A blue butterfly that settled just long enough on your left forefinger for you to be able to take that photograph which would eventually appear, 21 years later, on the frontispiece of the book that you had not yet written. Even without the proof of that grainy image I read this, your (his)story of the blue butterfly, as a wonderful conceit. The blue butterfly that becomes the *inspiration* for the book. Inspiration: to breathe in – like "[t]he breath whose might I have invoked in song" (Shelley 1974: 317). The blue butterfly that is (like) one of those nameless alien spirits that suddenly arrive from somewhere other (*UBL* 115) – another world? – and gently taps upon your shoulder. Or one of those magical voices whose inaudible whispers barely disturb the crisp autumnal leaves and yet, taking hold of your pen, begin to guide it mysteriously across the page. Or perhaps like *Mnemosyne*, the goddess of Memory, Mother-Goddess of the Muses, who sometimes visits poets in the deepest hollows of sleep, or trance, or psychosis and, silently whispering gentleness in their ear, beckons

---

[1] *Editors' note*: The essay by Slobodan Rakitić appears in this volume on pp. 315–324. For the full context of this quotation, see p. 319.

them towards the edge of some dark precipice. The blue butterfly that becomes an anthropomorphic shade, shadow, *pneuma, anima* or *geist*: one of those familiar unfamiliars who divine and change, move and have moved, shape and have shaped a multitude of poetries across so many distances and times. Like the *ombra* – the shade of Virgil – who guides Dante on his long and perilous journey (1961, 24/25 [1.66]). Or like the ghostly ghost of Hamlet (I, v) who haunts and goads his son towards his anguished bloody revenge. Or like the "Heavenly Muse", the "Dove-like" "Spirit" that Milton called down to "aid" his "adventurous song" (Bk I, 6–21). And now you, Richard with the blue butterfly, a winged insect that has become a messenger from the dead, settled upon your finger in order to call you, softly, urgently urging you, an English European Jew, to follow her into those forgotten distances of time and space and memory.

> Now my ears awakened in an alert
> attentive and percipient listening
> to scoured shells of voices, wholly prised apart
> from those dead mouths, pouring their testament
> onto spring wind, stirred by the *instrument*
> of the butterfly at rest on my finger, glistening.
> (*BB* 10, *italics added*)

ר

Here, then, is a conceit composed of many different threads. First came that blue lepidopteron which came to rest briefly upon your finger. Then in memory (eidetic, graphic and photographic) the blue butterfly (which now no longer exists) becomes the sign for a particular species which probably will never be positively identified (*BB* 124). By degrees it then becomes a name you use to christen a short poem (*BB* 8). This poem will then become part of a sequence which, when taken all together, will also bear its name. But this same sign can also be read as an *imago*, a symbol and/or an allegory of the *psyche* that dances between gaps and rents in some invisible firmament: or hovers over those silences that speak through "the language of flowers only" (Seferis 1973: 279). Or like Mercury who passes intelligences between friends and enemies: or the quicksilvered hermetic-tongued trickster who leads you to the very edge of that unknown abyss that lies between "no / man's land, contested gap between time-end / and time…" (*BB* 90). That blue butterfly that becomes, in its mercurial flight an ethereal messenger, like the wingèd Hermes (*UBL* 129), who arrives suddenly unbidden, carrying a cacophony of messages from wine-gods, or victims or survivors of a bloody massacre that took place somewhere near to where you once stood in time and place. And so, by degrees, that same blue butterfly will also become "…miraculously blessed / by the two thousand eight hundred martyred / men, women and children fallen at Kragujevac" in late October 1941 (*BB* 8). And once blessed, it will lead you into and through that long psychic journey that was not just "Kragujevac" but also *In a Time of Drought* and, at long last, finally to *Under Balkan Light*.

A blue butterfly that once landed "on [your] left forefinger" and beckoned you into "a different dimension … like Alice, / imperceptibly through some invisible screen / in an effortless slippage across time's barriers". For

> occasionally we too sense we reach right through
> time's surfaces or contours, even if not to its core,
> and the edges of our voices suddenly stretch out
> to reach and touch notes, albeit quavering, faltering,
> *they've never been capable even of approaching before.*
> (BB 77, italics added)

This blue butterfly that inspired you to sing the songs of those massacres which you had originally thought only to learn about in the museum of Šumarice.

> 'Listen,
> take me in, drink me,' and sometime entering you too,
> spreading drops on your hands, feeding your mouth with words,
> unclasping your throat in song's affirmation and harmony,
> like a blue butterfly (*BB* 76)

And so, Richard, what I now want to know is whether you believe, along with Stratis Thalassinos and Hölderlin and Seferis (and all those other old men) in The Harbour that "…the living are not enough for [you] / first because they do not speak, and then / because [you] have to ask the dead / in order to go further" (Seferis 1973: 279)?

ד

In one of Kafka's wondrous short stories (but are they not all won-drous?) a boat comes into a harbour and a bier is carried from the boat

108

and brought into the Burgomaster's house. In the bier is a man who "was probably dead". But the moment the Burgomaster is alone in his room, the man on the bier rises and introduces himself as the hunter Gracchus. "Are you dead?" asks the Burgomaster. "Yes," said the hunter, "as you see." "But you are alive too," said the Burgomaster. "In a certain sense," said the hunter, "in a certain sense I am alive too." But it transpires that the Burgomaster has already known that he will have this meeting because during the previous night a dove whispered in his ear: "Tomorrow the dead hunter Gracchus is coming; receive him in the name of the city." Gracchus then proceeds to tell the Burgomaster how he had been killed falling from a precipice whilst hunting a chamois. And then how his "death ship lost its way; a wrong turn of the wheel, a moment's absence of mind on the pilot's part, a longing to turn aside towards my lovely native country, I cannot tell what it was; I only know this, that I remained on earth and that ever since my ship has sailed earthly waters." Then, to the Burgomaster's enquiry as to whether the hunter had any "part in the other world", Gracchus replied:

> I am forever ... on the great stair that leads up to it. On that infinitely wide and spacious stair I clamber about, sometimes up, sometimes down, sometimes on the right, sometimes on the left, always in motion. The hunter has been turned into a butterfly ... I am always in motion. But when I make a supreme flight and see the gate actually shining before me I awaken presently on my own ship, still stranded forlornly in some earthly sea or other. (Kafka 1960: 104–110)

ר

At the heart of *The Blue Butterfly* lies Section Six, the 'Flight of the Imago' (*BB* 73–101): those seven 'dialogues' in which the living and the dead invoke you, Richard, a European Jew, to help them make sense of the senseless, give meaning to the meaningless, articulate what could no longer be thought of, spoken, remembered or denied. But I also believe that at the heart of the heart of section six lies 'Conversation Between a Blue Butterfly and a Murdered Man at One of the Entrances to the Underworld' ['Conversation'] (*BB* 89–98). It is a poem of paradoxical intensity in which a murdered man seeks to come to terms with the fact of his dying, of his about-to-be-dead, and to disappear from life. A dead man trapped between no-life and death in a "no / man's land, contested gap between time-end / and a time, a pause that is never a pause" (*BB*

90). A dead man, frozen forever at the instant he is about to pass into that "undiscover'd country, from whose bourn / No traveller returns" (Shakespeare, *Hamlet*: III. i. 79–80).

In my reading of 'Conversation' I found myself standing at an equipoise balanced on an edge of infinity. And in that moment I recalled another character from another of Kafka's "fairy tales for dialecticians" (Benjamin 1999b: 799) – not the un-dead Gracchus but the not-dead "man from the country who begs for admittance to the Law". And through the prisms of these readings I imagine how the blue butterfly might transform itself into that most powerful and yet very lowest doorkeeper of the Law (Kafka 1953: 235). And by degrees Kafka's gate to the Law will become "one of the gates, countless, unseeable, / that leads down to the Underworld, this being / *your special entrance, open for you only*" (*BB* 90, *italics added*). And like Kafka's sphinx-like and spectral shadow of a gatekeeper, the blue butterfly becomes protector, watcher and guardian of that *single* portal that might yet offer the murdered man his last hope of/for redemption. And through reading these writings which preface the Law (Kafka 1953: 235–244), I arrive, by less than six degrees of separation, at the *Angelus Novus,* Paul Klee's haunting painting, which Walter Benjamin reads as "the angel of history. His face … turned towards the past" (1999a: 249). And in this frame the blue butterfly also becomes the Avenging Angel ministering not only to the Living but also to the Dead: "*Angel of life or death, my blue butterfly, no matter*" (*BB* 98).

ר

But does it really *not* matter? And what of the Poet in *these* wretched times? Is he to become a *meshuggener* – a crazy man – in order to survive? And you, Richard, are you one of those *meshuggeners* who seek to stretch out the very Being of Language so as to squeeze each word through the thules of time? You, with your *mishegoss* – your crazy ideas – of talking with the dead. And why do you persist with this quest when, surely, you must know it to be *im/possible*? Maybe it is because there is always a nagging doubt that after all is said and done, it might just not be im/possible? Or is it because you believe the im/possible lies not in the im/possibility itself but inside those grimoires which the "*Lords of the far side*" (*UBL* 107), or maybe even the "Invisible Master" *himself* (*UBL* 110), have concealed somewhere in those "elsewheres" (*UBL* 62)? And if that is so then it might still be possible to discover even though it will always elude you. Or maybe you believe that the im/possibility exists only in the finitudes of Language with all its "gaps and holes", in which there "lurk / many incomprehensible expanses" (*BB* 91). But what if the im/possibilities have already been moulded into the very search itself so that your yearning to know all about death is paradoxically "ungrantable" because ultimately it is "the invisible / puppet-masters and mistresses who pull the strings / of the living, and the dead – who may even *be* / the dead" (*BB* 81)? And what if the im/possible also lies in our always being dependent upon not having (yet) learnt how to *read* the secrets of nature: "fluent in their clammy languages of indecipherable / signs and shadows that are to us wholly insoluble / and may only be traced in such ideograms and glyphs / as flower forms, wind scents and bee murmurs" (*BB* 82)? If you could only learn how to speak "the language of flowers", then *perhaps* you might yet learn how to communicate with "[t]he dead" (Seferis 1973: 279). But surely you can speak the language of flowers only if you first learn how to talk with the dead. But if you would talk with the dead you must first find "words like flowers leaping alive" (Hölderlin 1994: 269).

So when I enter my last mortal sleep,
after all dreams have gone, and I am dead,
will then I wake and, doubly waking, keep
some mirror of that garden in my head
and, back inside it, rising from the deep
distress of death, sleepwalk? Or wake instead? (*UBL* 84)

ר

During my reading of 'Ambassador' I turned one of your comments into this question: "Ithaca or Zion"? (*BB* 65).

There is a Talmudic tradition banning Jews from the "place of evil waters": or to put it more starkly, a Jew is forbidden to drink at the fountains of "Greek wisdom" (Epstein 1936: 269; Blackman 1990: 493). In his poem, 'Of the Hebrews (A.D. 50)', Cavafy (1976: 93) casts a wry glance at this rabbinical ruling, although I have no idea whether he did so with conscious intent. In this poem Cavafy has Janthis struggle to break free from "the beautiful hard hellenism" in order that he might "become the one I would always / want to remain: of the Hebrews, / of the Holy Hebrews, the son.… But he did not stay such a man at all. / The Hedonism and the Arts of Alexandria / kept him their devoted child." Does this mean, for the Jew at least, that Zion and Ithaca must always remain incompatible?

I venture a response by returning, once again, to 'Conversation', that powerful meditation on the murdered man's flight or slippage, into death: his passing out of life. Of course, had I paid attention to the full title: 'Conversation Between a Blue Butterfly and a Murdered Man at One of the Entrances to the *Underworld*' (*BB* 89–98, *italics added*), I would have realised much earlier that this was a poem that envisioned death as a voyage, or a journey, "that leads *down* to the underworld" (*BB* 90, *italics added*): and leading *down* it encompasses Classical Myth-ology. You christen "Fortune" not only "*Ananke*" but also "This elder sister of Hades" (*BB* 95, 97). And you name "grim Death" "*Thanatos, Hades, Dis, Charon*" and "plutocrat *Pluto*, brother to *Ananke*" (*BB* 96, 97). In the light of my previous comments I would now go so far as to say that this poem's entire ideological underpinning, if I could put it like that, is built firmly upon Ithaca. And if this is so then what of *Zion*? And why has she been occluded from your discourse?

ר

Wolfson (1994: 335) suggests that in the Jewish mystical tradition there is a belief "that at the moment of death the individual soul, freed from its physical encasement, sees the *Shekhinah*". He goes on to observe that "In zoharic literature, moreover, death is represented as the erotic union of the soul with the feminine *Shekhinah*. Just as the unitive experience of the mystic is a kind of ecstatic death, so in turn is death a kind of mystical union." For his part Guttmann (1964: 25) suggests that this mystical tradition can be traced back to the writings of Philo (20 BCE–50 CE), generally considered the first Jewish philosopher. Philo conceived God as standing "over and against the world in absolute transcendence ... and spirituality", a view which appears to contrast radically with the materialism and pantheism of many Greek thinkers. Philo also claimed (1993: 253, 258) that Moses taught that it was man's duty to "Take heed to thyself". Only by following this injunction could a Jew hope to free himself "from that base and polluted prison house of the body" thereby finding the way to come nearer to God. Guttmann concludes (1964: 28) that Philo's ideas were subsequently interpreted by a number of mystics as being an articulation of the "ideal of an *ascent* of the soul to the suprasensual world, culminating in a union with God" (*italics added*). This thread may well have inspired the subsequent concept of *devekut*, loosely defined as that private and mystical upsurge of the soul which brings man into "close and most intimate communion with God".

For his part Scholem (1995: 203, 227) has argued that this concept of *devekut* remains "without eschatological connotations ... for it can be realised in this life, in a direct and personal way". It is through a "state of *devekut* [that] man *finds himself* by losing himself in God, and by giving up his *identity* he discovers it on a higher plane". (*italics added*). What is important to note is that *devekut* is here considered to be a spiritual journey of "a strictly individual attainment" rooted neither in the belief in "Messianic redemption, nor ... in a hope or, for that matter, an anticipation of the Hereafter, of the World-to-come. In an eschatological sense, man can not be redeemed alone, individually". Or to put it another way, redemption can occur only with the coming of Messiah. *Devekut* becomes, therefore, the only possible response for the Jew who sits in a tradition that believes man can have no part in his own redemption. In this sense Life is lived as if in a waiting room, not for the World-to-come, but in constant anticipation of the Messiah, who is always *about to enter.* Which means that the life of the mystic seeking *devekut* is always "a *life lived in deferment*" (Scholem 1995: 35). Which, of course, returns me to that Benjamin quotation with which I started this letter.

ר

listen
to the petals
that have fallen
to the floor

listen
to
the souls
that have entered
death's last door

five white petals
untied the knot
from the rose
the dried
white petals
that dropped
from the red
of the rose

covet

the soul

the corpse

&

the rose

&

listen

to the knot

that ties

the living to the dead

&

to

the knot

of the living

&

not

to the dead

(kuhn, 'Diptych for Richard 2')

REFERENCES

Barnes, Jonathan. 1987. *Early Greek Philosophy*. London: Penguin Books.

Benjamin, Walter. 1999a. 'Theses on the Philosophy of History' in *Illuminations* (trans. H. Zorn). London: Pimlico: 245–255.

______. 1999b. *Walter Benjamin: Selected Writings 1927– 1934* (Vol. 2 trans. Rodney Livingstone *et al*). Cambridge, MA: The Belknap Press of Harvard University.

Blackman, P. 1990. *Mishna. Volume 4, Order Nezikin*. Gateshead: Judaica Press.

Blake, William. 1971. *Complete Writings, with variant readings* (ed. G. Keynes). Oxford: Oxford University Press.

______. 2000. *The Complete Illuminated Books*. London: Thames and Hudson.

Byron, George. 1905. *The Poetical Works of Lord Byron* (ed. E. H. Coleridge). London: John Murray.

Cavafy, C. P. 1976. *The Complete Poems of Cavafy* (expanded edition, trans. Rae Dalven). London: Harcourt Brace.

Cohen, Rev. Dr. A. (ed.). 1992. *The Psalms*. London: The Soncino Press.

Dante. 1961. *The Divine Comedy: Inferno* (trans. John D. Sinclair). New York, NY: Oxford University Press.

Deussen, Paul. 1980. 'Maitrāyaṇa a Upanisad' in *Sixty Upanisads of the Veda* (Vol. 1, trans. from the German, V. M. Bedekar and G. B. Palsule). Delhi: Motilal Banarsidass: 327–386.

Eliade, Mircea. 1969. *Yoga, Immortality and Freedom*. Princeton, NJ: Princeton University Press.

Engels, Frederick. 1947. *Anti-Dühring: Herr Eugen Dühring's Revolution in Science* (trans. E. Burns). Moscow: Progress Publishers.

Epstein, I. 1936. 'Sotah' in *The Babylonian Talmud: Seder Nashim* (Vol. 3). London: Soncino Press.

Freud, Sigmund. 1985. *The Complete Letters of Sigmund Freud to Wilhelm Fliess 1887–1904* (trans. J. M. Masson). Cambridge, MA, and London: The Belknap Press of Harvard University.

Guttmann, Julius. 1964. *Philosophies of Judaism: The History of Jewish Philosophy from Biblical Times to Franz Rosenzweig* (trans. David W. Silverman). London: Routledge and Kegan Paul.

Halsall, Guy (ed.). 2002. *Humour, History and Politics in Late Antiquity and the Early Middle Ages*. Cambridge: Cambridge University Press.

Heidegger, Martin. 1975. 'What are poets for?' in *Poetry, Language, Thought* (trans. Albert Hofstadter). New York, NY: Harper: 91–142.

______. 2000. *Elucidations of Hölderlin's Poetry* (trans. Keith Hoeller). New York, NY: Humanity Books.

______. 2002. 'Why Poets?' in *Off the Beaten Track* (trans. Julian Young and Kenneth Haynes). Cambridge: Cambridge University Press: 200–241.

Heraclitus. 1987. *Fragments: A Text and Translation with a Commentary* (trans. T. M. Robinson). Toronto: University of Toronto Press.

Hölderlin, Friedrich. 1984. *Hymns and Fragments* (trans. Richard Sieburth). Princeton, NJ: Princeton University Press.

______. 1994. *Poems and Fragments* (trans. Michael Hamburger). London: Anvil Press Poetry.

Homer. 1997. *The Odyssey* (trans. Robert Fagles). Bath: The Soft Back Preview.

Kafka, Franz. 1953. *The Trial* (trans. Willa and Edwin Muir). London: Penguin Books.

______. 1960. 'The Hunter Gracchus' in *Description of a Struggle And The Great Wall of China* (trans. Willa and Edwin Muir *et al*). London: Secker and Warburg: 104–110.

kuhn, philip. 2009. *at maimonides table*. Exeter: Shearsman Books.

Levinas, Emmanuel. 2000. 'Death and Time' in *God, Death, and Time* (trans. Bettina Bergo). Stanford, CA: Stanford University Press: 5–117.

Milton, John. 1968. *Paradise Lost and Paradise Regained*. New York, NY: Franklin Watts.

Nietzsche, Friedrich. 2006. *The Pre-Platonic Philosophers* (trans. Greg Whitlock). Chicago, IL: University of Illinois Press.

Philo. 1993. *The Works of Philo: Complete and Unabridged* (trans. C. D. Yonge). Peabody, MA: Hendrickson.

Rosenzweig, Franz. 2005. *The Star of Redemption* (trans. Barbara E. Galli). Madison, WI: University of Wisconsin Press.

Scholem, Gershom. 1995. *The Messianic Idea in Judaism and Other Essays on Jewish Spirituality*. New York, NY: Schocken Books.

Seferis, George. 1973. *Collected Poems* (trans. Edmund Keeley and Philip Sherrard). Bilingual Greek and English text. London: Anvil Press Poetry.

Shakespeare, William. 1982. *Hamlet* (ed. Harold Jenkins). London: Methuen, The Arden Shakespeare.

Shelley, Percy Bysshe. 1974. *The Poetical Works of Shelley* (ed. Newell F. Ford). Boston, MA: Houghton Mifflin Co., Cambridge edition.

Wolfson, E. R. 1994. *Through A Speculum That Shines: Visions and Imagination in Medieval Jewish Mysticism*. Princeton, NJ: Princeton University Press.

Zaharack, Brian. 1998. 'Skull Cup'. Museum #: 91.001.014. The Huntington Archive of Buddhist and Related Art (College of the Arts, Ohio State University, Columbus, OH). Online at: http://www.unc.edu/~benroger/tibetart/description.html. Consulted, 14 April 2008.

PART II

A Syntax of Stones:
Pre-Text, Edifice, and the Sacred Space in
Richard Berengarten's 'Avebury'

NELI MOODY

'Avebury' (*FL* 23–50, 219–220) was written in 1971 at Great Shelford, near Cambridge. On the most basic level, it is a poem about stones, stones being elemental products of the violent orogenesis of the earth. It is appropriately dedicated to Octavio Paz whose long poem, *Piedra de Sol*, or *Sunstone* (Paz 1991), Berengarten cites as one of his main influences ('Afterwords', *AVE*).[1] Paz not only strongly influenced Berengarten's work and helped him shape his own theory of poetics, he impressed Berengarten on a personal level too. During the Mexican poet's year at Churchill College at Cambridge as the Simón Bolivar Visiting Fellow in 1970–71, he and Berengarten often socialised, together with their wives (*OP*). The two stayed in touch after that visit and Berengarten describes the post-Paz Cambridge as duller, drabber and more insular.[2] The postcards and letters that passed between them were full of respect for each other as

---

[1] *Editors' note*: All references to the text of 'Avebury', in this essay, are to the re-published text that appears in the second edition of *For the Living* (Salt, 2008; reissued Shearsman Books, 2011). However, the author also refers to the 'Afterwords' that appear in the first published edition, *Avebury* (1972, London: Anvil Press Poetry). Whereas the text of the poem is identical in both editions, the 'Afterwords' are not included in *For the Living* and, therefore, the 1973 edition (hereafter *AVE*) is referred to where appropriate. *Avebury* has been republished by Shearsman as an e-book, at http://www.shearsman.com/ws-public/uploads/223_avebury.pdf.

[2] 'Notes on *Avebury*', an unpublished text sent to the author by RB, July 2008. Further references to this text are listed as *NA* 2008.

poets, combined with considerable personal affection and warmth. Paz wrote to Berengarten about 'Avebury', "I'm not a prophet, but I believe you have written a great poem."[3]

This essay suggests, first, that the arrangement of the stones themselves constitutes a kind of pre-verbal syntax, and second, that in this poem Berengarten has succeeded in capturing and expressing this 'patterning' in words, at least to some degree.

'Avebury' and *Sunstone* are both 'mystery' poems, in that their settings do not easily yield up their meaning. Both are concerned with what might be termed *architextuality*. Paz's *Sunstone* is about the relationships between architecture, cycles, ritual and culture. It is lush with vegetation and sexuality, tinged with violence, and written with a piquancy that is shared by other Latin-American writers, such as poets Pablo Neruda and César Vallejo, and novelists Gabriel García Márquez and Laura Esquivel. Like *Sunstone*, 'Avebury' contains imagery of fecundity and decay.

Avebury, a sacred site[4] larger than Stonehenge, becomes a place in which the poet seeks to unravel a mystery that is at once spiritual, communal and personal. Part of the allure of such sacred spaces, even today, is that they literally and figuratively stand for experiences beyond our comprehension. Their meanings, because pre-textual, are elusive to us; yet it is clear that their structures are based on significant numerical formulations. Thus, as if aiming explicitly to enact and embody these numerological significances, *Sunstone* is composed of 584 hendecasyllabic lines. The first six syllables are repeated at the end of the poem. The importance of this number is that it is equal to the synodical revolution of the planet Venus (Paz 1985: 57). The Mayan calendar begins with

---

[3] Unpublished correspondence from Octavio Paz to RB, 28 July 1973.

[4] Strictly speaking, Avebury is not a single site but a complex of Neolithic monuments from at least two millennia, spread out across several square kilometres of the chalk uplands of Central Southern England (specifically, the Marlborough Downs in Wiltshire). In addition to the stone circle that surrounds the village of Avebury itself (built some time in the third millennium BC), these include Silbury Hill (the largest prehistoric artificial mound in Europe, probably built at around the same time), West Kennett Long Barrow (a chamber tomb from the fourth millennium BC) and Windmill Hill (a causewayed enclosure from the fifth millennium BC). Given RB's comment (*NA*, 2008) that "we made a point of stopping off at Avebury for a break from the driving" (*en route* from Cambridge to Devon, in Summer 1971), and the imagery of the poem itself, it appears that the stone circle that surrounds the village of Avebury was the inspirational trigger. Other poets (e.g. Jope 1996: 76, 82–86) have written about this complex of sites from a more 'place-specific' perspective.

this Venusian cycle. Berengarten's 'Avebury', on the other hand, is composed of 24 short sections, roughly divided thematically: this being the approximate number of hours it takes for the earth to complete one rotation. The cyclical trajectories of celestial bodies are mirrored in these recurrent patterns of words and lexical dualities, such as stone/dance, seeing/blindness, speech/silence, just as they are celebrated at Avebury and Stonehenge.

Numerous cyclic motifs in 'Avebury' are evident at a number of levels. For example, the second section introduces us to a speaker who is described as pacing – circling the stones, much as an animal might circle and sniff a place in order to discover its story, its meaning (*FL* 26). The speaker hopes to find answers to his questions, ostensibly about the sacred circle, but, on a deeper level it soon becomes apparent that this quest is a search for self, for one's place in the universe. 'Avebury' begins with static images of ancient stones in the grass, but these images suggest that here is a story waiting to be told. Furthermore, the idea of telling and saying is hinted at by words that have to do with the mouth, such as "yawning", "tongued" and "cracked jaw" (*FL* 25). 'Avebury' ends with the imagery of water or, perhaps, of light: "waves / expanding, re-echoing / *including / us here / enclosing / us here /* say the stones / *now every / where centre*" (*FL* 50). Hence, the movement is from circle to circle, centre to edges and back, physically, just as the text itself is arranged on the page.

These patterns suggest that, like *Sunstone*, 'Avebury' concludes where it began. Although the silent ghostly setting at the beginning of the poem is replaced by a site potent with life, teeming with creatures and resonant with echoes, breath, and words, the final stanza seems to answer the unspoken question of the first. However, this is not a return to the exact same spot. It cannot be. The speaker is changed. "You are not the same people who left that station," writes Eliot in 'The Dry Salvages' (Eliot 1952: 134). Rather, the movement is a spiralling inward towards self-discovery. As Eliot writes in 'Little Gidding',

> We shall not cease from exploration
> And the end of all our exploring
> Will be to arrive where we started
> And know the place for the first time.
> Through the unknown unremembered gate
> When the last of earth left to discover
> Is that which was the beginning. (Eliot 1952: 145)

Metaphorically and symbolically, the stones are polysemous: they stand not only for culture, but also for deities, portals to heaven and hell; and ritualistically, the stones circumscribe sacred spaces where communal experiences were once enacted. Such rituals in themselves perform multiple functions. One is that, through religious experience, an individual defines and affirms lineage, i.e. blood connection to the community. In addition, the stones literally *mark time*. In the same way that the river becomes a vehicle for Eliot to examine concepts of time in 'Dry Salvages', Berengarten uses the stones of Avebury, the place, to perhaps discover something about the mystery of time as a non-linear event, because they have been invested with a power beyond their own time and function. The stones at such sacred sites are aligned with celestial events, such as the solstices, with an accuracy that today almost defies our sense of the possible, given the knowledge and manpower that must have been needed both to move and to set these huge slabs in place. In a sense, then, all such ancient stone artefacts are attempts by human beings to honour the patterns of nature. And quite apart from conceptual and religious factors, such matters were of clear practical relevance: it has been argued, for example, that such edifices were built on or near the flood-plains of Egypt and China in order to perhaps exercise some power over the cycles of flooding by appealing to various deities. But they also speak to social and cultural concerns, such as the well-being of the community.

In the case of a site such as Avebury, it is difficult for us even to imagine the connections that it embodied for its builders – for example, those between sky and earth, goddesses and gods, timelessness and time, dead ancestors and the living – partly because we are so removed from the family and kinship relationships that prevailed at the time when it was built, and partly because later paternalistic institutions more or less obliterated practices that sanctified the feminine, that is, other than within the acceptable dualistic frame of 'virgin/whore'. In fact, the speaker in 'Avebury' challenges this duality in the penultimate section, when he states "this was no whore" (*FL* 49).

'Avebury' freely moves through time, from pre-textual history to descriptions of art and civilisation, in the same way that Olson's *Maximus Poems* and all of the poems in Eliot's *Four Quartets* envision history as an event that is taking place now and always, past and present simultaneously existing. In the last stanza of Part 1 of 'Little Gidding', the speaker theorises about a pilgrimage where "the communication / of the dead is tongued with fire beyond the language of the living. /

Here, the intersection of the timeless moment / is England and nowhere. Never and always" (Eliot 1952: 139). This is also a conception of time that G. R. Levy discusses in relation to ancient peoples and their sacred spaces in *The Gate of Horn*, as we shall see later. Avebury was (and, to the sympathetic visitor, remains) a ritual space, in which people were (and are) transformed, reborn as more realised versions of themselves.

℘

To understand how the architecture of Berengarten's 'Avebury' unravels the mystery of the stones, we must delve into the poem's origins. This process will necessarily involve exploring motifs of fertility and creativity, of cyclic pattern and ritual, and of art as message and meaning.

Berengarten states that he was "heavily involved" in concrete poetry in the early 1970s:

> One of the tenets of concrete poetry as I understand it is that letters and words stop being merely *alphabetic* signs denoting sequences of phonemes and lexemes, but become iconic, mimetic and pictorial in themselves – though not necessarily representational in any crude sense. It might be said: they become more *ideogrammatic*. (*NA*)[5]

Berengarten's comments suggest a way into 'Avebury' that involves the use of pre-literal skills; through encountering the text as visual composition, arrival at the metaphorical heart of the poem, through its iconicity, becomes easier. Berengarten goes on to say that the act of making the poem a 'visual text' opened the poem 'spatially' for him, so that it was no longer 'linear' – which is the 'normative' way we read text. By giving the poem spatiality, Berengarten has opened the poem temporally as well. In this context, Olson's practice of field poetry intrigued Berengarten and, arguably, no form could have been more suited to the content of 'Avebury' than the Olsonian open form.

Berengarten uses words like "mime", "embody", "encapsulate" and "enshrine" to describe the process of building his 'Avebury'. He refers to this process as "composing" as he says, "in the strict etymological sense [of] putting together". In this connection, Berengarten also mentions the poet W. S. Graham (1970, 1977), although he wrote the poem before he became familiar with Graham's investigations of the "phenomenal world

[5] Other comments by RB in this paragraph and the next are taken from the same source.

123

itself [as] language". Thus Berengarten implies that, just as language is a code that must be deciphered, so are these stones 'coded', and it is the speaker's task to recover the key and discover the meaning of the 'text'. Eliot, however, writes in 'East Coker' of "old stones that cannot be deciphered" (Eliot 1952: 129).

Conceptually, Berengarten also specifies that much of his thinking in this book derives from his reading of G. R. Levy's *The Gate of Horn*. He incorporates phrases taken directly from Levy's work, specifically from Chapter 1, which informed Berengarten's writing about the Palaeolithic 'Venus of Willendorf' figurine (*FL* 30), as well as his descriptions of caves as sacred spaces of ritual and transformation (*FL* 35–40). The title of Levy's book refers to the two Homeric entrances to the Underworld. In the *Aeneid*, Virgil describes these entrances to sleep as the "Gate of Ivory" and the "Gate of Horn" (Levy 1963: v). The Gate of Ivory is the gate of false dreams and the Gate of Horn leads one to truth (Book VI: ll. 1235–1240). Similarly, in 'Avebury', there is a descent into the underworld, a journey often required of initiates in 'primitive' spiritual ideologies, for it is only by dying, going down, that one can be reborn. Such a belief echoes as a predominant theme through Berengarten's text, especially with the embedded quotation from Heraclitus: "and the way / up is way / down" (*FL* 35). There is likewise a descent in Eliot's 'Burnt Norton': "Descend lower, descend only / Into the world of perpetual solitude" (Eliot 1952: 120). Furthermore, this downward journey is the prerequisite to transformation and is certainly one required of the artist in order for the creative process to take place. Such a journey is also interpretable as a return to the womb, the site of one's conception. In Christianity the Mother Goddess has been divested of all real power and replaced by a figure who is more a repository than an initiator. When Nicodemus asks Jesus how it is possible for an old man to be born again and wonders if he must re-enter his mother's womb in order to do so, Jesus replies: "Except a man be born of water and of the Spirit, he cannot enter into the kingdom of God" (John 3: 5).

Another source for Berengarten is the epic of *Gilgamesh*. Nancy. K. Sandars' introduction explores the story, its origins and her approach to the translation of the text which, she writes, necessitated some overlapping and editing (Sandars 1960: 51). Berengarten references this multi-authored ancient text in his exploration of duality, specifically embodied in the characters of Gilgamesh and his 'savage' brother, Enkidu, especially in sections 12–14 of the poem (*FL* 36–39). Gilgamesh's journey is that of the hero. This Sumerian/Babylonian world is darker than the Egyptian one, in that the Sumerian Heaven is reserved only for the gods; and it is this darkness that pervades *Gilgamesh*. Gilgamesh's journey operates on many levels, as allegory, as a great adventure story, as a quasi-historical account of possible events. It contains a flood which predates the Biblical account by a thousand years, a river that must be crossed, and a forest through which the hero must find his way to the mountain. There he will find wood for the temple he is building. The mountain is the "seat of the gods and [entrance to] the underworld" (Sandars 1960: 33). It is also the "sender of dreams". The line between sleep and wakefulness is blurred both in the epic and in 'Avebury'. Indeed, the oneiric realm is as important as the conscious world in both texts, as well as in *Sunstone*. Dreams provide clues to unravelling the mystery.

The first two sections of 'Avebury' also suggest that the site of the stone circle is itself an opening to some other realm. What is therefore clear to the reader at this point is that there is something to be figured out. At the same time, it could be argued that no one ever really wants the answers to the mystery. Its impenetrability is its source of power over rational beings. In the second section, the questioner enters the text in person. The living walk among the dead, and the ancestorless speaker wonders what the beings search for, "looking for what / the riddle? / the question?" (*FL* 26).

Section 4 introduces one of the ritual motifs of the poem, dancing, and establishes the idea of stone as syntax: "metaphor on metaphor / silence / anagrammatised / measured | spaced out / in this syntax of land / this plot of time" (*FL* 28). Dance and time are both motifs of Eliot's *Four Quartets*, in particular the first and second stanzas of 'Burnt Norton'. He writes, "there is only the dance" (Eliot 1952: 119) and earlier, "Time present and time past / Are both perhaps present in time future, / And time future contained in time past" (Eliot 1952: 117). Here the sacred space, ritualised through dance and the marking of time, is a place of death, as in section 2: "ossified dreams", "dead memorials" (*FL* 26). From the outset, as we have already seen, words associated with the mouth reveal another motif, and these appear throughout the poem: in section 5, "sky's throat", (*FL* 29); in section 8, "protecting her cave / the mouth of her", where the mouth/cave is imaged as vaginal opening (*FL* 32); in section 14 "mouth of stone" (*FL* 39); in section 20, where the stones are "defying discourse" (*FL* 45); and in section 21, where language is stuck "in my throat" (*FL* 46) and the stones and words become one as the man is reborn from the cave he was immured in

                    break
            speech
in a tide on these stones
                        wash
clean   break
            word
into stone
            out of stone (*FL* 46)

Fertility and ritual are the themes of sections 6–10. Images of fertility and the duality of male and female appear in these five open-field 'sonnets' about sculptures: two are concerned with male and two with female images, while the fifth concerns musicians who, it might be argued, join the sexes together through art. Thus we have moved from images of stasis and death to ones of life. However, one of the male figures, from Michelangelo's series of *Prisoners*, has

            genitals
                        trapped
under unhewn rock
                        the arms
            unable to heave
        backbreaking
            stone off his head (*FL* 31)

In contrast, when it comes to the goddesses, the 'Venus of Willendorf' (*FL* 30) is pregnant and/or full breasted and bellied, and the 'Nike' ('Winged Victory of Samothrace') has

        incredible arrogant breasts

        and the breakers
                        confluent
        under the belly
        forming   like an unseen hand
protecting her cave   the mouth of her (*FL* 32)

Nike is ready to fly. Interestingly, both male and female statues are featureless. Does this anonymity make them more universal? Does it remove them from the constraints of time and place? The speaker does not seem distressed by the headless, faceless statues. The *phalloi* of section 9 would seem potent images save for the last lines, "one of the shafts / broken / above the marble scrotum" (*FL* 33). In spite of this seeming impotency, the poet appears to join the dance of section 10, a joyful celebration, even though the flautist is chinless.[6] The image of the female here is striking: "great dusky sea, so many pebbles round your neck / so many glinting jewels in your hair" (*FL* 34). These last lines are taken from 'Amorgos', a poem by the Greek poet Nikos Gatsos (Keeley and Sherrard 1966: 99), whom Berengarten cites as an influence on this work (*NA*).

Sections 11–14 are inward journeys. The speaker is not sure whether he is awake or asleep. He is "in / the cave, tomb / and temple" (*FL* 35). The word "tomb" here suggests its opposite, "womb". It is a tenebrous world of shades and shadows, just as it is for Dante in the *Divine Comedy* and it is a theme Berengarten visits often in *FL*, especially in 'Transformations' and 'Black Light'. This is the journey deep into the psyche, where one expects to encounter versions of oneself; Berengarten also cites Jung's work with dreams as an influence and it is here that the speaker is not sure which way is up or down.[7] He also encounters ghosts of his own past much as the speaker of 'Little Gidding' encounters the familiar compound ghost in section II of the poem (Eliot 1952: 140). This is the first time that the speaker of 'Avebury' is aware of his own place in time. Ironically, the ghosts are preceded by the line, "where I lost my memory" (*FL* 35). Many wisdom traditions assert that one must lose one's self to find one's self. Paradoxically, it is through forgetting that the poet remembers. In section 12, the "corridor wound like a horn" appears, the entrance to truth (*FL* 36). The visions of the poet are strange:

> you touch but don't believe,
> nor shadow of a glimmer down beyond them
>   your eyelids
>   jumping like fish
> well nothing here: you are the very
>   shadow you discarded (*FL* 36)

[6] The same figure appears in 'Male Figure Playing a Double Flute' in RB, *Against Perfection* (1999: 43).

[7] RB's 'Croft Woods' (*FL* 197–2009) revisits many of the themes of 'Avebury'. The slipperiness of language, the seductive charms of music, the journey downwards into Self and even the gates of ivory and horn reappear in this later work. The journey in the latter poem, however, seems more lateral than circular. The light is a "slanted source" and "hangs diagonally down" (*FL* 199).

By becoming blind, one sees. In this same section, the speaker shields his eyes "against a blaze of inner noon". A transformation has taken place. Blood is introduced as part of the ritual of sacrifice. The speaker wonders if it is his brother he hears in the darkness and, in section 13, an unnamed Enkidu, feral brother and darker self of Gilgamesh, and protector of the forest which stands between Gilgamesh and the Cedar Mountain, appears. In the epic, it is the temple priestess who 'tames' Enkidu, separating him from his animal companions through sexual initiation, and it is this separation from the beasts, which have no language, that marks the civilised man. Enkidu is given the double-edged sword of language, a highly significant gift but one that alienates him from his former companions.

In the following section, Berengarten alludes to the Medusa myth. The only mortal of the three Gorgons, Medusa is also seen as the guardian at the threshold of the underworld (*Odyssey*, XI: ll. 633–635; Dante's *Divine Comedy* [*Inferno*, IX: ll. 55–57] and Milton's *Paradise Lost* Bk. II: l. 611). It is Athena who, in a jealous rage, enacts her vengeance on Medusa, not Poseidon, for raping the Gorgon in Athena's temple. She is the one who transforms Medusa into the snake-tressed monster who can turn men to stone. Yet she so believes in the apotropaic powers of Medusa, whom some have theorised is the embodiment of a dissociated self (Neumann 2003: 96–99), that she carries the face of the defeated 'Mother Goddess' on her shield (Hesiod, Book 11: ll. 32–40):

> before she came
> with her ear-rings
> of amber   her breasts bared
> her armpits scented
> let down her braided hair
> and struck you with that gaze of stone
> taught you the art of her stone smile
> woke you with language
> of cattle
> byre and cave (*FL* 38)[8]

---

[8] Garber and Vickers' book *The Medusa Reader* (2003) chronicles the fascination writers and thinkers have had with the Medusa myth from Homer to Versace. Tobin Siebers' essay, 'Medusa as Double', from his book *The Mirror of Medusa* (University of California Press, 1983) reprinted in *The Medusa Reader*, is of particular interest for its study of Medusa and Athena, and Medusa and Perseus, as doubles. One of countless poems about Medusa is Shelley's 'On the Medusa of Leonardo Da Vinci' (Shelley 1901: 369). RB might have been thinking of Shelley's poem when he wrote these lines. Here, Shelley

An entire chapter of Levy's book is entitled 'Cattle Byre and Milk-Yielding Tree'. In this chapter, she discusses the Isis/Osiris myth and especially the importance of the Mother Goddess, who was a divinity of vegetation and fertility as well as death. This duality is embodied in Ishtar and the Sumerian Innana, goddess of love, fertility and war. Sections 13 and 14 refer to Gilgamesh's search for his brother/other: "brother, you / were the axe at my side" (*FL* 39). Gilgamesh has to use trickery to defeat his brother, who has control of the woods. It is not difficult for him to enlist the aid of the gods because he is two-thirds god himself. Embodied in the persons of Gilgamesh and Enkidu are both god and beast. Here, too, we find the image of the mouth, "standing in this cave of light / this mouth of stone / that eats me" (*FL* 39). And just as Enkidu is civilised by language, so the speaker becomes full of words: "words you rush in on me like a surf / into my core like semen to the uterus / like torchlight on these stones" (*FL* 40). Berengarten alludes to Botticelli's *Birth of Venus* in this section, who comes "riding / in on the foam this long haired / green creature who brings me / back again among the scattered seasons". And underground the speaker finds the mother:

> down in the pit I have seen your face   mother
>   your skull in the rockface
>
>   and who is that other
>   face in shadow (*FL* 40)

Sections 16–21 are particularly influenced by Paz, especially by passages of *Piedra de Sol*, where Paz writes of the goddess / mother and the dreamer (1991: 51 and 53) and also by Peter Russell's unpublished

confronts the dual nature of Medusa as seductress and destroyer:

> Yet it is less the horror than the grace
> Which turns the gazer's spirit into stone;
> Whereon the lineaments of that dead face
> Are graven, till the characters be grown
> Into itself, and thought no more can trace;
> 'Tis the melodious hue of beauty thrown
> Athwart the darkness and the glare of pain,
> Which humanize and harmonize the strain.

Ephemeron (*NA*). Section 16 moves from spiritual to scientific enquiry. As the stone is an elemental product of earth, the poet queries his own substance, "you too / a monad / atom / as I am / what is the sum / of these quanta? / I am not just / my body" (*FL* 41). In the philosophy of Leibniz, the monad is the elemental spiritual substance from which all material properties arise; thus, by choosing this particular word, Berengarten seeks to embody (textualise) the substance of the inquisitive speaker.

Sections 17–20 describe the ritual that precedes the transformation. Section 18 returns to the circle and the dance:

> stone in me
> stone that I am
> centre or periphery
> nomad and society of atoms
>
>   eyed by stone
>   eaten by stone
>   loved by stone
>
> danced in the dance
>   by the dance
>   of stone
>
> by stone
>   uttered
> by stone
>   dreamed (*FL* 43)

In this passage, the appearance of the word "nomad" suggests punning wordplay on the previous term "monad", and perhaps the sort of trick that the mind plays in dream and on the threshold between waking and sleep. As in the lives of the ancients, the dream is of vital importance to the poet, who is at the threshold between the conscious and subconscious mind. The poet has been spoken and dreamed. The "blood" of section 19 brings the poet back to the altar of sacrifice, and the death of the ancestors is recalled. The durability of the stone and of the ancestors is contained in the last lines, which describe the elemental forces at work: "the sun's hammer / the frost's nails / the wind's arsenal" (*FL* 44). These images are reminiscent of the power of Enlil, who in *The Epic of Gilgamesh* is the god of the storm and wind and of the breath and word of Anu, father of the gods (Sandars 1960: 120).

In the longer sections 20 and 21 the poet returns to the themes of the mysteries of coded text and the literal and figurative silence of the stones. They are "defying discourse", "telling nothing" and "giving nothing", "being of absence / core the dream" (*FL* 45). The speaker refers to the stone as "subversive", "uprooting / word from language / winding down / time to rubble". (*FL* 45). We have begun to circle back to the "time's teeth" of the first section. In section 21, the speaker is 'reborn'. Images of birth, of the throat and mouth and of speech dominate:

        in my throat
        the man rises
            from the cave he was immured in

                break
                speech
        in a tide on these stones
                wash
        clean   break
                word (*FL* 46)

By the end of this section, the speaker has been reunited with the "ghost gone at end / of childhood" (*FL* 46) and his ancestors. He rejoins the community as a new being. Section 22 is a departure from the spiritual community to the secular society and the edifices of the modern world, i.e. "The Labour Exchange", "The Square and Compasses", a pub (*NA*), and the "Maplan Supermarket".[9] The supermarket is presented, ironically, as the "sacred space" in the modern world, because it "sells everything", "with just room to move / from corner to corner / in a web of gravities / thick as a word" (*FL* 47). Olson writes in the *Maximus Poems*, "The corner magazine store / (Oconnell's, at Prospect and Washington) / has more essential room in it than programs" (Olson 1983: 379). The shimmering commodities of daily life curiously call the poet back to his ancestors who are "locked in stone". Now it is we who "struggle out of / measuring / immeasurables" (*FL* 48). And now, in section 23, the goddess figure returns. She has been introduced as "Venus / of the hunters" in Section 6, and has been present in various manifestations of femininity throughout the poem; but here it is recognised that she "was no whore".

---

[9] Interestingly, the name "Maplan" recurs 28 years later in RB's long poem *The Manager* where, as the company that employs the protagonist, Jordan Charles Bruno, it is an ironic acronym: "Market Advice Planning for Living And Necessity (MAPLAN)" (*TM* 145).

Now, significantly, there is "no gap / between speech and her mouth", as "lips touch / speech / tongues" and "the world" is "born". Blindness has been replaced by "light of eyes / eye of light / child of elements" and the affirmation "anywhere centre / say these stones / of Avebury" (*FL* 49).

The italics of the last section highlight what the speaker has found as a result of his 'death and rebirth': "*any / where*" is "centre" and not only the poet but the world awakens to this newness. Echoes are heard from "out of galactic range / creatures awake on distant shores". Not only has the poet been reborn but he has found his place among the others.

> *including*
> *us here*
>
> *enclosing*
> *us here*
>
> *say the stones*
>
> *now every*
> *where centre*
>
> I do not tell   *I say* (*FL* 50)

⁀

We have come full circle. "For the first time in our history we are contemporaries of all mankind" writes Octavio Paz (1967: 194).[10] Of the three epigraphs to 'Avebury', in my view this quotation from Paz would seem to be the most significant. Elsewhere, Berengarten writes about Paz's *Sunstone*, *Blanco* and *The Labyrinth of Solitude*:

> [T]hey have contributed to forming a key aspect of my poetics – especially in my current researches and explorations for what I now

---

[10] Paz's intriguing and well-informed essay, *The Labyrinth of Solitude*, delves deeply into the roots of Mexican identity, in particular, the tension between the public and the private self, the isolated individual and the need for community: themes RB also explores in 'Avebury'. First published in Spanish in 1950, and in English in 1961, and written in a prose both poetic and scholarly, *Labryinth* crosses the boundaries between disciplines. Part history, part sociological study, part economic analysis, part political commentary, its message is as relevant today as it was half a century ago. It would seem that 'Avebury' strives to express this same all-encompassing view of humanity and history.

132

call *Universal Poetics*. Some of these ideas about universality (that centres are everywhere) are first expressed in my work in 'Avebury', where they are encoded into the end of the poem. (*NA*)

Taking the standing stones of Avebury both as his point of departure and the locus to which he returns, Berengarten discovers that the *architext* of the sacred circle is inclusive. The sacred space is indeed anywhere and everywhere.

Martin Booth, reviewing *Avebury* on its first publication, wrote that the poem poses challenges to the reader, but that recurrent images provide grounding, create tension and sustain the themes (Booth 1973). Aged only 28 at the time, Berengarten undertook the difficult task of writing a long poem. Yet there is a timeless quality to the work in its attempt to understand pre-literate syntax and place oneself in an historical context: to find meaning in the stones.

References

Alighieri, Dante. 1939. *The Divine Comedy: Inferno* (trans. John D. Sinclair). New York, NY: Oxford University Press.

Booth, Martin. 1973. 'Self-placement in time and order', *The Teacher* (18 May).

Dryden, John (trans.). 1961. *Virgil's Aeneid*. New York, NY: P. F. Collier and Son.

Eliot, T. S. 1952. *Complete Plays and Poems*. New York, NY: Harcourt Brace.

Garber, Marjorie B. and Vickers, Nancy J. (eds). 2003. *The Medusa Reader*. New York, NY: Routledge.

Graham, W. S. 1970. *Malcolm Mooney's Land*. London: Faber & Faber.

______. 1977. *Implements in Their Places*. London: Faber & Faber.

Homer. 1953. *The Odyssey* (trans. A. T. Murray). Cambridge, MA, and London: Harvard University Press and William Heinemann, Ltd.

Jope, Norman. 1996. *For the Wedding-Guest*. Exeter: Stride Publications.

Keeley, Edmund and Sherrard, Philip (trans.). 1966. *Four Greek Poets*. London: Penguin Books.

Levy, G. R. 1963 [1948]. *The Gate of Horn: Religious Conceptions of the Stone Age and Their Influence upon European Thought*. New York, NY: Harper and Row.

Milton, John. 1929. *The Poetical Works of John Milton* (ed. John Beeching). London and New York, NY: Macmillan and Co. Ltd.

Neumann, Erich. 2003 [1949]. 'A Jungian view of the terrible mother' (trans. R. F. C. Hull) in Garber and Vickers (2003): 96–99.

Olson, Charles. 1983. *The Maximus Poems*. Berkeley and Los Angeles, CA, and London: University of California Press.

Paz, Octavio. 1961 [1967]. *The Labyrinth of Solitude and Other Writings* (trans. Lysander Kemp). London: Allen Lane.

_____. 1991. *Sun Stone* (trans. Eliot Weinberger). New York, NY: New Directions.

Sandars, N. K (trans.). 1960. *The Epic of Gilgamesh*. London: Penguin Books.

Shelley, Percy Bysshe. 1901. *The Complete Poetical Works of Percy Bysshe Shelley* (ed. George Edward Woodberry). Boston, MA, and New York, NY: The Riverside Press and Houghton, Mifflin and Co., Cambridge Edition.

Richard Berengarten's 'The Rose of Sharon':
"…by any other name…"

P. S. Sri

A poem that captivates by its rhyme, rhythm and meaning all at once is hard to come by. Such a rare gem of a poem is Richard Berengarten's 'The Rose of Sharon'. The poem won the Keats Memorial Prize in 1974 and was translated into Italian by Roberto Sanesi and included in his anthology, *Almanacco internazionale dei poeti* (1975). It is easy to see why the poem has garnered accolades and gained international recognition. Not only does it have intriguing rhymes and memorable rhythms, but also multi-faceted symbols and mystical themes that tease us out of thought into a contemplation of eternity.

The title 'The Rose of Sharon' is from the opening line of the *Song of Solomon* in the Old Testament. It may be read on a microcosmic level as an impassioned acclamation of physical love between a man and a woman as well as on a macrocosmic level as a joyous celebration of metaphysical love between Creator and Creation, Heaven and Earth, Spirit and Nature, the One and the Many.

Judging by the author's note to the published poem, 'The Rose of Sharon' is a symbol of "the *Shekhinah*, the feminine aspect of the divine presence in the Kabbalah" (*FL* 221). Berengarten has clarified that this poem was directly inspired by his reading of Gershom Scholem's scholarly work on the Kabbalah, *Major Trends in Jewish Mysticism* (1955). In Judaic tradition, the *Shekhinah* refers to the dwelling or settling of divine presence, so that, while the aspirant is in proximity to the *Shekhinah*, the connection to God is more readily perceivable. Thus the *Shekhinah* is manifested as a form of joy, connected with prophecy and creativity and is often depicted as the Glory that surrounds the Divinity, not only in the Hebrew Bible, but also in the Christian New Testament. The *Qur'an* mentions the *Sakina*, or Tranquillity, referring to God's blessing of solace and succour to both the Children of Israel and Mohammed. Hindu philosophy reveres and extols the *Shakti*, the dynamic female energy that is inseparably and indissolubly united with its male counterpart, *Shiva*. In the loftiest conception, the *Shekhinah* is clearly related to the redemptive Mother figure as in the Beatrice of Dante, the Madonna of Christianity and the Kali *Ma* of Hindu thought. It is noteworthy that while the Great Mother can redeem us and bestow joy, we must also be responsible enough to reclaim her and integrate her fully into our consciousness. This appears to be the overarching theme of Berengarten's poem.

The epigraph, "*The fire, the fire is falling!*" (*FL* 91) is from William Blake's *The Marriage of Heaven and Hell* (Abrams et al. 2000: 83) and underscores the *leitmotif* of the purifying fire of the *Shekhinah* or the Holy Spirit that resonates throughout the poem and enables the reader to partake in her heavenly radiance.

The simple yet haunting rhythms of the poem mirror those of yet another poem by Blake – 'The Tyger' – which, in turn, imitates the rhythms of the nursery rhyme 'Twinkle twinkle little star'. The awesome mystery of Creation and the innocent wide-eyed wonder of childhood are thus simultaneously evoked in Berengarten's poem, so that we, the readers, are drawn into the poem in a mood of reverence as well as excitement.

✢

In the first part of the poem, we may well imagine the *Shekhinah* or the Great Mother herself addressing every one of us fondly as "my love" and depicting the Creation of the Universe. At the very outset, she evokes the fierce energy expended by the primordial Being in the Act of Creation, in language that mimes the act of procreation and impregnation between a man and a woman:

> When primeval dusts were formed
> and the stars sprayed on the skies
> and the fallow clays were warmed
> and grew temples, feathers, eyes,
>
> O what shrinkage of his power,
> through what waste and in what rages
> were the seeds of my love's flower
> scattered down deserted ages. (*FL* 93)

This eloquent description by the *Shekhinah* herself of the creation of the universe as a "shrinkage of his [i.e., God's] power", is an audacious and paradoxical notion. The idea may be explicated thus: God is, by definition, eternal and infinite. His Creation cannot exist apart from him. Hence, the Universe cannot be an extension of the primordial divinity. It must be a diminution. So, from at least one perspective, the Creation involves an act in which the Supreme Being voluntarily diminishes himself (Scholem 1955: 260–263). The suggestion not only evokes our sadness over the "waste" of the "seeds" through the "deserted ages", but also summons our awe over the heavenly Father's magnificent act of self-sacrifice in engendering the Universe. Fondly addressing us all as "my love", the *Shekhinah* or the Great Mother calls on us to behold the ecstatic outcome: "how he laughs, my love, to find / a word alive, a man awake" (*FL* 93).

God "laughs" joyfully, in short, if he finds even one human being among us "awake" to the potential of his Universe and striving to complete in the form of "a word alive" the unfinished sentence of God's Creation. In other words, nothing pleases God more than his seeds falling on fertile soil, sprouting, flowering and bearing fruit. By implication, therefore, all of us have a responsibility to offer our love and devotion to God in return for his self-sacrifice. Not only is the *Shekhinah* celebrating the role of humanity in Creation, but She is also wordlessly inviting all of us to love and serve God.

The second part of the poem is couched as our possible response to the *Shekhinah*'s silent – and thus all the more potent – appeal to love and serve God. We are called to visualise the Great Mother as Moses saw her on Mount Sinai, in the form of "jewels" blazing at the throat of God and of "ornaments without a flaw" (*FL* 94), and to scan the words God wrote on the tablets, addressing the *Shekhinah*. Like Moses, we too are bidden to see her as one who crowns God's "loveliness",

> spreading perfume round his name,
> garment for his nakedness,
> diadem around his flame (*FL* 94)

We are encouraged to see her, in other words, as the feminine aspect of Divinity, as the Great Mother, as the Glory of God. Simultaneously, we realise with immeasurable sadness that "generations of repose" on our part have "veiled" her, not only from "his naked eye", but also from our vision. We recall with a shock of recognition Hopkins' statement that we no longer reckon with "the grandeur of God", because "Generations have trod, have trod, have trod; / And all is seared with toil; bleared, smeared with toil" (Abrams *et al.* 2000: 1651). We also remember with anguish what Yeats highlighted towards the end of his apocalyptic poem, 'The Second Coming' – the fact that "twenty centuries of stony sleep / Were vexed to nightmare by a rocking cradle" (Abrams *et al.* 2000: 2107).

We mourn the fact that the purifying fire of the *Shekhinah* has been almost put out due to our ignorance and indifference; that radiant "multifoliate thornless rose" now lies on her "bed of ashes" (*FL* 94). We are insistently reminded, through an intertextual echo of a dominant image in Eliot's poem 'The Hollow Men', that we have plummeted to the level of those who are sunk so deep in inertia that they dare not meet, even in "death's twilight kingdom", the eyes of a Saviour – eyes that resemble a "multifoliate rose" (Abrams *et al.* 2000: 2384–2385) – a multi-faceted symbol of the ecstatic union of the human and divine.

The "multifoliate rose" is linked with Dante's image of the saints in Paradise, clustered together like the petals of a white rose. When Dante steeps his eyes in the river of light and looks at the celestial rose (Canto XXX), he sees the eyes of the myriad Christian saints reflecting the glory of God, so that the rose appears to be a vast shining circle. This is the image Eliot evokes when he equates the eyes, the star, and the rose. Together they symbolise the reality of God, whose absence is keenly felt by the hollow men in their cactus land. Sunk in inertia, however, they decline to strive towards this reality.

The single rose is essentially "a symbol of completion, of consummate achievement and perfection" (Cirlot 1967: 205); it figures prominently in Western mystical literature as an image of unity. To Dante, the "white rose" (*candida rosa*) represents the end of his long journey, the fulfilment of his quest for the eternal Being of God. The "multifoliate rose" as a symbol of the reality beyond appearances is the Western equivalent to "the thousand-petalled lotus" (*sahasrara*) of Tantric mysticism. Eliot fuses Dante's "white rose" and Tantrism's "thousand-petalled lotus" (*sahasrara*) to create a particularly arresting synthesis, in his image of the "multifoliate rose", of Eastern and Western symbols. Berengarten not only echoes Eliot, but also goes a step further in singing of the *Shekhinah* as "multifoliate *thornless* rose" (emphasis mine), for he seems to suggest that the waning of the Glory of the Great Mother does not even 'prick' the conscience of all of us "hollow men". Simultaneously, he may also be using the 'thornlessness' of the rose to represent the *Shekhinah's* awesome compassion.

The third part of the poem begins by acknowledging that the radiance of the *Shekhinah* once spanned centuries and traditions. The same "fire" that manifested itself to Moses on Mount Sinai and instilled a divine glow into the Jewish religious tradition also inspired the pre-Socratic visionary philosopher, Heraclitus, and imparted a spiritual fire to the Greek philosophical tradition. The poem continues, however, in mournful accents to record the gradual waning of the Glory of the *Shekhinah* in our lives, so that she "who bore his burning oil" and was "chalice for his sword", along with her "wedding glory", lies "withered now and nearly dead" (*FL* 95). That the blazing glory of the *Shekhinah* and her grand saga of divine unity should have been shrunk and debased by us humans over time to the status of "a children's story / Buried in a madman's head" (*FL* 95) is a poignant tragedy for all humanity and is enough to fill our hearts with anguish.

The fourth and final part of the poem, however, at the very outset counterbalances our despair with hope, by evoking dawn through the image of the cock crowing in Hades and implying the regeneration and resurrection of our souls by a Christ-like Saviour. Consequently, the poem suggests that even "the sleepy hooded owls" – those mournful heralds and omens of death and destruction – "sicken" (*FL* 96). Meanwhile, the dark night of our souls gives birth to Adam Kadmon, the Primordial Man of the Kabbalah, comparable to the *Anthropos* of Gnosticism and Manichaeism, and equivalent to the *Purusha* of the Hindu Upanishads, denoting the Manifest Absolute itself. The poem goes on, therefore, to urge us to hearken to "the fire falling / from his breath in searing rain" (*FL* 96). Then it makes an incontrovertible and yearning appeal to the *Shekhinah*, the attendant Glory of God, to purify us, to re-energise us to go on living meaningful lives: "Pour your fire through us again!" (*FL* 96).

The poem ends by hailing the *Shekhinah* as a "jar of nights and jar of days" (*FL* 96), as a vessel and container of our souls, and by pleading with her to gather up the cracks in the jar and to "yoke and seal them, heal and mend!" (*FL* 96). In other words, the poem concludes by invoking the Great Mother to heal and mend our imperfections. Only then may our souls be yoked and sealed with her compassion, and divine love course like fire through our veins.

&

'The Rose of Sharon' may be seen to be structured like the Kabbalistic Tree of Life, with its three 'pillars'. The first part, which reinforces the idea of the Creation as a voluntary self-diminution of God, may be read as the central 'pillar'. The second part may be perceived as the left-hand 'pillar', which represents the Judaic religious tradition through Moses. This tribute to the Glory of God is counterpointed with the lament that the *Shekhinah*, the Great Mother, is now veiled from our vision due to "generations of repose" (*FL* 94). The third part may be understood as the right-hand 'pillar', which acknowledges the *Shekhinah* as the fountain-head of the Greek philosophical tradition; here, the praise of the radiance of the *Shekhinah* is offset by the tragic recognition that the Glory of God, the Rose of Sharon, is "withered now and nearly dead." (*FL* 95). The fourth part may be interpreted as a reversion to the central 'pillar', which celebrates the dawn of hope that the Glory of God may yet resurrect itself, course through our veins like a purifying fire, mend our shortcomings through love and manifest itself as radiant joy in our lives.

It is noteworthy, however, that the poem has an admirable symmetry, with each of its four parts containing three four-line stanzas; hence, the poem is more appositely seen to resemble a *mandala*.

The word *mandala* is Sanskrit and means 'circle' or 'completion'. It is a term used to refer to various diagrams. It is of Hindu origin, but is also used in other offspring of the Hindu way of life such as Buddhism. In practice, the *mandala* has become a generic term for any plan, chart or geometric pattern that represents the cosmos, metaphysically and symbolically, as a microcosm of the Universe from the human perspective. In various spiritual traditions, the *mandala* is employed as a spiritual teaching tool for focusing the attention of aspirants and adepts, as well as for establishing a sacred space and as an aid to meditation and trance induction. Its symbolic nature can help one "to access progressively deeper levels of the unconscious, ultimately assisting the meditator to experience a mystical sense of oneness with the ultimate unity from which the cosmos in all its manifold forms arises" (Fontana 2005: 10). The psychoanalyst Carl Gustav Jung saw the *mandala* as "a representation of the unconscious self", and believed his paintings of *mandalas* enabled him to identify emotional disorders and work towards wholeness in personality (Jung 1962: 186–197).

In Tantrism, an esoteric branch of yoga in Hindu and Buddhist mysticism, the *mandala*, "a composition of complex patterns and diverse iconographic images", is often used as an aid to meditation. *The Tantric Way* gives a vivid description of the structure of the *mandala*:

The predominant shape is the circle, or concentric circles, enclosing a square, which is sometimes divided into four triangles; this basic composition itself is contained within a square of four gates. Painted in fine brush-strokes between the spaces in hot reds, evanescent emeralds, soft terracottas and pearly whites, are labyrinthine designs, serene and static images of deities in meditative postures or terrific deities spewing out aureoles of smoke and flame … all with symbolic meaning. The centre of the mandala projects the cosmic zone; it may be represented by a ring of lotus as the seat of Vajrasattva, the embodiment of the supreme wisdom, immersed in union with his Sakti in a fathomless ocean of joy. (Mookerjee and Khanna 1977: 62)

In fact, the original poster of the poem, 'The Rose of Sharon', features a mandala at its exact centre. At its northern gate is placed the first part of the poem with its depiction of the Creation of the Universe. The second part of the poem, focusing on the Jewish religious tradition, is placed appropriately at the eastern gate. The third part of the poem, focusing on the Greek philosophic tradition, is placed with equal aptness at the western gate. The fourth part of the poem, with its emphasis on hope for the restoration of the radiance of the *Shekhinah* in our lives, is placed at the southern gate.

The mandala, moreover, is more than a mere geometric pattern; it is full of psychic significance:

The mandala indicates a focalization of wholeness and is analogous to the cosmos. As a synergic form it reflects the cosmogenic process, the cycles of elements, and harmoniously integrates within itself the opposites, the earthly and the ethereal, the kinetic and the static. *The circle also functions as the nuclear motif of the self, a vehicle for centering awareness, disciplining concentration and arousing a state conducive to mystic exaltation … The mandala is a psychic complex* which conditions the return of the psyche to its potent core. Hence *the initiation process is often referred to as a "march towards the centre" so that the adept can interiorize the mandala in its totality,* counterbalance the opposing dimensions projected in its symbolism and finally be reabsorbed in the cosmic space represented symbolically in the inner circle. *The process of interiorization is a matter of orderly progression,* wherein each inner circuit marks a phase in spiritual ascent … To evoke the universe of the mandala with its wide-ranging symbology accurately, the artist has to practice visual formulation … *The image, like a mirror, reflects the inner self which ultimately leads to enlightenment and deliverance …* the actualization of this awareness is known as "liberation through sight." The act of seeing, which is analogous to contemplation, is in itself a liberating experience. (Mookerjee and Khanna 1977: 64–66, *italics added*)

Clearly, the poem is meant to evoke "the psychic complex" of the *mandala* in order to urge us on a "march towards the centre". This process of interiorisation may lead us to a momentary apprehension of the *Shekhinah*, if not to a total emancipation from a time-bound existence; it may enable us, along with the poet, to reflect deeply on Creation and Creator, on earth and heaven, on time and eternity. In short, through its symbolism of the *mandala*, the poem as a whole may be seen to lead the poet, as well as his readers, towards a progressively greater awareness of unity in diversity.

Ultimately, 'The Rose of Sharon' reinforces the harmony, the unity and the joy that prevail in the universe when we let the Glory of God, envisioned as the redemptive power of the *Shekhinah* or the Great Mother, operate freely among the imperfections of our lives and our world, to gather up the "broken rays", to "yoke and seal them, heal and mend!" (*FL* 96). As a whole, therefore, the poem's form matches its content perfectly and urges us to participate wholeheartedly in the joyous dance of life.

REFERENCES

Abrams, M. H. *et al.* (eds). 2000. *The Norton Anthology of English Literature* (Vol. 2, seventh edition). New York, NY: W. W. Norton and Co.

AAE. 1980. *Academic American Encyclopedia*. Princeton, NJ: Arête Publishing.

Armstrong, Karen. 1991. *Muhammad: a Biography of the Prophet*. London: Harper Collins.

Bible, The (American Standard Version). Online at http://www.ebible.org/ bible/asv Consulted, 1 February 2016.

Blake, William, 2000. *The Marriage of Heaven and Hell* in Abrams *et al.* (eds): 72–84.

Cirlot, J. E. 1967. *A Dictionary of Symbols*. London: Routledge and Kegan Paul.

Fontana, David. 2005. *Meditating with Mandala*. London: Duncan Baird Publishers.

Jung, C. G. 1962. *Memories, Dreams, Reflections* (ed. Aniela Jaffé). London: Collins.

Mookerjee, Ajit and Madhu Khanna. 1977. *The Tantric Way*. London: Thames and Hudson.

Oxford English Dictionary. Online at: http://www.oed.com/ Consulted, 1 February 2016.

Sanesi, Roberto (ed.). 1975. *Almanacco internazionale dei poeti*. Pesaro: La Pergola.

Scholem, Gershom. 1955. *Major Trends in Jewish Mysticism*. London: Thames & Hudson.

Yusuf Ali, Abdullah (trans.). *The Holy Qur'an*. Online at: http://www.islamicity.com/mosque/SURAI.HTM. Consulted, 1 February 2016.

Explicit and Implicit: Ezra Pound's Influence on Richard Berengarten's 'Angels'

John Gery

One of Ezra Pound's early poems that has often stymied me, despite its relative popularity, is 'The Return'. The poem, which first appeared in the *English Review* in 1912 and then in Pound's collection *Ripostes* (Ruthven 1969: 25), was praised by W. B. Yeats in a speech in Chicago for *Poetry* magazine that same year as "the most beautiful poem that has been written in the free form, one of the few in which I find real organic rhythm" (Stock 1982: 153). But besides being admired as accomplished *vers libre*, the poem has been held up as an example of Pound's early "Greek" style (Ruthven 1969: 204), as a predecessor to the lean poetics of early Imagism (Grieve 1997: 9), as evidence of the impact of the *Song of Songs* on Pound's early verse (Witemeyer 1969: 128), and as embodying rhythms later prominent in *The Cantos*. Pound himself referred to the poem as "an objective reality [that] has a complicated sort of significance" when he attempted to distinguish Vorticist poetics from the "mushy technique" of French symbolism (1970: 85). As one of Pound's most often anthologised pieces, 'The Return' remains a showpiece of bold poetics and rhythmic lyricism; it was even set to music in 1913 (Ruthven 1969: 204). Yet its actual subject is not so easily discernible:

> See, they return; ah, see the tentative
>   Movements, and the slow feet,
>   The trouble in the pace and the uncertain
>   Wavering!

See, they return, one, and by one,
With fear, as half-awakened;
As if the snow should hesitate
And murmur in the wind,
            and half turn back;
These were the 'Wing'd-with-Awe,'
            Inviolable.

Gods of the wingéd shoe!
With them the silver hounds,
            sniffing the trace of air! (Pound 1990: 69–70)

While the "tentative / Movements", "slow feet", and "trouble in the pace" of those returning here are made quite explicit, it is not, in fact, until line ten that the poet actually names who "they" are, and even then only by way of the (apparently Dantesque) appellation, the "Wing'd-with-Awe", the "Gods of the wingéd shoe". Aligning the poem with related early poems by Pound, such as 'Surgit Fama' and 'Apparuit', Hugh Witemeyer notes how 'The Return' presents "a figure entering the speaker's field of contemplation from afar" (1969: 128), so that, as in experience, one must read virtually the entire poem to recognise who the figures are, these gods returning from not only another world but another era, as Pound dramatically envisions them becoming manifest, and "with them the silver hounds, / sniffing the trace of air!" (1990: 70). In the end, the poem offers nothing so pedestrian as an account of where these gods have come from, why they are re-emerging now, nor why they disappeared in the first place; rather, it vividly dramatises their incarnation, even as it then closes with an explicit series of epithets for the silver hounds as the "swift to harry", the "keen-scented", and the "souls of blood", restrained by "the leashmen". As an Imagist or Vorticist piece (despite having been composed before either of those 'movements' was born), 'The Return' explicitly dramatises the *moment* of its subject, while allowing the larger context to remain implicit.

After the publication of Pound's *Hugh Selwyn Mauberly* (1918), and T. S. Eliot's *The Waste Land* (1921), famously edited by Pound, readers soon attuned themselves to the allusive, elusive Modernist technique of constructing a poem from a plethora of texts and materials; and in order fully to appreciate *The Cantos*, of course, it has become mandatory to use, if not an extensive library of one's own, the invaluable guides, compendia, and reference books that help situate Pound's work literarily, historically, politically and biographically in the context of its composition. Still, taken on its own – approached as, say, a young poet might, free from its ornate aesthetic, social and mythic trappings – 'The Return' simultaneously confronts a reader with its direct language and tantalises him or her with its indeterminate subject matter. Such a paradoxical mix of directness and ineffability creates in the poem an almost prophetic tone, as though the poet knew something of a 'complicated sort of significance', outside the purview of his readers.

&

Among the many features of Richard Berengarten's poetry that bear the mark of Pound's influence, what I wish to examine here is this understated Poundian tone in Berengarten's work. While we can trace clear evidence throughout his poetry of the impact of Pound's experiments in rhythm, the ambitious reach of his subject matter, the play of multiple languages and cross-linguistic phrasing, the 'bric-à-brac' design of *The Cantos* (most obviously evident in Berengarten's *The Manager*), the preoccupation with economics and politics, and the assertions of poetic authority, what prevails, I think, as the most resonant Poundian quality – especially in Berengarten's early to mid-career poetry – is this striking balance between the explicit and the implicit, between the seen and the not-seen.

To read Berengarten in relation to Pound, however, requires first an acknowledgement of the more prominent *other* early influence on Berengarten as a poet, namely, Peter Russell. Not only was it Russell who introduced Berengarten to Pound's work, but in a formidable way, the elder poet also positioned himself early, from what I can tell, as the lens through which Berengarten would see (and *not* see) Pound himself. As is well-documented, Berengarten spent part of two years, 1965–66, living in Venice, primarily to 'serve' a literary apprenticeship under Russell, who himself resided in Venice primarily because of Pound's living there (Grant 2002: 50–51). In his own short biography of Pound from this same period, Russell writes of categorising Pound's work "under three headings – critical, economic-historical, and poetic" (Russell 1968: 14); but then, after discussing Pound's dismissal of most criticism and his endorsement of Mussolini's fascist state, Russell concludes, "Whatever the value of Pound's criticism and historical or economic writing, his chief and lasting attainment is as a poet" (1968: 17). Clearly, whatever Russell thought of Pound's politics (as suggested, for instance, in his pub-

146

lishing Pound's economic tracts in *Nine* after the war), what really drew him to Pound was the American poet's energy and artistic spirit.

This admiring attitude surfaces in Russell's longer, more anecdotal memoir of Pound in Venice, written shortly after Pound's death in 1972. In this affectionate piece, Russell confesses to becoming after the war "not only a devotee of Pound's poetry and of the poet himself, but a convert to his principles" (1973: 270), even though he also openly condemns Pound's "extreme political acts" before 1945 and "his foolish, impetuous statements with respect to Jews" (1973: 270). Here, what most impresses Russell about the Pound he knew, besides his energy, is his reserve (in contrast to the bombastic character more often attributed to Pound), as well as his generosity. When discussing with Pound the value of "modernist" poetics, for example, Russell recalls extolling to Pound how his juxtaposing discordant images in poetry "set up new voltages"; but he reports, in his reply, that Pound

> seemed dubious about this. He didn't deny it. ... Without dismissing the subject as simply irrelevant, however, Pound added, "A man must have something to say out of himself, over and above the facts he's collected and sorted. This is the important thing". (1973: 284)

Indeed, reflecting on Pound's achievement and his silence late in life, Russell observes:

> The best artist is presumably one who can say the most of significance in the fewest words. Some people have attributed his increasing silence in old age to guilt, or dissatisfaction with himself.... But it was as much for the continuing restless and violent state of society and the world as for himself – far more, I would say – that he grieved.... His personality was forceful but he never let it determine his aims and ideals (1973: 304).

What Russell so fiercely admires here about his mentor, even beyond his dedication to "ideas in action", is, surprisingly, Pound's sense of *discretion*.

In his own memoir, 'With Peter Russell in Venice, 1965–1966' (*PRV*, 1997), Berengarten portrays *his* mentor in opposite fashion to Russell's Pound, when he lauds Russell's expansive, didactic, often explosive nature. To be sure, Berengarten's Russell comes across as at least as generous and as "unassumingly genteel" (*PRV* 119) as Russell's Pound, yet through Russell, the young, ambitious Berengarten for the first time "felt in living touch with the only world I had ever really wanted to belong to, unfiltered by academics" (*PRV* 122). Besides introducing Berengarten to contemporary poets he knew little or nothing about, Russell as a "Pluralist" exposed him to an impressive range of historic writers, from Mandelstam to Plotinus, Rumi to Erich Neumann: "This hugely knowledgeable and likeable man was talking to me as though this kind of conversation was perfectly normal fare," notes Berengarten, "and by implication, he was inviting me to share more of it with him. I relished every morsel" (*PRV* 122). Berengarten and Russell also exchanged poems and soon became each other's critics and editors.

Before long, Russell invited Berengarten (who was then teaching in Padua) to share his flat in the Castello district of Venice, which Berengarten and his partner at the time, Kim Landers, agreed to do. Strangely, though, despite all three now living but a *vaporetto* ride or brisk walk across the Grand Canal to Dorsoduro, where Pound resided with Olga Rudge, Russell never asked Berengarten to accompany him to meet Pound. About being excluded, Berengarten writes:

> He never offered to take me or Kim round there and, even though I was curious, I kept this to myself and asked no questions at all, in order not to seem to be putting pressure on him. The matter of these visits to Pound always seemed delicate for Peter, and of deep importance to him; and he was somehow secretive about them, as though he were an initiate privileged to enter some kind of inner sanctum. I would glimpse Pound occasionally on the Zattere from the other side of the Grand Canal, out for a walk on Olga Rudge's arm. Only once were Kim and I introduced to him by Peter, more or less by accident, among a larger group of people during an interval of a performance by the New York Living Theatre company at *La Fenice*. (*PRV* 126)

It is impossible to say, of course, whether, in choosing not to introduce his protégé to his mentor, Russell felt compelled to protect Berengarten from Pound, Pound from Berengarten, or himself from either or both. What's revealing, though, is Berengarten's own impression of the relationship between Russell and Pound as "somehow secretive", involving "some kind of inner sanctum" from which he, the youngest of the three poets, was being excluded. Indeed, Pound's association with cults – for instance, the Eleusinian Mysteries and the Knights of the Templars, or Masons, invoked throughout *The Cantos* – is much debated among Pound scholars, and I cannot help but wonder how the remoteness not only of Pound's person, but of his poetry, must have impressed the younger Berengarten, who after all, like both Pound and Russell before him, was now putting his own livelihood and survival at risk in pursuit of his art outside an academic milieu. To be sure, in a more recent, unfinished essay reflecting again on his apprenticeship in Venice (*TDP* 2008), Berengarten discreetly characterises his own reaction to Russell's veneration for Pound as, at best, a cool one, for at least two, somewhat contradictory reasons: first, though only in his student days, Berengarten was familiar at Cambridge with "educational hierarchies" among his elders and was ready to defer to them. And yet, second, as part of the 1960s "generation", neither his partner Kim nor he "were really the types to go in for unadulterated hero-worship" and, in fact, "were decidedly critical" of such a practice. To the young Berengarten, it seemed increasingly incongruous that Pound, "a man who'd been an iconoclast himself", should be "surrounded by acolytes of any sort" who would regard him "as if he were some kind of little tin god just because he'd grown old" (*TDP* 2008).

Whatever Berengarten's reactions to Russell's high regard for Pound at the time, the poetry of both continued to have a significant impact on his own work. As Berengarten notes in a letter to me:

> Ever since that time [living in Peter Russell's flat in Venice in 1965–66], I think I've had two approaches to Pound's poetry. The direct approach as a reading *bricoleur* is reflected in Pound's direct influence on my own poems. The other is the filtration of Pound into my own work and thinking through Peter Russell, who by my deliberate and conscious choice was my poetic mentor and *majstor* in those years.

Of course, any "direct approach" to Pound necessarily involves coming to terms with Pound's peculiarly Modernist *indirection* as a poet, as I have already suggested, and surely, for Berengarten this indirection was further reinforced by Russell's own complex posture as a poet.

One of his own early poems that Berengarten attributes to Pound's influence is 'Mythos', included among his 'apprentice poems' in *Double Flute* and shaped by his reading of Pound's *Personae*, especially its first poem, 'The Tree' (Pound 1990). 'Mythos' develops as a series of subordinate (relative) clauses – which might also be read as a series of unpunctuated questions:

Who spoke to me
through the gauze of flesh

Who hammered the earth
on my eyes' anvil

Who dreamed me into carbon
out of ore   dusty with bloodclots

Who danced to silent music on my lips
and poured the wind into my wine

Whose the rhythm   whose the pace
of my clear breath speckled with dew

Who clutches me on the other side
of pain's wall in this embrace

Who lifts my head as though it were winged
[...]
Who sings this (*DF* 9)

In Pound's 'The Tree', the speaker recalls being transformed from a man into a tree, alluding to two of Ovid's tales on the same subject (Baucis and Philemon, Daphne and Apollo) as precedent to his own mysterious, if not mystic, metamorphosis. That earlier poem works as both an explicit account of pagan experience and an allegory of literary indoctrination for Pound. Similarly, Berengarten's poem begins by plunging into a mythic landscape; yet it, too, portrays physical experience – of being spoken to (through not the ears, but the skin), of having eyes "hammered on" as on an anvil, of being dreamed up, of having lips danced upon, and of being embraced. However, the diction and figurative tropes of Berengarten's poem strike me as notably *not* like Pound's: phrases such as "gauze of flesh" (where Pound would be likely to have deleted "of flesh"), "my eyes' anvil" (a visual metaphor), "silent music" (an oxymoron), and "on the other side / of pain's walls" (personifying an abstraction) – irrespective of the poem's beginning *in medias res* – render this poem far more explicit, yet less allusive in its figuration than in the mythic lines of 'The Tree'. Furthermore, composed as a litany of fragments, 'Mythos' recalls Pound's rhythmic techniques less than it does passages from Whitman's *Song of Myself*, Chidiock Tichborne's 'Tichborne's Elegy', and Christopher

Smart's 'Jubilate Agno' for his cat Jeoffry. And most significantly in comparing the two poems, they each end differently.

Pound's poem closes conclusively, "Nathless I have been a tree amid the wood / And many a new thing understood / That was rank folly to my head before" (1990: 3), clearly asserting the poet's authority, albeit one gained from a supernaturally natural experience of metamorphosis. In sharp contrast, Berengarten's poem's closure bears the mark of a prescient postmodernist diffidence, not only by the way the poet attributes his own 'new thing understood' to the myth's power to lift "my head *as though* it *were* winged" (italics mine), but in the last line's irony, when he hails his own voice at the very moment that he also questions, by virtue of his ambiguous syntax, whether it is really *he* who is singing.

Another early Berengarten poem that expresses an ambivalent approach to Pound's (and Russell's) influence is the longer, dual-columned 'Actaeon', also composed in Venice in 1965-66 (*FL* 15–21, 219). This poem treats the same figure who appears prominently in Pound's Canto 4 (and reappears in Cantos 17 and 80): the hunter Actaeon who, upon encountering the goddess Artemis (or Diana, in Ovid's version) while she is bathing, is turned into a stag for his curiosity and then pursued by his own dogs. Surely Berengarten must have appropriated this character knowing Pound's rendition, especially given how his own poem employs a series of concise phrases that recall Pound's prosody: "And air pawing blind, held", "*You sang in the wine flask*", "Black stag and hind / *Those fleeing animals* / And roebuck and mottleback" (*FL* 18–19). Otherwise, Berengarten's poem distinguishes itself from Pound's in large part through its dramatic play of two voices in two distinct columns, speaking simultaneously, or interactively, as well as in its explicit attempt to resolve, not just depict, Actaeon's tragic outcome; in short, 'Actaeon' expresses a thematic closure in a manner rarely found in Pound's treatments of myth,

By the time Berengarten comes to write his own poem entitled 'Tree' in 1978 (*FL* 117–130, 222), he seems to have absorbed Pound's devotion to the concreteness of poetic language enough to have made it his own, even as he cultivates a separate mythic vision. Indeed 'Tree' is prefaced with an epigraph from Carl Gustav Jung, although literally ascribed to the pseudonymous 'Basilides of Alexandria', an historical figure whom Jung identified as an "inner voice" dictating to him (Jung 1967: title page). Here again, as in 'Mythos' and 'Actaeon', in terms of its mood, a heavily ritualistic overtone predominates – as it does for Pound's trees throughout *The Cantos*, from "the apple, maelid, / Through all the wood" where "the leaves are full of voices" in Canto 3 (1993: 11) to the "sounds of the forest" with which the speech of the Na Khi people "fit in … unperceived by the game" in Canto 104 (1993: 758). Yet in 'Tree', a lengthy paean to the almost infinite powers of trees, Berengarten exploits a diction that, despite the poem's lack of punctuation and dramatic stanza breaks, adeptly interweaves the literal with the archetypal:

> to sing darkness's
>   molten core
> of ice
>   moss and coal
> fossil fern
>   and dinosaur
> time tree
>   revolving burning
> prising open
>   history's lips
> drilling its jaw
>   to spit pips
> needle twigs
>   and wiry shoots
> earthed in its seams
>   and blood routes *(FL* 122–123)

More than an allegory for natural, or aesthetic, experience, Berengarten's poem bursts with apostrophic appellations, as it indefatigably celebrates, even deifies, "the green world", leaving little doubt as to the poet's enthusiasm for his subject. Still, despite its obvious association with Pound's more Classicist portrait of pastoral experience, 'Tree' displays little or no Poundian prosody.

However, in his earlier poem, 'Angels', composed, according to Berengarten, between 1974 and 1976 (*FL* 51–56, 220–221), he strikes a Poundian balance between the explicit and the implicit through a fantastic narrative. Just as Pound does in 'The Return', Berengarten composes 'Angels' as dynamically efficient, creating no overt historical or mythological context for the poem, even as he invents a world remote from the one most of us know. One reviewer ranks both 'Tree' and 'Angels' among Berengarten's best works, praising them for their "meditative, almost mystical dimension" and finding "the subtlety of Berengarten's language, the interplay of syntax, metre and rhyme…

richly satisfying" (Anonymous, 2002: 118). But what stirs the "almost mystical" in Berengarten, as in Pound, is not so much his subject and prosody, but what he omits – that is, the way (or ways) in which the poem evokes a vivid landscape without locating it anywhere, while the poem's speaker makes assumptions that a reader must accept on faith. The poem's setting combines the *very* specific conditions of the speaker's world and the archetypal *human* existence it insinuates, despite being spoken by an angel. The causes behind the poem's apocalyptic story are left to the imagination, creating a kind of pre-history that seems oddly familiar, despite its being unknown. Yet given its account of the eradication of angels, arguably no other rendition of the story of their demise would be as appropriate. After all, annihilation is a condition as remote and 'mystifying' as it is compelling.

In structure, 'Angels' incorporates several Poundian features, however loosely applied. For one thing, it is exactly one hundred lines long, creating an odd, even eerie symmetry for a poem about extinction. Yet this numerological patterning serves to reinforce the poem's authority. Pound's 'The Seafarer', for instance, another poem undoubtedly related to this one, is only ninety-nine lines long, making it oddly asymmetrical. Still, Pound's poem is a translation of an Old English poem, whereas 'Angels' has no such discernible precedent, so its length has been determined entirely by the poet. What both poems share is that, in each, the persona freely mixes narrative with commentary and pure description with expressions of unabashed grief. More poignantly, both exploit Anglo-Saxon alliteration. In lines devised as much through sound as through imagery, Pound's beleaguered seafarer laments:

> Hung with hard-ice-flakes, where hail-scur flew,
> There I heard naught save the harsh sea
> And ice-cold wave, at whiles the swan cries,
> Did for my games the gannet's clamour,
> Sea-fowls' loudness was for me laughter
> The mews' singing all my mead drink (1990: 61).

Here the hard-edged *h, s, w, g,* and *m* blend with open vowel-sounds, especially *a* and *i*, to create a gruff, worn voice. Indeed, Berengarten's speaker at the opening of 'Angels' employs some of these same consonants to depict the hunters' slaughter of his companions:

picking us off, first one by one,
then scourging by hundreds as they closed in,
burning, smoking us from the homelands,
hounds baying, snapping our heels,
till, blood-glutted, gorged on our meat,
wearing our hides, copying our calls
and rubbing our fat, death-scented,
into their flesh to charm and ensnare us,
[…]
their glazed eyes deep, ice-covered pools
where our charred valleys were drained moistureless
and our own murders measured and mirrored,
as we scattered to barren tundra. (*FL* 53)

Like Pound, Berengarten clusters his alliterative phrases (the *h* of "hundreds", "homelands", "hounds", and "heels", the *g* in "blood-gutted, gorged", the *m* of "murders measured and mirrored"). He also follows Pound's practice of devising kennings and epic tropes. In 'The Seafarer', the phrases, "Bitter breast-cares have I abided", "not heart from harping, nor in ring-having" and "Over the whale's acre, would wander wide" (1990: 60, 61, 62) anticipate similar phrases in 'Angels': "the closed circles / of their web-knit formations", "moving henges of hurlers and missiles" and "breath longer, blood beat slower, / the whole skin another ear drum" (*FL* 53, 54).

Furthermore, like Pound, Berengarten composes his poem in accentual tetrameters (or dipodic hemistichs) more akin to the meter of 'Caedmon's Hymn', *Beowulf* and the original 'The Seafarer' than to blank verse. Such a rhythm creates a tone of otherworldliness not echoed in, say, the more discursive pentameter of Milton or Wordsworth. Pound's poem opens, "May I for my own self song's truth reckon, / Journey's jargon, how I in harsh days / Hardship oft endured" (1990: 60), declaring its theme up front; Berengarten's poem begins equally straightforwardly, as it plunges us into the angels' harrowing predicament:

We were a multitude, until the hunters,
scouting the immemorial pastures
with hewn weapons, on foot and horseback,
tracked us down where we ambled grazing
and fell upon us with poisoned javelins…. (*FL* 53)

Finally, also like Pound, Berengarten employs a cagey syntax to en-snare his reader in the narrative. Pound uses twenty-seven sentences, Ber-engarten only eighteen. One of Pound's longest sentences occurs toward the end of 'The Seafarer', a nine-line sentence (itself, in fact, appended to the preceding one) concerned with men's yearning to create a legacy through words. But he then truncates that reflection with four brief sentences on the power of oblivion:

> Waneth the watch, but the world holdeth.
> Tomb hideth trouble. The blade is layed low.
> Earthly glory ageth and seareth. (1990: 63)

Using a similar rhetorical strategy, although one that shows as much the influence of Milton's expansive style as that of Pound's, Berengarten opens his poem with nothing less than a twenty-line sentence (much of which I've already quoted). But he then follows it with a half-line sentence: "And there evolved" (*FL* 53). This abrupt syntactic shift recalls not only the Anglo-Saxon hemistich and similar prosodic variations in *Paradise Lost*, but Pound's modernist technique of fragmentation used as a cross-cutting device – when for instance in Canto 25, in the midst of a documented history of the Ducal Palace in Venice, he suddenly and abruptly refers to the life of Christ in a single, isolated line: "Also a note from Pontius Pilate dated the 'year 33'" (1993: 116). While Berengarten sustains his narrative more than Pound usually does, syntactic interpolation such as this works both to invigorate the rhythm and to intensify the poem's drama.

So what exactly *happens* in 'Angels', then? As far as content is con-cerned, the poem most resembles Pound's 'The Return', with its vivid portrayal of a primal world, but in this case one permeated by violence. To be sure, although never explicitly identified as either angel or human, Berengarten's speaker seems more animal than ethereal, as he tells of the decimation of his kind as though they were a herd of gazelles or bison, slaughtered for their "meat", "hides" and "fat", whose "calls" are imitated so that they can be tracked down by those "on foot and horseback", with their "hounds baying" (*FL* 53). Lines twenty-one through twenty-nine describe the angels' initial response, in phrases again marked by a lack of subjects for verbs, as though to emphasise the speaker's self-effacement, in reporting how, coerced into fleeing their homeland, the angels

... kept watch, and by winds smelled them,
learned their shadow shapes and cunning
and when to rush through the closed circles
of their web-knit formations (*FL* 53)

By evading rather than resisting their pursuers, the angels soon become
"leaner, hardened, lighter-footed" and learn to weave "secret speech of
our own" (*FL* 53). This latter phrase introduces, I think, a significant di-
mension of the poem. Having had their "calls" co-opted by the hunters,
the angels resort to a coded language, which aligns them not only with
indigenous tribes eradicated by invaders throughout history – from
Genghis Khan to Pizarro – but more aptly, with African slaves brought
to the Americas, Jews shipped to Nazi concentration camps, and other
incarcerated groups who have devised their own "secret speech" in order
to avert detection by their captors.

In 'Angels', however, this agile response does not prevent further
carnage, as the speaker recounts yet more atrocities – the "hacked off
limbs" of young and old, and the "crippled mutilated bodies / hung for
trophies on bark-stripped poles" (*FL* 53–54). Meanwhile those who
were able to do so fled "through the few remaining trees, / stumbled
aimless over moors and heathland / into deserts to die of thirst ... / or
perished in forests / beyond borders of the known world rim" (*FL* 54).
Curiously, as they are driven further from their "homeland" and as their
numbers diminish, the landscape itself becomes increasingly forbidding,
while the poem invokes not only genocide but the devastation of their
environment. By line forty, only "ten, twelve, sixteen" angels survive,
"now wild in willpower and aware of [their] destiny", though only to
be annihilated. When they reach "land edge", they plunge "for refuge in
deep waters / under the ice floes" (*FL* 54). Again, to convey this primeval
scene, Berengarten creates an austere voice here, using phrases without
articles, for instance ("to land edge", "in deep waters"), a voice more akin
to Eliot's evocation of 'What the Thunder Said' in passages of *The Waste
Land* or Ted Hughes' in the more apocalyptic moments in *Crow* than to
the urbane voice we come to expect later in Berengarten's *The Manager*,
or the meditative one he cultivates in 'Only the Common Miracle' and
'Croft Woods', both of which show Peter Russell's influence.

Mid-poem, yet more angels disappear, and the few who remain evolve
into a new, sea-born species, their "limbs attuning to water's rhythms, /
building fat under sealed pores, / muscles till now unused growing firmer,
/ breath longer, blood beat slower" (*FL* 54). At this point, the poem turns

in a new direction. Breaking away from apocalyptic doom, it now heralds a metamorphic future, touting the angels' survival not only from their sheer strength, as Darwin might have it, but through the unique power of poetic invention itself:

> Self-delighting in a borrowed world,
> slow to learn grace, we received as a rite
> water's gift, laughter, that drowns weeping
> and engulfs memory of all time but presence
> which, itself a flood, buoyed us up
> to sing across aeons, and our long calls
> spanned oceans' depths and embraced the other
> depths we embraced in and through one another,
> till our speech took on the pitch and resonance (*FL* 54–55)

Becoming amphibian, at least temporarily, liberates the few surviving angels. (Are they mermen and mermaids now?). This eleven-line sentence from the middle of the poem includes some of its longest lines, shedding the predominantly Anglo-Saxon diction Berengarten uses earlier in favour of grander, more Latinate terms. It recounts the angels' successful transformation that literally leaves their enemies behind. Yet before long, the angels come to languish in their isolation, more like Tennyson's lotus-eaters than the inhabitants of a post-apocalyptic netherworld; they grow "sleek and lazy, / vast in girth, living only for music", so that once again the hunters' "sensors" are able to detect their new "frequencies" (*FL* 55).

What exactly is signified here by the angels evolving to a new state, only to be found again by their pursuers? Is Berengarten insinuating that a life devoted to poetry ("living only for music") dooms one, whether to becoming decadent or to becoming vulnerable to wrathful forces from outside? Or might he be obliquely alluding to Pound's tirade in Cantos 45 and 51 against 'usura' (the practice of money-lending which Pound believes strangles production, individuality, and art): "Usury rusts the man and his chisel / It destroys the craftsman, destroying craft; / ... / Usury brings age into youth; it lies between the bride / and the bridegroom / Usury is against Nature's increase" (1993: 250)? Of course, the conflict between art and money, or more precisely, between working at one's art and making a living, becomes a central theme later for Berengarten in *The Manager*, in which the white-collar speaker, for instance, unleashes his wrath against not Usury but his boss, as "*Dictatorial Power-Hungry Stingy Selfish Unscrupulous Manipulative Conniving Nefarious Flagitious*

Amoral Pasty-Faced" (*TM* 66); eventually, in fact, the manager resigns from his job and, among other things, circulates a petition for a "great new team" to be "[c]ompletely made up of unpaid / volunteers" (*TM* 153), who "by dowsing, through air, / invisible threads of light, / … / Might rediscover the heart's well, once-upon-a-time called Meaning" (*TM* 152).

Regardless of what causes their demise, the angels in 'Angels' inevitably suffer for their idleness and singing, and lines seventy-one to eighty-two return us to their terrible slaughter. Even though they have reverted to an aquatic existence, having adapted to "the soft / inverted womb the seas ha[ve] become", their oppressors rediscover them. What ensues is more violence in the angels' struggle to prevail, as they drag the hunters' "bucking vessels leashed behind [them] / across the waves' vertiginous surface" and dash them against "coastlines / where our hauled wrecks [are] carved and heaped / in messes on the beaches, till the creeks [stink]" (*FL* 55). Here, in depicting these horrific events, the speaker narrates his own species' annihilation with an historian's unshakable authority, in a voice much different from the more skeptical voice in 'Mythos'.

Yet because this poem is neither strictly allegorical – in that it registers no *single* set of reference points – nor aligned with any particular prophecy, at least so far as I can tell, it finally remains as oblique as Pound's 'The Return'. While it resonates, it distinguishes itself – at least, for me – from any explicitly *singular* literary, psychological, or mythic context. Rather, it invokes tradition without reiterating it. Is Berengarten re-imagining the world's end-game here: a world threatened by ethnic and technological holocaust, the desiccation of faith as well as of the natural world, and the tragic diminishment (if not eradication) of art as a vital source of thought? I am convinced that the angels in 'Angels' really are angels, or creatures that evolve toward angels before they become extinct. But what *else* are they? Where *else* do they take us?

Despite the angels' temporary resurgence, the last eighteen lines of the poem portray their incipient demise. Once their numbers have been reduced to "three, perhaps, four" (with the uncertainty of "perhaps" being especially provocative), the speaker drifts from being "wild in willpower" into "zones unhaunted, by no fish followed, / where water's weight and sheer blackness / pressed till we shrank and merged with shadows" (*FL* 55). Then these few survivors dive to a place "deeper than terror"; and when only two of them remain, they entertain each other by singing "of Tiphareth, of the Throne, of the Glory" (*FL* 55). Here, for the first time, the poem provides three proper nouns, linking its narrative to the *Kabbalah*. "Tiphareth" (meaning 'beauty') can refer to "the sixth Sphere (sephira) of divine emanation" or to the Sun, the "sphere of the Messiah/redemption", where it can also signify "perfected humanity". Tellingly, the term is associated with the Kabbalistic 'Tree of Life' and can serve as "the gateway to the Causal Plane of Universal Mind, or the Self" (Stone 1982). The more familiar terms that follow, "Throne" and "Glory", evoke heavenly associations in both the Old and the New Testament traditions, as these last two angels, on the brink of extinction, spend their time imagining eternity. In fact, this one line seems crucial to identifying the poem's allegorical, as well as its Kabbalistic realm of discourse, since for the first time it opens up a frame of reference other than the immediate world thus far depicted. In the same way that 'The Return' reveals its context only toward the end of that poem, it only now becomes clear that the speaker in 'Angels' is telling us this story at an Apocalyptic moment akin to that in *Revelation* 21.4–5, when "the former things are passed away / And he that sat upon the throne said, Behold, I make all things new. And he said unto me, Write."

In addition, perhaps coincidentally, by invoking a tree here, Berengarten places this poem into the same metamorphic world of Pound's and his poems on trees. Yet I still contend that, despite its turn at the end toward Judeo-Christian symbology, 'Angels' finally rests less on *allusion* than on *imagery*. Berengarten's speaker closes the poem by characterising the last two survivors as

> the uncounted, the unaccountables,
> sons and daughters of the starry heavens
> become a lost calling without a name
> drifting among unfathomed valleys (*FL* 55)

until at the last, one alone remains – a figure akin to the 'last Jew standing' – who then explains how he

> on a still sea trumpeted, took air
> and dived for ever. And you'll not find me
> nor you nor you, till the almond tree flowers
> on the mountain, and there is no more sea. (*FL* 56)

Despite being relegated to the "uncounted" among "the unaccountables" – certainly a term equally appropriate not only for the Jews in Auschwitz, but for the millions of other victims of genocide and 'disappearances' over the last century – the speaker here remains defiant, even in his erasure, determined not to be taken as the hunters' final trophy. Only when "the almond tree flowers on the mountain" (presumably a radical change) and earth itself is swept of its oceans, will the loss of the angels be entire; only when memory itself is erased will poets' voices be forgotten, though they may be for now unknown. In a variation on Zeno's paradox, the poem strongly suggests, without saying it, that until memory itself ceases to exist, any particular memory might still be recovered. Indeed, 'Angels' ends by *including* exactly what is left out, when the speaker ironically pledges the survival of one whose entire kind has been annihilated.

ɞ

Like Pound's 'The Return', 'Angels' closes by revealing in intense fashion the apocalyptic moment of its telling, while leaving its larger context conspicuously implicit. Nowhere does the poem's speaker actually mention God, for instance (though as in Pound's poem, gods seem omnipresent). Only line 89 and the final clause obliquely disclose the speaker's apparent awareness of a firmament familiar to us through other, mythic (or if you prefer, mystic) sources, while the bulk of the poem dramatises the physical and natural world. "Go in fear of abstractions," wrote Pound in 1913, in what has become a catch-phrase for poetry after Modernism, whether poets accept, dispute, or reject his thinking otherwise (1968: 5), and Berengarten in this poem seems to have absorbed that dictum almost wholeheartedly. Suppressing an abstract frame of reference through most of the poem, of course, contributes to the poem's aura of mystery, even as it also allows for a direct encounter with the angel's narrative. What may appear remote is presented in its immediacy. The result is not a poem cloaked in secrecy or the occult, despite the difficulty a reader may have in discerning its larger literary, social or theological context, but (as with Pound's own work) a paradoxical grafting of the intimate with the otherworldly, of one's own identity with separateness. Whether 'Angels' means allegorically to imagine twentieth-century genocide, the extinction of the human species, or the end of time, it conveys not the *idea* of the thing but the *experience* of it.

Recognising and realising the otherworldly in individual experience is certainly one of the chief motives behind Pound's epic quest for *paradiso terrestre* in *The Cantos*, as it is throughout the later poems of Berengarten,

160

often through the reappearance of angels speaking, in fact. In 'Only the Common Miracle', for instance, the poet writes, "the way I want to talk / to you, and you to me, is only a small sight away from angelic voices" (*FL* 160). Similarly, in the second of the 'Seven Blessings' in *The Blue Butterfly*, the poet concludes the poem by calling for "a voice pure as impossible / harmony of human / made angel" (*BB* 106). True, by the time he comes to write *The Manager*, Berengarten is less Poundian in his prosody, more comfortable with discursive writing. But as his tribute to Pound in Part Ninety-Two of that epic attests, the younger poet's powerful yearning for the "blue flash" of the divine, for "the moment *benedetto*", as he calls it, has not diminished from his days in Venice. At a turning point of the poem, immediately after the manager resigns from his job, the poet alludes to the lines in Pound's last complete Canto, CXVI, in which "the old man", as he refers to Pound, avows the preeminence of divine light ("i.e. it coheres all right. Even if my notes do not cohere" [*TM* 146]). Then Berengarten's speaker, looking at his immediate environment, affirms the same presence:

> This seedling on my windowsill turns constantly towards the light.
> Its green moment is blessed. And weightless the light's true
> quality. There is order in being.

> I wish I could grasp it forever, this glory the real world inflects.
> I lose it then find it then lose it. It will not come ever again
> like this. Ever. (*TM* 146)

What Berengarten has absorbed from Pound, beyond technique, poetic ambition and musicality, is how remote may be that which is immediately before us, and how valuable to us is "this glory the real world inflects", not only when we can see it but, even more poignantly, when we cannot.

References

Anonymous. 2002. 'Poetry Comment', *Acumen* 43 (May): 117–118.

Blau, Ludwig and Kohler, Kaufmann. 1906. 'Angelology' in *The Jewish Encyclopedia*. Online at: http://www.jewishencyclopedia.com/articles/1521-angelology. Consulted, 1 February 2016.

Dennis, Geoffrey W. 2004. 'Angels' in *Encyclopedia Mythica*. Online at: http://www.pantheon.org/articles/a/angels.html. Consulted, 1 February 2016.

Grant, Alexandra. 2002. 'Well Versed: Alexandra Grant Meets Cambridge Poet, Richard Burns', *Cambridgeshire Journal* 86 (April): 50–51.

Grieve, Thomas F. 1997. *Ezra Pound's Early Poetry and Poetics*. Columbia, MO, and London: University of Missouri Press.

Jung, C. G. 1967. *Septem Sermones Ad Mortuos* (trans. H. G. Baynes). London: Stuart & Watkins.

Kenner, Hugh. 1971. *The Pound Era*. Berkeley and Los Angeles, CA: University of California Press.

Pound, Ezra. 1968. *Literary Essays of Ezra Pound* (ed. T. S. Eliot). New York, NY: New Directions.

______. 1970. *Gaudier-Brzeska: A Memoir*. New York, NY: New Directions.

______. 1990. *Personae: The Shorter Poems of Ezra Pound* (eds. Lea Baechler and A Walton Litz). New York, NY: New Directions.

______. 1993. *The Cantos of Ezra Pound*. New York, NY: New Directions.

Russell, Peter. 1968. *Ezra Pound*. New York, NY: Haskell House.

______. 1973. 'VINGT-CINQ ANS APRES: An Editor's Personal Retrospect' in Peter Russell (ed.) *An Examination of Ezra Pound: A Collection of Essays*. Revised and enlarged from 1950 edition. New York, NY: Gordian Press: 267–304.

Ruthven, K. K. 1969. *A Guide to Ezra Pound's* Personae *(1926)*. Berkeley and Los Angeles, CA: University of California Press.

Stock, Noel. 1982. *The Life of Ezra Pound: An Expanded Edition*. San Francisco, CA: North Point Press.

Stone, Philo (*aka* Richard and Iona Miller). 1982. *The Holistic Qabala*. Online at: http://zero-point.tripod.com/holistic/Tiphareth.html. Consulted, 1 February 2016.

Surrette, Leon. 1979. *A Light from Eleusis: A Study of Ezra Pound's* Cantos. Oxford: Clarendon Press.

'Tiphareth'. *About.com: Alternative Religions*. Online publication: http://altreligion.about.com/library/glossary/bldeftiphareth.htm No longer available.

Tryphonopoulos, Demetres, P. 1992. *The Celestial Tradition: A Study of Ezra Pound's* The Cantos. Waterloo, ON: Wilfrid Laurier University Press.

Turco, Lewis. 1986. *The New Book of Forms: A Handbook of Poetics*. London: University Press of New England.

Witemeyer, Hugh. 1969. *The Poetry of Ezra Pound: Forms of Renewal, 1908–1920*. Berkeley, CA, and London: University of California Press.

Roots and Rings:
Under the Shade of Richard Berengarten's 'Tree'

STEFANO MARIA CASELLA

e chi la scure
asterrà pio dale devote frondi
men si dorrà di consanguinei lutti,
e santamente toccherà l'altare.[1]
   (Ugo Foscolo, *Carme dei Sepolcri*, 1806/1807)

The most recent recension of Richard Berengarten's 'Tree' appears in *For the Living* (2008: 77–88).[2] According to the author, the poem bears the influence of a trip he made when staying on the West Coast of the United States: "During my first and only visit to San Francisco and the Bay Area in California in Spring 1978, my friend Robert Hass drove me out to Muir Woods, and this experience led to the writing of 'Tree'."[3] These are the basic facts. But as with any poem, there are deeper roots at work – the word roots being apposite in this context for obvious reasons, though it is hardly possible not to adopt botanical metaphors in approaching and discussing this text and its multiple themes, echoes and sources.[4]

---

[1] "and he who piously / shall keep the axe away from the consecrated foliage / less shall he mourn kindred losses / and saintly shall he approach the altar." (author's translation).

[2] 'Tree' was composed in Cambridge in 1978–1979 and first published as a pamphlet in 1980 by the Menard Press, London, with an explanatory note (*FL* 222). It has also been published in Spanish, German and Serbian. Italian, Russian and Swedish translations have been made, but are still unpublished.

[3] Personal communication to the author from RB, March 2008. The author is also indebted to RB for making available other unpublished material and comments.

[4] RB's indications on his very wide range of sources include Carl Gustav Jung, Wilhelm Reich, Norman O. Brown, the Bible, the Kabbalah, and oriental religions and philosophy. For more extensive research into the rich symbolism and seemingly endless associations of the poem, I would also suggest Guenon (1962) and Brosse (1989). For the list of

After thirty years, 'Tree' scarcely appears to have aged, dated or lost its vigour. On the contrary, as often happens with poetry of high quality, its main themes continue not only to be relevant but actually to anticipate contemporary concerns. This is very much the case in relation to current ecological and environmental issues, with the emphasis on respect for "the green world" of trees and plants.[5] Berengarten's poem itself arises out of the sense of the communion and interdependence of all living beings, both on Earth and even beyond it. 'Tree' explores correspondences not only between microcosm and macrocosm, but among all creatures. It calls up the image of a chain of beings, all closely connected.

Typographically, the poem resembles a long cascade of very short lines, consisting mainly of two or three short words, though the number varies from one to five. The theme unravels through a phantasmagoria of details. Sounds echo one another, at times assonant or onomatopoeic, but always evocative. Images spring from one another, sometimes in dreamlike fashion. And intentionally ambiguous and polysemic meanings and concepts are arranged and re-combined, based on free associations that trigger and recall one another, shaped and organised more according to an analogical pattern than on any logical sequential principle.

As regards the precisely calculated number of lines, 365, the author stresses that "*Tree* has the same number of lines as a year has days," adding: "This makes it three lines longer than the height in feet of the tallest tree in the world, the coast Redwood Howard Libbey Tree in Humboldt State Park, California." (*FL* 222).[6] Being intimately bound up with the cycle of seasons and the life of nature, the poem also has a chant-like quality and lends itself to recitation.[7] As far as this quality is concerned, Berengarten acknowledges the influence of the American poet Anne Waldman's 'chant poem', *Fast Speaking Woman* (1978):

> In 1979, I did my first reading tour of America. In the years between, I was specially impressed by the voice of one American poet. This was

precious and semi-precious stones (ll. 59–67), see Wallis Budge (1992, ch. XV).

[5] *Editors' note*: a reference to Ezra Pound's *Pisan Cantos* (Canto LXXXI): "Learn of the green world what can be thy place / In scaled invention or true artistry…" (81/535).

[6] The note adds: "The Californian tree should have caught up by now" (*FL* 222).

[7] The author of this essay was one of five speakers, including the poet, who took part in a syncopated, polyphonic, multilingual reading of extracts of this poem, at the British Institute in Florence (January 2008). The languages were English, German, Italian, Serbian and Spanish.

Anne Waldman, in her extraordinary celebratory chant-poem 'Fast Speaking Woman'. ... This poem had an extraordinary effect on me. To me, it was faultless: moving, dramatic, gripping, profound and exciting. And it was also flamboyant, funny and intelligent, in that it even deliberately parodied its own procedures. As Anne Waldman had celebrated femaleness in *Fast Talking Woman [sic]*, in my own chant-poem 'Tree', I set out to celebrate both female and male principles, in a direct response to her work. (*JLI*)

Reading between the lines of this statement, one intuits that, in 'Tree', Berengarten shares with Waldman the attempt to recuperate the ancestral and original dimensions of shamanic chant, rhapsodic monody, sacred celebration, healing magic and spell.

Although the style appears to be simple and plain, it is in fact highly elaborate and calibrated, thanks to the extensive recurrent use of assonance, alliteration and onomatopoeia. In this respect, although the poem's musicality is not always melodic, it is certainly effective:

blood and sweat
  sighing shivering
shuddering tree (*FL* 128)

  blood bathed
breath blown
  bone fibred
body tree (*FL* 119)

clawed through crust
of cliff and crag (*FL* 122)

moss and lichen
mould gathering
  mushroom tree
mother of orchids
  and mistletoe (*FL* 129)

In each of these passages, insistent repetitions and re-combinations of bilabial, dental and velar plosives /b/, /d/ and /k/, of the unvoiced sibilants /s/ and /ß/, and of the nasal /m/ and lateral /l/, all imbue the images with unique musicality. Clearly, Berengarten has learned such patternings from Old English and Middle English alliterative poems. At times, alliteration provides the opportunity for exuberant punning, which can also bring out thematic motifs – as in the first of the following examples, which economically yokes together elements of two mythologies: the tree nymphs of the Greeks and the oak-worship of the Celts:

tree of Dryads
  tree of Druids (*FL* 129)

depthless tree
  deathless tree (*FL* 130)

In patterning and flow, 'Tree' has an apparently seamless continuity. Yet the poem also seems to be open to almost endless variations, permutations and rearrangements, especially in an oral reading. It almost seems that it could be read backwards, as if it were a palindromic text. It can be split into various cuttings, the only difficulty being where the semantic breaks should occur. And it can be re-grafted into a different patterning. Even so, its essential meaning will not be substantially altered. Try, for example, the simple experiment of reversing its opening and closing lines. Within the poem's overall scheme, neither the musicality nor the meaning seem to change substantially; and this observation itself reflects the cyclic quality of the poem's theme.

Tree planted
  in my core
spreading growing
  tree of songs (*FL* 119)

tree of justice
  human rainbow
blossoming (*FL* 130)

Similarly, the poem's syntax may appear to be simple, but on closer examination one realises that the total absence of both punctuation and of any main clause with a finite verb indicates in itself the endlessly flowing spatial and temporal rhythm possessed by both any natural tree and this poem. Through the entire text, verbal movement occurs mainly by means of the present and past participles: the former stressing the tree's ceaseless 'becoming', its inexhaustible motion, as *process*; and the latter its rooted stillness, its 'perfectedness' and its resilient passive endurance. Furthermore, the regular deployment of enjambment itself iconically and synaesthetically emblematises continuity – or, rather, embodies it – simply by abolishing any hiatus, whether formal or semantic, throughout the flow of discourse. Sometimes, the tree's active and passive aspects appear in immediate contrastive proximity:

creaking tree
  enduring thunder
wind eroded
  snow bound (*FL* 119)

insect gnawed
  rot infected
lightning blasted (*FL* 126)

In these passages, sweepingly powerful atmospheric elements and microscopic enemies and parasites, both continuously menacing a tree's survival, are juxtaposed. However, other lines consist of pairings of either present or past participles, as if separately to stress the tree's active and passive attributes:

revolving burning…   crowded stunted…

ringing singing…   raped mutilated…

sighing shivering…   uprooted felled…

   (*FL* 123, 124, 128)   (*FL* 126, 127)

As might be expected, juxtaposition of dialectically opposed themes, images and characteristics is also a marked feature:

tree of creation   quiet tree
    tree of destruction (*FL* 123)   of yes of no
                                 of this of that
nailing hell   of black of white
    to paradise (*FL* 127)   confluence
                                 of pasts and futures (*FL* 128)

These patternings are all the more apt since the tree, both naturally and symbolically, is connected with both soil and air. This simultaneity of upward and downward directions in itself suggests the blending of opposites (*coincidentia oppositorum*) and of the elemental and mythical motifs of Underworld and Heaven. Since a tree grows continuously upwards towards the sky and downwards into the earth, in terms of 'vertical' alignments, the poem embodies a 'mirroring' element.

In connection with this theme of the blending of opposites, the poet has commented on the influence of the Romantic painter Samuel Palmer: "I think I may also have been subliminally influenced by Samuel Palmer's visionary painting, *The Magic Apple Tree*, in the Fitzwilliam Museum in Cambridge."[8] Palmer's painting is undoubtedly fascinating, conveying as it does the fecund, maternal and protective aspects of the tree, that are entirely consonant with the author's comments on Waldman's *Fast Speaking Woman*. Personally, I would wish to add another more modern representation of a tree, of which I was reminded when reading the poem: Charles Rennie Mackintosh's *The Tree of Personal Effort* (1890s,

---

[8] Personal communication from RB to the author, March 2008. Samuel Palmer (1805–1881), painter, etcher and printmaker, was an example of markedly visionary Romantic landscape painting. He was influenced by William Blake, and together with other friends (E. Calvert, F. O. Finch, G. Richmond and F. Tatham) formed a group of artists called the 'Ancients'. *The Magic Apple Tree* can, in a sense, be considered as an emblem of his visionary and dreamlike sensibility.

Glasgow School of Art).[9] This watercolour, in my opinion, suggests the hard/complex work Berengarten carried out in the arrangement of his long poem and offsets a more 'masculine' perspective against Palmer's quasi-magical interpretation.

೦೩

As should already be apparent, form and content are so inextricably intertwined and harmonised in 'Tree' that their unity is inseparable. The richness of the resulting composition, however, almost exceeds expectation. Berengarten's poem is virtually a compendium of the most significant symbolic, mythical, religious and esoteric motifs that have been attributed to trees since ancient times. Foremost among these is the tree as symbol of a fixed world axis around which everything turns:

> pivot fulcrum
> axial roof tree
>   probing pharos
> ever turning (*FL* 122)

Lines like these almost suggest that here Berengarten has found a point where 'things do *not* fall apart', where 'the centre *can* hold'.[10] Yet, a tree is also constantly exposed to the atmosphere and all its vagaries; and, higher still, it seems to connect the earth to the celestial bodies:

> high skies   sun cradle
>   cirrus strewn   moon basket
> milky ways   cloud blanketed
>   and birds returning   cask of stars
> (*FL* 119–120)   rocking meteors
>   shaking planets
>   ploughing galaxies (*FL* 121–122)

[9] Charles Rennie Mackintosh (1868–1928), Scottish architect, painter and designer, is a representative of the so-called 'Glasgow Movement'. *The Tree of Personal Effort*, both in its straight and sinuous lines and its quasi-evanescent chromatic nuances, represents, in my opinion, another visual counterpart to RB's poem.

[10] W. B. Yeats' poem 'The Second Coming' (1920) opens with the image: "Turning and turning in the widening gyre / The falcon cannot hear the falconer; / Things fall apart, the centre cannot hold". The poem continues with images of turmoil, violence and destruction (1989: 187). On the contrary RB's 'Tree', Yggdrasil-like, stands undaunted and unshaken by adversities.

169

Moreover, the way that a tree spans and bridges *space* encompasses not only the highest and hugest regions of the skies but also the smallest and humblest aspects of nature on the earth's surface, with its unceasing and minute life of small plants, fungi, insects and animals:

> nurturing
>   moss and lichen
> mould gathering
>   mushroom tree
> mother of orchids
>   and mistletoe
> [...]
> where the spider weaves
>   and the rooks nest
> and the bat flitters
>   and the kestrel waits
> tree of lives (*FL* 129)

And with regard to *time*, Berengarten implies that not only past geological eras are registered and recorded by the tree's immemorial presence, secretly engraved in its growth rings, but also deeper origins, going back to particles ("baryons") that are thought to have existed only in the wake of the Big Bang itself:

> baryons
> kindling speech
>   of origins
> to sing darkness's
>   molten core
> of ice
>   moss and coal
> fossil fern
>   and dinosaur
> time tree (*FL* 122–123)

Intertwined with these motifs from the natural world, multiple references and allusions link 'Tree' to human culture and history. These range from classical myths, for example the golden apples of the Hesperides (*FL* 125), to ancient religion, esoteric lore, Hermetic doctrines and alchemy. Biblical associations from both Old and New Testament abound: for example, the serpent from *Genesis* (*FL* 120, 128), Israel's flight from Egypt ("pillar of wisdom / of smoke of cloud / desert beacon", *FL* 120), and allusions to the crucifixion:

tree of madness	blood spattered
tree of passion	royal trunk
set with thorns	nailing hell
sweating blood	to paradise
pain tree	gallows tree
evergreen (*FL* 126)	rising again (*FL* 127)

In another passage, Kabbalistic and Biblical references combine; but not only Judaism and Christianity are covered by this tree: it also spans Buddhism, Hinduism and Oriental philosophy:

> rod of aeons
>   of Adam Kadmon
> Jesse David
>   and Sataniel
> and Moses
>   on the high mountain
> Buddha tree
>   Tilopa tree
> zen tree
>   tantric tree
> Kali's tree
>   dancing on skulls (*FL* 129)

Matriarchal and mystery cults of the Middle East are also present, along with Hermetic symbolism:

volcanic tree	tuned wand
of Ashtaroth	alembic
Lilith	caduceus twined
Ishtar and Astarte (*FL* 129)	branching vessel
	[…] mercurial sap (*FL* 125)

Furthermore, Heraclitus' inimitable paradox is encapsulated in the double oxymoron: "I descend up / and ascend down" (*FL* 128).[11] And apropos of Hermeticism and Occultism, the alchemical imagery of precious stones and of their "virtues" is present, as is the tree's essential connection with the four elements:

---

[11] Also quoted by T. S. Eliot as an epigraph to *Four Quartets* (1942/1943).

from evening
    gathering emerald
carnelian
    and diamond dews
and in the studded
    bowl of dawn
with pearl and opal
    dissolving them
[...]
    tree of earth
water fire
    of air of airs (*FL* 121)

Other patterns of imagery establish parallels and proximity between the vegetable life of the tree and the physical and bodily life of man, in procreation and sexuality, and in his mortal remains after dissolution:

tree of creation
    tree of destruction
temple planted
    in an upturned skull
worming woody
    fibres through
eye socket
    and mandible (*FL* 123–124)

flesh tree
    rimmed in muscle
blood and sweat
    sighing shivering
shuddering tree
    generous
sperm tree
    life pump
ever brimming (*FL* 128)

Berengarten's sturdy and dauntless tree is also connected with human culture and artefacts: it becomes a ship, sailing and moored (*FL* 121); a quill, illuminating a manuscript (*FL* 122); and a tabernacle and a cathedral (*FL* 124). It is endowed with energy (*FL* 123); it has its own voice and music (*FL* 124), and it mirrors and emblematises the growth of human language (*FL* 129–130). It is also useful even after its death, performing a kind of self-sacrifice on behalf of mankind (*FL* 127); and it is the 'arbre de la Liberté' of the French Revolution, whose apotheosis is celebrated in the fully human triad of "freedom", "love" and "justice" (*FL* 130), before it finally arches upwards and outwards into the concluding metaphor of the "rainbow / blossoming" (*FL* 130).

Specific literary echoes also sound through the poem. The lines "threaded with voices / and children's laughter" (*FL* 120) recall the "[c]hildren's voices in the orchard" in T. S. Eliot's 'New Hampshire', the first of his five *Landscapes* (1985: 138). In both these passages the echoes of muffled whispers, laughter and voices hidden among the branches and the leaves of a tree convey an atmosphere of childlike innocence and, mythically, an echo of the Golden Age.

At the other end of the arch of human life, in the image of "blind man's staff" (*FL* 127), an attentive reader can perceive a remote echo (even though it is impossible to quote exact verbal correspondences) of literary characters of Old Men wandering and staggering, such as Shakespeare's King Lear or Sophocles' Oedipus.

So in its frame of reference, just as in its linguistic and formal techniques, 'Tree' embraces and blends opposites.

❧

It is a challenging task to describe this long poem. Here I have offered only a sketch of a much broader and richer tapestry of words, sounds, images, meanings and echoes. In conclusion, it is perhaps best to call on metaphor again – as the poet himself does – if one is to do even minimal justice to the poem. 'Tree' is a psalmody, a ritual sound-rhapsody, an incantatory healing mantra, a spell-spiral turning in an ascensional vortex, a column of wafting incense, a mountain waterfall tumbling into a narrow stream, a spring jetting out incandescent rainbow sprays, an illuminated scroll unravelling miniatures, a gothic stained glass, a glance upwards through foliage to its crown, and a glimpse of the sky beyond. This tree's branches and roots mirror each other in a Heraclitean dialectic. This poem is a unique and original 'tree encyclopaedia', not in the scientific-botanical, but rather symbolic, mythological and archetypical sense. Above all, it is an affirmation and celebration of a miraculous living being.

REFERENCES

Brosse, Jacques. 1989. *Mythologie des Arbres*. Paris: Plon.

Eliot, T. S. 1985 [1969]. *The Complete Poems and Plays*. London: Faber and Faber.

Guenon, René. 1962. *Symboles fondamentaux de la science sacreé*. Paris: Gallimard.

Nichols, J. G. (trans.). 2009. *Sepulchres: Ugo Foscolo*. Oxford: Oneworld Publishers.

Pound, Ezra. 1989. *The Cantos.* New York, NY: New Directions.

Waldman, Anne. 1978 [1975]. *Fast Speaking Woman & Other Chants.* San Francisco, CA: City Lights.

Wallis Budge, E. A., 1992. *Amulets and Talismans.* New York, NY: Citadel.

Yeats, William Butler. 1989. *The Collected Poems of W. B. Yeats* (ed. Richard J. Finneran). New York, NY: MacMillan/Collier Books.

The Black Light of the Poets

Nasos Vayenas

Translated from Greek by Michael Eleftheriou

Above all else, it is the light that impresses most visitors to Greece. A light cleaner, brighter and stronger than in any other European country, it bestows a profound vividness on the colours of Greece's landscapes and cityscapes, and a vision-like translucence on its atmosphere that survives even the hottest days of summer. As C. M. Bowra notes in *The Greek Experience*, the light is central to the experience of every foreign visitor to Greece:

> What matters above all is the quality of the light. Not only in the cloudless days of summer but even in winter the light … sharpens the edges of the mountains against the sky, as they rise from valleys or sea; it gives an ever-changing design to the folds and hollows as the shadows shift on or off them; it turns the sea to opal at dawn, to sapphire at midday, and in succession to gold, silver, and lead before nightfall; it outlines the dark green of the olive-trees in contrast to the rust or ochre soil, it starts innumerable variations of colour and shape in unhewn rock and hewn stonework. The beauty of the Greek landscape depends primarily on the light, and this had a powerful influence on the Greek vision of the world. (Bowra 1957: 23; quoted in *FL* 149)

The native Greek, of course, registers none of this. To anyone born and bred in this land, its light feels as natural as the air one breathes. Only when one has lived awhile far from this country is it possible to understand the impression its light makes on visitors from abroad. I remember the sensations that coursed through me on my return to Athens after my first extended stay abroad. I had come back for the Easter holidays, one bright afternoon in 1971, after six months in Italy. The Roman light that day had been so bright and fine that on the bus out to Fiumicino Airport I told myself it was the brightest day I had experienced in Italy, a day as bright as Greece's brightest. And yet, emerging from the plane an hour and a half later, I had to shield my eyes with my hand as they readjusted to the intensity of the Greek light. I felt it wasn't the same as the light of Italy. Nor was it simply more powerful. This was the first time when I felt that descriptions of the "Greek sky beyond brightness", which abound in our text books and travel books, were not as exaggerated as I had thought. In retrospect, I think that the difference is to do with what I can only describe as an 'epiphanic' quality – by which I mean that, in and under this Greek light, 'things' are and remain precisely *what they are*, while simultaneously taking on qualities of both *revelation* and *otherness*. At the same time, Seferis' line, "Angelic and black, light", from 'Thrush' (Seferis 1982: 336–337), and the poet's explanation of it, which had been engraved on my memory since the very first time I happened upon it in *Days* (his diary for 1945), resonated within me even more profoundly:

> There is a drama of blood played out between the light and the sea, all around us here, that very few sense. It is not sensualism; it is something much deeper than the fleeting desire and the so persistent smell, let's say, of woman that prisoners yearn for. There is a drama of blood much deeper, much more organic (body and soul), which may become apparent to whoever perceives that behind the gray and golden weft of the Attic summer exists a *frightful black*; that we are all of us the play-things of this black. The stories we read about the houses of Atreids or Labdacids show in some way what I feel. Attic tragedy, the highest poetic image of this hemmed-in world, constantly striving to live and breathe upon this narrow golden strip of land, meanwhile, with little hope of being saved from sinking to the bottom, This creates its humaneness. (Seferis 1974: 31; 1977: 42)

I was talking to Ilias Lagios about this one spring morning in 2004 as we sipped our coffees in the sun outside a *kafeneio* in Theseion. We were talking about 'Black Light', the collection of Richard Berengarten's poems inspired by his experience of Greece and Seferis' poetry, as is made clear both from the collection's subtitle, "In memory of George Seferis", and from the epigraph, which consists of the two quotations above, by Bowra and Seferis. I had given Lagios a photocopy of 'Black Light' the previous day, and he had called me that same evening to tell me that he had read it and we simply *had* to meet to discuss it.

Lagios told me that he liked 'Black Light' very much, because he recognised in it his own perception of the "*enílios skótos*" [darkness within the sun]: his own reading of Seferis' "angelic and black light". It came as no surprise when, despite the fact that 'Black Light' was the only work by Berengarten that he had read, Lagios expounded on his poetry with the insight of someone who had studied the entire *oeuvre*. For Lagios had a keen nose for poetry that enabled him to deduce a poet's entire identity from a single poem. So before I could tell him that I considered 'Black Light' to be at the core of Berengarten's work, Lagios had beaten me to it, adding for good measure that *The Manager* – Berengarten's most ambitious and lengthy poetic composition, which I'd spoken to him about at length on an earlier occasion and which many considered to be the poet's most important work to date – ought to be read as a development of the experience charted in 'Black Light'. Lagios also believed that the quotation from Seferis that follows the one from Bowra in the epigraph was in fact an ironic commentary on the English writer, and that Berengarten had chosen to juxtapose the two quotations in order to highlight to his readers just how superficially the British philhellenes had engaged with the atmosphere of Greece.

We talked about 'Black Light' and themes triggered by it, and found that our thoughts coincided on most things. We agreed that, just as Seferis had had such a close rapport with the Greek light because he had lived so long outside Greece, Berengarten was able to feel Seferis' poetry as he did because he had lived so long in Greece – long enough to be in a position to see the "frightful black" in the "angelic" brightness of its skies – and we also agreed that the "drama of blood" that Seferis had caught sight of behind the "golden weft" was present, too, in the verses of 'Black Light':

> What is that voice from Hades down the street,
> wafting up through a basement on the chords
> of a baghlamá or bouzouki plucked by racing fingers…? (*FL* 154)

> Remember the soul's wings are fragile as an insect's
> and may be withered by excess of light, or darkness. (*FL* 155)

We spoke about Berengarten's angels, too, Lagios saying the angel in the introductory poem reminded him of Klee's *Angelus Novus*, and me replying that, above all else, it called Hugo Simberg's *Wounded Angel* to mind. Still, there was something about our conversation that bothered me: the odd persistence with which Lagios kept steering us back to 'Black Light' every time I tried to move on to a new subject. I suspected that his loquaciousness, so out of keeping with his customary sparse precision, was his way of preparing the ground for a declaration to the effect that he wanted to translate the book – even though I had already told him that I had started work on a translation myself. And indeed it was not long before he broached precisely this intent, with a formality so droll that it made him laugh. Lagios insisted the task should fall to him, because the act of translation would help him return to his 'genuine poetic self'. Needless to say, I disagreed, especially since, only a few days previously, I'd read some of the poems from his new collection (*The Man from Galilee*, then nearing completion) which he had told me he considered his finest work.

After various failed attempts on both sides to persuade the other to give up the desire to translate the work, we reached a Solomonic solution: we would each translate some of the pieces, in order to keep our poetic voices separate. So we decided to divide up the thirteen poems in the collection between us, so that each of us would translate the poems allotted to him in his own way. I agreed he should take seven to my six. It was Lagios who, half-seriously, half-jokingly, had come up with the idea of sharing out the poems in this way, at precisely the point when our respective refusals to back down had reached their most adamant. As we talked the idea over, at first we were both ready to reject it as flippant, because it ran contrary to the principle of stylistic unity in a poetic work. But slowly we began to see that an experiment in translation of this kind might have something to be said for it. After all, the work we would be translating might itself be viewed as the result of a similar 'collaboration'. Indeed, it could be argued that the poems in 'Black Light' were not 'just' the work of Richard Berengarten, seeing that they expressed not only an English poet's lived, *personal* experience of the Greek light, but also his poetic, *literary* experience – though of course this was one that was no less uniquely 'lived'. In this case, the literary experience consisted precisely of Berengarten's readings of poems, diary-entries, lines and snippets of lines by Seferis – which explored exactly the same subject.

Viewed from this perspective, then, 'Black Light' could itself be rightly interpreted, or rather re-interpreted, as a *translation* of those poems and verses which had so clearly expressed Seferis' own sense of the Greek light, and of his experience of that mysterious quality which transformed this particular light into a symbol – first for Seferis and then for Berengarten – of light in general, of the centrality of light to human beings. Swiftly, then, and suddenly motivated by this set of insights, we realised that 'Black Light' was interpretable as a *synthetic* poetic work: one that embedded the interplay of two voices, Berengarten's and Seferis'. In 'Black Light', the voices of these two poets unite in a single breath. Yet while the text brings them together, it simultaneously leaves parts of each voice separate, unmerged – which enables each to 'refract' within the other.

In retrospect it is clear to me that this curious and singular 'inter-refraction' was another element that drew us both into this intertextual discourse. For, since we had both been brought up with (and within) the Seferian sense of the Greek light, and since we both felt an equally profound kinship with the 'black light' in Berengarten's poem, we decided that it was *appropriate* for us to add our voices to this translingual dialogue. It might also be said, with full appreciation of our multiple sources, that we found ourselves engaged in *re-appropriating* into Greek what Berengarten himself had appropriated from Seferis into English.

Curiously and subtly, then, in its Greek translation (*Mavro fos*, hereafter *MF*), 'Black Light' celebrates not only a linguistic retuning and transformation of the English text, but also its return to its Greek source. And in so doing, it also becomes a synthesis which merges and refracts not just *two* voices (Seferis' and Berengarten's), but *four* – in a quadrophonic 'game' of echoes and reflections, whose experimental nature also serves the function, we hope, of legitimising our own relationship – that is, Lagios' and my own – with Seferis' poetry.

I say 'hope', though the present tense no longer holds for Lagios. A few months after our translation was published (in May 2005), Lagios passed away. The poet who had, in his final months, clearly expressed his desire to experience the depths of the abyss, finally did so: he fell from on high into a fathomless hole of the black light, which had shone on him all his life and lent his verses their unique warmth and energy. And it is certainly no coincidence to my mind that the poet who began his career by rewriting a poem entitled *The Waste Land* in Greek terms and a Greek setting should end it delivering a volume called 'Black Light'.

REFERENCES

Bowra, C. M. 1957. *The Greek Experience*. New York, NY: Mentor Books.

Lagios, Ilias. 2005. *O ánthropos apo tyn Galiléa* [*The Man from Galilee*]. Athens: Erato.

Seferis, George. 1974. *Days of 1945–1951: A Poet's Journal* (trans. Ethan Anagnostopoulos). Cambridge, MA: The Belknap Press of Harvard University.

______. 1977. *Méres E: 1 genári 1945–19 apríli 1954*. Athens: Ikaros.

______. 1982. *Collected Poems* (trans. Edmund Keeley and Philip Sherrard). Bilingual Greek and English text, third edition. London: Anvil Press Poetry.

In Light of Hellas

Paschalis Nikolaou

> I have mentioned these names as though they were talismans that, upon being rubbed, bring to life images, faces, landscapes, moments. And they are like certificates: a testimony that my education in India lasted for years and was not confined to books. Although it is far from complete and will remain forever rudimentary, it has marked me deeply. It has been a sentimental, artistic, and spiritual education. Its influence can be seen in my poems, my prose writings, and in my life itself.
>
> (Octavio Paz, *In Light of India*, tr. Eliot Weinberger)

The sun is *kinging* : Greekness experienced

The dialogue between poetry and translation has been a more than productive one across the centuries – not only in the vital sense of exchanges of worldview and sensibility, of forms that travel between national literatures, but also in terms of literary voices that find themselves between languages and cultures and then go on to relate a consciousness informed by otherness. As I have argued elsewhere (Nikolaou 2005, 2008), experiences in geographical and linguistic relocation and dislocation may lead to themes and forms that engage a felt duality, to compositions that more readily deploy multilingual modes of expression, and to translations that exhibit autobiographical proclivities. Such instances manifest translation itself not just as a disembodied activity of textual transfer, but rather as a wholly lived and experienced condition, as a state of being – and, indeed, as an essential function of human thought, communication and artistic aspiration and ambition. Octavio Paz asserts that "[p]oetry is waiting not only for a translation but for another sensibility. Poetry is waiting for the translation of a reader" (cited in Barnstone 1993: 15). In reading this we realise relations that are as organic as they are essential.

Such understandings are reflected in the works of authors and poets like Nabokov, Beckett, Pound and Lowell – all of whom have consciously dealt in translation, in its *literariness*: in its locations within their own locutions, in its place within a poetics.

Even as we should be wary of 'biographical readings' that might seduce us into critical reductionism, it is also counterintuitive to dispute that poets' living circumstances (at home and abroad) may anticipate or lead to the work they produce; the passage extracted from Octavio Paz's essays on India that opens this essay already suggests as much. In the case of Richard Berengarten, his "poems for friends in Greece 1967–1971" collected in the pamphlet *The Return of Lazarus* (1971) show how the stay of an English poet in Greece has influenced the content as well as the forms delivered in his output of that period. Here, we witness an outsider's perspective coinciding with a desired naturalisation: the poet not only *inhabits* the realities of late-sixties Greece, and especially the repercussions of the military *coup d'état* of 1967, but also voices aspects of a national character that he has observed and participated in:

> Freedom is not a birthright or a gift of gods
> but must be fought for again and again
> Four Easters ago I was free and did not know it
> I was young enough to think myself immortal
> never having tasted death in my wineglass
> I walked then on the olive covered hills
> and wallowed in the hazy ouzo evening
> and Rigas and Byron and Kolokotronis
> were textual problems for the classroom. ('Eleftheria', *RL* 13)

While Greece has become a frame of reference that has affected Berengarten's poetry ever since, even if more subtly and sporadically, these early poems more evidently double as a translation of the land and its people, permeated as they are with political-historical and socio-cultural references, ventriloquisms of spoken language, considered analogies of tradition, and recollections of everyday experiences. And yet, even though the tone may be confessional in places, the poems are far from autobiographical or topographical recordings. The poet has always been more interested in meaning-making, and all too well realises the imaginative transformations that define literary art; how it furthers originating experience and how it needs to reach for a wider and deeper relevance.

In *The Return of Lazarus*, as well as in some poems on Greek themes that appear in Berengarten's collection *Double Flute* (1972), the overriding sense of Greece is that of direct presence and identification. Poems such as 'Eleftheria' (*RL* 9), 'In his Ancestral Garden' (*DF* 52), 'Three Songs of Exile' (*RL* 7), 'The Funeral' (*RL* 13), 'Male Figure Playing a Double Flute' (*DF* 43) and 'Zeimbekiko' (*RL* 9) (the last two of which resurface in later collections) chronicle an intimate relationship that goes much deeper than mere idealisations of Hellenism or adoptions of antiquity. Rather, Berengarten's Greece, like, for instance, Seamus Heaney's, is a living and lived space, where the ancient past remains contemporaneous and the present is also one of encompassed histories: Byzantine, Ottoman, Vlach and Balkan inheritances share the space and shape the people who inhabit it. Berengarten is enamoured with the resulting *Romiossyne*, that is, with the 'Greekness' he encounters in all its multifaceted manifestations: the landscape and the light, and the food, music and singing beside the quiet, weathered marbles. Taken together, these elements whisper a felt continuity that includes countless survivals, revolutions and resurrections – all of which, subsumed, also appear to connect to Berengarten's awareness of Judeity. Indeed, for the poet, whether as Brit, Jew, Slav, Greek, or as an inheritor and bearer of each of these conditions, the dialogue between sensed identities and shared experience can prove productive, and uniquely so: 'Ode on the End of the Third Exile', the long, closing poem in *Learning to Talk* (1980: 75–79; see also *FL* 57–63), is an ambitious amalgam of eastern Mediterranean settings, both Italian and Hellenic, and Jewish tradition and Greek myth. Here the first-person protagonist is pictured as a kind of travelling musician, a *jongleur* or *troubador*, who embarks on a sea voyage. As the poem unfolds, the figures and stories of Arion, Jonah and Dionysus seem to merge. More recently, in *The Blue Butterfly* (2006, 2008), Berengarten's major sequence on a massacre of Serbs that took place at Kragujevac in October 1941 during the Nazi occupation of Yugoslavia, we come across translations of two songs from *Mauthausen* (1965) by the Greek poet Iakovos Kampanellis, who was himself deported to that concentration camp (*BB* 45–46). Such moments of convergence – here found within what is perhaps the most potent synthesis of cultural elements, literary traditions and poetic forms of Berengarten's career – imply the wealth of recognitions assimilated in the course of the poet's wanderings. Embeddings of translation within a larger poetic whole, or across a body of work, make manifest the poet as a *reader* while also contributing to creative intention. Furthermore, they are suggestive of a common, expressive core in both poetry and translation.

Such instances in Berengarten pronounce a mind that integrates disparities, and a poetics that, beneath the drone of different languages, cultural perspectives and ethnic identities, strives to locate the core values and psychological responses that should name – or remind us of – our collective self as humans. When asked to 'put in order' his many 'identities' – male, Jewish, English-speaker and so on – it is no coincidence that Berengarten places 'human' first (*JL* 18). Here, the poet's self-description registers a conscious preference to identify himself as "a European poet writing in English" (*AP*, inside back cover). From the beginning of his career, Berengarten's native sensitivity to meaningful encounters of language, literature and culture as they realise, employ or deploy one another, comes to draw fully on his varied experiences of 'living in translation': mainly in Greece and former Yugoslavia, but also in Italy, France and even the USA. This sensitivity, which may perhaps be likened to a kind of porosity, or semi-permeable receptivity, makes possible the empathy and inclusiveness that define his poetry and are reflected in its formal variety. Furthermore, this quality not only helps us to understand his main themes of unity and justice, but also to contextualise his search for 'human constants', as well as his related search for universals in poetic expression. This is not to mention a striking ability to understand and depict the diverse contents and manifold agitations of a modern consciousness, as he does to great effect in his book-length poem *The Manager* (2001).

Berengarten's early poetry is shaped by his experience of Hellas while also benefiting from the perspectives of the wider European tradition that he brings with him to Greek landscapes and seascapes. In turn, Greek elements find diverse entry points into his work, contributing to its multicultural reach, to its discoveries of what is shared in difference. This is what happens in 'Nada: hope or nothing' (*BB* 9), in which the poet's discovery of the meanings of the same word in two different languages (Serbo-Croatian and Spanish respectively) reaches an affirmation in a last line that is also a string of further translations of the word 'hope': "*Nada, Elpidha, Nadezhda, Esperanza, Hoffnung*" (the second is Greek). Thus, Hellas, its artists and its poets weave their way through Berengarten's poems. Among numerous examples of such references, echoes and inter-textualities, there is the translated excerpt from Nikos Gatsos' 'Amorgos' (1943) in the tenth section of 'Avebury', which ends in the lines "great dusky sea, so many pebbles round your neck / so many glinting jewels in your hair" (*FL* 34); and the (mis)quoting of Nobel laureate George Seferis in the penultimate section of *The Manager*: "So I've gone on trying till now. One has to go on trying. No it's not / the past I'm talking about. I'm trying to talk about love." (*TM* 156). The influence of Yannis Ritsos can be felt in *The Return of Lazarus*; the rhythms of Odysseus Elytis can be heard in 'Avebury'.

The popular composers Mikis Theodorakis and Manos Hadjidakis are evident too: household names to Greeks because their music and lyrics are experienced as capturing and expressing what, earlier in this essay, I have referred to as *Romiossyne*. Furthermore, genre songs that frame Greek life, in their marriages of words and melody, can be sensed through references to the *rebetika* tradition, especially to one of their major interpreters, Sotiria Bellou (see 'Zeimbekiko' in *RL* 9 and *LT* 41). Ancient thought (Heraclitus, Basilides of Alexandria), figures from myth (especially Orpheus) and the remains of the past (the winged *Nike* of Samothrace, two *phalloi* on the island of Delos, as well as Cycladic sculptures, all of which are set among the 'stones' of 'Avebury') surface throughout Berengarten's *oeuvre*, finding their analogies and their references in the actual present and in the landscapes the poet inhabits or imagines. The occasional borrowing of Greek linguistic structures and rhythms, the encountered traces of Greek poetic forms, the frequent transliterations of everyday items and actions: these complete the picture and serve to embed the reader in experiences that often coincide with their verbal construction.

Together, such entries speak collectively for translational moments and movements, separate instances and singular episodes that ultimately form and inform a wider and experiential sense for translation. This is also defined in terms of an intertextuality that reflects cultural identifications, and witnessed in instances where translating becomes part of creative expression itself. At the same time, 'translation proper' is never far away and often provides its own starting points for a 'literary life'. Berengarten's living in Italy, Greece and former Yugoslavia, his immersion in their languages, give rise to and coincide with translations undertaken: notably, of Italian poet Roberto Sanesi[1] (1983), of Antonis

---

[1] Of interest here is Berengarten's essay on translating Sanesi, together with comments on the influence of Welsh poets such as Watkins and Thomas on Sanesi's work (*RS*). The essay is followed by 'Elegy for Vernon Watkins', Berengarten's translation of Sanesi's 'Elegia a Vernon Watkins' (*EVW*). Not only do we discover in the essay an affinity with the image of an Italian poet in dialogue with Wales, but also insights into the practice of Berengarten himself as a literary translator, who takes liberties and may be less than literal, though he aims to 'restore' in English the expressive constitution and creative history of the original. Berengarten eventually edits a selection of Sanesi's shorter poems in 1983 (*IVI*). It should also be noted that Sanesi had already created an Italian version of Berengarten's own *Avebury* in 1976 (*AVI*).

Samarakis' novel *To Lathos* (1965), co-translated with Peter Mansfield as *The Flaw* (1969), and of Tin Ujević and other twentieth-century Yugoslav poets (see *Out of Yugoslavia*, 1993). Even more interestingly, a meeting with Greek poet and academic Nasos Vayenas in Cambridge in the late 1970s instigated a dialogue between poetry and translation as a conversing of poets: in 1978, Berengarten translated Vayenas' second collection, *Biography*, into English, published in the same year. By Berengarten's own admission (in *JL* 21–22), the reading of each other's work has led to both translation and inspiration: *The Manager* owes a great deal to (the translating of) *Biography*, especially in terms of style (the 'verse-paragraph') and the treatment of experience. A similar pattern occurred on Vayenas' side: in his 1989 collection *I Ptosi tou Iptamenou* ('*Flyer's Fall*', a project of interest in itself, as it combines originals and translations in exploring the relationship between the two), the Greek poet includes a translation of a poem by Berengarten.

That poem is 'Only the Common Miracle', from *Black Light: Poems in Memory of George Seferis* (*BL* 1983), which brings us to an elective affinity that Vayenas and Berengarten share, and to the latter's most sustained articulation of Greek culture, people and landscape. Here, in a series of poems that involve translation in all its senses, the voice and eyes of Seferis are added to the thematic and stylistic preoccupations first encountered in *The Return of Lazarus*. The first epigraph to *Black Light* is taken from C. M. Bowra's 1957 study, *The Greek Experience*. The second is an epiphany that Seferis described in his journal in June 1946.[2]

This passage was later transformed into the poem 'Kichli' ('The Thrush', 1947; see Seferis 1982), a crowning moment both in Seferis' *oeuvre* and in Greek literary modernism. Then, in 'Black Light', Berengarten converses with the Greek poet, further exploring Seferis' intimations and associating them with the 'Greek experience' he has filtered through his own linguistic and cultural perspectives. The result can be read as homage to a land loved and remembered; the sequence was written in the summer of 1982, after Berengarten's return to Cambridge. It also clearly involves a deepening integration into the poet's awareness of what has surrounded him:

> *Blood*, they insist through day, *Sperm. Sweat. Salt.*
> Crazy birds chirping, old crones cackling,

---

[2] *Editors' note:* The epigraph from Bowra, as well as the entry from Seferis' diary, are quoted in full on pp. 175 and 176 respectively.

village philosophers full of homely wisdom,
bright eyed and red cheeked, children laughing,
they purr, miaow, bark, they whinny, roar and howl:
Write, write, they wail. *Sing with us*, they hum.
Do not forget your origin. The gold sun, they shriek
is a black apple buried under the lake of darkness
and we its pips, the black seeds of the sun.

Without them, no sky, no sea, no land, no light,
no wisdom no madness no love no breath
without them no song or poem
No   they will never leave me (*FL* 172).

The intensity of feeling in this poem, as in others, is matched only by its textual complexity. Lines from Seferis become epigraphs to each poem in the sequence, and are also found embedded and transmuted within almost all of them. English language and Greek wording keep reaching meaningful unions. Transliterations evoke landscape and people, importing the textures of a lived-in Hellas. And Berengarten's "notes and acknowledgements" at the end of the early small editions of *Black Light* (retained and extended in *FL* 222–225) confirm a wealth of Greek literary, cultural and critical absorptions, among them Nasos Vayenas' study of Seferis, *The Poet and the Dancer*, published in Greek in 1979. So, in these various ways, Berengarten pursues this awareness of how death's blackness not only shadows this light and this life, but also enables them, providing the backdrop that they need to truly exist, in poetry that evidently functions too as an attempted *translation* of Seferis' vision. Above all, what is understood here, via the writings of Seferis as other, is the relationship between living and creating, between experience and the literary imagination. The intertextual and metatextual eddies and shimmerings that suffuse *Black Light* provide answers of their own to Berengarten's elective affinity, showing how necessary the workings of empathy and identification may be within the poetic condition. At the same time, these poems are both 'in memory' and *made of memory*, responding to its callings, while place-names, events and surroundings are powerfully recalled – as is a light that stands (as shorthand) for everything Hellas comes to mean.

More recently, the second of the 'Nine Codas' in *Book With No Back Cover* (38–39) recounts a leisurely evening spent "on the waterfront at Milina" by what appears (from the names) to be an international group of tourists on holiday in Greece's Pelion area. The poet is among them, eavesdropping on their dialogues and moods, as he evokes the sense of the place. In line 9 of the poem he writes: "And now the sun, as the Greeks say, is *kinging* into sea haze" (*BWNBC* 38). The italicised word here is a literal translation of the verb *vasilévei*, as found in the exact Greek equivalent of the English phrase 'the sun is setting'.

Poetry and poets strive for a renewing of language, for (re)translations of the world; they aim to enrich our experience, which may mean: to explore the possibility of experiencing what is familiar *differently*. In Berengarten's work, the relationship between poetry, translation, and a Hellas construed as one of the poet's 'formative readings', runs deep; thus verbal invention coincides with a translation that allows us to perceive, through Greek eyes, what has always been part of our experience.

Epistrophe: translation returns

The dialogue between poetry and translation is ongoing: later, the act of translation returns to Berengarten's poems in a reciprocal arc. Since his work is so open to Greek and other socio-cultural elements, linguistic patternings and literary traditions, and since so many transfers have already been made into and within 'original' compositions of his, such as *The Blue Butterfly* and *Black Light*, it is hardly surprising that these originals readily lend themselves in turn to a 'translation proper'. This, inevitably, involves a *return* to the first ground of their expression, that is, to the bedrock of their constituent cultural environs and underlying languages. Here, the inter-linguistic movement itself illuminates and comments on significances first conveyed in Berengarten's English poems; and at the same time, in this context, the methods and meanings of translation both as process and as literary topos are more deeply enriched and more subtly clarified.

With reference to the 'Greek aspect' of Berengarten's *oeuvre*, and more specifically, *Black Light*, here I return to its translation by Nasos Vayenas and Ilias Lagios. In my review (2006: 168–171) of *Mavro Fos: Poiimata eis mnimin Yiorgou Seferi* (*MF*, 2005), I wrote of the sense of 'homecoming' generated by this bilingual edition, in which poems already drenched in Greekness now undergo and simultaneously come face to face with their own translation – a procedure that often inevitably coincides with a kind of '*un*-translation' or '*de*-translation'. For here, I emphasise, "the fragments of Seferis in English revert to the originals, italicised transliterations of words like *koré* or *tsípouro* and other cultural appropriations disappear into a 'target language' now claiming its own fabric" (Nikolaou 2006: 170).

Already in literary dialogue with Berengarten, already translated by and having translated him, Vayenas here produces versions of poems permeated by yet *another* poetic voice that has helped shape Vayenas' own; and in that sense, this project also constitutes the repayment of a debt to Seferis. Both the six translations by Vayenas and the seven by Lagios are based on the preliminary general awareness, and subsequent more finely-tuned realisations, of how the translator is required to un-ravel the original in re-creating its essences, and how translation must re-think itself in order to really take place. At certain points these versions inevitably trace their translators' own poetic accents; yet together they also constitute a *new* cohering entity, which not only presents a further manifestation of Seferis' "black light" but returns his mediating vision, now joined to Berengarten's own 'Greek experience', to Hellas, to its language and literature, and to Greek readers. In my review, I concluded that *Mavro Fos* therefore resembles a game of mirrors, in which

> originals conspire with translations toward scenes of recognition: the translating that attends the poetry is allowed to surface, translations reveal what they share with literary creation, the two poet-translators glimpse their own reflection in what Berengarten has made. We confront a quartet of sensibilities in multi-layered, many-sided conversation that lays bare interdependences of poetry, translation, and influence (*ibid.*: 171)

The resulting reader-experience is compounded not least by the bilingual presentation on facing pages: this kind of 'mirroring' simultaneously identifies and expands the intertextualities of the source text. And so it is fitting, too, that the translation coincides with a furthering of the original: at the end of *Mavro Fos* we now find Berengarten imagining an encounter with Seferis, in a new prose piece entitled 'An Old Man in the Harbour', facing a translation by Vayenas (*MF* 58–63) that reaches us as a sort of textual afterthought, a reflection perhaps assisted by the occasion of translation, twenty years after the publication of the original, English *Black Light*.

We may well suspect Berengarten's satisfaction with this progression, which is also an *epistrophé* – and one in which truths of translation and those of poetry enact each other. In this connection, another short sequence by Berengarten entitled 'Transformations' (*FL* 105–116), which he dedicates to the memory of the artist Frances Richards, clearly implies both the senses and the roles of translation within creative composition. The six parts of this sequence include responses to four of a set of ten lithographs by Richards (1975) inspired by Rimbaud's *Les Illuminations*. Richards' loose-leaf folio includes sheets on which the relevant excerpts from Rimbaud, translated into English, are copied in her own handwriting, together with an illustrated title page announcing: "Prose poems from *Les Illuminations* of Arthur Rimbaud put into English by Helen Rootham". In their turn, Berengarten's poems, inspired by Richards' images, are subtitled: "from Rimbaud's *Les Illuminations*". This consolidates the fact that these poems already have two transubstantiations as their source texts. 'Transformations', then, witnesses experience and imaginative thought travelling not only from one creative mind to another, but also from one artistic medium to another: from poetry to painting, and back to poetry. Here, Frances Richards' visual interpretations of the French poet are incorporated into Berengarten's own attempts to render visible in poetry the essentially translational effort that motivates projects of art. At the same time, any translation, as Derrida and many others remind us, involves transformation, metamorphoses. And so does the epigraph Berengarten uses for 'Transformations' (*FL* 105), a dialogue between Quince and Bottom in Shakespeare's *A Midsummer Night's Dream* (Act 3, Scene 1) in which Quince exclaims, "Bless thee, Bottom! bless thee! thou art translated."

References

Barnstone, Willis. 1993. *The Poetics of Translation: History, Theory, Practice.* New Haven, CT, and London: Yale University Press.

Bowra, C. M. 1957. *The Greek Experience.* New York, NY: Mentor Books.

Gatsos, Nikos. 1943. *Amorgos.* Athens: Aetos.

Kampanellis, Iakovos. 1965. *Mauthaousen* [*The Mauthausen Chronicle*]. Athens: Themelio.

Keeley, Edmund and Sherrard, Philip (trans.) 1966. *Four Greek Poets* (Cavafy, Seferis, Elytis, Gatsos). Harmondsworth: Penguin Books.

Nikolaou, Paschalis. 2005. 'From the many lives of self-translation', *In Other Words, The Journal for Literary Translators* 25: 28–34.

______. 2006. 'Review of *Black Light* and *Mavro Fos*', *Modern Poetry in Translation* (third series) 5: 168–171.

______. 2008. 'Turning inward: liaisons of literary translation and lifewriting', in Paschalis Nikolaou and Maria-Venetia Kyritsi (eds), *Translating Selves: Experience and Identity between Languages and Literatures*: 53–70. London and New York, NY: Continuum.

Paz, Octavio. 1997. *In Light of India* (trans. E. Weinberger). New York, NY, San Diego, CA, and London: Harcourt Brace.

Richards, Frances. 1975. *Les Illuminations, Ten Lithographs and a Title Page*. ('Prose poems from *Les Illuminations* of Arthur Rimbaud put into English by Helen Rootham'). London: The Curwen Press.

Samarakis, Antonis. 1965. *To Lathos*. Athens: Eleftheroudakis.

______. 1969. *The Flaw* (trans. Peter Mansfield and RB). London: Hutchinson; New York, NY: Weybright and Talley.

Sanesi, Roberto. 1981. 'Elegy for Vernon Watkins' (trans. RB), *Poetry Wales* 17(2): 52–53.

______. 1982. *In Visible Ink: Selected Shorter Poems* (ed. RB), *Prospice* 13 (special issue). Skye: Aquila.

Seferis, George. 1982. *Collected Poems 1924-1955* (trans. Edmund Keeley and Philip Sherrard). Bilingual Greek and English text; third edition. Princeton, NJ: Princeton University Press.

Vayenas, Nasos. 1978. *Biography* (trans. RB). Cambridge: Lobby Press.

______. 1979. *O Poiitis ke o Choreftis* [*The Poet and the Dancer*]. Athens: Kedros.

______. 1989. *I Ptosi tou Iptamenou* [*Flyer's Fall*]. Athens: Stigmi.

Foreign in Our Own Country[1]

Maria Filippakopoulou

Initially, what attracted me to *Black Light*, the collection of *Poems in Memory of George Seferis*, in the bilingual English and Greek edition that introduced me to the work of Richard Berengarten, was, I suppose, what would attract any literary academic to a work rich in dealings with foreign cultures and poetries. This was a series of poems which clearly entered into conversation with canons and people outwith its own native traditions, a work growing by ceding its voice to that of others, from other places and times. Its ability to acknowledge the poetic fruits of other sensibilities without cancelling them out by appropriating them would be appealing to any student of literature, especially this particular one, trained in literary translation and criticism, keen on types of writing that surpass the national. As a bilingual myself in Greek and English, with French as my third language, academically primed to read national literature through the lenses of its influence on or reception by others, I eventually came to focus on translation as the means by which I could best explore and understand literature and poetry. I was particularly interested in this collection because it seemed to be a prime example of translation as creation, thriving on reflections of individual affinities, and perceptions of each interlocutor's origins.

In the context of Berengarten's oeuvre, *Black Light* was all the more intriguing for me not only because it was written in honour of Greek poet laureate George Seferis, but also because it carried its own afterlife in its translation by Ilias Lagios and Nasos Vayenas who – by the very act of

---

[1] The title of this essay is taken from 'Only the Common Miracle', a poem in RB's sequence *Black Light*. For the most recent monolingual English publication of this sequence, see *FL*. For the first English editions, see *BL*. Many references in this essay are to the bilingual Anglo-Greek edition of *Black Light* entitled *Mavro Fos* (*MF*), translated by Nasos Vayenas and Ilias Lagios, both poets in their own right.

translating these poems – were themselves honouring both Berengarten and Seferis.[2] This bilingual edition's main metaphor, *translation*, facilitated by the ease of comparing versions on facing pages, made the entire project endlessly fascinating. This book was, surely, a striking record of a self-perpetuating pleasure drawn from the poetry of the Other, a pleasure so uncontainable that it had to go back to the original source of attraction and address it, producing ripples and reflections in constantly changing combinations.

The writing of this present essay, from note-taking for it, to further readings of it, and thence to alternate and/or cancelled drafts, occurred between two deaths[3] and the birth of my daughter. Death and birth, when they concern you and your (extended) family, put you irrevocably, and at one stroke, in the ranks of the grown-ups – ranks which until then you might have felt free to join or leave at will. No matter how oblique or imperfect, the slant these events gave to my reading of Berengarten's poetry was inescapable. By that time, I had to admit to myself that the largely unanticipated emotion that it burned into me had more to do with loss than with the celebratory effects of its tapestry of poetic voices. *Both* the theme of loss *and* the concomitant elegiac motif are part of the core of *Black Light* itself, since the thrust and intention of Berengarten's book constitute a *memorial* homage to Seferis.[4]

Admittedly, the excitement generated in this edition of *Black Light* for a bilingual reader, by the multifaceted encounter with its facing presences in both languages, gains substance with every reading through its textual layering. This effect results not only from the accumulated work of the men who, in retrospect, can clearly be seen to have played a part in the making of this volume – that is, Berengarten and his Greek translators Lagios and Vayenas; and Seferis and his English translators Edmund Keeley and Philip Sherrard – but also the source of both Seferis' and Berengarten's attraction, the 'black light' itself:

---

[2] *Editors' note:* This collaboration is also discussed in the essay by Nasos Vayenas on pages 175–180 and by Paschalis Nikolaou on pp. 181–191.

[3] During the period which intervened between my first and second readings of the bilingual edition of *Black Light*, Ilias Lagios, one of the book's two translators, died unexpectedly in Athens in 2005. In 2006, I also learned of the death of my close personal family friend, Kyria Christoula.

[4] This element in the text itself could, at least partly, account for the affinity I felt with the book at my own time of loss.

> [I]f the original of this book is not [only] Seferis' poem 'Kichli' [Thrush], but the black light of the Greek landscape, whose experience is shared with equal exaltation and dread by all those men…, then it is an original and originating/generative experience, fractured in the poetic testimonies carried forth by all the texts, and textual fragments quoted, glimpsed at, translated, back-translated, or glossed in this book: namely prefaces, explicit and implicit quotations, translations of epigraphs, verbatim quotation, and postscript. The interlingual translation by Vayenas and Lagios is only one of these convoluted chains of identification with, say, Seferis' 'Kichli' (Filippakopoulou 2005: 47–48).

There is an unyielding power in the central metaphor of the black light, whether in its linguistic, referential, existential, or poetic guise. I believe that the source of infatuation it represents to each of these poets and translators and – through their skilful mediation – to readers such as myself, is its power to *reflect*. Furthermore, what it reflects, paradoxically, it reflects in *distortion* or, rather, in a series of distortions: it is black, the opposite of clarity and luminosity. That the coined phrase is a combination of two words which lend themselves easily to translation – *black*, *light* – does not detract from the fact that this mesmerising, twisted phrase acts upon Berengarten's poetry in ways not always foreseen: perception of agency, poetic will in this case, is, therefore, changed in a manner that I shall examine shortly. For the moment, let me simply say that to accept this premise – 'black light' intimated by Seferis, reiterated in English by Berengarten, back-translated by Lagios and Vayenas – is to see Berengarten's poetry proposing and experiencing a *wilful* alienation which merges with a process of transformation affecting poet and reader(s). In the course of this discussion, I aim to flesh out these abstract thoughts, for they have helped me reckon not only with the lasting appeal of Berengarten's poetry but also with editorial manifestations such as the bilingual edition of *Black Light*. I also aim to show how the effects of *Black Light*, the different types of distortion it allows (call it, if you will, refraction, alienation, or transformation), can stand as a system of ethics for the writing of poetry.

In the context of this set of aims and, more particularly, given the 'overarching' perspective of a reader responding to both English and Greek texts, I have come to view this bilingual edition primarily as an exercise in *reflection*. A reflection, by definition, on lost poets and their respective works, is more precisely an effort to counteract the deadening of a language – a deadening which has come to register the fact of death. To make such an attempt is to engage in an open-ended dialogue with the foreign; here 'foreign' is expanded to include the foreign within ourselves (Kristeva 1991), in terms of identity, self-perception, and (native) language. Its key element is the cross-lingual dialogue of poets, whether or not through translation; hence the relevance of looking closely at the bilingual rather than the original monolingual edition.

The alienation brought on by death, whether remote or intimate, makes visible the manner in which one's relation with one's mother tongue has become stilted, blunt and merely 'communicative'. In this respect, the loss of childhood that I hinted at earlier is simultaneously the inability to keep language alive by speaking it with those one loves; as Seferis himself put it, "as the years go by and you converse with fewer voices, / you see the sun with different eyes" (Seferis 1982: 168). What is lost by growing old(er), by accepting changes, by continuing to live after loved ones are gone, amounts to a withering away of language, especially "the native tongue". Hugo von Hofmannsthal in *The Lord Chandos Letter* spoke eloquently about this deadened language and the ensuing self-estrangement, the reduction in the sharpness with which the world used to present itself when language seemed to be organically linked to the sensations conveyed by the world (Hofmannsthal 1995: 19, 20).

❧

I can recollect with some effort the roughness of the grey woolly blanket my brother and sister and I used to cover ourselves with, when we slept outside on the veranda on hot summer nights, how pleasant its warmth became when we finally fell asleep in the gathering dark, and how oppressive when dawn finally came, bringing with it the growing heat of the morning. Is the recollection of the peach juice running down my chin as I lay on warm pebbles after a long swim, as the light was fading, imagined? Real or constructed memories, the sensuality of the images, their very *presentness*, all stand, nonetheless, for a reality that language now can neither hold nor capture any longer; and recollections such as these point to a clarity of emotion inseparable from a language quick to catch at the core of emotions that surfaced at the time, but have now become evasive. It is a mixed blessing that Berengarten has come up with the very definition of the kind of language-as-lost-happiness that I have in mind. It is found in the poem called 'Salt':

> [F]or here desire and fulfilment are stitched in one weft of light,
> cross-woven, stilled and impossible to unravel

195

> from this seamless tide of days which flow in one movement
> together (*FL* 164)

But it would be ill-advised to point too quickly to a success, as there is
nothing neat about what is beneath this project. I would rather speak about
the mechanics of how the tribute to a lost poet is paid, how the act of
preserving life in the face of its cessation is carried out. For it is necessary
for poetic composition to *enact* the alienation referred to, before it can
bring back traces of the enchanted 'place' where death was not yet a factual
reality. I would like, therefore, to structure this discussion on the basis of
themes and tropes, especially those found in *Black Light*. I will try to recover
evidence of the book's main (emerging) themes: distortion, transformation,
loss, sensuality, and celebration. Simultaneously, I will be looking for the
tropes which are largely responsible for what I would call the *undeadening*
effects of Berengarten's poetry. Foremost among them are immediacy, land-
scape, the undoing of clichés and, last but not least, translation.

❧

'Distortion' leads the series of underlying themes in Berengarten's
poetry. The word itself has risen to my consciousness largely thanks to
the foreword by the two Greek poets/translators, in which they refer
to the way in which Seferis' voice is "deflected in the voice of Richard
Berengarten. The distortion of *de-* makes one wonder why Berengarten's
voice should be *deflected* rather than *reflected*. Do we consider it normal
for voices to be deflected as they cross geo-linguistic borders? If so,
should we be at all concerned with or about this change? Part of the
change certainly involves the decontextualisation of, say, Seferis' poetry,
seen through the lens of Berengarten's English. That alone brings out
the potential of a re-reading, whereby Seferis' poetry is purged from the
inevitable baggage of its own historical genesis, and in particular his use of
T. S. Eliot's high modernistic idiom to re-energise Greek letters.[5] Already,
unexamined notions of native perception, supposedly self-sufficient –
what is commonly referred to as the 'self-same' – are put into question, as
deflection is seen to have already acted on the Greek original, which came
into being by its very will to reflect the foreign.

---

[5] In Greek criticism, Seferis' 'Kichli' [Thrush] is considered to be nothing less than "the
Greek equivalent of *The Waste Land*" (Vayenas 1989: 99).

196

To broaden the picture, the deflection at work can also be seen in Berengarten's stated amazement at the way in which the new becomes familiar while at the same time being an engine for productive self-distancing – i.e. self-alienation. Significant in this respect, is a compact note in his 'Postscript' to *In a Time of Drought*, which, interestingly, like *Black Light*, is another work by Berengarten that involves 'multiple acts of translation', this time from south-Slavonic and other Balkan languages:

> When I started working on *In a Time of Drought*, an idea had come to me, a hunch, a theme, accompanied by a little (*too* little) knowledge. So, during the composition of the poem's first drafts, I set about finding as much as I could about the rain-making practices and songs. Their occurrence in cultures of which I had shallow or scant experience, and their location in languages I understood either imperfectly or not at all, added to their attraction. But as soon as I started exploring, I found myself entering areas not only so new but also, simultaneously, so wholly recognizable and so warmly hospitable that my set of enquiries began to turn into an activity with its own separate direction and momentum. More than once I was astonished to find that images which had been cropping up spontaneously in my own mind during composition turned out to belong to the sources themselves, and even to be part of their stuff or grain…
>
> Given the nature of the material that has gone into the making of *In a Time of Drought* and my involvement in it – whether as fascinated guest, baffled foreigner, or both – I believe in retrospect that this plaiting or weaving together was a necessary and inherent part of its composition. But as I began to have inklings from my first notes and rough drafts of what was going on, when it came to working on them, and at the same time taking the poem forward, I found myself wanting to turn subliminal process into willed procedure, and so gradually watched myself aiming to embed as complex a web of associations in the writing as possible. And this self-watching got caught up in the poem's making too, formulating itself, as I see now, as an attempt to eliminate any remnants of my own voice. (*ITD* 76–77)

Berengarten moves from observing all things foreign to manipulating them as poetic sources by following a willed procedure, and through this process he clears his voice of what has been his own. Once again, as with the 'deflection' operating in this open dialogue, the poetic route seems to pass through something of a distorting channel before the final composition is offered.

Similar unlikely pairs are found in 'Poem at the Autumn Equinox':

[A]nd the one [dream] containing a word
clearly heard and recognised
from a language unknown,
which I can never pronounce. (*UBL* 36)

The mystery of a word in a dream is conflated by sets of unknown and unknowable elements: though mutually exclusive in normal usage, the two adjectives, "recognised" and "unknown", qualify the same noun, "word". Equally significant, the "word" is "heard" – and therefore must have been spoken – but it is impossible for the poet to repeat it: he can "never pronounce" it. The realm in which the recognition of the "unknown" word occurs is surely very different from that of *logos*, the Greek word that means 'rationality' and 'speech'. Rather, a process of physical and imaginative dislocation is in motion here. The scenario is one of teasing or torment depending on where and how you look at it. It hints at language as hindrance, even lack, thus presenting readers with two nearly impossible puzzles: one is the source of seduction (a word), that is unattainable; the other is the need to access it by language even when language is not forthcoming.

One even wonders here whether English, or indeed any other *single* language, is capable of fully illustrating the obvious truth of the poet's insight. Might not a cross-lingual dialogue be more suited to the task? In 'Only the Common Miracle', the realisation of failure takes a dramatic turn when, "at passion's crest", one lover opens her/ his eyes: the realisation becomes a material tear on the page, when "a gap opens for a voice" (*FL* 161). The split is there for both lovers to behold, causing a nagging sensation because this voice is one that "isn't yours or mine, but we both hear quite clearly, and recognise". The phrasing here is very similar in lexical choice to 'Poem at the Autumn Equinox', thus suggesting a deeper affinity between the two poems. But further on in 'Only the Common Miracle', we read that this is a voice [which we both] "understand, and adore, because you know as well as I do, my love, that it's your voice, not mine" (*ibid.* 161). The gap seems to be bridged here, albeit briefly, as the poet's persona reaches over to her/his lover. However, the disconcerting spectre of alienation even on one's own native ground remains, and, with it, the threat of not mastering "the language of love", as the next, and last, stanza illustrates:

                                                      but people like
          you and me have been travelling
    like this for years, along the same dirt track through the same
          city streets the same weary beds
    foreign in our own country, *no longer recognising the speech of*
          men or women we know, of our own flesh,
    so how then can we be expected to converse with angels or even
          with old friends, long dead,
    let alone speak the language of love, let alone the language of
          love? (*ibid.* 161; *italics added*)

'Cicadas (I)' singles out, I believe, the moment in which "a gap opens
for a voice", and enlarges that moment to a whole poem. The first stanza
reads as follows:

    The men play *távli* and drink *tsípouro* or coffee,
    skéto, métrio, glykí vrastó. Above our heads
    the *nichterídhes* flitter among the plane trees
    and every table but mine in the square is full.
    Through voices' thrum, laughter, clatter of board
    and counter, clink of glasses, and fork against plate,
    where the bald, bullied waiter runs, scurrying, sweating,
    tonight I sit alone, trying to write a letter
    home to my son and daughter: *Dearest Children*… (*ibid.* 159)

There is a cacophony of voices here, which could indicate an attempt to
alert us to the gap as discussed earlier, as a representation of language's
eventual failure to communicate – or rather, failure because language, a
mundane instrument, *primarily* communicates. First, there is a series of
transcriptions of Greek words, which, although ordinary, would mean
very little to an English reader: *távli, tsípouro, skéto, métrio, glykí vrastó,
nichterídhes*.[6] Repetition of the 't' sound, which is probably the single
most overwhelming sound heard when a Briton overhears two Greek
people chatting, together with their sheer accumulation in the first three
lines, helps to impress the point of alienation by direct illustration. Then
the level of foreignness/estrangement drops from actual human (foreign)
speech, through "voices' thrum" and "laughter", to the inanimate noise
in the café: "clatter of board and counter", "clink of glasses", "fork

---

[6] However, RB is careful to add the English meaning of these words in his notes to the
poem: "*távli*: backgammon; *tsípouro*: an anis drink, like ouzo; *skéto, métrio, glykí vrastó*:
sugarless, medium, sweet-boiled (terms used for coffee); *nichterídhes*: bats." (*FL* 224)

against plate". There are, of course, human beings behind these noises, but crucially the imagery reduces them to simple auditory effects. The non-human movement seems to have engulfed even the emergence in the poem of the waiter in the form of two sets of alliteration – "bald, bullied" and "scurrying, sweating" – to the extent that he is entirely made up of sensory signals. Against this background, it would be very difficult not to take the last sample of speech – the form of address in the narrator's letter to his children, "*Dearest Children…*" – as yet another expression of inane human language, blunt with overuse. Of note also is the corroborating line-break splitting "letter" and "home", exposing their uneasy cohabitation. Symmetry alone in the stanza structure means that the italicisation of the Greek loan words mentioned above, on the one hand, and the typographical relief of this standard phrase, on the other, link them to each other as illustrations of spoken language which has ceased to signify effectively, or affect authentically.

ω

No poem speaks more eloquently about loss than the prose poem 'Shell' (*FL* 170). This is as much about the fossilisation of memory as it is about the frustration of human action when it comes to remembrance. The clinical exactitude of the English lines[7] encapsulates the meticulous nature of striving to pin down material traces of the past, so prone to fossilisation, so close to death:

> The golden giant shell hangs nailed against your wall, more than a little cracked, though you mended it with glue, and drilled two clean holes there for memory's green cord to loop through, and hammered the nail in firmly to make sure it wouldn't fall. (*FL* 170)

Ilias Lagios has tightened the precision of the foredoomed action by rendering the "cord to loop through" as the kind of rope used to hang people. The artefact that the shell has become is a sad substitute, "like a tarnished mirror, [that] no longer quite shows true" (*ibid.*). Once again, the poet returns to the metaphor of language to explain the inability to

---

[7] This line of analysis fails to acknowledge properly that the poem actually takes the precise form of a fully rhymed sonnet, embedded within the prose; its rhythm is alexandrine (hexametric). The fact that this feature has not been carried over in the Greek translation may certainly account for my content-heavy approach.

revive the past by referring to the ornament on the wall as "souvenir of some place you passed or *name you thought you knew*" (italics added). The confluence of place and name suggests that there can be no lived experience separate from its relating, its naming, the language with which it comes to be understood and shared. If this language escapes us in the end, then we have to content ourselves with the complacency of what the first lines of 'Shell' describe.

No matter how desperate the need to ascertain the reality of lived experience, Berengarten's poetry incorporates the flimsiest of its echoes, mostly in the form of a half-forgotten, or half-heard speech – also remarkably caught in 'Shell' in the metaphor "the sea's secret speech" (*FL* 170). 'Only the Common Miracle' highlights the moment "when you turn round and wonder who spoke to you but / nobody's there", or, later on, "when you stand astonished, in a street in some foreign city, / thinking you heard a friend / greet you in your own language, someone very familiar once, / you haven't seen for years…" (*FL* 160). In 'Neolithic', a similar moment occurs when "you lifted your head suddenly, thinking / you heard a mule bray or smelt goats on the downwind" (*FL* 165). These moments, highlighting silence, are fraught: only a hair's breadth separates them from admitting loss or the desire for the elusive word that will transform reality. The last of these occurrences marks the appearance of the old man with his dog – a prophet figure who will hint at rather than fully divulge the meaning of the Greek light. His prophecy is, of course, the next best thing to a full revelation, for it both heralds and postpones the moment of the actual transformation of life by the miracle of light.

ɔ૯

Not everyone would agree with the slant I have given to Berengarten's poetry, a hemmed-in reading that insists on the *dark* part of the 'dark light'. It is, however, a matter of emphasis; and emphasis is necessary if the existential reading I am offering is to balance itself out. The fraught moments of realising what is lost, of observing the Seferian moment that "cuts through time", of contemplating memories as mere fossils of bygone times, of desiring the faces of "our own flesh" (i.e. our own kin) to the point of thinking we hear their voices in an unlikely place – all these are moments that would eventually put an end to all dialogue if no actual transformation were to follow. The climax of *Black Light* – the proof, if you prefer, of its thorny fertility – is, for me, 'Volta', a poem about falling

201

in love again, or being able to (*FL* 157–158). Transformation is required to achieve a language defying loss, evident in this poem when the narrator becomes "porous", to receive the light of a radiant evening. The tone of the poem is rightly elegiac, and its pivotal position in the collection is evident if we consider that it is a comment on a very unstriking line by Seferis: *now that dusk falls…* (*ibid.* 157). I would like to risk the argument that a nondescript epigraph for, in effect, a sublime poem should surely lead us to a moment of intense dialogue between poets, which is also the moment at which Berengarten's creativity is sharply ignited by the Greek light – a light he refers to in a filigree of images such as "[k]ing sun", "sweet evening skyglow", "shimmering light", "darling evening", "light thousands of years old", "clear throated singer", "a mould that sculptures all it touches". The understatement of the Greek epigraph – strategically designed to have this effect[8] – has led to an excess of emotion in Berengarten's response to the light, a response in turn to the effects of light on people before him and his time: the cumulative effect is such that the observer/recipient of light becomes a web of exposed senses. His realisation is expressed in the lucid, composed language of a well-rounded citizen of the city in question, and one cannot help but think of another famous citizen, no other than Constantine Cavafy, and Alexandria.

The unashamed rawness of emotions – impacted and reflected – is on a par with the fundamental rawness of senses rendered naked, their very functionality. Looking closer, one notices how the internal rhyming through the repetition of the 'o' sound, climaxing at "the pool of gold you pour", uncovers the porous quality of the poet's transformation:

> King sun, rosy-cheeked, day's sovereign coin,
> you touch me, and my skin becomes a cornea,

---

[8] In a personal response to the author (3 April 2008), RB has noted that if the epigraph taken from Seferis is "understated", it was chosen to be so, deliberately. He continues: "because, for my purposes, I needed to highlight the simplest elements of Seferis' line and so to remove them from their (from my point of view, over-specified) surrounding context. So perhaps the part quoted does *appear* 'uninteresting'. But I've always thought the whole of this line to be among Seferis' most wonderful, most fabulous achievements, for its purity of music (with the sibilant sounds of ships' sirens) and its transparent simplicity, as well as its centred, embodied love of the aural and visual…. I suppose you could even say that my poem, in some respects, attempts to retranslate back (i.e. both 'honour' and 'give back') the 'open secret' of physicality redolent in this epigraph." The entire line by Seferis reads as follows: "Σφυρίζουν τα καράβια τώρα που βραδιάζει στον Πειραιά," which is transliterated as 'Sfirízoun ta karávia tóra pou vrathiázei ston Pieiraiá' – "The ships hoot now that dusk falls on Piraeus." ('In the manner of G. S.', Seferis 1982: 110–111).

my spine an optic nerve, and my body trembles
half dazzled by the pool of gold you pour
over this sea and city, and I'm blinded. (*FL* 157)

In my initial reading of this poem, I considered it significant that there was a semi-obscure female presence acting as a catalyst on what women readers would undoubtedly perceive as 'an encounter of male poets' in the context of Greek history (Filippakopoulou 2005: 48). But now I am convinced that, although this remains true,[9] the sensuality of these stanzas far exceeds sexuality, especially in terms of heterosexual desire and lust. In this respect, the language of the poem is exuberant in its impact for it can bring both female and male readers back to the way life used to be experienced, through the senses, to the point that the senses themselves become a synonym for outer reality. The narrator's ecstatic exclamation: "I drink you, shimmering light" (*ibid.* 157) sums up the celebration of senses that is the poem; it concludes a few lines further on: 'And, thirsting to drink you wholly, I would fill / every pore with your radiance..." (*ibid.* 158). It might be that Berengarten has discovered, in this "porous" condition, the appropriate state and a new means of honestly and creatively translating another culture and literature, in the dual sense of both 'honouring' and 'giving back'.[10]

The theory of translation is historically grounded on a discourse that sexualises the translating and translated sites in the image of unequal sexual pairs. Metaphors in use, such as *les belles infidèles*, illustrate that "western culture enforces [the] secondariness [of translation] with a vengeance, insisting on the feminized status of translation" (Chamberlain 1988: 477). Understanding the role of such metaphorics does not, however, mean that it can be easily transgressed, especially in the case of a male author. But here we have an instance of translating a trademark trope – Seferis' "black light" – in such a way that there is neither invader

---

[9] This is especially so in the translation, because in Greek all nouns are gender-specific – most either masculine or feminine, with a smaller number that are neuter. Thus, when one is translating from English, gender differentiation sometimes yields unexpected results in terms of meaning: for example, the "[k]ing sun" is masculine, the city is feminine, and "darling evening" is feminine. This means that the narrator's enamoured adoration of these elements can unexpectedly convey hints of heterosexual or unidirectional attraction. Roman Jakobson, among others, has commented on the poetic implications and mythological connections bound to the gender of inanimate nouns (Jakobson 1992: 149–151).

[10] Cf. note 9 above.

nor invaded. The transformation of Berengarten's narrator into a porous being who has willed his body and senses to take in the universe cast by the Mediterranean light, to become its "slave, if not [its] citizen" (*FL* 158), is a valid, robust proposition out of the deeply ingrained sexism found in translation practice.

The light that the narrator cannot help but adore is what "liquefied stone" in 'Salt': it is "as if the statue's marble body were dancing" (*ibid.* 162), an additional intimation of the miraculous capacity of light to do and undo what death fixes forever, matter. The function of the statue in Berengarten's poetry is quite strategic in that it suggests a notion of perfection in gestation. Statues – the effects of light – are simultaneously fixed and liquid, and in this capacity they help avoid a cliché in their imagery in relation to the representation of Greek literature and culture. In this he takes his cue from Seferis himself, who famously undid the fixity of statues, that is to say, the rigidity of the Greek ancient past, by giving statues human attributes, especially in section II of the 'Thrush' (Seferis 1982: 163).[11] The entire landscape of 'Volta', both human and inanimate, is defined and signified by the effects of light, and the poet's willingness fully to acknowledge these effects results in the poetic expression of a perfect day on a fishing boat. 'Salt' might commence and finish with the phrase "all I know" (*FL* 162, 164), but it embodies a type of knowledge beyond cognition; it is rather the wisdom, imparted by the senses, to receive the world rendered naked by light's miracle. Earlier, I suggested that Berengarten offers nothing less than a definition of happiness as experienced by a long-lost internalised child of five, savouring a ripe fruit in front of the sea; we read in 'Salt':

> and all I know is, I'm helplessly
>   in love with this mountain and this sea,
> for here desire and fulfilment are stitched in one weft of light,
>   cross-woven, stilled and impossible to unravel
> from this seamless tide of days which flow in one movement
>   together, its whole fabric soaked and doubly strengthened
>   in salt,
> and mine is its crusted harvest with the perfect inner sheen,
>   although I have gnawed summer down to its black core.
>
> (*ibid.* 164)

[11] For a discussion of statues in Seferis' poetry, see Beaton 1991: 46–49.

Naivety aside, I would argue that Berengarten forces his language to recreate the core of the world as uncovered by light in a superb description – its fabric being not ethereal, but heavy with the crust of salt, the lived-in experience, a tactile memory of summer. Because tactile, virtually epidermal, it has to be talked about in the first person: the narrator is obliged to exclaim, with a child-like reversal of the proper word order, "*mine* is its crusted harvest with the perfect inner sheen" (*ibid.* 164, *italics added*), transformed because transported to a near-orgasmic state, recalling the wild joy of once savouring the moment while registering the consuming desire to regain it. In another poem, 'Song, for Petro', the glorious experience is digested down to an "appetite, unearthly, / for speech, which makes men human, / and music, which makes men gods, / to devour the core of the world" (*ibid.* 168) – in their quasi-universal appeal, these lines are justly proverbial. Behind them lies a sure-footed existential itch, drenched in the legendary stuff that great narratives about cultures are made of: in such narratives, as in this poem, the man celebrates with his tribe, only then to go and "weep by the sea at sunrise" (*ibid.* 168). I can still remember stories I heard as a child about a shepherd who, wild from months of isolation high in the mountains, would occasionally come down to his village, drink for a whole week in the only *tavérna* of the village, emptied for the occasion from its regulars, while singing loudly and thumping his *glítsa* (crook) on the earthen floor; or the seaman who, when asked about his age, answered with the question "are you asking me about my age when at sea, or ashore?" This semi-legendary manner brings to mind Seferis' note about rural Greece, an 'enclosed', idealised space: "A boatman's chat, a fisherman's gesture have an authenticity for me that I have felt only very rarely in the company of so many ministers or professors or intellectuals. They belong, even today, to a ceremonial world" (Seferis 1974: 38).

Paramount among such perspectives, *Black Light* is also a collection of poems that has *attracted* its translation by the two Greek poets. The series of moving mirrors, no matter how "tarnished" they might be ('Shell', *ibid.* 174), helps to strengthen Berengarten's essential virtue: of mastering a language enchanted enough by the foreign and surrendering enough to the foreign to invite its own deflections. The project has enabled difference – the mark of the foreign – to bring on a transformation, unexpected in its results, that owes much to the multiplication of lines of attraction and intersection between the native/self and the foreign. My argument has been that the transformation depends on assuming a problematic affinity between childhood (and the native tongue upon which it is grounded) and the remote foreign landscape (spatial and human): as suggested in my introductory comments, the alienation that primarily marks adulthood can be accentuated by a plunge into a foreign landscape – here 'black light' as a metaphor from/for Greek poetry. An ideal illustration of this is the first stanza of 'Song, for Petro':

> What moves, though still, yet sounds,
>   what, breathing, blows mysterious,
> perfuming this whole valley
>   channelling mountain waters
> to race and tumble, child-like,
>   down to your beach, through memory,
> and plunge into the sea – this gift,
>   old friend, is yours:
> let nobody take it from you. (*ibid.* 168)

Every time the poem is read, its meticulous language brings together an already existing landscape and seascape for the first time; the quickening fluidity of the description helps keep at bay complacency, the banality of a picturesque holiday destination. To turn the familiar into the unfamiliar is a fine achievement. Here, senses co-operate with movement to build a specific emotion in the brain and the heart, which would then recognise the flow of the water as it comes down from secret mountains to reach you. Readers are, at one stroke, transformed into small children who, wobbly feet and all, run to join *floísvos* [the sea's edge]. The encounter should be child-like for a good reason: the ancient elements become recognisable only to a sensitivity susceptible to enchantment and enamoured with the matter as it finds it; this must be the metaphor *par excellence* of unadulterated perception.

Besides the invocation of the landscape, another aspect of translation in its extended sense is the illuminating dialogue between poem and epigram, of which 'Cicadas (I)' and 'Cicadas (II)' represent a case in point (*ibid.* 159, 171–172). The figure of the cicada itself as an allegory is rather ambiguous. In both 'Cicadas (I)' and 'Cicadas (II)', the incessant, inane singing of the cicadas can function either as a metaphor for the annihilation of human language against which poetry struggles,[12] or

---

[12] 'Cicadas (I)' finishes with the couplet '[t]hey are hollowing a cave out of these night covered hills / and they will hole us up in it, until we drown in darkness' (*FL* 159).

as the very essence of *poeisis* [creation].[13] Although these are plausible interpretations, one should, more importantly, account for the fact that the two poems offer a commentary on the epigraph to 'Cicadas (II)': "...*the way the cicadas stop suddenly and all together*" (Seferis 1982: 338–339). The issue here, then, is not the allegorical figure of the cicadas but the question of what the exploding silence, the momentary cessation of Nature's 'voice', means – and, most importantly of all, where this leaves the poet. His is a miraculous position, to create on the basis of the exposed, artificial silence as a site both vacant and full: vacant through the absence of meaningful human language, and filled with what human language is not, be that nature, musicality of sounds, or dreams. Berengarten gestures towards both possibilities while at the same time illustrating how the potential of translation can be fruitfully, suggestively exploited here.

☙

In rare moments of physical and mental clarity, perhaps daydreaming or through intense concentration, one can half-imagine, half-reconstruct the sensation of the "seamless tide of days which flow in one movement together" (*FL* 164) – the connectedness with nature and people through language encapsulated in these fortunate verses. Trying to recapture this lost order is the constitutive war of adulthood. Since the time of Sappho, armies of people have known that this war is lost, though the manner of losing it makes all the difference. Poetic language partakes of this crucial task, to wage war on *líthi*, on forgetting. *Black Light*, not to say Berengarten's poetry in its entirety, shows that managing this Promethean task cannot be done through one language, no matter what that language might be.[14] If lyrical language is to have any success in bringing about its undeadening effects, it needs a catalyst to rehearse the reality of loss, to *enact* self-alienation. In the translation by Lagios and Vayenas, the

---

[13] 'Cicadas' is the grammatical subject of a string of verbs: "they groan / like the dead", "they whine like the unborn outside my window", "hover... over the surrounding hills", "argue my destiny", [are] "creaking under snow / breaking up glaciers", "roped like slaves, heaving slabs of silence / into pyramids of music to celebrate a pharaoh / across deserts on the ocean's chilly floor" (*ibid.* 171–172).

[14] In an early poem, 'Guest', we read: "He said he had opened himself to the light, / that the light was a poem, was everywhere presence, / a silent language with its grammar of waves and particles / of which our speeches were dialects..." (*LT* 1980: 21).

enterprise is played out in a format which obliges bilingual readers, at any rate, to look first into the face of the British poet turned towards the Greek poet laureate, before they can contemplate the work of the Greek translators and be struck by its manipulative energies.[15] The multiple and zigzag reading is truly illuminating for it is responsible for the joy of recovering, partly at least, one's native tongue in the very midst of estrangement.

The emotion stirred at the moment of empathy with the poet's infatuation with light and light's inflections is not dissimilar to the moment in which one encounters words unnoticeably forgotten in the course of life, words that one will never speak again with people now perished, "outside of being, in that radiance".[16] These spoken words are haunted, as Berengarten very appropriately stresses again and again. Of all the themes and tropes I have discussed here, translation proves to be the most revealing for bilingual readers, a true key to Berengarten's poetry: in 'Cicadas' and 'Volta', the respective dialogue between the poems and their epigraphs was conducted across a gaping difference. But it is precisely through the lack of equivalence that an excess of meaning has been uncovered – the breaking of silence and the mystery of language in 'Cicadas', understatement and ecstatic recognition in 'Volta'. Berengarten's poetry invites readers to glimpse the mechanics of multivocal, multilingual poetry: its attraction works by bringing one closer not simply to what is not one's own, but also to what is. It is not simply that what is native – that which belongs unthinkingly to a national literature and language – needs the foreign in order to enrich its traditions and gain in originality. The ethics of this poetry is that a single language / literature should work through another language/literature to let in alienation, in order to chisel new life out of death. Today poetic dialogue with the Other is not simply one literary option or device among many others; it is a bare necessity.

---

[15] Elsewhere, I have discussed the clear deviation of Nasos Vayenas, who reinstates syntactical order by omitting the comma in the lines "[a]ngelic and black, light… / Angelic and black, day", the epigraph of RB's 'In Memory of George Seferis (I)' (*FL* 147), as a mark of "a predominantly *native* experience of the Greek light", perhaps even "of *Seferis' verses*" (Filippakopoulou 2005: 50).

[16] 'Radiance, palpable. In memory of Ilias Lagios' [*sic*] (see 'Poems', RB online).

References

Beaton, Roderick. 1991. *George Seferis*. Bristol: Bristol Classical Press, and New York, NY: Aristide D. Caratzas, Publisher.

Chamberlain, Lori. 1988. 'Gender and the Metaphorics of Translation', *Signs* 13: 464–472.

Filippakopoulou, Maria. 2005. 'Common miracle', *In Other Words. The Journal for Literary Translators* 26: 46–51.

Hofmannsthal, Hugo von. 1995. *The Lord Chandos Letter* (trans. M. Hofmann). London: Syrens.

Jakobson, Roman. 1992. 'On Linguistic Aspects of Translation' in Rainer Schulte and John Biguenet (eds) *Theories of Translation. An Anthology of Essays from Dryden to Derrida*. Chicago, IL, and London: The University of Chicago Press: 144–151.

Kristeva, Julia. 1991. *Strangers to Ourselves* (trans. L. S. Roudiez). New York, NY, and London: Harvester Wheatsheaf.

Seferis, George. 1974. *A Poet's Journal. Days of 1945–1951* (trans. A. Anagnostopoulos). Cambridge, MA: The Belknap Press of Harvard University.

_____. 1982. *Collected Poems* (trans. Edmund Keeley and Philip Sherrard). London: Anvil Press Poetry.

Vayenas, Nasos. 1989. *Poiisi kai Metafrasi [Poetry and Translation]*. Athens: Stigmi.

All Art Ever Meant:
Richard Berengarten's 'Against the Day' and Johannes Vermeer's *The Guitar Player*[1]

Dídac Llorens Cubedo

Richard Berengarten's 'Against the Day' (1986) could be defined as an attempt to translate into poetry the artistic singularity and power of Johannes Vermeer's *The Guitar Player* (c. 1669–1672).[2] The Vermeer scholar Albert Blankert dismissed this painting as mannerist and rather clumsy in its composition, clearly not one of Vermeer's best works (Bozal 2002: 289). With his poem, however, Berengarten vindicates the striking communicative potential of *The Guitar Player*, even in its imperfections. Hence, most probably, the title of the collection in which the poem was first published, *Against Perfection* (*AP*), which has a reproduction of Vermeer's painting on its front cover.[3]

It would be misleading to reduce the poem to a mere exercise in *ekphrasis*, if we take the most common definition of *ekphrasis* as "descriptions of works of art" (Preminger and Brogan 1993: 320), most often through the medium of poetry. However, the term *ekphrasis* is currently applied to poetry that responds to artistic stimuli, rather than simply describing them. The appreciation of the work itself may lead to comments about its composition or about the artist, to subjective associations that reach through time and space, to unrelated thoughts, etc. (Szczepanek 2006). Therefore, 'Against the Day' could be considered *ekphrastic* – if

---

[1] Research for this study was funded by a grant from the Universitat Jaume I de Castelló.

[2] Johannes Vermeer, *The Guitar Player*, Kenwood House, Hampstead, London (Iveagh Bequest).

[3] 'Against the Day' is found in four editions: *AP* (1999: 11–19); *FL1* (2004: 121–129); and *FL* (2008 and 2011: 185–195). For references to and quotations from the poem in this essay, the number of the section is given in Roman numerals.

our reference is this broader definition of the concept – although not exclusively or primarily descriptive, as we will see. Its author has referred to it as "*among other things*, a *commentary* on Jan Vermeer's painting" (*AP* 85; *italics added*; and see *FL* 225).

ಉ

The poem is divided into eighteen highly cohesive sections; their number equals the age of the girl (the poet's daughter) to whom the poem is dedicated: "*To Lara, on her eighteenth birthday*" (*AP* 11; and see *FL* 225). Each part is made up of ten lines, mostly iambic pentameters, with the occasional rhyming couplet.

Further cohesion between the eighteen ten-line divisions that make up the whole sequence is achieved through the echoing of verse lines. Berengarten has explained that this device was inspired by the Middle English poem *The Pearl* (*Perle*, late 14th century). This anonymous poem is made up of twenty sets of five stanzas. Within each set, the closing lines of the five stanzas end in the same word or phrase; this word or phrase is also at the beginning of each stanza, so that the effect is that of a string of stanzas, or pearls. In 'Against the Day', the last line of each section (except the last three) reappears three sections later – always slightly modified – as the opening line: according to this pattern, the last line of I is the first of IV, the last of II is the first of V, and so on. The linking of the poem's sections, based on the number three, was intended to represent the plaiting of a girl's hair.[4]

The similarity between *The Pearl* and 'Against the Day' is not only structural: fatherly love and marriage are themes in both poems. The *Pearl* poet mourns the loss of his young daughter (his pearl), who, in his vision, appears as one of Christ's brides, wearing pearls that symbolise sanctity. In 'Against the Day', there is no such sense of mourning or loss, only a sense of anticipation, and celebration of (the power of) art and poetry.

ಉ

[4] For this and other information about the poem, its composition and influences, I am indebted to its author.

211

Two traditional metaphors appear in the first two sections to characterise the girl. She is first compared to "a pearl, offset against the day" (I); then, to a rose; and, in a new, subordinate metaphor, the dew drops on its petals are compared to pearls: "some sturdy, dew-pearled rose // gathering light towards her" (II). The image of pearls appears in all three metaphors (these could be formulated as THE GIRL IS A PEARL, THE GIRL IS A DEW-PEARLED ROSE, DEW DROPS ARE PEARLS), as it does in a good number of female portraits by Vermeer. In some of these, women and girls, sometimes also playing musical instruments, are dressed in the same way as the guitar player: yellow or gold silk, ermine and pearls. This is the case with *Woman with a Lute*, *Woman with a Pearl Necklace*, *A Lady Writing*, *Mistress and Maid* and *The Love Letter*.

In section VI, more attention is paid to the girl's jewellery, hairstyle and dress. Her wearing a pearl necklace and her bare hands are interpreted to symbolise innocence:

> pearls round her neck, but no bracelets or rings,
> whose absence may mean, imply or suggest
>
> an innocence: in her ringleted hair,
> ermine and silk, she is wearing her best… (VI)

The pearl and the rose, the target domains of the two main metaphors, are rejected later in the poem, in order to stress the naturalness conveyed by the teenage girl: "no pure pearl or bloom // could possess such composure" (VIII). Finally, in the penultimate section of the poem, the girl is equated to a gift contained in an "envelope of luminous air" (XVII), addressed to whoever is prepared to appraise the work of art in all its beauty and significance.

The painting has captured the girl in her transition from a still manifest innocence to an already latent, wished-for adulthood – she is "turning from us into womanhood" (X). The relevance of this idea has been indicated from the very beginning of the poem, through its dedication to a girl who turns eighteen, as well as through the epigraph from Edmund Spenser's 'Prothalamion' (late 16th century), from which Berengarten's poem takes its title. There, and recurrently, Berengarten uses the preposition 'against' as Spenser famously does in his refrain: "Against the Brydale day, which is not long: / Sweete Themmes runne softly, till I end my Song" (Maclean and Prescott 1993: 643). Here "against" introduces a time adjunct "with some idea of preparation", and is synonymous with 'in view of; in anticipation of, in preparation for, in time for'.[5] The poet perceives in the guitar player her yearning to become a woman, her readiness for an imagined bridal day, despite her obvious youth and naivety:

> Against
> Her bridal day, no girl could seem so ready
>
> as she, in certain hope, so qualified
> by all but nature, for her womanhood. (XI)

Towards the end of the poem, the girl's coming of age is compared to the reception of the painting over the coming years and centuries; to be durable in its value, the painting must continue not only to appeal emotionally, but to challenge the coolly rational examining eye. Thus, both the girl's reaching womanhood and the painting triumphantly reaching the modern viewer are comparable examples of fulfilment. The girl's father is proud that

> This child of his will meet her adulthood
>
> by playing her being's pattern quietly through
> the centuries, until she reaches you. (XVI)

The identification between the girl's father and the artist reveals itself effortlessly in reading these lines, probably in allusion to the likelihood that the guitar player was in fact Vermeer's elder daughter Maria, at the age of seventeen or eighteen. The poem's dedication also juxtaposes the painter and the poet, and their creations, since Lara is, as mentioned above, Berengarten's elder daughter.

The portrayal of the girl is so vivid that it even allows for conjectures as to her state of mind, her thoughts and her intentions in playing: "whether she aims to impress or attract / or simply to please, or just doesn't care" (III). We have seen how an element in the girl's attire (the pearl necklace) is made to correspond with a personality trait (her innocence). Similarly, a physical feature (the eyes) is, to the poet, indicative of an intelligence that causes the girl to rebel against the prospect of remaining a passive object, hanging on a wall:

[5] Definitions are taken from *The Complete Oxford English Dictionary*, 1989: I, 242.

                              Those deep eyes
    are burdened with too fine, alert intelligence

    and too prepared, in willing mute obedience
    to wait forever in her drawing room. (VIII)

❧

As the poem progresses, associations between key images crystallise, especially those connected with space, light and music. This is so with the girl and the room where she is playing the guitar: "as though she were the space she occupies" (VIII). Towards the middle of the poem, a total integration between the girl, the room and the light of day is achieved. Light imagery pervades the whole sequence, causing the different sections to cohere.

Early in the poem, the daylight is said to compete with the light irradiated from inside the girl's body: "she glows / against the day, which settles in her core" (II). In connection with these lines, it should be noted that Vermeer is generally praised for his unique representation of light, which becomes as it were an attribute of the things portrayed, as if internal to them (Bozal 2002: 206). In subsequent sections of the poem, the light is identified with youthful desire, driving the girl towards her future as a woman. Desire "radiates through her skin" (VII) and "a warm human longing fills her gaze" (X).

Against the day, the girl's light of desire glows more intensely: she is the true source of light. The light is identified with the girl, both metonymically and metaphorically, and so is the music that she plays, which becomes the girl's being – her existence like a musical score: "playing her being's pattern, she plays true. / She is the song she plays" (XV).

The imaginative coalescence is further enriched through the association of the girl's light with her music, a non-visual image that flows so consistently through the poem that it becomes central to it. The motif appears in section I, as a sign of love: "her song which binds unguarded love to you". In the last couplet of section II, the light that has permeated the girl's body and her song are paralleled. The beauty of the music played by the girl is attributed to the light she is imbued with ("as if the day itself had overspilled / itself through her to make those fingers skilled"), and ultimately, to a transcendental being or force: "a more intelligent, kinder love" (V).

214

In 'Against the Day', several sets of basic opposites are made to coincide. Those who might be listening to the girl playing, somewhere in the room, out of sight, are "distant and yet near" (XIII). The apparent immediate fixity of the painting is suddenly animated by an impression of (imminent) movement: the girl is "ready to move yet still seem[s] at rest" (VI); and she is "balanced between action and repose" (X). Finally, and more importantly, the painting combines the actual silence with the evidence of implied sound. This is expressed through the oxymoron "silent music", which is in tune with some critics' comments about Vermeer's portrayal of musical scenes. The Dutch artist "is able to represent not the sound, but the silence that music requires, and without which it cannot exist" (Bozal 2002: 208).[6]

This music, like the girl's light dissipating the distancing darkness, bridges the spatio-temporal gap that separates the guitar player from those contemplating her. The light radiates from the girl's fingers, and she plucks the strings "to reach across the broken, varnished years / in silent music no-one really hears" (VIII). "[S]hadows and gloom" (III) separate the work of art from its modern receivers, but the obscurity can and must be overcome. There exist invisible currents along which the light and music will reach 'us' as we contemplate Vermeer's painting:

> [the light] collects
> within her forehead, pools beneath her skin
>
> and radiates towards us, quiet, strong,
> delicate, but untouchable, as her song. (II)

Whoever approaches *The Guitar Player*, years or centuries after it was painted, must not only look at, but also listen to the silent music, for the aesthetic experience to be complete:

> Come, hear her subtle playing
>
> Unlock the solid shutters of the years
> And open them, light-wrought, in filigree (XV)

℣

6 My translation from Spanish.

Ideally, the painting, with its music and light, will reach an "audience" that is receptive and appreciative. The presence of an audience here is a theme itself worth commenting on. It has been pointed out that the motif of the girl playing a musical instrument is recurrent in Vermeer's work. Several of these girls seem to look into our eyes as we look at the painting: for example, *A Lady Standing at a Virginal* and *A Lady Seated at a Virginal*.

Exceptionally, *Woman with a Lute* looks through a window as she plays and *The Guitar Player* looks towards her right. At first, the object of her attention is declared to be a "mystery":

> she looks away. What there she sees or knows
> offstage, in her own private, secret place,
>
> waits there, without embodiment or history
> and is not for the telling. It's her mystery. (X)

But the poet later assumes that the girl is looking at someone else in the room. Another oxymoron, "absent presence", is used to refer to this person or these people, presumably enjoying the girl's music. It has been argued that the girl's unusual expression, her blush, are indicative of a love theme in the painting: "Perhaps the girl's flirtatious expression suggests the presence of a male listener nearby" (Janson 2007: online).

Both the invisible listener or listeners (father, friend, relative or groom, the poet suggests) and the space they occupy are associated with the girl's music. Although neither the "listener" nor the "space" occupied is immediately perceptible, they both become powerful through subtle implication: "whoever may be listening, manifest / space as the sound her silent song must claim" (XIII).

There is another audience more external or distant than those for whom the girl might be playing: we, the present-day viewers – or all subsequent viewers – of Vermeer's work. In a note on his poem 'The Man with the Blue Guitar' (1937), Wallace Stevens explains that the guitar is a symbol of the imagination (transforming "things as they are") and of "the individuality of the poet" (Stevens 1997: 998). In 'Against the Day', whose author has acknowledged Stevens' poem as one of his major sources, the guitar is identified with us as the external audience, and the music is compared to the effect of emotion that the work of art has the power to produce.

The two audiences, those listening in the girl's room and those contemplating Vermeer's portrait, are finally assimilated: "You are the absent audience in her wings" (XVI), as if to imply that the girl's interaction with the people in the room, made present by her gaze, also indicates her awareness of us, outside her room, beyond the moment captured and framed.

಄

In the final sections of the poem, the girl and the music that is part of her being are described as a gift offered to her more external audience, who are conceived as both collective and individual, general and specific: "her music plays to *all* of you *alone*" (XVII, *italics added*).

But what if this gift, offered out of love ("This music binds unguarded love to you", III), is ignored or not gratefully accepted? The girl is reduced to mere image on a flat surface, paint on canvas. She is not given the chance to project herself beyond the painting itself, even beyond the artist's intentions. If the encounter between the guitar player and an ideal audience were never to take place, she would remain always pubescent, against the bridal day and against womanhood:

> To wait for ever in her drawing room
> could be her destiny, always: poised steady
>
> as a dart to pierce the adulthood
> she leans against... (XI)

As explained above, the girl's fine intelligence prevents her from waiting passively and perpetually. If she were regarded simply as the product of a skilled artist, if she were prevented from coming to life under the eyes of a viewer, her limited representation would be comparable to that of the framed tree behind her. However, the girl is potentially very different from the plain tree: she was not painted to be forever static and fixed, trapped in two-dimensional space. She reaches out for the viewers, for each one of them, to find common ground – in what the poet calls the "fourth [dimension]" (XII). Here she is finally alive, freed of spatial constraints.

This dimension, which opens up when and only when the girl is received as a gift, is the context for the supreme moment of communion between the subject–receiver and the artistic object (which in this case, is also a subject, the girl). Such communion, of course, correlates with the marital union, against the bridal day. As a result, the work of art is transformed from inert artifice into an active force that reaches us, crossing spatial and temporal boundaries – against the day. The poet stresses that this is the essence and purpose of art; this

> is still and always all art ever meant,
> and only you have natural power to call
>
> her being from its painted artifice
> created by the man who patterned all
>
> he knew in her (XIV)

In section XVIII, we as viewers are encouraged to surrender to this magical, ritual moment of artistic reception: "Come, join her in the gift of this, her moment" (XVIII). In the closing lines, the emphasis is on the girl's music, which, by always being played beneath the level of physical sound, represents the painting's power to appeal to the viewers' emotions, to be meaningful and relevant to them, through the ages. Only art can communicate that sort of power:

> and, though this be impossible, confess
> how well you hear and understand these songs
>
> she plays to you through everlastingness
> on soundless subtle chords no aural sense
>
> could ever pluck, except against the heart,
> against the day, against desire, in art. (XVIII)

ᴥ

In summary, Berengarten's 'Against the Day' results from the poet's deep appreciation of Johannes Vermeer's *The Guitar Player*. The poem progresses through imaginative associations: the girl and the room, the girl and the light, the light and the music, the listeners and the viewers. These associations combine visual and auditory elements (both perceived and imagined), which arguably constitute the very essence of poetry.

The poet's contemplation of this girl, whom he identifies with his own daughter, leads him to explore the themes of innocence and fatherly love, through involvement in her transition from adolescence to adulthood. Finally, the poem poses the question of the reception of art, its permanence and timelessness. The link established by inspiration between 'Against the Day' and *The Guitar Player* is paradigmatic of the power of art to arouse fascination, cause emotion and defy the passing of time.

References

Andrew, Malcolm and Waldron, Ronald (eds). 1987. *The Poems of the Pearl Manuscript*. Exeter: University of Exeter Press.

Bozal, Valeriano. 2002. *Johannes Vermeer de Delft*. Madrid: Tf. Editores.

Janson, Jonathan. 'The Guitar Player". Online at: http://www.essentialvermeer. com/catalogue/guitar_player.html. Consulted, 1 February 2016.

Maclean, Hugh and Prescott, Anne Lake (eds). 1993. *Edmund Spenser's Poetry*. New York, NY: W. W. Norton.

Preminger, Alex and Brogan, T. V. F. (eds). 1993. *The New Princeton Encyclopedia of Poetry and Poetics*. Princeton, NJ: Princeton University Press.

Stevens, Wallace. 1997. *Collected Poetry and Prose*. New York, NY: The Library of America.

Szczepanek, Anna. 2006. 'The old masters and young viewers, visual tradition in American ekphrastic poetry', paper presented at *New Literatures of Old: Dialogues of Tradition and Innovation in the Literatures in English* (Universitat Jaume I de Castelló, 23–25 November 2006).

The Descent through Croft Woods

CRAIG WOELFEL

In its opening stanzas, Richard Berengarten's 'Croft Woods' appears to tread a path that will lead through familiar, if hallowed, ground – the poet's walk through the woods. This place is green and beautiful, and the reader listens, with the speaker, for the sound of the breeze through the branches. "But no" (*FL* 200). Not yet midway on our journey, the speaker falls into a rabbit hole of silence, and the reader discovers that a walk through Croft Woods is something quite different – a descent into the underworld. While this may be an equally familiar motif, here the meditative walk is transformed by Berengarten's unique poetic and intellectual preoccupations into something entirely new. Seeing the way that those preoccupations shape the content and form of the poem provides an interpretive key not only for unlocking the meaning of 'Croft Woods', but also for bringing its music to the surface and understanding Berengarten's poetics.

The poem's essential conceit is that the descent is not into the ground (at least, not only into the ground), but into the depths of the psyche and the dream-world of the unconscious. According to Berengarten, the trigger for the poem came from the work of the neo-Jungian James Hillman, especially *The Dream and the Underworld* (1979), the informing argument of which is that the mythical underworld can be read as being co-terminous with the world of the psyche. Berengarten first encountered Hillman's work in 1987 and, while this was an important stimulus for 'Croft Woods', the poem is very much Berengarten's own creation.[1]

---

[1] I was directed to Hillman's work as an influence on the poem by the author himself. For further reference, see Hillman's *Re-Visioning Psychology* (1977), as well as *The Dream and the Underworld* (1979).

'Croft Woods' can also be seen as a kind of imaginative *ars poetica*, the representation of Berengarten's belief that the descent into the psyche can lead to a transcendence of the self and, ultimately, that it constitutes an integral part of the act of artistic creation. The journey is archetypal, but it is also self-reflexive and deeply personal, as any descent into the self must be; and its pattern and direction are shaped ineluctably by Berengarten's path as a poet. Appropriately, many of the poem's images and ideas incorporate explorations that Berengarten has made elsewhere; and the world of the woods is haunted by the ghosts of his own poetic memory – not just of Dowland, Wyatt, and Shakespeare, but of Mandelstam, Virgil, Blake, and Dante, Shelley's Aeolian Harp,[2] Keats' nightingale, and Goethe's (and Marlowe's) Faust.

ℰℬ

Hillman may have provided a seed, but Berengarten's interest in the aesthetic implications of Jungian psychology was already integral to his poetics. The most notable and relevant exploration is his monograph on Ceri Richards and Dylan Thomas, *Keys to Transformation* (*KT*, 1981). There Berengarten discusses the connections between exploration of the repressed and/or unconscious aspects of the psyche that are manifest in dream images and the opening of possibilities for overcoming the blindness of limited consciousness. He focuses in particular on explicating Jung's *Septem Sermones ad Mortuos* ('Seven Sermons to the Dead'), in which a god that "mankind forgot", ABRAXAS, represents the transcendence of standard binary categories and valuations through its simultaneous embodiment of seeming opposites.[3] This Heraclitan acceptance of the paradoxical co-identity of seeming opposites is the 'key to transformation' from which the monograph takes its title (*KT* 100–106). The result is not just an expansion of self, or the harmonising reconciliation of intellect with the unconscious, but the unlocking of a powerful creative energy.

[2] In 'Ode to the West Wind' (1820). See also Coleridge's meditation on the subject in 'The Eolian Harp' (1795).

[3] RB explains this idea in *KT* (100 ff.), where he cites several textual examples from Jung. For relevant works by Jung, see the bibliography in *KT* (135–137). My interest here, however, is in exploring RB's creative use of these influences rather than in engaging in a critical discussion of them. To track this Jungian presence directly through 'Croft Woods', see especially stanzas 19–23 (*FL* 203–204). Note also the allusion to the *Aeneid*, Book VI, with its images of the gates of sleep and dream: "*Pass, through the gates of ivory and horn*" (*FL* 203). The entire poem is full of references to sleep and dream states.

The subject of that monograph and the time of its writing frame Berengarten's explanation of a Jungian/Heraclitan aesthetics in particular reference to issues of gender. According to Berengarten, the expressed goal underpinning Ceri Richards' work and, perhaps by implication, his own at that time, is an acceptance of the feminine-gendered depths of the psyche in order to correct the "one-sidedness" of that moment's "contemporary consciousness, with its over-valuing of the [masculine] intellect at the expense of the 'deeper' [feminine] zones of the instincts and basic passions, which are just as important keys to the 'higher' spiritual zones as the intellect itself" (*KT* 103):

> ...it is the job of the artist and poet to lift our jaded images of femininity out of the secret places we have hidden them in, to air them afresh, to rethink and reinterpret them, and to follow them, not blindly, but awarely, and so ourselves become creative, embodying creation and self-transformation in every corner of our lives, and in our ends as in our beginnings. (*KT* 104)

The provisional title of 'Croft Woods' was 'The Deepening', and its connection to the 'deeper' zones of the psyche is fundamental.[4] However, in 'Croft Woods' Berengarten's attention has shifted from the explicitly gender-inflected engagement of *Keys to Transformation*. More importantly, the work is not a critical explanation, but an exploration of Berengarten's own creative process.

As in Ceri Richards' painting *Afal du Brogŵyr* [Black Apple of Gower] and as with the Jungian god ABRAXAS, both transcendence and the subsequent release of creative power in 'Croft Woods' are dependent upon an initial engagement with what is traditionally viewed as negative, repressed or feared. The initial contrast with the Dantean model that the poem seems to invoke is indicative: the speaker's attention is initially focused on "a slanted source / of sunlight", echoed again in the statement that the light in the woods "hangs diagonally down" (*FL* 199). The image of the shaft of light penetrating the dark wood evokes the opening setting of Dante's *Divina Commedia* and its thematic opposition between light and dark.[5] What marks the descent *in* 'Croft Woods' is that the speaker

---

[4] This working title was provided by RB in comments to me about the poem.

[5] This Dantean contrast is ubiquitous throughout 'Croft Woods'. For Dante, hell is light-less, and God is envisioned as a point of light, etc. In a later poem by RB, 'Diagonal' (*BB* 70), the connection of the image of the slanted shaft of light to Dante's universe is made explicit. The poem is written in a variant of Dantean *terza rima* and features a prominent Beatrice-like figure.

does not begin in a state that is lost in the dark wood, but moves from a zone of light into a darkness that, though daunting, "calls [him] deep into it" (*FL* 199).

In stanza 6, the descent begins in earnest, as the speaker is swallowed into the silence of the woods that runs beneath the song of the wind in the trees. The evocation of Shelley's Aeolian Harp and the mention of Dowland, Wyatt and Shakespeare in stanza 5 emphasise that the speaker's descent into silence has tremendous psychic weight; its direct consequence is the sense of total loss of identity (*FL* 200–201). However, even in its very beginnings, the poem expresses a paradoxical promise of rebirth that will come *within* this loss, not *after* it. The speaker "stop[s] and start[s]", for the silence contains music. He descends into a "complete silence" that becomes pregnant, "magnified", "full" (FL 200) with a "stranger, eerier music from the forest"; and this seems to hold a secret (*FL* 201). The apparent oscillation and even identification between silence and sound are developed further in stanzas 6 and 7, which offer a series of paradoxes and oxymorons in an attempt to gather and grasp the experience: "stop and start", light in darkness, pouring "upwards", birth from nothing, "a screen that is no screen", and "images that cannot be imagined" (*FL* 201).

In stanzas 11–14, a section that can be seen as a *coda* for the greater poem, these oppositional, paradoxical and oxymoronic elements cohere into a composite set of images of harmony. Here, a composite image provides a key to the entire journey down into the psyche that 'Croft Woods' represents. Because of its importance, I reproduce it in full.

> Our speech is built on spirals spun of air,
> voice-pillars that support whole architectures
> of meaning on their shoulders, caryatids
> without whose weight the topless roofs of thought
> would crumble and cave in, as mountains might
> be one with valleys, on the Day of Judgement.
>
> But in the forest, mother of cathedrals,
> in starred, sky-tented glade, in cultured garden,
> in orchard, copse or grove, high moor or fen,
> curtains dividing speech and silence fall,
> and colloquies of oxygen and carbon
> counterpoint chants of plants and breaths of men.
>
> And these translucent symphonies of sap
> print negatives of speech, gaps, absences,

> unstitching and unweaving human voices
> to dim inverted echoes of our origins,
> as shimmering escarpments, cliffs and peaks
> reflect in lakes through which the abyss speaks.
>
> On still lake surfaces lie twin perspectives,
> both open simultaneously to view:
> what seems, reflected by superior light,
> and all that really lives and moves below.
> So, in the fugues of plants we trace both bright
> marks of our own world, and a more mysterious glow –
> (FL 201–202)

Here, apparently oppositional relationships occur between the following paired elements:

speaker	Croft Woods
world above	underworld
voice or speech	silence
intellect	unconscious
meaning	unmaking of meaning
civilised man	primeval man

On first reading, the latter components of these binaries would appear to be favoured, in keeping with the motif of 'welcoming' the descent into the underworld. However, a closer look reveals that a considerably more complex understanding is necessary. The initial movement of descent is clearly positive, but the implied movement away from the left half of these pairs does not involve an abandonment. The world of the woods is on the one hand outside the speaker, but on the other it also precipitates a 'deepening' into something that is universally human, reached through a search for "echoes of our origins" that have been forgotten or become hidden, like Jung's ABRAXAS. The goal is an eventual transcendence in which both the seemingly positive and negative are apprehended as one. This Heraclitan oneness defines both the poem 'Croft Woods' and the woods themselves as a "space within" the poem; and recognition of this oneness is broached precisely where "curtains dividing speech and silence fall" (FL 201), where the binary oppositions of thought are dissolved and reconciliation occurs. The language of the poem reflects that goal: the silence of the wood is also the "chant" of plants, and later the "fugues of plants"; and its darkness is also the locus in which we trace "bright /

[marks]" of the upper world. The simultaneous presence of "the chants of plants *and* breaths of men" (*FL* 201, *italics added*) creates a contrapuntal energy, whose transcendent music symbolises the journey's goal.

The section climaxes in the Heraclitan motif carried between stanzas 13 and 14, an image of simultaneous reflection and transparency – not just the cliffs seen inverted on the surface of the lake, but the world below the lake that appears through the same single surface. The movement is both downward and upward, like the expression of desire for otherness that initially frames the descent.[6] The result is a more complete understanding of the totality: what "seems" (the upper world) is now reflected off the lake-surface by "superior light", just as "all that really lives and moves below" is now visible by conscious means, moved into the 'view' of sensory perception (*FL* 202).

The lake image is visual, but the language of the passage is also careful to maintain the aural and vocal framing of the journey: silence, speech, voice and, of course, music. At this point, this music finds its way directly into the language of the poem itself. Extending from the end of stanza 13 through stanza 15, the breakthrough of this transcendent vision corresponds with a crescendo of rhymed verse. There is no consistent scheme, but a clear progression from the couplet of 13 to the fully-rhymed stanza 15. These bursts of rhyme, shifting in pattern, are functionally and thematically important throughout the poem. As points at which the music of 'Croft Woods' becomes an integral part of the poem's own creation, they strongly suggest that this imagined journey is to be seen as a direct expression of Berengarten's own poetics.

As the music of Croft Woods finds its way into the language of 'Croft Woods', so too does its paradoxical nature. As the protagonist of the poem falls into a "full" silence, Berengarten continually presents the reader with the language of paradox and oxymoron. This dialectic can be seen as a 'materialisation' of the journey itself – the woods moving *out* onto the page – but also as an appeal to the reader to escape his/her own conscious expectations of language and thought in order to descend *into* the experience of Croft Woods. More obvious and direct statements, such as stanza 8's "I am a shell without a listening child / To hear the sea in" (*FL* 200), evocative of Zen koan, are supplemented by description through

---

[6] In hindsight, it becomes clear that the initial descent has strong intimations of this double movement: before falling into the silence, the speaker expresses the desire to be "a ghost", becoming a full part of the underworld. Conversely, the underworld of the wood cries for a "release" that the tread of the speaker seems to offer (*FL* 203).

repetition with variation. Berengarten deploys different oxymoronic and paradoxical word pairings and phrases to suggest mirroring, inversion and flux. Stanza 17, the first attempt to describe the music of the underworld, is exemplary. The music is:

> …not sound, but mirrorings of sound
> an anti-music, music's twin and opposite,
> fluid in meanings, filled with coded messages
> of bodiless bodies, dry dews, airless airs. (*FL* 203)

The multiple attempts to name the sound (here, four), and the series of oxymorons that ends the stanza, are both typical of 'Croft Woods'. There are also more subtle shifts between unity and multiplicity, such as the choice of "mirrorings of sound" instead of simply 'the mirror of sound'. This movement towards a fluid possibility of multiple meanings is emphasised and expanded in the next line. Thus, in the language of the poem itself, the Heraclitan principle that "everything is in flux" is actualised, and experienced by the reader.

Traditional models in myth and epic, as in *Gilgamesh*, the *Iliad* and the *Divine Comedy*, suggest that the movement from descent to ascent is not only dialectically oppositional but also purposeful. Furthermore, the descent is a necessary precondition for the consequent progressive movement, which is 'returned to' after the task of descent has been completed. But in the 'turn' to ascent in 'Croft Woods', Berengarten is careful to maintain the emphasis on paradox and flux:

> and listening to this music is descending
> a ladder dangling in an endless void,
> to reach its end, let go, and still to tumble,
> throughout one's self until all self is blown
> like breath from dying lungs or a balloon,
> and further fall, a meteoric stone.
>
> Deeper than self entirely, made transparent,
> the dreamer enters unsleep, a new zone,
> and in so doing, *climbs*! If this is falling,
> it is a falling upwards, a dawn breaking,
> a dream undreamed, redressed, a double-waking,
> and through fear so far gone, fear is unknown. (*FL* 204–205)

Here the dream-world is made to undo itself, becoming "unsleep", yet without the dream stopping: so, paradoxically, in the very process of being dreamed, the dream itself is "undreamed". Mirroring this shift, the oxymoron of "falling upwards" maintains the descent within the new process of ascent itself.[7] Thus, in 'Croft Woods', another Heraclitan dictum is actualised: "the way up and the way down are one and the same" (1994: Fragment 108).

This Heraclitan message is enriched by the introduction of the notion of self-annihilation, introduced here through the Buddhist concept of the self blowing out (*nirvana*). This seems an appropriate elaboration: the exploration of the self culminates in dissolution of the fusion between self and other. The speaker of the poem becomes one with the world of the wood, touching the leaf to "become other", joining the "dream-cast" and himself becoming silence, "unspeaking" (*FL* 205). But, even as the speaking 'I' proclaims its otherness, identity is maintained (as in stanzas 6–10), and the voice proclaiming silence is contained within one of the poem's characteristic breaks into musicality through rhyme. Like love in the ecstatic proclamation at the end of the poem, the self simply is, even as it seems to experience its own negation, or shift into the other.

❧

The transformation wrought by the descent unlocks the poet's creative powers, as celebrated in the impassioned language of stanzas 31–33:

> And now, I have the key – of songs perpetual
> accompaniments to our own human music
>
> [...]
>
> Here is the score, and now I have the words –
> prelude, crescendo, finale, strewn from silences
> that lie behind dumb sources of the wind.
>
> This song of plants builds tuned keys for the chords,
> threads to the maze, and figures to the dance,
> scales to the stars – and scaffolds to mortality.
> These boughs and trunks are valves the underworld
> allows the dead we tread on underfoot

---

[7] Croft Woods is a fictional place. Whether the entire episode is a dream of the speaker, or the descent is a dream, or a dream within a dream, are all questions left open. Several passages that draw attention to dream and sleep states, as well as to waking or dreaming within dreams, suggest that this potential for multiple readings is intended.

to breathe a little through from atmospheres
funnelled from earthy moistures. Each porous
bulb, root, tuber is a well sprung door
hinged between death and life and keyed by dream.

[…]

blossoms and flowers, like astral telescopes,
in petalled bowls snatch impulses from stars. (*FL* 206–207)

Like the lake surface in stanzas 13–14, plants themselves are zones for the union of opposed movements, doors "hinged between death and life and keyed by dream". Berengarten's image of stars can once again be usefully contrasted with Dante's. The caesura bridged by the strong Anglo-Saxon rhyme in the line "scales to the stars – and scaffolds to mortality" exemplifies the poem's inversion of Dante's progress in *Paradiso* upward and away from the body and created matter. Berengarten embraces everywhere the material thing. A shift of perspective leads to the insight that plants not only grow 'up', but down as well. Energy from light and air is taken down into the underworld through the root structures, just as water (that originally falls from above) is taken up the roots to bloom into the leaves that absorb sunlight. The model is organic, even photosynthetic. Light is absorbed by the organic, and the result is growth – creation – coming from below and moving upward, but dependent upon a corresponding movement downward. Thus, rather than overvaluing the 'higher' at the expense of the 'lower', there is a constant two-way flow between celestial or heavenly qualities above and material and chthonic attributes below: the spiritual is cultivated both through a movement downward and a corresponding and simultaneous movement up.

Three times in this important passage Berengarten uses the symbolic word "key", familiar from *Keys to Transformation*. The double-meanings of 'unlocking a transformative experience' and 'finding the appropriate musical expression' are both intentionally in play, reminding the reader that the creative power that results from this transcendent experience has a crucial aesthetic element. The speaker who first became lost in silence has found, in that silence, "'the words'". Thus, through and as a consequence of the descent, poetry has moved 'up' into consciousness. This process may be experienced by any person but as the journey is ultimately into and through the self, the transformation here finds expression in words that are deeply personal for Berengarten – "I am at one with Keats and

Mandelstam / I am the bloodless rose inside the rose" (*FL* 205).[8] The images of the breathing dead and of the aerated earth link this creative energy with that of the wind brushing and plucking its instrument, "the usual / English lute", that the speaker has fallen away from in stanza 5. We have come full circle.

Through the descent into the psyche and a deepening of self-awareness, Berengarten seems to suggest a model by which the artist is guided by the material world itself towards the pattern and mode of its proper expression or representation.

> I touch a world inside the veins of rock
> which Michelangelo knew before he chiselled
> to dig from them his perfect Rondanini. (*FL* 205)

Here, the creation of Michelangelo's *Rondanini Pietà* is paradoxically both an act that comes from within the artist and from the material of the natural world (here, the rock). The *Rondanini* is 'his' (Michelangelo's), and it is his act of shaping that transforms it into something 'perfect', into art. But the verb and preposition in the third line are telling — it is not that Michelangelo cut or chiselled faces and forms into the material, but that he found a way to dig *out* forms already there. For the artist, then, the positive and creative movement is thus simultaneously negative, a kind of surrender to what is inherent in the material.

To borrow a term from mathematics, the compositional process here could be described as 'iterative', in that the answer to the problem emerges from continual *return to the problem itself*, using information from the 'journey' to do so. That is to say, in 'Croft Woods', the poem's pattern comes directly and 'organically' out of the 'music' of the wood itself. We see such a pattern emerging gradually, in fits and starts, through the poem's fluctuating shifts in rhythm and, more especially, rhyme. As I have suggested, the poem often breaks into moments of noticeable musicality in key sections, and this musical energy is released full-force in the poem's final three stanzas.[9] Following the poem's triumphant sum-

---

[8] In another near-contemporaneous poem, 'In the room suddenly' (*AP* 41–42), RB explores an image of 'the fullness of silence' to express the ineffability that, paradoxically, poetry can at times make material through language. In that poem, he writes: "Description fails, / For gaps in time like these defy defining", even though hope persists in the injunction to continue to struggle. 'Croft Woods' inhabits just such a "gap in time".

[9] This suggestion is furthered, I believe, by the extreme musicality and more regular rhyme attributed to the imagined speech of the woods themselves that comes in stanzas 20–23 (*FL* 203–204).

mary declaration that "love cannot grow, die, be reborn. *It is*" (*FL* 208), the poem finds final confidence in its ability to be the poetic mirror of the music of the woods. Appropriate to the theme of accepting inversion, stanzas 39 and 40 (allowing the assonance of "husks" with "fluff") are near-perfect mirrors of each other's rhyme-scheme, except for the rearrangement of the rightly named 'thorn line' (the one line in each stanza that doesn't rhyme with any other): ABCABB, AABACB. This mirroring gives way in the final stanza to rhymed couplets, which in turn culminate in the final burst of iambic pentameter: 'These voices call from zones where dews have dried / And guiding hope and love rest purified' (*FL* 209).

In the end, what makes the descent of 'Croft Woods' unique is Berengarten's scope. Although in all respects this descent involves a quest that may be called heroic, the protagonist is not portrayed as a classical demi-god or the founder-of-a-nation-to-be; for the poet, there is no privileged assertion of an eternity, basking in endless light, beyond the material world and time. Quite to the contrary – knowledge, hope, love, and poetry are all found down in the dirt, among the dead and in the dream, and must be made from what is, in all of us, always now.

References

Heraclitus. 1994. *The Complete Fragments*. (trans. William Harris). Online at: http://community.middlebury.edu/~harris/Philosophy/ heraclitus.pdf. Consulted, 1 February 2016.

Hillman, James. 1977. *Re-Visioning Psychology*. New York, NY: Harper Paperbacks.

______. 1979. *The Dream and the Underworld*. New York, NY: Harper Paperbacks.

Jung, C. G. 1963. *Septem Sermones ad Mortuos* (trans. H. G. Baynes). London: Stuart and Watkins.

A Spectacular Variety of Registers[1]

Angus Calder

Chambers, I think, for succinctness, rather than the OED: "*manage* ... v.t. to train by exercise, as a horse: to handle, to wield: to conduct: to control: to administer, be at the head of: to deal tactfully with: to husband, use sparingly (*arch.*): to contrive successfully: to have time for: to be able to cope with: to manipulate: to contrive: to bring about. – v.i. to conduct affairs: to get on, contrive to succeed."

Several of these meanings have pejorative overtones, and these echo in the neutral usage 'to administer'. In the middle of the last century, there was a drive among some writers on politics to extol the manager. James Burnham wrote an influential book, *The Managerial Revolution* (1941), which envisaged the immanent domination of the world by managers. Orwell built this theory into his nightmarish *Nineteen Eighty-Four* (1949). Yet even the milder arguments on behalf of managers failed to make their image wholesome or exciting. They were not entrepreneurs, creative heroes, or vile, but dashing buccaneers. Unlike engineers-by-degree, they did not devise great structures. Unlike engineers-by-apprenticeship, they did not create and maintain useful and lively machines. Yet no pathos attached to their role as 'contrivers'. Unlike the men at the coalfaces, whom they administered, they were not oppressed. Unlike the young women in their typing pools, they could never be seen as 'downtrodden'.

Nowadays, I suppose, the word conjures up a chap in early middle life flushed with booze in a saloon bar or brasserie, boasting about his car and making coarse suggestions to the female staff. His substantial

---

[1] *Editors' note*: The original version of this essay was published in *The London Magazine,* January 2004, as a review of the first edition of *The Manager* (*TM1*, Elliott and Thompson, 2001). In this essay, all quotations have been updated to refer to the second edition in the *Selected Writings* series (*TM*, Salt, 2008; reissued Shearsman Books, 2011).

income gives him a big suburban house in which his children begin to wonder why daddy has to make so many 'business trips', when, on expenses, he is shagging secretaries or clients or his colleagues' wives. In larger enterprises, his key tool for 'manipulating' and 'contriving' will be the alienated and alienating newspeak of modern business, transmitted by computers which infest it with their own jargon.

Let us suppose that this brute might have a soul. Many years ago, in Nairobi, I was approached by an expatriate manager who wanted me, as a teacher of literature, to comment on his poems. He had been drawn to display his soul. His poems were dreadful.

Richard Berengarten's huge poem *The Manager* is predicated on the daring idea that such a creature may not only have a soul, but have *our* soul, be archetypal man. Adam Kadmon *aka* Jordan Charles Bruno.[2] Bare-forked animal, *moyen sensuel*, he may represent us in the arenas of love, beauty and death, fear and joy. In section 88, the devil he sees in the mirror, his detestable *fratello* (*sembable, frère*), tells him to bugger off: "become your own father, i.e. Manager of Your Self.… // Inherit your own damn fatherdom" (*TM* 141).

In a cycle of a hundred poems, with three very fine detached lyrics, Berengarten takes Jordan Charles Bruno from cynically philandering middle management through marital and mental breakdown to the point where he speaks as a prophet in the *Old Testament* sense, winning past death to endorse life.

The original edition was handsomely produced, as a broader-than-usual trade paperback, and pleasantly printed (in Malta). The poem has been accumulated over decades, sections having appeared in a score of magazines and books; and the first book-length version came out in Serbo-Croat in the former Yugoslavia in 1990. On the back cover of the first edition are quotations of praise from Frank Kermode, Alan Sillitoe, Zygmunt Bauman, Elaine Feinstein – and, would you believe, *Management Today* ("challenging but rewarding read"). So why, when it first appeared late in 2001, was it not widely reviewed as the major work which it certainly is? Not Faber, nor Carcanet, nor Bloodaxe published it, but a new firm called Eliott & Thompson, specialising in fiction and prepared to take it on as a verse novel.

---

[2] The character was named for the sixteenth-century Italian philosopher, mathematician and astronomer Giordano Bruno, who was burned at the stake for heresy in 1600 (see, e.g. Francis Yates, *Giordano Bruno and the Hermetic Tradition* (University of Chicago Press, 1964).

Sillitoe claims that it is "not beyond anybody's comprehension". I don't find the storyline as clear as some seem to, but then, I have never been much good at reading novels. My own statement would be that Berengarten has pulled off the rare feat of creating an experimental poem which is at every point wholly accessible. No doubt, as his text is taken up for study in universities and schools, cribs will appear on the Internet plotting the story, and patterns of imagery and allusion will be explored in articles or learned journals. Meanwhile, having admired its components, I can repeat that none individually is baffling. When section 78, after Bruno's breakdown, presents a page cast in the wake of Finnegan:

> *Weave Die egg Nosed ass Haiku matty con Dish hunk cold Hiss tory list ness, witches dee Finders Toe cull Lucker Reel eyes Asian 'em piss pecked Yvonne* (*TM* 124)

the facing page obligingly provides the Medical Newspeak version:

> We've diagnosed a psychosomatic condition called history-lessness, which is defined as total lack of realisation and perspective

> *On...* (*TM* 125)

and a bright school student should be able to spot an interesting kind-of-pun on Witchfinders, those early psychiatric practitioners.

As these brief quotations exemplify, Berengarten uses throughout what he calls "*verse-paragraphs*" which, he has said on more than one occasion, are "related to the *verset* of French poetry" (*TM* 161).[3] They vary between two and seven lines in length and prove capable of presenting well-parodied business-speak, as in this draft of a job-ad from the Chairman of the Board for a corporate call-girl:

> 2. Hostess/Consort for international clients. Official duties to include travel/reception arrangements at Heathrow/London City/Gatwick also hotel & theatre bookings cultural/industrial visits etc. Also to provide

---

[3] *Editors' note*: For example, in a review entitled 'The Manager, a poem' on the now defunct *Terrible Work* website, Steve Spence commented: "The Manager is written in what RB calls the 'verse-paragraph', loosely based on the French verset."

3. Individualised secretarial service throughout client's GB stay accompany evenings as & when necessary offer attentive personal support entertainment hospitality etc. I have in mind… (*TM* 16)

or these declamations reminiscent of Neruda:

> shout at
> shutters brick walls drainpipes gutters. No at pavements lamp-posts shop-fronts passing cars. (*TM* 99)

> And if I were to greet you with my whole voice evolved and empty. As ready to be occupied as a cello or a hive. (*TM* 100)

– and an idiom recalling at once the King James Bible and R. M. Rilke:

> Sir. Since the living are flesh-enmeshed, the dead cry out to be heard. They paint summer rose. They groan

> Through creaking trees. They bleach the stars in dawn. They dye evening henna. They place sweet-smelling suns

> In a pot of herbs by our gate. (*TM* 108)

But the school student will be primarily struck, as I was, by lots of horribly convincing imitation of pub-speak and phone-speak, pages of evocation of suburban dystopia, most vividly in Sarfeast England, 'novelistic' or TV-esque mimicry of The Way We Live Now:

> Well Charles what'll it be. You must be bloody joking. Put a squirt of vodka in it. Hair of the dog. Hail Mary. (*TM* 10)

and from somewhere between Hardy Country and Larkinland:

> Auntie Mimi has died leaving a full freezer. Frozen bones for stock. Stews for a rainy day. Half a kilo of home-made meat-balls flavoured with oregano. Her favourite apple pie, heavily spiced with cloves. (*TM* 142)

It is famous that no other bard, not Bottrall nor Sitwell nor Bunting, has ever successfully imitated the form of Eliot's *The Waste Land*. But Berengarten here recalls the range of that poem, from Lil's pals in the pub and the typist home at teatime to voices of prophecy and adumbrations of the end of time. The cover of the first edition shows a crowd of men in suits flowing over what may be London Bridge. There are ample verbal echoes: Bruno waiting at an airport for a client; "Never upon This World had I known life had un- // leashed so many" (*TM* 88); Bruno bedding said client, a comely lady from Czechoslovakia, "the nipples on her long breasts spread out in glowing points" (*TM* 91). It is worth noting that in both these cases Eliot's pessimism is modulated towards optimism, but also that the geographical range of Berengarten's poem – from London through southern and eastern Europe to Soviet Asia – while it falls short of Ganga, largely matches that of *The Waste Land*. I catch echoes also of 'Preludes', 'Coriolan' and *Four Quartets*.

One can distinguish between poets who accept the necessary fiction of chronological, linear time, and such as Eliot who presume to work outside it. Berengarten seems, as his sequence ends, to be on the verge of Eliotic timelessness, when Bruno very explicitly holds back – he has "not surrendered – nor shall abandon – History". (*TM* 154). Most movingly, he affirms what is not transcendent over but immanent in "the grammar underlying our world's common parlances". (*TM* 152). The final post-sequence lyric evokes two tots, boy and girl, in "Hope Street", entering their future, naming themselves, one reincarnating that aunt:

> Mimi, *she says*. Mi mi. *The boy drops his stick. Stands up*. Yoshi,
> *He replies*. Yo shi. (*TM* 159)

ℰ℈

Now it is time to attempt to do justice to Berengarten's detail. He traverses a great deal of life in 142 pages of text, and does so in a spectacular variety of registers. Section 18, for instance, mimics most plausibly the voice of a master at a fee-paying school shouting on the rugby team, until the young Bruno gets the ball and produces imitations of both Devil and Soul:

> ...Yes all the way out. Fifteen seventeen. This
> must be our last chance to score. That Bruno on the wing
> can fly like an archangel. Now for God's sake don't waste it.
> Go Go Go Boy. Go.

> What in hell is he doing. He's standing gawping stock still with it.
> Two yards from their line. Not a soul within miles of him.
> He's turning around he's laughing he's twirling it in his hands.

235

> I just don't believe it. He's gone and knocked it on. Deliber-
> ately, I'd say. (*TM* 30)

Section 20 shows how Berengarten can express passion with detachment, or detachment within passion – in this case through play with internal rhyme. Bruno is involved in tender adultery:

> The fields the rivers the forests the unassailed peaks. And all the
> tarnished metaphors
>
> Are somnolent in your smile. They shimmer there, made radiant.
> Ah yes, the latitude of platitudes.
>
> The glens and the dales. The vales and the veils. And the silence
> between them. This light that nothing fails.
>
> Tell me how have you been. And how are your children. Have you
> missed me. I've missed you. You haven't. I have, you know.
>
> Yes I do know yes. Your touch is white light and you smile upon me
> the rainbow. Your naked body clothes
>
> Your naked body in glory. (*TM* 32)

Berengarten's skill with cadence should be evident from that.

The skill of satirical mimesis is more unexpected. As homunculi go, Berengarten's Sarfeastern cits and citesses are remarkably substantial. A female lecturer at Corsington Polytechnic University gives an extramural lecture on 'Linguistics for Everybody':

> The rather unwieldy, archaic Latinisms and even ha *Chomskyisms* of
> masculine-dominated linguistics, and – here, let me write it
> for you onto this slide so you can all get it off the screen and
> all just jot it straight down, I'll use this nice green marker
> I think, – is S/H/IT. (*TM* 58)

Suburban man is deserted by suburban wife. Bruno goes to comfort him:

> To Hell With Her, blurts Sam, flinging open the door. Eyes hollow,
> eyelids bloated. Am Glad The Bitch Is Gone. Far Better Orf
> Without. Ho Me, The One-Night Stud. That Creep She's Run
> Off With
>
> Is Just A Third Class Wally. (*TM* 68–69)

This is serious, as we shall see. Sam will commit suicide. And his outburst of banal demotic is framed by Bruno's allegorical car drives to and from him:

> Back via Puritan Place. Imperial Way. Exploitation Boulevard. Past Hope Street (No Entry). And, at long last, Atlanta Road. (*TM* 69)

The corporate culture of Prospect International, which employs Bruno, is evoked with measured hatred. I don't think I need to quote another deft pastiche of management jargon, just Bruno's musing after he has blown up and broken down.

> I have tried to make sense of my life…
>
> Kept spreadsheets straight. Kept the in-tray clear. Infallibly chosen the right tie. Not tying too showy a knot. Sounded neither too officious nor too forward on the phone. Skied in the Alps and The Dolomites. Toured The Rhine The Loire The Rhône. Not to mention The Ardèche. And the Isère.
>
> Invested in Hocks and Moselles of recommended vintage.
>
> (*TM* 132)

It cannot be said that Charles Bruno alias Adam Kadmon alias Cadman is a 'consistent' or 'rounded' character. Which is, I take it, part of Berengarten's point. Each in his own prison, to bring in Eliot again, experiences himself as multiple. Escaping the prison to face up to our Usness entails not 'rounded' barging but open-eyed dissolution, as far as possible, into the life around us. Well, that's how I'd put it, and I wouldn't have phrased that thought this way if I hadn't been thinking hard about Berengarten's truly remarkable poem.

REFERENCES

Burnham, James. 1941. *The Managerial Revolution: What Is Happening in the World*. New York, NY: John Day.

Chambers Dictionary. 1988. Edinburgh: W. & R. Chambers.

Eliot, T. S. 1959. *Collected Poems*. London: Faber and Faber.

Orwell, George. 1949. *Nineteen Eighty-Four*. London: Secker & Warburg.

The Manager:
Tradition and the Individual Talent

Manana Gelashvili

&

Temur Kobakhidze

In 'Tradition and the Individual Talent', T. S. Eliot wrote: "No poet, no artist of any art has his complete meaning alone. His significance, his appreciation is the appreciation of his relation to the dead poets and artists. You cannot value him alone: you must set him, for contrast and comparison among the dead" (1975: 38). Eliot's viewpoint on tradition provides a good starting point to write about Richard Berengarten, for two reasons. First, Berengarten himself has referred to his major poem *The Manager* as "at least in some sense my conscious attempt to 'answer' *The Waste Land*." (RB online[1]). This statement clearly offers a key. Second, Berengarten's understanding of tradition, which is apparent in his poems as well as his various essays and comments on poetry, appears to be in line with that of Eliot. In a conversation at his home in Cambridge in August 2006, Berengarten said that he perceived history as an unfinished sentence,[2] a comment which suggests that, in his view, individual works are not to be regarded as static but as dynamic entities, whose status and meaning constantly change as they are reinterpreted by new generations of artists.

The aim of the present essay is to study and evaluate *The Manager* by setting it within and against the modernist tradition, particularly vis-à-vis *The Waste Land*, in order to throw light on the author's "conscious

---

[1] '*The Manager*: Eliot's "influence"'. http://www.Berengarten.com/site/Eliot-influence. html (consulted 19 October 2007), hereafter RB, 'Influence'.

[2] Editors' note: an observation based on the *Kabbalah*.

attempt to 'answer'" his predecessor. Such an exploration suggests that some of the most interesting modernist influences on *The Manager* may be neither superficial nor obvious; for Berengarten's poem attempts not merely to follow and imitate the tradition, but to "make it new" (Pound 1934). Accordingly – and since we consider content and form inseparable – in what follows, we analyse some of the main themes and techniques in this work.

❧

The Manager consists of 100 sections and three that are unnumbered, which the author calls "buffer pieces" (*TM* 161). What obviously unites them is the protagonist, a middle-aged manager named Jordan Bruno, who works for a large company. On closer inspection, however, it becomes evident that the unity of the poem lies at a deeper level, and that all the pieces are wrought together by means of recurring themes, motifs and images, and interwoven into a subtly unified texture.

The poem is an attempt to render a particular set of experiences at the end of the twentieth century. The protagonist, who calls himself *Homo aspirans* as distinct from *Homo sapiens*, may well be viewed as a quest-hero – even though here the 'quest' is totally secular, and partakes of none of the Eliotic motifs of sainthood, saintliness and martyrdom. What Berengarten's protagonist is after is to "rediscover the heart's well, once-upon-a-time called Meaning" (*TM* 152). This aim involves a search for the joy lost somewhere in childhood, along with simple human understanding and sympathy.

The urban world of the poem every now and then opens out into a striking oasis: for example, in the trees that form "latticed temples", when "…the light shining on, through, across them, particle or wave, makes music" (*TM* 153). The sense of a subliminal pattern running through the work is suggested by juxtapositions: for example, the sudden yoking of various voices, fragments and allusions to the myths of the Fisher King and the Grail (*TM* 148–149); and the offsetting of realistic descriptions of the rush and bustle of a modern metropolis against the highly suggestive recurring image of "Hope Street" – at first with and later without its *"No-Entry sign"* (*TM* 69, 144, 148, 149, 159). Indeed, "Hope Street" becomes one of the poem's central symbols. Situating the poem within a modern city or metropolis is significant too; the function of the descriptive focus on half-deserted streets is to modulate attention

239

back to the hero's alienation. Indeed, dissociation of sensibility, one of Eliot's major themes, proves to be more relevant than ever here, at the end of the twentieth century.

The Manager depicts the dissociation between Bruno's public outward personality and his thinking, sensitive self. In his attempts to attain self-understanding, Berengarten's protagonist has no choice but to conduct a constant dialogue with himself, which only reveals his divided and disturbed psyche:

> When did I last see myself? Myself, did I say? Last night I looked
> in the mirror and saw a slice of cardboard. Cartoon eyes
> painted in, and all proper features. Looking really natural.
> Really relaxed. And on its forehead, printed in shiny letters,
> like a tattoo: I AM. (*TM* 140)

This inner conversation between Bruno and his *alter ego*, who ironically calls himself "His Eminence the Arch-Trickster and Sorcerer Doctor Lord Editor Me", takes place in the mirror, when the protagonist's "enantiomorph" blames him for not being "ironic *enough*" and not "[hating himself] *hard* enough". This dialogue also makes it apparent that in "hiding behind appearances", Bruno has become deeply aware of how involved and complicit he is in bourgeois society, with its materialism and betrayals (*TM* 140–141). As an insider, gradually he grows disgusted *by* being inside. But only towards the end of the poem, after he has decided to resign from his unsatisfying managerial job, does he find himself once again in "Hope Street", this time with its "houses transformed in late March sun" (*TM* 144). Only then can he become "Manager of [His] Self" (*TM* 141) – after he has resigned from his job as "Floating Manager" of "Market Advice Planning for Living And Necessity (MAPLAN)" (*TM* 145). From this point on, he apparently no longer needs to define himself "within the Current Comparatively Defined Sociopolitical Ethnomorphic Blah Blah Context!" (*TM* 141). However, before this self-realisation can take place, Bruno has to pass through many instances of lies and betrayals, "loss and despair" (*TM* 129):

> If No could change history I'd dial God and tell him my No. Hey
> You there God I'd tell him. No to this pile of rubbish. No to
> tomorrow's promises lies the same as today's. (*TM* 99)

Even so, in most cases, Bruno's revolt and irony are followed by his uncertainty as to whether either of these responses makes sense. His ironic tone and timidity, or rather, his hesitation and doubt about whether it is even worth making any attempt to break free at all, call to mind Eliot's early poem 'The Love Song of J. Alfred Prufrock'. But whereas in Eliot, futility of effort is central and Prufrock's characteristic tone is one of weary, ironic self-deprecation, Berengarten's protagonist moves in a much more positive direction:

> Do not approach. Not yet. I am still actively waiting for a call
>   on the other line...
> [...]
>
> ... I have scarcely set out.
>
> Have too much yet to do. Have not proved myself, even
>   anything. And have not surrendered – nor shall abandon –
>   History. (*TM* 154)

The "waiting for a call" mentioned here – with the constant underlying presence of the telephone as another key motif – runs as a refrain throughout the whole poem and is associated with a search for human understanding that involves at least the possibility of finding another person to communicate with. The missing person, the "you" whom Bruno "wanted to speak to" (*TM* 156), might be a friend, a loved one, or – more interestingly and significantly – even someone, an interlocutor, from the past or the future. This theme is consonant with Berengarten's view of poetry and time.

♋

In several of his texts on poetics, Berengarten cites a phrase of Octavio Paz as a key:[3] "For the first time in our history, we are contemporaries of all mankind" (*ALF, ALF1*). To this, Berengarten adds his own gloss: "'All mankind' can scarcely not include the living and the unborn – and the dead."[4] And he continues:

---

[3] *Editors' note*: This line from Paz has resonated for RB for many years, and is one of the two epigraphs to *Avebury* (1972).

[4] *Editors' note*: For RB's additional comments on the poem's "addressee", see also 'Coda 9', *BWNBC* 48), with its echoes of Mandelstam and Celan.

241

This *toi* who is 'I', who is the poem's addressee, clearly includes (incorporates, embodies) the unopened eyes of the unborn. Each response, which is a reading of the poem, and a new writing, happens in what Eliot calls an *eternal present*. It might equally well be called: an atemporal *contemporaneity* – even if that doesn't sound quite so pretty. (RB online)[5]

In this explicit reference to *Four Quartets*,[6] by arguing that new writing enters an 'eternal present', Berengarten deliberately follows in Eliot's footsteps. Indeed, Eliot's idea of the recycling of past literatures to create a modernist literature and his understanding of the historical sense,[7] which he thinks indispensable to a poet, both lie close to Berengarten's postmodern poetics. Berengarten has stated on several occasions that he thinks of himself as "a European poet who writes in English".[8] Furthermore, in his keynote speech delivered to the Conference 'Une Poétique Mondiale de la Poésie?' at the National Library in Paris,[9] by exploring the pronoun 'toi', Berengarten goes so far as to propose his basis for what he calls a "universal poetics". Paraphrasing Arthur Rimbaud's famous statement, "Je est un autre", he presents his own response, "l'autre qui est je s'appelle toi."[10] He then goes on to argue that, "ever since Sappho", indeed "ever since *Gilgamesh*", poetry has always been addressed to *toi* – i. e., to the 'you' that is both singular and intimate: *toi* not *vous* (RB, 'Pour toi'). Thus Berengarten implies that the poet's claim to universality, across both time and space, is not only linked with the irreducible singularity of the reader/ interlocutor, but is wholly dependent on such an implicit presence across and despite time. While the voice at the end of *The Manager*, calling out to and for "somebody real on the other end of the line", is wholly in character, it is also interpretable as the voice of the poet calling to and

---

[5] 'Pour toi'. http://www.Berengarten.com/site/Pour-toi.html (consulted 19 October 2007), hereafter RB, 'Pour toi'.

[6] "If all time is eternally present" ('Burnt Norton', l. 4).

[7] Consider the phrase from 'Tradition and the Individual Talent': "feeling that the whole of the literature of Europe from Homer [...] has a simultaneous existence" (Eliot 1975: 38).

[8] For example, the inside back cover of *AP* and http://www.richardBerengarten.com/ Biography.html (consulted 9 October 2007).

[9] 13 May 2002: organised by Michel Deguy, editor of *Po&sie*, Paris.

[10] In a letter to Georges Izambard dated Charleville, 13 May, 1871, Rimbaud wrote: "I is another" / "I is someone else" (Rimbaud 1966: 304–305). RB says literally: "The other [the someone else] who is called I is you [singular]."

for his singular interlocutor. "No it's not the past I'm talking about. I'm trying to talk about love" (*TM* 156).

❧

To return to other aspects of *The Manager*, one of the names – or facets – of the protagonist is "Adam Kadmon", the primordial man of the Kabbalah. He appears several times, always in simultaneous reference and ironic contrast to Bruno (*TM* 73, 76, 118); and on the third of these occasions, he is announced by the striking image: "Adam Kadmon hangs upside down in the Sistine of my skull." The protagonist's journey of self-discovery is a complex one. Moving backwards and forwards in the labyrinth of history, it is expressed, in various sections, as lost childhood (e.g. *TM* 104–107), understanding (e.g. *TM* 152–153) and joy (e.g. *TM* 155). This movement necessarily takes place through experience; and, in this process, love and sexuality are of considerable importance (*JL* 19). Bruno's abundant amorous adventures might well be viewed as his search for his lost rib embodied in a woman.

Berengarten has stated that one of his quibbles with Eliot is the earlier poet's treatment of sexuality:

> …as far as Eliot is concerned, there's the question of the treatment of sexuality and attitude to it, throughout all of Eliot's poetry. Without wanting to demean the huge achievement of his work by carrying out spurious archaeological digs back into his biography, so far as I can make out, encounters with women seem to work positively in Eliot's poems only when they're approached on a symbolic level – 'in the rose garden', as it were. As for *The Waste Land*, all the sexual contacts and encounters are unhappy, unfulfilling or depressing. I think that Eliot viewed *all* women as frightening, even terrifying. In *The Manager* I've aimed to present not just the misery and suffering attendant on sexual love – of which there's plenty around for all of us – but its funny side too, and its pleasures and joys – and even its revelations and transformative powers and effects. (RB, *JRL 1*).

Indeed, *The Manager* displays a marvellous co-existence of the tragic and comic. One of the achievements of the poem is surely its inclusiveness of lines expressing both pain, such as "Married couples tearing each others' [*sic*] hearts out" (*TM* 87), and the funny side of male/female relationships, as in "What's a woman like me to do, she said. This whole town's choc-a-bloc with fragile graduate wimps / Sporting overblown egos" (*TM* 44).

243

The poem can also oscillate swiftly between wry irony and the lyricism of lines like "As she stripped she seemed to take off everything. Including death and memory." (*TM* 31).

☙

As for Berengarten's concern with language itself as the medium of poetry, this is evident in another of his texts on poetics:

> Languages have gaps and holes and render reality imperfectly. To make a poem, a poet needs to travel through them into silence and to return through them from silence back into language: to test (tear) the boundaries between language and silence. This two-way movement between language and silence means that every poetic journey is a Heracleitan return, not a one-way flight. (*ALF*, RB online)

In *The Manager*, Berengarten's need to find adequate means of expression leads him to experiment with wider resources of language that may seem traditionally 'non-poetic'. The incorporation of snippets of TV and radio broadcasts, business jargon, a horoscope, memos, faxes, phone conversations – and many other modes of communication – involves a wide range of language registers and varieties. The overall effect is to create a kaleidoscopic picture of contemporary language use and contemporary life. Here, one can only wonder at the author's technical inventiveness and experimentation. As a result, *The Manager* encapsulates two tendencies of post-modernist poetry: on the one hand, the complexities of persona poems, where diction is character, and on the other, a modulated and discursive lyricism. Jeremy Hooker, one of the first to write on the poem, remarks that with "its linguistic versatility, and … by virtue of the [poet's] command and knowledge of words, and ability to imitate a wide range of speech forms…, the poem calls to mind James Joyce" (Hooker 2003: 115).

A related issue is the poem's allusiveness. In this respect it seems almost impossible not to mention Eliot and Pound and their techniques of recycling a wide variety of sources. However, in any discussion of poetic allusion, it is essential not only to identify the source of the allusion but also to enquire why a poet alludes and how the allusion functions in the poem. In these respects, there is an essential difference between modernist practice and that of Berengarten; and this is not simply that Eliot's and Pound's works contain more allusions than *The Manager*. In Eliot and Pound, allusions are essential to the structure of the poem and thus serve as considerably more than a means of reinforcing meaning. Similarly, in *The Manager*, allusions enrich our understanding: the more of them we recognise, the closer we come to discovering the poem's immense field of reference. On the other hand, our understanding of the poem as a whole, or any part of it, is not *crucially* dependent on deep familiarity with its sources. For example, if in Section 92 (*TM* 146) we do not catch the quotations and adaptations from Pound's *Cantos* in such lines as "The light sings eternal" (cf. Pound 1970: 24), or "Saw the blue flash of kingfishers. And the moment benedetto" (*ibid.* 31), or if we miss the allusion to *The Waste Land* in "O Lord Thou. Dresden Nagasaki Sarajevo. Burning Burning Burning" (*TM* 49) – which offers an implicit critique of two passages ('The Fire Sermon' and 'What the Thunder Said') – our understanding of the poem still feels secure and the text still has an emotionally and intellectually meaningful impact on the reader.

Here, we might well refer again to Eliot, who was the first to distinguish between two ways of deploying allusion. In 'A Note on Ezra Pound' (1918), Eliot wrote about the "deliberateness of Pound's allusions and Joyce's 'sudden' allusions", that opened "the vista … to the imagination by the lightest touch" (Eliot 1918: 5–6). Although in both cases the function of the allusion is to open a vista and thus create a hypertext, Pound's allusions (like those of Eliot himself) seem much more deliberate, in that they represent a major component of the poet's aesthetic, whereas in Berengarten (as in Joyce), 'sudden' allusion is just one among various devices. At any rate, the allusiveness of *The Manager*, for example to Blake, Eliot and Pound, certainly projects the world of the poem into a wider context. This 'enlarged' effect is further emphasised by the three buffer sections, which give the poem a philosophical or metaphysical dimension.

༄

Jeremy Hooker has rightly noted that at times Berengarten's language "…rises to the cadences and vocabulary of the Psalms and the Song of Songs" (Hooker 2003: 116). In conversation with Joanne Limburg,[11] Berengarten recollects how he came to use the verse-paragraph, with its suggestion of these models. It was when he was translating a poem by the Greek poet Nasos Vayenas, who himself had adapted it from the Byzantine Bible.

---

[11] *Editors' note*: All references to this interview are to the published text (*JL*).

Then I suddenly realised what should have been obvious all along: that Blake and Whitman had both derived their own long lines from the King James Authorised Version and Ginsberg from the Hebrew or Yiddish Bible and so on. So, curiously, it turned out that the Bible in various languages, was the key to my own long line too. (*JL* 21)

It might be said that parataxis was both a way of seeing and a mode of composing developed by modernists such as Eliot and Pound. One of the characteristics of *The Manager* is precisely its 'absence of continuity', and this even appears to be the patterning principle of the whole book. The author ascribes this partly to the way in which the poem was created: "It often seems to me that life *consists* of interruptions" (*JL* 21). Furthermore, this experience would appear to be true not only for the protagonist of this particular poem, but for modern man's general perception of the world as chaotic and fragmentary. Berengarten adds that this "absence of continuity is what patterns it [the poem] and what it is all about" (*ibid.* 21). Yet here again form reflects content: it is as if the author of *The Manager* were inviting the reader to make thousands of connections, yet without destroying the fragmentary character of the poem. The sense of complex subliminal connectedness that ensues is both the source of the particular textual pleasure in the poem and a representation of the ways in which experience, knowledge and understanding are received and absorbed by the protagonist. Probably this is the reason why Berengarten pointed out to Limburg that he had thought of publishing the poem as "a loose leaf album or as a set of unbound pages in a box" (*ibid.* 21). However, structural discontinuity does not mean that there is no movement or ordering principle in the poem. Section 92 (*TM* 146) begins: "I cannot make it cohere is what the old man said. Try though as he did through his art." Here not only the direct appropriation of the opening lines from the later *Cantos* is significant (Pound 1970: 26). For the "old man" in this passage is Ezra Pound himself. And Berengarten develops his theme by directly quoting Pound's answer to 'himself': "The light sings eternal… i.e. it coheres all right, Even if my notes do not cohere" (Pound 1970: 24, 25). These lines enable Berengarten to conclude: "There is order in being" (*TM* 146) – which, so he implies, every poet would wish to "grasp… forever", in spite of pain, despair and change.

Berengarten is well aware that the modernists' endeavour involved them in actively "[w]illing that bridges be built where none had ever existed" (*TM* 146). He has also recognised clearly that Pound's and Eliot's break from the coherent narrative and clear structure characteristic of the conventional, narrative long poem have provided him, if not exactly with a model, then at least an example and a spur for *The Manager*. Furthermore, as suggested above, despite discontinuity, the poem does move towards a positive goal – or, rather, in a positive direction. In the wake of "betrayal" and "bereavement", "[a]fter nights of panic and weeping" (*TM* 129), after the ironic parody of a crossing of "The Original River Styx" (*TM* 130), and after eventually realising that "[t]he situation is desperate" (*TM* 153) – Bruno's various ineffectual and conventional attempts "to make sense of [his] life" (*TM* 132) eventually lead to three final pieces that are filled with serenity and acceptance, regardless of how difficult life may continue to be.

A long poem written at the end of the twentieth century can hardly be expected to resolve itself into an orderly conceptual-moral scheme with a clearly defined *Inferno* and *Paradiso*. As Pound put it, he could not use "an Aquinas map: Aquinas not valid now" (Pound 1971: 323) – by which he meant that, in the anarchic modern world, any equivalent of the Dantesque journey, from darkness and despair towards light and affirmation, could be no longer be modelled on an orderly, still less hierarchically arranged, topology. The greater probability would be for paradisal and infernal elements to exist alongside each other – just as they do in *The Manager*. Even so, whilst two of the twentieth century's great epics, *The Waste Land* and *The Cantos*, are strongly in evidence throughout the poem – in its immediate background, as it were – their presences can hardly be interpreted simply in terms of 'influence'. They are present, rather, because Berengarten conducts a polemic dialogue with both these predecessors, in terms of (and by means of) the very paradigms that they have set up for the 'modern' poem. Berengarten puts this as follows: "[I]f *The Waste Land* and *Cantos* were to be taken as paradigms of the modern / modernist poem, then *The Manager* might be read as a critique of both modernity and of modernism" (RB, 'Influence').

However, Berengarten is not merely critical: it may equally well be argued that he not only grasps what is limited and problematic in Eliot, but also what becomes possible *through* him. One of Eliot's most important innovations was to find a form and expression for the complexity of the modern sensibility and the related breakdown of individual consciousness. Yet, for the post-modernist Berengarten, his 'way through' Eliot involves more than an attentive 'triggering and sparking' from the *technical* aspects of his predecessor's work – which have provided him with his means, including different voices, deploying varied speech rhythms, registering details, and assembling fragmentary elements into a coherent whole. Berengarten's directedness 'out of' Eliot towards a more 'positive' goal is clearly evident in the final unnumbered italicised section, which describes a small girl and a small boy in "Hope Street". These figures – particularly the girl, who is "[*i*]*nspecting moss and green grass blades between two slabs in the pavement*" (*TM* 159) – return us yet again to two of the central themes of the poem: the male/female relationship and the search for hope as meaning. The poem, which starts with a highly suggestive symbol of an old woman knitting our destiny, ends with yet another striking image that implies love, life and futurity. In this sense, at least, while the refined impersonality of Eliot's authority – which shaped an entire era in poetry and literary criticism – is challenged and demystified by Berengarten, *The Manager* may equally well be interpreted as a continuation of 'tradition' as Eliot himself viewed it.

References

Eliot, T. S. 1918. 'A Note on Ezra Pound' in *To-day* 4 (September): 5–6.

______. 1940. *The Waste Land and Other Poems*. London: Faber and Faber.

______. 1975. *Selected Prose of T. S. Eliot* (ed. Frank Kermode). London: Faber and Faber.

Hooker, Jeremy. 2003. 'Handling Experience', *The Swansea Review* 22: 114–118.

Limburg, Joanne. 2002. 'Human Above All: Richard Burns's *The Manager*', *Jewish Quarterly* 185 (Spring): 17–23.

Pound, Ezra. 1934. *Make It New*. London: Faber and Faber.

______. 1970. *Drafts and Fragments of Cantos CX-CXVII*. London: Faber and Faber.

______. 1971. *Selected Letters* (ed. D. D. Paige). New York, NY: New Directions.

Rimbaud, Arthur. 1966. *Complete Works: Selected Letters* (ed. and trans. Wallace Fowlie). Chicago, IL: University of Chicago Press.

Form and Redemption in *The Manager*

PATRICK QUERY

In *The Manager*, Richard Berengarten embarks on a project, the long poem, that is at once very close to his heart and one of the most difficult for a poet writing in the twentieth (or twenty-first) century. While the long poem has retained its attraction for a considerable number of contemporary poets, the structures of understanding that had sustained the composition and reception of long poems since their epic beginnings have been, if not entirely obliterated, at least rendered as tenuous and contingent in the modern world as anything else passed down from our classical forebears. There are certain key features of the epic poem that the modern long poem simply does not have at its disposal. For instance, it can hardly even posit a teleological sense of history or a hero – still less a culture – with any coherent and unified identity or shared and common myths. Still, Berengarten has had an abiding attraction to the long poem form, and his comments on the subject evince far more confidence in its worth than anxiety about its viability in the modern world: "[W]hatever one's thinking on the relative importance of 'inspiration' and 'perspiration' ('work') in the composition of a *short* poem, it's obvious that an effective long poem can't avoid being a consciously wrought, deliberately and patiently made thing, a sustained intellectual and imaginative construct, which requires complex overall design and intricate patternings" (*JLI*).[1] Given the potentially oppressive associations of 'epic' and the relative unhelpfulness of the term 'long poem', is 'lyric

---

[1] The author is grateful to RB for providing him with access to the series of unpublished typescripts that made up his interview with Joanne Limburg on *The Manager* (Dec. 2001–Jan. 2002). *Editors' note added for second edition*: The drafts of *JLI* have been collated and revised as the interview 'Managing the Art' in *International Literary Quarterly: English Writers 3* (2016) (hereafter *MTA*).

sequence' perhaps a better choice for categorising *The Manager*? Here one must proceed with caution. As his *oeuvre* affirms, Berengarten is obviously not averse to lyrical writing as such, but he has a very clear sense of its limitations: "I've never been happy with any view of poetry that suggests that production of this kind of thing [the short lyric] is the highest or most valuable thing one can aspire to: flawless gems, timeless instants out of time, mountainous moments, and so on" (*MTA*). Yet it can hardly be denied that *The Manager* is constructed of small, lyrical units; none of the one hundred numbered sections of the poem is longer than a couple of pages, and some are the very definition of lyric. Still, virtually everything else about the book's arrangement indicates that this is indeed one long work. Nowhere is the reader encouraged to think of the book as simply a collection of lyric poems on a common theme. So either *The Manager* sits in some highly ambiguous formal territory, or it has created a territory of its own. I am inclined, for reasons I will explain, to believe the latter. This essay will raise some questions about the form of *The Manager* and suggest some provisional answers to them. In the process, it may begin to be apparent that *The Manager* itself is a kind of provisional answer to some of the most vexing questions about the place of poetry in the contemporary world.

§

In a recent book about post-modernist long poems, Brian McHale (2004) argues that a common factor that draws contemporary poets to the long-poem form is a feeling of "obligation toward the difficult whole". The phrase, which McHale uses as his title, is particularly suited to begin addressing just how form creates meaning in Berengarten's own longest poem, a work that demonstrates the difficulty of wholeness but even more powerfully underscores the poet's sense of obligation toward finding it. Berengarten has stated in no uncertain terms that he feels *The Manager* to be a "specifically *post-modern* and *post-modernist*" poem (*JLI*), and virtually all of McHale's chosen descriptors for the postmodern long poem apply very well indeed to *The Manager*: for example: "a fascination with erasure and unmaking" (quoted in Reed 2005: 341), randomisation as an element of composition, sampling, and the disoriented and disorienting progress of narrative.[2] In a prototypically

---

[2] Another productive point of contact between McHale's idea of post-modernity and

250

post-modern way, *The Manager* is obsessed with lack of communication, with interruption, with absence and disconnection: from oneself, from others, from order of all kinds. Still, there are some crucial ways in which the poem departs from McHale's rubric for the postmodern long poem, even if these are admittedly more descriptive than explanatory. The most prominent is the steadfast regularity of the form of *The Manager*, which works so powerfully to counteract the post-modern tendencies toward disconnection as to suggest an altogether different intention. In claiming the poem as "post-modern", however, Berengarten also affirms that "*The Manager* might be read quite legitimately *as a critique of modernity and of modernism*" (*JLI*). What follows may suggest that the poem is also very much a critique of the vertiginous worldview generally associated with *postmodernism*.

I will now focus on some of the most important formal features of *The Manager* – the *verse-paragraph* primary among them, but also others, including the epic scale of the poem itself. All of these features work in concert to create a dominant impression of order and pattern redeeming chaos and isolation, an impression that one may observe in the way the poem treats the personal imagination, psychological disorder, the bombardment of impressions and information that one might call the postmodern situation, and the relationship between the poem and the reader. An essential paradox of *The Manager* is that the emotional subject matter of many sections – rage, lust, madness, ecstatic joy – is emphatically the kind of stuff that might be expected, as in most other post-modernist poems, to blow apart any ordering structure the poet might attempt to impose upon it. More exactly, such material would seem better suited to a far looser structure than the regular one immediately apparent in the poem. "I cannot make it cohere" – a line borrowed from Ezra Pound's 'Canto CXVI' – is not only "what the old man said" (*TM* 146) but what the speakers of the poem seem to believe; yet the strength of poetic form keeps countering with a demonstration of coherence.[3] Every section of *The Manager* owns its form, maintains it securely, at any cost, never surrendering to the tendency toward dissolution that its

RB's view of the long poem is the prominent attention they both pay to architecture as an organising but also complicating model for composition, especially in light of a line like "This is the place of my belonging. I must make it liveable" (*TM* 144). See McHale 2004: 6–17.

[3] Even the number of sections in the poem, a round one hundred, bespeaks a reassuring completeness.

material is always calling up. Virtually every thematic element of *The Manager* is contingent, shifting, negotiable, ungovernable. The form, though, is never negotiable, and from that tension emerges the special genius of the poem; and this is why Berengarten may be said to have written, against impossible odds, a great poem of hope.

⟡

The formal structure that propels *The Manager* is the *verse-paragraph*. It is perhaps the first thing one notices about the poem. A glance at any page or a flip through dozens will signal immediately that, whatever it may be about, this is a poem organised around a regular structural unit. Berengarten locates his contact with the *verse-paragraph* as coming from Greek oral poetry by way of George Seferis first, and then Nasos Vayenas (*MTA*), and from the French *verset*. He cites the verse-paragraph's adaptability for the rhythms of modern English as one of its most helpful features ('Postscript', *TM* 161). Indeed, in Berengarten's hands, the range of voices that the form is able to accommodate is one of its most remarkable features. That all the poem's voices speak through the same medium, without losing any of their idiosyncrasy, is another. This is one way in which the *verse-paragraph* performs its work of redemption in the poem, and it is a mode of redemption that is very much in keeping with Berengarten's mistrust of the lyrical impulse in isolation. The strong form of *The Manager* also redeems the personal from preciousness, from too much faith in what Berengarten calls "magic moments" (*JLI*), in which the romantic lyric tends to operate. The *verse-paragraph* is supple enough not to miss the delicate and the personal, yet structured enough to fend off both meandering and insularity. For example:

> One street on my citymap always eludes me. Though it lies in a
> zone I know. Between avenues lined with plane trees. At a house
> in that street I have to deliver a package. A box that rocks and
> rattles. Wrapped in glossy brown. Sealed with red wax and string.
> (*TM* 148)

In this paragraph, the length of the line – the whole paragraph is essentially one long line – keeps any individual sentiment from standing out; each thought is subjugated to the structure of the whole. The intensely personal note of the passage is rescued from dissolving into self-referencing interiority by the shape of the paragraph itself, which, like a

252

vessel, shapes what fills it. The note of confusion introduced by the first sentence is similarly kept from dominating by the force of the form, which keeps things moving along despite the speaker's diffidence. One is never quite sure where *The Manager* (or the Manager) is headed, but the *verse-paragraph* reassures the reader that it is headed somewhere. Indeed, this section, Ninety-Four, ends with the affirmation: "Now blessèd I backwalk / up Hope Street, alive. My cup runneth over" (*TM* 149). A beauty of form in *The Manager* is that another *verse-paragraph* is always ready to catch such emotional overflow; the poem never runs out of spaces to hold it. Thus *The Manager* literally embraces the lyric impulse, while consistently coaxing it to be something more.

This dynamic is poignantly visible, as the central consciousness of the poem descends into psychological breakdown and madness before the reader's eyes. Mental chaos beckons throughout the first seventy-five sections of the poem as the Manager's psyche threatens to slip loose from its moorings in objective reality. It climaxes in section Seventy-Eight, where language's communicative power appears to shatter into mere frag-ments of sound:

```
Weave Die egg Nosed ass Haiku matty con Dish hunk cold
    Hiss tory list ness, witches dee Finders Toe cull
    Lucker Reel eyes Asian 'em piss Pecked Yvonne
                                            (TM 124)
```

Even so, the fragmentation of an individual mind, the subject of so much modern and postmodern poetry, is not beyond redemption thanks to the formal integrity of *The Manager*, that is, the pattern of the work that shores up such ruins along with all the others over which it ranges. Here again, content mirrors form, as despair is once more denied the last word, which, in this case, is "patience" – as in "The only cure really is patience" (*TM* 125). *The Manager* earns the reader's patience even with apparent insanity, by virtue of the poem's implicit promise of a return to order; and, to be sure, love, coherence, and identification – between the speaker and the objects of his attention, between poet and reader – do prevail by the poem's end.

Individual madness is symptomatic of the general lack of logic defining the modern society the poem describes, where human communication is rarely full or effective or supported by the material world. Such difficulties in intelligibility regularly characterise the relationship between the text and the reader in post-modernist poetry, much of which, in the impenetrability of its design, wilfully defies meaningful communication (see, for instance, Armand Schwerner's *The Tablets*). Berengarten, however, has chosen a different course. *The Manager* takes great pains to invite the reader in, to establish contact in the teeth of the evidence for disconnection. One touching example is section Seventy-Eight quoted above. Even though the bizarre homophonic passages are just about decipherable with some effort, the facing page offers a translation into 'normal' speech, as if to provide a safeguard against the reader's potential alienation. The first passage briefly estranges the reader; the second extends a hand inviting him/her back in. The presence of the "Glossary of Some Foreign Words" appended to the first edition of the poem also signals a similar concern for the reader's comfort.[4] Despite its strangeness, *The Manager*, one might say, is a thoroughly hospitable poem.[5] Underscoring its magnanimity are several lines that seem to address the reader directly. Sections Ninety-Eight through One Hundred all but explicitly invite the reader into a relationship with the speaker, as in the poignant "The aeon lies torn in pieces but you shall mend it with me" (*TM* 155), and "You who sit waiting for me at the other end of my story ... // Who are you out there? I cannot scry your features. But how / infinite your patience. And how replete in acceptance your / interiorised smile" (*TM* 157). The penultimate section, in a very small space, identifies both the difficulty of contact and the necessity of striving for it:

> I've been trying to get through for ages but your line was engaged. And you know I can't say a word into an answering machine.
>
> My voice dries up. There has to be somebody real on the other end of the line. No, anybody won't do at all. It's you I wanted to speak to
>
> So I've gone on trying till now. One has to go on trying. No it's not the past I'm talking about. I'm trying to talk about love.
>
> (TM 156)

---

[4] *Editors' note*: This glossary is not included in the second edition. Instead, non-English terms are translated within more extensive page-notes.

[5] This idea may well be considered central to RB's entire poetics, as reflected in 'A little further? Twelve propositions' (*ALF, ALFI*), especially this from the second proposition: "Ancient laws of reciprocity, hospitality and magnanimity are necessary to the poetry of this time and this place too. Anything else or less is not good enough and will not serve adequately. A poet without such qualities can only be second-rate, however clever, skilled and cunning."

Trying to establish loving contact in the face of all the loss, cruelty, anxiety, and futility of the Manager's relationships evinces a hope beyond the ordinary, as does the writing of a poem like *The Manager*, which clings to the bracing power of form not as a drowning man clings to a line but rather as the rescuer does.

In all kinds of situations, the speakers of the poem seem to be fighting a losing battle against the meaninglessness of modern life; the phrase "What difference does it make" occurs in the course of at least two exchanges (*TM* 53, 122). Each of these, though, is followed by a full stop instead of a question mark: "What difference does it make." It is a striking choice that seems consistent with the poem's overall commitment, even against intense opposition, to hope. "What difference does it make" is not a real question but rather a momentary pause on the way to an answer that is made to seem inevitable by the relentless forward movement of the poem. "What difference does it make?" is the kind of question that can stop a poem, if not all creativity, effort, indeed life, in its tracks. *The Manager*, however, does not formulate this utterance as a question but rather acknowledges that the difficulty of finding meaning is to be interpreted as an obstacle. The language suggests that the difficulty has already been partly addressed by dint of the effort of searching, and moreover that it will be fully overcome within the space of the poem by the commitment to form: "So I've gone on trying till now. One has to go on trying" (*TM* 156). The reader knows that this poem will go on trying, to the end of each line and each *verse-paragraph*.

The figure doing most of the trying within the poem is its central character, the one I have been referring to as the Manager. One thing the poem does is trace this figure's efforts to manage his existence, to hold together the rebellious and at times hostile elements of his experience – jobs, relationships, memories, a barrage of sense impressions, a diffuse sense of self. Much of the poem is about what he must do "…So you can become your own father, i.e. Manager of Your Self" (*TM* 141). As I have been suggesting, the poem's form has a similar function, managing what is everywhere threatening to become unmanageable. Yet *The Manager* is about more than managing, more than simply hanging on. It is also about the deliberate search for a meaningful order that includes both life's fractious material and its capacity to support beauty and joy:

> I wish I could grasp it forever, this glory the real world inflects. I
> lose it then find it then lose it. It will not come ever again like
> this. Ever. (*TM* 146)

This is the reality with which the lyric poet must contend and which, in other contexts, can lead to despair. *The Manager*, however, can tolerate the impossibility of existing forever in such glory. Its lines extending out into the future like hope itself imply that what is lost will be found again. Its form not only fends off despair but actively seeks the redemption and wholeness of every aspect of modern experience – an endeavour as far from despair as one can imagine, yet anchored to the prosaic business of life in a way that makes the effort to try seem within the ordinary person's capacity. Whether or not things cohere when bidden, the poem, the search, will go on.

References

McHale, Brian. 2004. *The Obligation Toward the Difficult Whole: Postmodernist Long Poems*. Tuscaloosa, AL: University of Alabama Press.

Pound, Ezra. 1970. *The Cantos*. New York, NY: New Directions.

Reed, Brian. 2005. 'When All the Pieces Fail to Fit: The Puzzle of the Postmodern Long Poem', *Contemporary Literature* 46(2): 346–357.

Schwerner, Armand. 1999. *The Tablets*. Orono, ME: National Poetry Foundation.

A Reading of
Book With No Back Cover[1]

Mark Pirie

There's a side of Richard Berengarten which is pure raconteur, entertainer, and there's nowt wrong with that.

(Steve Spence, August 2003)

Can a book have no back cover? Moreover, should a book *require* a back cover, or even an end? These are the entertaining and innovative questions behind Richard Berengarten's *Book With No Back Cover*.

These questions deserve discussion, not just for the original book design and for the thinking behind the poems, but also because of the way the book brings together two 'sets' or sequences (one 'complete'), to challenge concepts and conventions of book production and writing that we often take for granted. Such an approach is not only original and peculiar to the book at hand, it is also markedly different from Berengarten's other sequences and poetic constructs, which operate in a more traditional sense; and it adds a 'newer' and postmodern dimension to his already considerable *oeuvre*. And, quite apart from its placement in this *oeuvre*, the fact that some of this book's features are interesting and unusual, and perhaps even provocative – in terms of how we think about and perceive 'the book' – suggests that it is worth opening up an exploration of these features.

These are the ideas I would like to explore, but first let us go back to my initial encounter with Richard Berengarten and his *Book With No Back Cover*.

---

[1] *Editors' note*: In the printed edition of this book (2003), the title is presented in lower case (*book with no back cover*). Since this was a designer's decision, in the current volume the title is consistently referred to as the author intended it.

℣

In March 2005, I visited England for the first time to attend the London Book Fair as a New Zealand poetry publisher (*HeadworX*). That year the London Book Fair featured Australasian publishers, and a 'Kiwi contingent' arrived in London to promote their authors and catalogues. Via email, my contact at Salt Publishing, Jen Hamilton-Emery, recommended that I meet the poet Richard Berengarten. One morning in London, I went to the Poetry Library and looked up his work. On the library shelf there, I found numerous collections of his, dating back to the 1970s. As I glanced through them, their technical skill and intellectual depth impressed me. I knew by skimming through the pages that here was a poet of considerable power and gifts, who was capable of writing poems often without the wilful obscurity of much academic poetry, and who conveyed a certain honesty and compassion about the human condition and its accompanying tragedies, i.e., war, massacres, genocides and political injustices.

I then made a point of contacting Richard when I visited Salt (which published us both) in Cambridge that month. He struck me as generous and very sociable. He enjoyed showing me his recent work and book collection, which I noted had an East European influence. We traded books and notes. He swapped two books with me, one of which happened to be *Book With No Back Cover*.

This particular book continues to intrigue me. The design is eye-catching and many visitors to my home have stopped in their tracks when I have shown them a copy. As a 'commodity', Berengarten's book is a collection of poems, no more, no less; but it also has the quality of an 'art object', and this in itself suggests that the author's intention is that the book's design and form should complement and *extend* the ideas behind the text. Charles Olson, quoting the young Robert Creeley, has stressed that "FORM IS NEVER MORE THAN AN EXTENSION OF CONTENT" (1966: 16); and Berengarten, in following this idea, opens up interesting challenges to (and questions about) the 'commodification' of the book in the market-place.

℣

I suppose you might say, before looking closely, that Berengarten's book is commonplace in its design. The book is in A5 size with the author's name and title on the cover, in black and white and, below, a quotation from the text sprawling diagonally across it. *Commonplace? Ordinary?* Hardly. On closer inspection, turning to the back cover … hold on … there is no back cover! Where are the blurb, jacket information, price and bar code? They are missing completely, and instead, the front cover repeats itself on the 'other' cover of the book. Hence the concept of a "book with no back cover", brilliantly and faithfully exploited by the designer Will Shaman for David Paul Books.

The spine is unusual too. The author's name and title repeat themselves down the spine both ways, as if mirroring each other. Inside, the part of the book you start from (depending on which way you open it) reads like an 'ordinary' poetry collection. Yet half-way through, an arrow directs the reader to turn the text upside down and begin again from the other cover. So – turning it upside down, you can read the other part of the book in the opposite direction from the one you originally started from, and again find no 'end'.

Book With No Back Cover contains one more surprise in layout: the typesetting of the 'found' poem entitled 'Code of Practice'. This piece, positioned across a double-page spread, is at the centre of the book, and bases itself on an English legal text. On the verso page, the first line is printed left to right, the second line right to left in mirror writing, the third line left to right, and so on. (This form of script, known as *boustrophedon*, occurs in some ancient Greek legal inscriptions.) The entire text mirrors itself on the facing recto page.

Here, you can sense that Berengarten is having fun and loving it. He has produced a seemingly postmodern text with 'two beginnings, a middle and no end', while at the same time pushing the boundaries of his art form, but in a very different manner to other more consistently postmodern L=A=N=G=U=A=G=E poets. To me, as a publisher, typesetter and designer, this book's design and concept extend the possibilities of what a book can look like and do.[2]

~

Readers familiar with Berengarten's recent work will also recognise the form of one of the book's halves, as well as its human and metaphysical

---

[2] In New Zealand, Scott Kendrick's *Cold Comfort Cold Concrete: Poems & Satires* (2007) has a design similar to that of RB's book, though Kendrick's book divides itself merely because it is two-books-in-one.

concerns. This part is divided into three sections: 'Sketches with Voice-overs', 'Nine Codas', and 'Code of Practice'. These poems continue a style that Berengarten developed in his earlier long poem, *The Manager* (2001). Berengarten calls this the 'verse-paragraph': a long unit, usually consisting of two to three lines of text, evolved from the models of Blake, Whitman, Ginsberg and the *verset* of modern French poets, e.g. Saint-John Perse.

For the most part, these poems consist of dreams and urban reports, and deal with observations of people and social situations. These sketches always firmly locate their central interest in the human and the meta-physical (the appearance of angels, for instance, with *Kabbalah*-like overtones). The poems are not as shocking in their subject matter as, say, the work of Peter Reading (1995, 1996), but instead become thought-provoking through the poet's incessant concern for the life around him and by way of the gradual construction of short imagistic sentences. However, one poem, number 16 from 'Sketches With Voice-Overs', a dream about Hitler (*BWNBC* 30–31), is very chilling and as graphic as any hard-hitting poem by Reading, e.g. 'Stet' (Paterson and Simic 2004: 162–164). Overall, this part of the book reveals how the world continues, regardless of awful truths and the presence of death. The sense of continuity across generations is a quintessential theme in Berengarten's work. He states in 'Coda 5': "I will speak. Yes I will. I will not, cannot be silenced. I am / responsible for this seed landed here called Human" (*BWNBC* 43). Implicitly, here Berengarten communicates a strong individual response to human tragedies, as he affirms hope and the power of the human spirit to prevail through history and over death. Berengarten, to my mind, wants the reader to be part of this commitment too: "'To Whom It May Concern' means you" (*BWNBC* 48).[3]

☙

The other 'set', under the title 'Following', features a spare, minimalist style, that connects more with the work of American poets William Carlos Williams, George Oppen, Louis Zukofsky and Robert Creeley,[4] and with Asian forms like the haiku, than with any contemporary British

---

[3] This type of inclusive address to the reader is also present in the American poet Peter Cooley's collection *A Place Made of Starlight* (2003). Cooley, however, includes the reader in his poems for different purposes to those of RB's work.

[4] Email from RB to author, August 2007. Contrast this work with the minimalism of British poets Ian Hamilton or early Hugo Williams, for example.

exponents of minimalism. In Berengarten's hand the minimal takes on a wrought and finely-tuned appearance on the page, much like the product of a sculptor who has chipped away at stone or of a gardener who has carefully removed branches from a bonsai tree. This Asian image is quite apt, in that these poems owe a great deal to Berengarten's readings of the *Yijing*,[5] and of Zen and Taoist thought. At the end of 'Following', he includes 'A Note on the Hexagrams', which relates each poem to a particular hexagram from *Yijing*. These poems also link with Heraclitus, Ungaretti and Jabès, three Western 'presences' who also appear to have had an impact on Berengarten's thinking.

A great deal of technical skill is required for the form Berengarten uses here. A good example is the poem 'Grace', which is also included in *The Blue Butterfly* (2008):

> Under the hills, quiet
> Fire. From their graves
> The dead awaken.
>
> Blessing on you
> Who live, they call
> Through our own voices,
>
> As in their places
> We too shall call
> Our own unborn.
>
> Under hills, this
> Grace flows
> Through everything.
>
> Chestnut and oak
> Bud, green
> Earth's carpet
>
> Red tulip petals
> Scatter. A blue
> Butterfly hovers. (*BWNBC* 50)

On the surface, this poem shows a refined elegance. It is carefully written. Each word counts and the style is pared of ornament. Its lean lines and

---

[5] Also known as the *Book of Changes* (*Yi Jing / I Ching*).

unforced enjambment are highly accomplished. 'Grace' is a fine example
of minimalist poetry, comparable to the best of Robert Creeley's work,
though perhaps more emotionally restricted than Creeley. Richard Ald-
ington's books of *Images* also come to mind, through the sensual appeal
of details like "chestnut", "oak bud" and "red tulip petals". To me, 'Grace'
is a poem of celebration for the living and for the dead. The poet refuses
to give an inch to mortality, wishing humanity to live on in song, in
poetry, in defiance of death. This recurrent theme in Berengarten's work
is no better expressed than here, in this new minimalist mode.

At times, these poems can read like small blessings and prayers: for
the living ('Lara's garden in August': 30); for migrants and the exiled
('Gathering' and 'Return': 24–28); for the massacred dead ('Grace': 50);
for the dying ('For Natalie, dying': 34); and for the natural world ('Thanks
to the wind' and 'Two lakes': 37, 38, and 'In Light/In Fire': 49). The fact
that Berengarten dedicates 'Following' to the memory of a friend, John
Blackwood, a Buddhist poet and contemporary from his student days,
also confirms the theme of a metaphysical continuum.[6] Even the blurb
consolidates the idea of continuity: "This is a book that flows in waves. It
cannot be concluded, only continued."

⇝

Book With No Back Cover differentiates Berengarten from poets who
have attempted to remove the personal voice from their poetry and the
metaphysical from their worldview. Instead, he shows how a poet can
combine metaphysical themes with postmodern forms of design and
thought; and in doing so, he urges the reader to be a part of what makes
and shapes the world we live in: "The label on the package / 'To Whom
It May Concern' means you" (*BWNBC* 48).

This passage, from 'Coda 9', is repeated in slanting lettering on
the cover that-cannot-be-a-back-cover. Berengarten has stated that his
readings of Mandelstam in the 1970s "transformed some of [his] ways of
thinking". The following passage, Berengarten states, holds the key both
to this 'Coda' and to the structure, meaning and coherence of the entire
book.[7]

[6] Email from RB to author, November 2007.
[7] Email from RB to author, August 2007.

262

Everybody has friends. Why doesn't the poet turn to his friends, to those people who are naturally close to him? The shipwrecked sailor throws a sealed bottle into the sea at a critical moment, and it has his name in it and what happened to him. Many years later, walking along the dunes, I find it in the sand, I read the letter, I learn when it happened, the testament of the deceased. I had a right to do this. I did not unseal someone else's letter. The letter sealed in the bottle was addressed to its finder. I found it. That means, then, that I am its secret addressee. (Mandelstam 1977: 60)

‽

Perhaps the only drawback is that some parts of the book give the impression of being experiments lifted from the poet's notebook. Steve Spence (2003) has suggested that some of these poems consist of 'residual' material from *The Manager* and some of the 'Sketches with Voice-overs' do read like out-takes from that book; while the minimal poems based on *Yi Jing* are not as compelling as Berengarten's earlier Olsonian 'field form' work in *Avebury* (1972). Nevertheless, the sequence of powerful 'codas' creates cohesion, even though the presence of 'codas' might seem an irony in a book with 'no end' and 'no back cover'.

Yet overall, the experiment of making his book with no back cover adds an extra dimension to Berengarten's central themes and *oeuvre*. It shows him to be a versatile poet capable of adapting contemporary post-modernist theories and practices as well as traditional forms, and subverting them not only in telling and thought-provoking ways, but also in a highly enjoyable and entertaining manner. *For the Living* (2004) also displays the rich adaptability Berengarten is capable of as a poet. From the earlier 'Avebury' (1972) to the tight villanelles of 'Black Light' (1983), Berengarten has always shown that his range as poet is vast and his technique accomplished. His excursion into the *Yi Jing* in *Book With No Back Cover* is similarly well wrought and skilled.

Berengarten has spoken against those who try to remove the heart from poetry, the human and personal from the poem, and the metaphysical from the poem's life.[8] In contrast, he would prefer to retain these qualities as central to the celebration of the world we find ourselves in, particularly at the beginning of the twenty-first century when we face many uncertainties in urban life, many 'an inconvenient truth' (as Al

---

[8] In 'A Little Further?' (*ALF, ALF1*), paragraph 9: "Who wants a heartless poetry?"

263

Gore puts it in his film of that title), as well as terrorism and human conflict. Berengarten's poetry shows commitment to the 'big' global issues around us, as it confronts, and deals with, issues that some readers and writers would choose to escape from.[9]

Book With No Back Cover offers a rewarding and innovative presentation of theoretical concepts that are carried into the book's design. The book is invigorating in its technique that both reflects and embodies its content. Its innovative nature and the challenges it makes to conventional ideas of 'the book' mean that it occupies a highly original and even a unique position in contemporary British poetry. *Book With No Back Cover* is a book we could all do well to complete.

> [The book] was meant specially
> for you, being the one who found it.
>
> This voice, no longer mine, is yours now. Take it, use it. Give it
> your own, far finer sound.
>
> In hearing these words, rewrite yourself. Having no back cover,
> now the book is yours to complete. (*BWNBC* 48).

References

Aldington, Richard. 1948. *The Complete Poems*. London: Allan Wingate.

Cooley, Peter. 2003. *A Place Made of Starlight*. Pittsburgh, PA: Carnegie Mellon University Press.

Creeley, Robert. 1991. *Selected Poems 1945–1990*. London and New York, NY: Marion Boyars.

Kendrick, Scott. 2007. *Cold Comfort Cold Concrete: Poems & Satires*. Wellington: Seraph Press.

---

[9] On his website, RB lists the influences behind the book's conception. Despite his Cambridge background, and apart from his citing of T. S. Eliot, these are not typical or traditional influences for a British poet: Osip Mandelstam, Borges, Paul Celan, Edmond Jabès and Nasos Vayenas. The website also lists his twin central themes in *BWNBC* as: "first, that no book has an end; and, second, that all books are part of the one *Book Without End....* Furthermore, *Book With No Back Cover* challenges notions of linear, 'progressive', 'developmental' time, as well as Aristotle's prescription in *The Poetics* about the need for 'a beginning, a middle and an end'..." (http://www.berengarten.com/ site/BWNBC.html).

Mandelstam, Osip. 1977. *Selected Essays* (trans. Sidney Monas). Austin, TX: University of Texas Press.

Olson, Charles. 1966. *Selected Writings.* New York, NY: New Directions.

Paterson, Don and Simic, Charles (eds). 2004. *New British Poetry*, St. Paul, MN: Graywolf Press.

Reading, Peter. 1995. *Collected Poems 1*. Newcastle upon Tyne: Bloodaxe Books.

______. 1996. *Collected Poems 2*. Newcastle upon Tyne: Bloodaxe Books.

Spence, Steve. 2003. '*Book With No Back Cover* by Richard Burns', *Terrible Work*. Online publication. Consulted, 16 August, 2007. No longer available.

Cross-cultural Numerology and Translingual Poetics: Chinese Influences on the Poetry of Richard Berengarten

CHEE LAY TAN

The Chinese language has a highly visual term to express the idea of 'maxim': *Zuo you ming* [座右铭]. This literally means the inscriptions 'on the right of the seat'; that is, written maxims which, positioned where an ancient Chinese scholar would sit, were meant both to remind him constantly of correct principles and to guide him accordingly. The first pages of the sequence entitled 'Following' in Richard Berengarten's *Book With No Back Cover* show calligraphed Chinese characters standing out prominently in the top right corner (*BWNBC* 13–51), just as if inscriptions of traditional Chinese maxims were being brought to bear on the text of a modern English book of poems. Not only do these Chinese characters remind readers of the influence of Chinese culture on Berengarten's poetry, they actually serve as a thematic guide to understanding his poetic texts themselves.

That these Chinese characters are actually the names of hexagrams from the *Book of Changes* [*Yi Jing* 易经], one of the oldest and most influential Chinese philosophical texts, reveals the philosophical outlook and inclination of Berengarten's poetic impulse. In the *Book of Changes*, the hexagram denotes the underlying structure of each of the sixty-four pictograms that constitute the book, and each hexagram is made up of two sets of three broken or continuous lines (trigrams). The many variations and permutations of these figures (384 in all, i.e., 64 × 6) are used to represent patterns that can emerge, shift and develop in a person's life, that is, in the world of events. More than being a source of inspiration, the *Book of Changes* has been 'followed' by Berengarten, as attested in the titles of this sequence itself. I believe 'following' here refers to his pupillage to the book in terms of its philosophical and structural patterning, and even its oracular teaching. Berengarten confirms such pupillage in his response to my enquiry: "*I Ching* [*Yi Jing*] is one of the VERY GREAT BOOKS of the world [...]. I have been a student of this book for the last 44 years."[1]

In this essay, I shall attempt to examine the cross-cultural poetics and philosophies apparent in the sequence 'Following' in Berengarten's *Book With No Back Cover*, in so far as these are evoked by his 'following' of 'maxims' from the *Book of Changes*. Furthermore, I will also look at Berengarten's poetic language and forms from the perspective of translation, since the process of translating some of these poems into Chinese has been an extremely challenging and rewarding one for me – as both translator and poet. Within my focus on translingual poetics and cross-cultural philosophical influences, Berengarten's many references to the numerological patterns and formal structures so crucial to the *Book of Changes* stand out as major and critical aspects – and in what follows I shall be emphasising them too. In addition to the *Book of Changes* in Chinese, the version consulted and quoted here will be the translation by Richard Wilhelm (1873–1930) (Wilhelm 1951),[2] which is also the version Berengarten prefers to use.[3]

༄

In the Foreword to Richard Wilhelm's book, the renowned psychologist Carl Gustav Jung (1875–1961) performed a highly intriguing experiment by asking the *Book of Changes* to deliver an oracular judgement on its own situation in being presented to Western readers in the form of Wilhelm's translation, accompanied by Jung's own introduction (Wilhelm 1951: i–xx). I do not intend to discuss the details or the validity of Jung's experiment here, but among the concepts he highlights, some appear to be highly reflective of how an educated Western reader is likely to perceive and utilise this Chinese classic – and hence, Jung's theory may

---

[1] Letter to author from RB, 3 October 2007.

[2] In fact, a 'double translation' is involved here: Wilhelm translated the Chinese text into German, whose English version was rendered by Cary F. Baynes. This translation is commonly referred to as the Wilhelm-Baynes version.

[3] Letter to author from RB, 3 October 2007.

be highly illuminating when we try to decipher how the *Book of Changes*, in turn, influences Berengarten.[4]

One of the main concepts that Jung ascribes to the *Book of Changes* is 'synchronicity', which, as he defines it, "takes the coincidence of events in space and time as meaning something more than mere chance, namely, a peculiar interdependence of objective events among themselves as well as with the subjective (psychic) states of the observer or observers" (*ibid.* iv). Although there is an unmistakably psychoanalytical overtone in Jung's definition, the concepts of interdependence, synchronicity, and even the tendency to harmonisation that he implies, actually run deep in Chinese tradition and cultural consciousness, and nowhere more so than in traditional Chinese poetics. The renowned Chinese scholar Pauline Yu has proclaimed that "implicit throughout the *Great Commentary*, as in the *Great Preface to the Classic of Poetry*, is the assumption of a seamless connection" (Yu 1987: 38–40). Such an interdependent and closely-linked relationship among many different aspects and elements of poetry, including images, subjects and objects, and even events, bears close resemblance to the 'synchronicity' which Jung brilliantly pinpointed.

Some of the more notable manifestations of the concept of 'synchronicity' in Berengarten's *Book With No Back Cover* occur in a poem entitled 'The Nonplussed Pleasures of Love':

And then to the sheer

Facts of my breath, of you
And me improbably being
Both here, together, alive. Is

Death the condition without
Which such a life would be
Unacceptable? (*BWNBC* 16)[5]

Grouped under the ninth Hexagram, *Xiao Chu* 小畜 (represented as ䷈ 'The Taming Power of the Small', and interpreted by Berengarten in his book under the heading 'An Acceptable Condition'), this poem

---

[4] RB's direct interest in other aspects of Jung's work, apart from the theory of synchronicity, is apparent both from the symbolist dimensions of many of his earlier poems, for example, 'The Rose of Sharon' (1973, collected in *FL* [91–96]), and from his monograph *Keys to Transformation* (*KT*).

[5] All quotations from *BWNBC* in this essay are from the section entitled 'Following'.

delicately offers at least three readings that may be considered concurrent, alternative, or even intertwined. The first of these suggests, quite simply, that the protagonist ("I") is dedicating the poem to his living companion or partner ("you"), who lives (is "alive") with and alongside him, in that they share their lives together ("Both here, together, alive"). Such a reading, then, would suggest that the poem has to do with *contemporaneity* and *communality*, and that it expresses gratitude for life, love and companionship, which it proudly, even defiantly, celebrates "in the face of death". Yet, simultaneously (of course, we can also think of it as 'synchronically'), the poem may equally well be interpreted in two further ways. In one of these, the voice of the living poet ("I") addresses the living reader ("you"); and, even though the poet himself may be dead by the time the poem reaches the reader, both are inevitably "here, together, alive" within, around and through the poetic text – by very virtue of the reader reading it. In this light, the poetic text has become the world of co-existence, concurrently, for both the poet and the reader. Thirdly, the poem may be read as portraying the subtle feelings of an implausible love between a living protagonist ("I") and a dead person ("you").

Interestingly, each one of these interpretations manifests a variant form of love and faith that possesses great "taming power" over the protagonist, the poet, or even death. And herein resides Berengarten's polysemous, multi-layered interpretation of the hexagram, 'The Taming Power of the Small', which fundamentally acknowledges the force of "the shadowy – that restrains, tames, impedes", as explicated by Wilhelm (1951: 41).

Besides following the overarching philosophical significance ascribed to '*Xiao Chu*', this poem also portrays Berengarten's take on the temporal and spatial concept of 'synchronicity' as he imagines the interdependence of I/you, life/death, and human/creature, and does so in such a way that the movement of time is not viewed as a one-way flow from the past to the future. For in this poem, such conventional perspectives on linear time are 'interlaced' by a form of communication (that of the poem itself) that cuts *through* and *across* them in (at least) three 'lanes' (or 'lines'). And insofar as it cuts through and across linear time, it also cuts through (and across) life and death. Thus, in Berengarten's poetics, it might be argued that the function of poetry, at least in part, is not only to query and challenge received ideas about the flow of time (as 'linear', 'historical', 'chronological' etc.) and mortality (that life and death must be mutually exclusive, etc.), but also to offer alternative perspectives through which events in the past, present and future may co-exist 'synchronically'. In fact, the symmetrical visual patterning and tight dialectical structure of *Book With No Back Cover* represent a defiance (and a criticism) of the Aristotelian notion (in his *Poetics*) that a book should have "a beginning, a middle and an end". A 'book with no back cover', by definition, can have no end. In such a book, linear time is countermanded and complemented in an invitation to play with 'other' modes of thinking and of connecting phenomena. Implicit in this defiance and criticism of linear time are, of course, the ideas of recursiveness, circularity and return that characterise the *Book of Changes* and the theory of synchronicity.

In this poem, it is quite palpable that a reader's concurrent (co-occurring) readings may point to a kind of 'synchronisation', that can indeed be derived from Berengarten's lines: for example, my memories of you are dependent on your absence or death, just as yours are on mine; so that any 'acceptable' life or mode of living must eventually come to be seen as dependent on the "condition" of death. When the dichotomies of I/you and life/death are not only juxtaposed, but emphasised in terms of mutual interdependence instead of difference, their coexistence becomes obligatory instead of coincidental.

Furthermore, such a philosophical connotation of the interdependence of life and death in Berengarten's poetry is reminiscent of the Buddhist perception that life and death constitute but one continuous cycle (and hence the two conditions are not mutually exclusive but interdependent). And this mutual I/you reliance is also parallel to the Taoist understanding of Yin and Yang – in every Yin (black), Yang (white) exists, and vice versa, as illustrated by the white/black dot in the larger portion of black/white respectively in the Taoist *Taiji tu* (literally, 'Diagram of the Supreme Ultimate') ☯.[6]

Another overarching concept inherent in the *Book of Changes* is transition – referring to the continuous changes or flow of *Qi* (literally 'air', but connoting 'energy') for the compositions of living and non-living things, and the interactions between them. In the *Book of Changes*, it is

---

[6] The *Taiji tu* is the visual symbol which best represents the twinned principles of *yin* and *yang* in Taoist philosophy, with the outer circle symbolising the entirety of perceivable phenomena, while the black and white portions within represent the interactions of the two main principles in the world, *yin* (black) and *yang* (white). Furthermore, each contains a smaller circle or element of the other, which shows that neither can exist without the other. In correspondence with me, RB has confirmed that he has read a considerable number of Taoist works over the last forty years, and has been strongly influenced by them.

held that such constant transformations or adjustments help to maintain the fine balance and harmony in the world. In Berengarten's book, his portrayals of transition take the forms of changes both as described by the text, and as changes in it. For instance, in the opening poem, 'Following' [随 ䷐], the "I" speaks to the "poems" and hopes that they will last and endure after "Death":

Throw away your
Craft, your tricks,

Your techniques, all
You have learned. I'm
Following your directions,

So when Death blows or calls
Me or anyone out, you
Will pass, last, endure. (*BWNBC* 13)

Here again, multiple interpretations co-occur, combining and recombining. Firstly, the "I" may be read as the 'voice of the poet' as he directly addresses his poems – this poem's addressees being his poems themselves ("you" in the plural), to whom the poet issues commands. It might be argued that the very fact that the poet speaks to his poems in this way implies that they are being treated as if they were sentient beings. Secondly, the "I" may be taken to be the voice of the poem (*this* poem) itself. Thus it may be construed that, here, this poem is speaking to other poems, as if in communication, through and 'by means of' poets and readers.[7] Thirdly, we may even think that the singular voice of "I" is speaking from the point of view of one poem, and that it is 'addressing' the poetics of its creator, the poet. Hence "you" becomes the encompassing pronoun for all the "craft", "tricks" and "techniques" that form the poetics of the poet. Ergo the poet hopes that his poetics in all its aspects (philosophical, linguistic and imaginative) will "last" and "endure", even if any one of his poems is somehow overlooked or lost in time (as if undergoing a metaphorical "death").

Furthermore, the complex pattern of transformations or changes as articulated by these addressed poems involves the throwing away of craft, tricks and techniques, which, as already suggested above, can also be

---

[7] The idea that 'poem addresses poem' across time is of course one way of defining tradition.

regarded as a transformation in the poet's perceptions of, and desires for, his own works. That the poet 'follows the poem's directions', instead of the poem following its creator's discretion, is yet another transformation in the writer/writing relationship. Finally, the passing, lasting and enduring of the poem (normally perceived to be completed and unchanged after it has been written) together signal that the poem is consistently evolving, in order to survive and be passed down from generation to generation. This idea of constant adjustment to suit all times has often been deployed to describe Confucius, who is called *sheng zhi shi zhe* [圣之时者] – meaning that he is the holy person of all eras, because his teachings and words have withstood the test of time and have been able to adjust to change, to speak to and for people in different eras and, in so doing, to evolve.

It is clear too that most, if not all, of Berengarten's poems written under the influence of these Chinese hexagrams also follow the interpretations of the hexagrams themselves, as phrases set down in the *Book of Changes*. One of the most prominent examples in *Book With No Back Cover* is inspired by the hexagram in the *Book of Changes*, *Dui* 兑 (䷹, 'The Joyous, Lake', or as Berengarten has interpreted it, 'Two Lakes'):

> Two lakes, joined
> One above the other
> Along the same river:
>
> Upstream, The Hayden
> And, below,
> The Ladybower.
>
> When two lakes join
> Together they
> Do not dry up.
>
> [...]
>
> Joyousness:
> Two lakes, joined,
> One above the other. (*BWNBC* 38)

The *Dui* hexagram, as elucidated in the *Book of Changes*, symbolises one smiling lake resting on another, which is why the hexagram's attribute is joyousness. Berengarten's depiction of two scenic lakes (or, strictly speaking, reservoirs) in the Peak District of Derbyshire, England – the

Hayden (Howden) and the Ladybower – appears to constitute a true physical manifestation, indeed, a fully realised embodiment, of the imaginary textual descriptions of our ancient Chinese classic, as the River Derwent joins the one lake in the north with the other in the south: "Two lakes, joined, / One above the other / Along the same river".

Furthermore, from the 'Judgement' and the explanation of the image (or hexagram) provided in the *Book of Changes*, the hexagram is interpreted as "true joy" which "rests on firmness and strength within, manifesting itself outwardly as yielding and gentle". The text continues: "Lakes resting one on the other: The image of THE JOYOUS … the superior man joins with his friends" (Wilhelm 1951: 238–239). Berengarten's interpretation, which suggests that 'unity means strength' ("together they / Do not dry up"), is certainly a reflection both of the 'image of THE JOYOUS' and of 'strength'. Additionally, his image of the river flowing between the two lakes projects a situation and a context in which transitions take place all the time, enabling an ideal state of constant harmony to be maintained.

℘

Two of the most striking Chinese-influenced aspects of Berengarten's poetry are numbers and highly patterned forms, which in fact are so closely related that they can be considered under the single broader category of numerological patterning. Berengarten is well aware that numbers and their manifestations are abundant in the *Book of Changes*, such as: the *Bagua* 八卦 (eight trigrams, normally drawn around the *Taiji tu* mentioned above); the sixty-four hexagrams; the numbers represented by the trigrams; and the six solid or broken lines of the individual hexagram. It is therefore hardly surprising that he utilises these numerical elements and their combinations effectively in these poems.

Firstly, all his Chinese-inspired poems gathered under the heading of 'Following' have six short stanzas, so that they correspond to the six-line structure of each of the sixty-four hexagrams in the *Book of Changes*. That is, every poem has six stanzas, each 'representing' and 'embodying' one line of the hexagram mimetically. Furthermore, each stanza contains three lines, so that it corresponds to the *Book of Changes*' smaller unit of signification, the three-lined trigram: in this way, each stanza manifests

273

the motif of a 'core' trigram.[8] Besides these deliberate efforts to emulate the *Book of Changes* in terms of form, almost all the poetic lines are trimmed short (often by enjambments) and are rather uniform in length, very much like the individual solid or broken lines in a hexagram. Their brevity also hints at another Eastern source – the patterning of Japanese haiku, which Berengarten describes as "a separate though connected influence".[9] Some poetic lines have a comma or a full-stop to break the line somewhere in the middle, and these punctuation marks make such lines further resemble the broken (*yin*) lines of a hexagram, not only in terms of visual appearance, but also as temporal and syntactic breaks. Below is a good example that shows the structure and short lines inspired by the image of the hexagram itself. It is the last poem in the sequence, which operates as a kind of *Envoi*, or concluding stanza:[10]

> May this work
> Move on
> Its winding way
>
> And these words
> Hold well together
> and, in their time
>
> Wherever they
> Carry, hold
> Constant
>
> At all points
> On this narrow strip
> Between blindness
>
> And sight, pain
> And joy, water
> And water, stardust

[8] My observation was later confirmed in a letter from RB, 3 October 2007.

[9] *Ibid.*

[10] In fact, this poem can also be regarded as the beginning of RB's forthcoming project. According to his email to me on 3 Oct 2007, the sequence 'Following' will be the "taking off point" for his future Chinese-influenced book that will contain 384 poems (64 hexagrams times six variant interpretations = 384 readings). The book will be based on his readings of the *Book of Changes*.

And earthdust
Void and air
Fire and fire (*BWNBC* 51)

'*Da Chu*' 大畜 (䷙ 'The Taming Power of the Great', or as Berengarten's interpretation, 'Still and On').

The layout and structure of this poem are highly reflective of the numerological patterning of a hexagram, with six stanzas, each composed of three very short and uniform lines. In fact, the maximum number of words per line in 'Still and On' is only four, while the minimum is actually one.

Moreover, the utilisation of the technique of enjambment is not only immediately apparent (for example "May this work / Move on / Its winding way"), but also highly effective in achieving three objectives: firstly, to keep the sentence uniformly short so as to correspond to the visual image of the lines of a hexagram; secondly, to inject an element of surprise (for instance by the juxtaposition of antitheses, such as "Between blindness // And sight, pain / And joy"); and finally, to modify clichés or patternings that have been become too predictable, rigidified or conventionalised. For instance, Berengarten breaks the conjunction into "water / And water" in different lines, but later connects the images of fire as "Fire and fire" in the same final line. His semantic connection and syntactic enjambment of stardust and earthdust ("stardust // And earthdust") project a refreshing element of surprise, without appearing awkward or forced.

Furthermore, it might be suggested that in interpreting this twenty-sixth hexagram *Da Chu* as 'Still and On', Berengarten is adopting precisely the kind of structural parallelism that underpins the dialectical world-view that has gone into the evolution of the *Book of Changes* by means of accretion and refinement over the centuries. Here are the six pairings of images present in the last lines of the poem, set out symmetrically:

blindness	and	sight
pain	and	joy
water	and	water
stardust	and	earthdust
void	and	air
fire	and	fire

Here, each paired unit contains either an opposition or an equalisation. Not only do such structural parallelisms constitute a form of numerological patterning in their own right, but they may also help in deciphering the poem's underlying signification. Indeed, they might be said to portray a kind of 'aesthetics of symmetry' and, in so doing, to project a 'recurring rhythm' into words/images, concepts/ideas and events/phenomena.

℘

Besides consulting the *Book of Changes* on a 'personal' level – that is, with regard to daily actions and events – Berengarten has also found himself consulting the book when actually composing poems, with regard to the theme, the poem itself, and the puzzles or uncertainties of composition. In Berengarten's words:

> *I Ching* [*Yi Jing*] has often helped me to articulate poems in a way that I think is correct and appropriate … my own belief is that this also means that these poems enter a 'mode of being' and a 'form' that are not merely rooted in my own subjectivity and opinions, but in a 'wider' / 'deeper' / 'higher' ('trans-subjective', 'intersubjective') field.[11]

Possibly because the poems' "mode of being" and "form" are rooted in a more profound and multi-subjectival field, Berengarten's poems are not easy to translate. At the outset, however, they can appear to be deceptively easy, thanks to Berengarten's unadorned language and his consciously articulated intention to achieve "clarity of thought and image by simple diction uncluttered by conventional tropes or devices" ('Statement for *Love and Justice*', 2002–2003; hereafter *SLJ*).[12] But once a translator delves further into the "wider, deeper and higher" field which encompasses the poem, it is easy to get lost.

Let me illustrate from my experience of translating Berengarten's poems (some of which have been published online and in the printed anthology of *PoetrySky*.com (*PS*), and *Singapore Chinese Daily, Lianhe Zaobao*). Berengarten is expert at word games, as we shall shortly see; and the new syntax that emerges from his linguistic experiments, combined with the reinvigorating of clichés to inject the element of surprise,[13] can

---

[11] Letter from RB to author, 3 October 2007.

[12] Provided by RB to author, 3 October 2007.

[13] Incidentally, in an email to me (19 November 2007), RB commented that this theme of "the reinvigorating of clichés" has always been one of his preoccupations. He believes

276

make the translation process difficult and laborious. As a result, it is not always possible to convey the puns, ambiguities, multifaceted meanings and other linguistic strophes of the source language. In particular, many of Berengarten's line endings deliberately avoid natural breath pauses or syntactic pauses, hence forcing two or more lines to be joined in the process of reading and comprehension. Conversely, Berengarten also introduces full-stops or commas into a single line in order purposely to break the line, and so force a pause in reading and decipherment. Such forced alterations to rhythms and syntax make it difficult for the translator to follow the positioning of equivalent phrases, let alone render them. The above-quoted poem, *Da Chu*, serves as a case in point to demonstrate Berengarten's use of enjambment both to break and to join up his poetic lines.

I shall further refer to my attempt at translating Berengarten's 'Untouchable Miraculous Air':[14]

    Air keeps spilling
    Out of this world
    Onto death, almost

    As if it were water
    From a leaking tap and
    Time were the wooden

    Floor it dripped and spilled
    Onto and soaked through
    And trickled between planks

    To puddle and pool in down
    In cellars and stream through
    Soil onto impermeable
    Rock. Since this un-
    Touchable miraculous
    Air that slips through my

it was first expressed in an early poem entitled 'To Another…' (1973), which serves as a parody and riposte to Yvor Winters' poem, 'To a Young Writer' (1930). Winters' poem contains this advice: "Write little. Do it well" and RB's response in 'To Another…' is: "Good poets should evade / Cliché, that master taught. / A lie: he was afraid, / And the worm gnawed his thought. // Stone cold, his dream, for what's / Without flaw or splinters./ *Redeem* cliché. Write lots. / And to hell with winters." See *LT* 25, and also Winters (1952: 73).

[14] My translation is published in the online poetry journal *PoetrySky* (*PS*).

Lungs will suddenly be
Taken from me, I drink it
All the more joyfully. (*BWNBC* 18)

Firstly, we notice that the common expression in line two ("Out of this world") carries polysemous significations which are, at best, cumbersome to translate, and, at worst, impossible to convey in their entirety in translation. This phrase's richness in meaning ensures that it can refer to one or all of the following connotations: 'uncommon', 'wonderful', and 'divine'. Furthermore, linked with the metaphorical 'spilling of air', this common expression makes the overall hermeneutics even richer and, hence, more profoundly complicated. As such, it becomes almost impossible to translate its full breadth of meanings and connotations into Chinese. In order to achieve a smoother flow in the movement of the poem, in my translation I decided on the phrase *cong zhe shijie yichu* [从这世界溢] which manages to convey no more than the literal meaning of 'spilling out of the world', with a tint of joyous or positive signification inherent in the word *yi* 溢 ['overflow']. This somewhat imperfect translational experiment reflects that Berengarten's syntactic patternings are indeed a constant challenge for any translator, and in fact, for any serious reader of poetry.

As another example to illustrate this point, we can return to the earlier poem 'Still and On'. Besides the denotation of 'continuing activity', the word "still" in the title could also be interpreted as 'motionless', which is an absolute contradiction of the first meaning. If "still" is indeed taken as 'motionless', then it actually becomes the direct opposite of the subsequent word 'on' in the title. Correspondingly, the six pairs of images (which were listed above), through structural parallelism, may also correspond to 'motionlessness' and 'continuity' respectively. In other words, "still" or 'motionless' corresponds to the first images of the pairs (i.e., "blindness", "pain", still "water", "stardust", "void" and still "fire"), whereas "on" or 'continuous flowing' (also linked to the concept of 'transition') corresponds to the second images of the pairs (i.e., "sight", "joy", flowing "water", "earthdust", "air" and spreading "fire"). The translation of this title, because of such polysemous, even contradictory, significations, becomes a most testing task. I have chosen to use *Duan·Xu* 断 · 续 ('Still / Discontinue-On / Continue') as its Chinese title, because this phrase, in my perception, encompasses the meanings of both 'motionlessness' and 'continuity' that are present in the English word 'still'. *Duanxu* [断续] is a Chinese phrase which refers to the intermitting of, or the alternation between, progression and stoppage. Consequently, not only can the phrase *duanxu* signify 'progression' (albeit in a somewhat intermittent manner), but the deliberately inserted dot – a specifically Chinese punctuation mark to signal a break or represent division – between the two characters *duan* [断] and *xu* [续], further emphasises the individual meaning of each of them. That is, the translated title succeeds in highlighting both "still" and "on" *separately.*

Interestingly, Chinese is an extremely condensed language with multiple meanings generated by the most economical of words. This is especially apparent in classical Chinese (which is the written language used in the *Book of Changes* and other Taoist classics), where a single character or word can sometimes have more than five different (though sometimes related) denotations – so that the number of connotations and implications may thus be expected to be far greater. That said, it is still impossible to find any corresponding phrase in Chinese for a polysemous English phrase such as "out of this world". We could, however, deduce that Berengarten's inclination towards, or penchant for, utilising highly-condensed and polysemous phrases may itself have been influenced, even if indirectly, unconsciously and subtly, by his reading of the *Book of Changes* and other Chinese classics, albeit in translation. Additionally, Berengarten has attested that he has been influenced by Ezra Pound – whose own poems were heavily influenced by the Chinese imagery system and the Chinese ideogram, especially through Arthur Waley's works, both as translator and as theorist of Chinese classical poetry. Berengarten also claims that his readings of Pound and Waley further led to his interest in the 'Chinese written character' or ideogram, which, in actual fact, is in itself a rich source of polysemous significations.[15]

Returning to the poem, 'Untouchable Miraculous Air', we further see a number of prepositions being enjambed to new lines to project a sense of separateness, dislocation, disjunction – even alienation. Such a technique is often found in other poems by Berengarten: not only does it create surprise (for example, the joy-implicating phrase "out of this world" seems to be transformed and negated by the phrase "onto death"), but information can be added that qualifies or changes the meaning of the previous line (for instance, the enjambed preposition "Onto" actually turns out to move the meaning of the previous two lines in a totally new

---

[15] Letter from RB to author, 3 October 2007.

direction: "…Time were the wooden // Floor it dripped and spilled"). The final line, "All the more joyfully", also provides a surprising or optimistic twist to the gloomy portrayal of the spilling air (which was earlier related to death, leakage, spillage, puddle and cellars, etc.).

Although the use of such prepositional enjambment enriches the overall poem, it is almost impossible to translate it well. My translational strategy has been, firstly, to keep the meaning of the sentence intact; and, secondly, to break the translated lines as closely to their originals as possible, without attempting to maintain rigid loyalty to the use of a preposition every time – simply because Chinese does not lend itself to the use of prepositions to anything like the extent to which they are deployed in English. Furthermore, this enjambment in Berengarten's poems also reminds us that, in each hexagram of the *Book of Changes*, individual lines are closely linked to other lines, and mutually influential. Their positioning and patterning (solid – *yang*, or broken – *yin*) affect the signification of the core trigram, as well as the overall meaning of the hexagram, in very much the same way as enjambed lines affect the overall meaning of a stanza and of an entire poem by Berengarten. In this sense, it might therefore be said that the principle of change (transformation) that is both subject and substance of the *Book of Changes* is itself reflected in Berengarten's poetic technique and applied even to its most minute details.

Finally, another of Berengarten's poetic techniques which proves challenging to a translator is his combined usage of hyphenation and line breaks. In the above poem, we see that in the fifth stanza, ambiguity is intentionally created with the breaking up of the word "untouchable" by a hyphen, so that "touchable" is enjambed to the second line, thus creating the impression that the air may actually be "touchable" if we read the line on its own. Such a technique of appending a negative prefix to reverse the meaning is actually particularly suited to Chinese syntax. Without even the need for hyphenation, inversion of meaning in Chinese is often achieved by affixing a *bu* 不 ['not', or 'un-'] before any verb, or prefixing any adjective with a *fei* 非 [equivalent to 'un-' or 'dis-']. Here then, it is fortunate that I have been able to translate "un- / touchable" into *wufa / chumo* [无法/触摸] – a solution that fits both layout and semantics. Although Berengarten may not be proficient enough in Chinese to have been directly influenced by this common pattern of Chinese prefix-negations, the many usages of such compounds in the Wilhelm-Baynes explications of lines in the hexagrams, such as

'Mis [-]fortune', 'No blame', 'No praise', 'No remorse', 'dis[-]quieting', 'dis [-]appears', may have unconsciously inspired Berengarten to explore and subvert such prefixes in English.

೮౩

As well as responding to the general and overarching influence of Chinese philosophies and culture, Berengarten has written individual poems which have been influenced by, or resemble, poems by Chinese poets. One such prominent example is his poem 'Bird up there black', which is likely to have been influenced by the works of Chinese exile-poet, Yang Lian, who is London-based and an acquaintance of Berengarten. Interestingly, Yang is another poet who, like Berengarten, has based his poetry collection, *Yi*, on the structures and philosophies of the *Book of Changes* (Tan 2007). Particularly, "black bird" is a recurring image in Yang's poetry, often acting as the agent between light and darkness. For instance, Yang's poem, 'Crow's Proposition' contains the lines: "each morning dies once again in crow's language / Crow uses darkness to display light." (Yang 1995: 25). This may be the impetus or inspiration for Berengarten's 'Bird up there black':

That bird up there
Black black black
Because of the sun

Behind it, is
Flying straight
On arcs of air

Into death (*BWNBC* 17)

Here the bird which is "black / Because of the sun" appears to be a modification and adaptation from Yang's crow which "uses darkness to display light". Furthermore, both poems portray death in the face of the sun/morning.[16]

In conclusion, we come to what I would like to call 'the reverse osmosis'. In just the same way that Chinese philosophies and cultures

---

[16] In an email to me (18 November 2007), RB confirms the influence of Yang Lian on this image and adds a query of his own: he asks whether this repeated image in Yang Lian's work may owe something to Ted Hughes' collection *Crow*.

influence Berengarten's poetry, we need to realise that Berengarten's marvellous renditions of these influences in his own poems, in turn, influence and determine their translations, as they travel 'back' to their Chinese 'source'. On the one hand, there can be little doubt that the Chinese influences on Berengarten's works are profound and far-reaching: they range from the *Book of Changes* and Taoist and Confucian classics to contemporary Chinese poetry. This observation is particularly apt and relevant in the approach to Berengarten's works, as his perspectives are known to have "consistently drawn on non-English poetic traditions" and to "combine English, Mediterranean, Jewish, Slavic, American and Oriental influences" (*BWNBC* inside cover). On the other hand, if the Chinese influence on Berengarten's poetry and thought is to be seen as a structural, philosophical and linguistic 'osmosis', then I believe that, as the translation of his works into Chinese garners more attention and a wider readership, a 'reverse osmosis' of Berengarten's influence on Chinese poetics may, slowly but surely, be taking place.

References

Aristotle. *Poetics*. The Internet Classics Archive. Online at: http://classics.mit.edu/Aristotle/poetics.1.1.html. Consulted, 1 February 2016.

Tan, Chee Lay. 2007. *Constructing a System of Irregularities: The Poetry of Bei Dao, Duoduo and Yang Lian*. Newcastle upon Tyne: Cambridge Scholars Publishing.

Wilhelm, Richard. 1951. *The I Ching or Book of Changes* (trans. Cary F. Baynes from German). London: Routledge and Kegan Paul.

Winters, Yvor. 1952. *Collected Poems*. London: Routledge and Kegan Paul.

Yang Lian. 1995. *Where the Sea Stands Still* (trans. B. Holton). London: WellSweep Press.

______. 2002. *Yi* (trans. M. Lee). Los Angeles, CA: Green Integer.

Yu, Pauline. 1987. *The Reading of Imagery in the Chinese Poetic Tradition*. Princeton, NJ: Princeton University Press.

PART III

In a Balkan Light: Richard Berengarten and the South Slav Cultural Space

Francis R. Jones

Richard Berengarten describes himself not as an English or a British poet, but as "a European poet who writes in English" (*TM1* inside back cover). The protagonist of *The Manager*, for example, despite being both product and victim of a superficially British every-man-for-himself late-Thatcherism, is also the European Everyman. In addition, Berengarten's Jewish heritage is also, almost by definition, a mainstream European one. However, it is to Southern Europe, and especially the Balkans, that his links are closest. Berengarten has lived in Italy and Greece, and his relationship with Greece marked an earlier phase in his poetic output – in *Black Light*, for example, his homage to Seferis.

But Berengarten's longest stay in the Balkans was in the late 1980s, in the last years of existence of the country then known as Yugoslavia. More recently his relationship with that country, or with what would now more accurately be called the 'South Slav cultural space', has come to the fore in his poetic writing. It is this Yugoslav period, and its poetic outcomes, that I discuss here.

Before I start, however, it is worth pointing out that no observers are neutral – myself included. One's involvement as an observer implies a certain point of view, a stance that is inevitably subjective. When dealing with recent Yugoslav history, this is more than a commonplace: the events and personalities one describes, and how one describes them, depend on one's own views and reasons for involvement in the region (for a discussion of the issues this entails, see Jones 2004). Hence I should point out that my own political views on the wars of the Yugoslav succession are, at least in part, conditioned by my having lived in Sarajevo, though I also have personal links with Serbia. Also, my knowledge about the poetry of Mak Dizdar, Vasko Popa and Ivan V. Lalić derives in no small measure from the fact that I have translated their works into English.[1]

℘

As a basis for analysing the interplay between Berengarten's works and his Yugoslav experience, it is worth sketching the cultural background of former Yugoslavia in the 1980s and 1990s – particularly of Serbia, the component republic of the Yugoslav Federation where Berengarten spent most time. In this sketch, the cultural is never far from the political. One reason is that the two became ever more closely intertwined during Yugoslavia's final years. This is when the socialist politics of *bratstvo i jedinstvo*, 'brotherhood and unity', disintegrated into nationalist political movements based on 'ethnic' differences which, particularly in the case of Serbia, Croatia and Bosnia, were rooted primarily in cultural heritage. But a more important reason is that, for Berengarten as a poet, the aesthetic is never far from the political, and both find their reflections in his Yugoslav verse.

From 1945 to the late 1980s, Yugoslavia was a Communist state and, until 1980, when Josip Broz Tito died, it was governed under the autocratic leadership of one man. In the mid-1950s, however, under pressure from young intellectuals – such as the poet Vasko Popa – who subscribed to socialist ideals but resented the straitjacket of socialist realism, the Communist Party relinquished control over the cultural sphere. This resulted in a creative upsurge, particularly in poetry and the novel, an upsurge the effects of which were still felt in the 1980s, when many young writers who had come to prominence in the 1950s were at the height of their mature powers. The Yugoslav literary and artistic scene of late-Tito Yugoslavia, in fact, was exceptionally lively and multi-stranded. Though hard-won liberties had given it an added impetus, it drew much of its strength from Yugoslavia's diverse cultural, ethnic and religious heritage. Indeed, the expression of local identity, far from being suppressed (as some ill-informed commentators assume), was not only permitted but actively encouraged in the cultural sphere.

Thus, in the 1970s, Bosnian poet Mak Dizdar was constructing what might be called 'existentialist cosmologies' – atavistic myth-worlds that addressed the wider human condition – from the beliefs of medieval

---

[1] See Lalić 1996, Popa 1997 and Dizdar 1999.

286

Bosnian heretics, who saw the earth and the human body as created by the Devil. *Kameni spavač* (1973), translated as *Stone Sleeper* (1999), is a dialogue between the heretics who lie dead in the Devil's earth, awaiting Judgement Day when their spirits will be raised to God's right hand, and the modern poet who sees in death merely a comfortless eternity:

> Born in a body barred in with veins
> Dreaming that seven heavens descend
>
> Barred in a heart bound into brains
> Dreaming the sun in dark without end
>
> Bound in your skin ground into bones
> Where is the bridge
>
> To heaven's thrones? (Dizdar 1999: 29)

Meanwhile, in Serbia Vasko Popa was building similar cosmologies of universal significance from Serbian ethnic myths – be these mythicised historical events, such as the 14th-century fall of the Serbian kingdom to the Ottoman Turks in *Uspravna zemlja* (*Earth Erect*, 1973), or myths proper, such as the Serbs' pre-Christian wolf totem in *Vučja so* (*Wolf Salt*, 1980):

> The she-wolf lies
> In heaven's foothills
>
> Her body a live coal
> Is overgrown with grass
> And covered with sun-pollen (Popa 1997: 225)

In a comment on an early version of this essay, Berengarten writes that "Vasko's influence on me has been *precisely* in modelling and validating the attempt to construct"[2] such myth-worlds of universal significance in his own poetry, as we shall see particularly when we look at *In a Time of Drought* below.

Berengarten, however, sees Ivan V. Lalić as the Yugoslav poet with whom he had the closest poetic affinity. Lalić (1931–1996) was born and lived in Belgrade, the Serbian and Yugoslav capital, but studied and met

---

[2] Personal communication from RB to author.

his wife in the Croatian capital Zagreb. Lalić, however, saw himself not only as a Serbian and a Yugoslav poet, but also as a Mediterranean poet. He sited his poetic identity in a space that linked Serbia and the Croatian seaboard with the wider pre-Christian and Judaeo-Christian heritage of Italy, Greece and the Eastern Mediterranean. This is a space in which personal and historical memory intersect to define our present identity, as with the exiled medieval chronicler who writes:

> I have composed a homeland,
> piece by piece,
> Of the signs which overtake me like justice
> From the other side, where love needs no excuse
> And love is our daily bread (Lalić 1996: 178)[3]

❧

In the 1980s, the Yugoslav dream was souring. Tito, wily autocrat and charismatic symbol of Yugoslav unity, was now dead. As the Cold-War confrontation eased, it was no longer in Western interests to shore up Yugoslavia against a Soviet threat. Prosperity previously underwritten by international loans and access to Western markets collapsed, and politicians from the various republics in the Yugoslav Federation became mired in mutual recrimination. Few suspected, however, that Yugoslavia would fail to muddle through this crisis as it had muddled through others, and no one foresaw how swift and savage the end would be. In retrospect, a transition from autocracy to democracy at a time of deep economic depression proved to be a fatal mix that would do for Yugoslavia as it had done for Weimar Germany a half-century before. In the late 1980s, the regional cultural identities that had been Yugoslavia's strength became the basis for a particularly virulent form of politics. The unscrupulous and bigoted ambitions of those such as Serbian Communist leader Slobodan Milošević and his Croatian nationalist alter-ego Franjo Tudjman gradually fanned inter-ethnic tensions into ethno-nationalist hatred. In 1991, the year Berengarten left the country, Yugoslavia finally imploded, with the secession of Slovenia and the start of the Serb-Croat war.[4]

---

[3] Source text published in Lalić 1969.

[4] For analyses of the economics and politics of the Yugoslav breakdown, see Woodward (1995), and Silber and Little (1997).

Berengarten visited Yugoslavia at various points during the 1980s. Crucial encounters for his relationship with the region occurred through the international Cambridge Poetry Festival, which Berengarten had founded in 1975. Three Yugoslav poets appeared at this event between 1975 and 1983: Vasko Popa, Miodrag Pavlović and Ivan Lalić. All three became Berengarten's friends. In 1982, 1983 and 1984, Berengarten appeared at the Belgrade October Writers' Meeting. His links with Yugoslavia and Yugoslav writers over the next few years, together with – as Berengarten points out – the experience at Kragujevac in spring 1985 that eventually led to the writing of *The Blue Butterfly* (see below), culminated in his decision to work as a British Council Lector in Belgrade from 1987 to 1991. Here he married Jasna Mišić (his second wife), and their daughter Arijana Mišić-Burns was born in 1989, further strengthening his ties with the country. During this period he and Ivan V. Lalić also became close friends.

During Berengarten's time in Yugoslavia, a corpus of poems began germinating. These were not to reach full fruition until over a decade later, after the wars of the 1990s. They finally found print form in what Berengarten calls his 'Balkan Trilogy': *The Blue Butterfly*, *In a Time of Drought*, and *Under Balkan Light*. One might speculate on reasons for this time lag – perhaps, for instance, because the break-up of the country that had become his second physical, intellectual and emotional home was so traumatic and murderous that it was difficult to give a proportionate poetic response while it was happening.

The delay is more apparent than real, however. Several of the poems in these volumes took their first form during Berengarten's Yugoslav years. On the publication of *The Blue Butterfly*, for example, he wrote that "the book has been twenty years in the making".[5] Other poems show how his concern with the South Slav cultural space lasted through the intervening years. *In a Time of Drought*, for example, is "to do with the [1999 NATO] bombing and break-up of Yugoslavia and finding alternatives to the culture of war".[6] Instead of a delayed poetic reaction, therefore, it is probably better to talk of a gradual poetic maturation.

Artistically, the flow is not merely from Yugoslavia into Berengarten's poetry, but also the other way. A good number of the poems in these three books have been translated into Serbian. Indeed, *U vreme suše* (Radojević,

[5] E-mail communication from RB, 2006.

[6] *Ibid.*

2004), the Serbian translation of *In a Time of Drought*, actually appeared in print before the English original.[7] Conversely, Berengarten has co-translated verse from Yugoslavia into English; for example, poems by Tin Ujević (1891–1955), one of Croatia's twentieth-century master poets:

> Listen how in this perfumed dark
> Our nerves' thin wires are twanged to flame
> As if struck by a nettle's spark.
> For wounding us, they'll take the blame. (Ujević 1990: 52)

Though Berengarten is known mainly for his original English verse, few verse translators into English have his sonic gift – that of making a translated poem sound both foreign and as if it were originally written in English.

❧

During his time in Yugoslavia, Berengarten travelled and worked in every one of the country's component republics. Nevertheless, his base remained Belgrade; hence it was with Belgrade writers and poets that he appears to have had the closest contact and to have felt the closest affinity. After he left Yugoslavia in 1991, Berengarten maintained a strong personal concern with further acts in the tragedy of the Yugoslav break-up. With most of his Yugoslav friends in Belgrade, however, and after 1996, his ex-wife and daughter too, it was perhaps inevitable that his sympathies during the wars of 1991–1999 should lie primarily with the Serbs. Hence an episode that affected Berengarten particularly deeply, at least on the evidence of his writing, was the NATO bombing of Serbia in 1999 in an attempt to force the Milošević regime to loosen its grip on Kosovo (cf. *INR* 1999).

This sympathy, however, does not descend into apologism for the evils unleashed by that regime, even though – as Berengarten points out in an interview with the Belgrade magazine *Glas javnosti* – in the United Kingdom of the late 1990s, it was "hard in intellectual circles to present yourself as being against the NATO bombing, and at the same time being

---

[7] The translator, Vera V. Radojević (see 'Poet in the Power of a Butterfly: An English Poet in the Balkans' and 'Wonderland Through a Cracked Mirror: An English Poet in Yugoslavia', pp. 315–324 and pp. 302–314 below respectively), also translated *The Blue Butterfly* into Serbian as *Plavi leptir* (*PL*).

opposed to Milošević" (Milosavljević 2007).[8] It is obviously simplistic to reduce the complexities of three of a poet's mature books to one theme. However, if there is a single socio-political current running through what Berengarten calls his 'Balkan Trilogy', it might well be characterised as that of opposition to the bringers of death and the burners of books, whoever they may be, and, in their stead, an insistence on the value of the fragile and the ordinary. This value is perhaps most clearly encapsulated in the image of the blue butterfly, which supplies the title of the first book in the trilogy – and on which, like William Carlos Williams' red wheelbarrow, "so much depends" because it simply *is*:

> a blue butterfly simply fell out of the sky
> and settled on the forefinger
> of my international bloody human hand. (*BB* 8)

The socio-political current that I have noted above is precisely what I believe makes Berengarten's poetry special, conveying it out of the backwater of British (or, more precisely, English) poetry into a more exciting, risk-taking European mainstream. Furthermore, this mainstream involves the tradition of both the democratic dissident and the impassioned humanist: that is, of an individual "international bloody human" (*BB* 8) in concordance and harmony with other international bloody humans, and in opposition to the inhuman and inhumane. And the current is also a poetic one. Typical of Berengarten's more recent verse is his skill in implementing a rich variety of forms, from fixed to free, to channel this passionate humanism into what Lalić (in the title of his 1984 volume) called the "passionate measure" of mature poetry.

Underlying this is a spirit of risk-taking, in life as in poetry. The power of post-war Yugoslav poetry was rightly recognised by British and North American poets. However, Berengarten's choice to live in the Yugoslav capital during Yugoslavia's deepening economic and political crisis in the late 1980s, shows substantial courage – even though few, myself included, realised quite how bad the crisis would get. A characteristic of poetic risk-taking, of course, is that not all risks pay off. But when they do, Berengarten's voice is worth listening to. For all these reasons, Berengarten's Yugoslav trilogy is an important work in recent English poetry – particularly in what might be called 'Anglo-European' poetry, in

---

[8] Quotation translated from Serbian by the present author.

that it explicitly places itself in the European poetic mainstream. I will consider each work briefly in turn, therefore, commencing with *The Blue Butterfly*.

☙

The title and cover of *The Blue Butterfly* are based on an encounter with such a creature, which settled on Berengarten's hand while he was visiting the Serbian town of Kragujevac in 1985. Kragujevac is notorious for being the site of a massacre by Nazi occupying troops in October 1941. In retaliation for an attack by resistance troops on a German platoon, about three thousand citizens of the town and surrounding area were shot – most of them male, including over 200 high-school pupils and some of their teachers. This incident of epiphany, at a place where mass murder is recent and public memory still raw, inspired the poem 'The Blue Butterfly'. This poem in its turn seeded a book. The book powerfully charts the massacre itself, but also the deeper existential sense of the industrial-scale killings that so scarred mid-twentieth century Europe.

Its opening poems have a documentary air, establishing the modern witness's outrage: "Darkness flowered / in cruelty. Gracelessness / numbed hope" (*BB* 3). The breathtaking facts themselves are outlined in found poems that echo the pseudo-documentary style of some parts of Berengarten's previous book, *The Manager*:

> Each man who behaves kindly
> sins against his dead friends and regardless of rank
> will be held responsible before the Court Martial. (*BB* 4)

The fourth poem, titled 'The blue butterfly', reaches beyond the historical event itself, to link the poet's Jewish heritage, his English upbringing and the reality of a specific place and time in Serbia:

> On my Jew's hand, born out of ghettos and shtetls,
> raised from unmarked graves of my obliterated people
> [...]
>
> on my pink, educated, ironical left hand
> of a parvenu not quite British pseudo gentleman
> [...]

a blue butterfly simply fell out of the sky
and settled on the forefinger
of my international bloody human hand. (*BB* 8)

The three 'attempts' in 'The telling' transmute this image further: what does this epiphany mean? how can it be held in a poem?

> Ah, but plausible
> though it may be to trust most of the time
> in language, in telling…
> […]
>
> how shall miracle, resistant, absurd,
> ring clean through the slickened varnish of rhyme? (*BB* 14)

These two moods intertwine through the book: reflections on Europe's mid-century death-fest, of which this was but one small phase, and a poetically more complex reflection on its wider meaning. This reflection incorporates a dual insight: how every massacre, say – be it Kragujevac 1941, Srebrenica 1995 or New York 2001 – leads to the same "destiny, but not a destination" where suddenly, undeservedly "the trains of space-time halt" (*BB* 49). And how this can coexist with random, unmotivated moments of grace and epiphany – such as a blue butterfly settling one spring on the poet's finger as he visits the site of the massacre?

❧

In a Time of Drought, a shorter volume, is a sequence of poems based around rural rain-making ceremonies which used to take place in many parts of the Balkans, and in Bulgaria and Serbia survived at least until the 1960s. The direct inspiration came from a child's drawing, by Berengarten's daughter Arijana, showing a rain-maker girl dressed in a garment of leaves. In his postscript 'Arijana's Thread', however, Berengarten also describes the poems as "a response to the events between 1989 and 2001 in Yugoslavia", citing the political background of when the poems were written: between NATO's 1999 bombing of Serbia, and Milošević's 2001 extradition to face war crimes charges in The Hague (*ITD* 73).

The book is tightly structured. There are seven cycles, each of which contains seven poems (as in *The Blue Butterfly*). Each poem has four

rhyming quatrains and a chorus. The auditory repetition of rhythm
and rhyme pitches somewhere between incantation and folksong, and
stays in the ear long after reading. And the content pitches between two
cultures, or rather in two cultures simultaneously, merging British and
Balkan ritual and myth: for instance, Queen of the May and Dodola, the
rain-making girl:

> Who on the Spring Lord's holiday
> Shall be called out as Queen of the May
>
> Who shall be stripped and dressed in green
> The fairest young woman that ever was seen (*ITD* 3)

or Guy Fawkes and petty dictators everywhere:

> Then stuff and sew a doll upon
> A stake and put old leggings on
>
> And call him Lord and *Gospodar*
> And souse him in vinegar
>
> And call him Prince or President
> To send him where his cronies went
>
> The favourites he raised and made
> And those he tortured or betrayed (*ITD* 36)

The underlying theme is the struggle between the conjurors of life and
the bringers of death:

> And what if the laws of our bitter blood quarrel
>
> Demand more revenge and bitter blood feud
> Deny them and dance for the day that's renewed (*ITD* 46)

The poems feel both familiar in terms of form, and strange in terms
of content. This is perhaps why they seem to me, as a translator, to read
like perfect verse translations (much in the same way as Berengarten's
translations of Tin Ujević mentioned above). This, to my mind, is more
than coincidence. In Berengarten's work, as with Ted Hughes', there is
a sliding scale between verse that is 'translated from', 'inspired by' and
'imbued with' the foreign. In any case, the effects are similar: when

translating, a poet aims to make the strange familiar; and when writing 'original' verse, to make the familiar strange.

This strange familiarity, however, is not merely an effect of combining English verse with non-English content. It is also an effect of Berengarten's use of homely and outlandish myth and ritual (in this case, the figures and actions in a pan-Balkan rain-making ceremony, but also British May-Day ceremonies) as a route into the universal. In what Berengarten calls *In a Time of Drought*'s "public cosmology",[9] he shows the clearest echoes of Vasko Popa, whose poetics exposed the atavistic and universal just beneath the surface of folk-belief and legend. This debt, or sense of affinity, is acknowledged explicitly by Berengarten's dedication of one of *In a Time of Drought*'s cycles, 'For the Green Rider', to Vasko Popa (*ITD* 11).

⁊

Under Balkan Light, the third book in the trilogy, is dedicated to Ivan V. Lalić. In comments on a draft version of this essay, Berengarten explained that some of the earlier poems in the volume were written as direct addresses to Lalić. Berengarten's 'The Voice in the Garden', for example:

> The dead themselves need no miracles. They are
> what we shall once become, when we have learned
> our final lesson: that to stand alone
> is the only genuine source of grace, or love (*UBL* 71)

responds to Lalić's early poem 'A voice singing in gardens':

> As for the dead, whom I am afraid
> To ask in case they know much, too much,
>
> They do not notice us as they concentrate on
> Carefully dismantling their former fates,
> Like watchmakers... (Lalić 1996: 36)[10]

Later in the book, the cycle 'On the death of Ivan V. Lalić' gives what Berengarten (in comments on a draft version of this essay) describes as his "cumulative response in the wake of [my] friend's death in 1996".

[9] Personal communication from RB to author.

[10] Source poem first published in Lalić 1958.

295

Here Berengarten sees himself as addressing Lalić in these poems "just as directly as the living friend … in the earlier ones". Thus Berengarten's poem 'Lords of the Far Side' –

> *Lords of the far side.* How formally
> you addressed them. But it isn't their plural
> hordes, interminable multitudes, or even select
> representatives I call for, call to, call on here,
> but you, my close, loved, unique friend (*UBL* 107)

– explicitly echoes Lalić's 'Song for the dead', the translated opening lines of which Berengarten uses to preface this cycle in homage to his fellow poet:

> Nobody dies too late, O lords of the far side
> Of curiosity, nobody ever dies too late
> To find an open door. Someone will be waiting to wipe
> The blood from his frightened lip, to name
> Him once and for all. (Lalić 1996: 42)

Though their tonalities are superficially different – Lalić's more meditative, Berengarten's more *engagé* – they clearly share common ground.

Yet *Under Balkan Light* is more than a poetic homage to a fellow poet. "I think Ivan Lalić's poetry epitomises the Balkan way of being, perceiving and experiencing", Berengarten writes in his postscript (*UBL* 140). The figure of Lalić, in other words, also acts as a lens that focuses Berengarten's relationship with the Balkans – or, more properly, Yugoslavia – onto the printed page, as the book's title indicates. In *Under Balkan Light*, the most complex and ambitious part of his Balkan trilogy, Berengarten comes to terms with what Yugoslavia means to him. Yugoslavia, it seems, is a site of personal, historical and ethno-religious memory. It is the homeland of his friends and daughter. It is a place where the scars of Europe's mid-twentieth-century bloodletting, including that of the Jews and Serbs, still smart with the tenderness of living memory. And it is a country where, in the 1990s, just as across most of Europe fifty years previously, similar political pressures (nationalism coupled with deep economic depression) led to a similar bloodletting, whilst Berengarten, I and many others who had loved that complex, cussed, exhilarating crossroads of a country, looked on helplessly.

The first, long poem 'Do vidjenja Danitsé' ['Goodbye Balkan Belle'] (*UBL* 1–15) gives the wide view. One of the most accomplished poems in the volume, it traces the fictional life story of Danitsa,[11] symbolic Balkan everywoman, from girlhood to cronehood. In doing this, it traces the story of Yugoslavia's last half-century, marked by place names in the margin. Danitsa, who is addressed directly throughout (hence the vocative ending -*é*), is imprisoned in Tito's notorious prison camp on Goli Otok ('Bare Island') and then released:

> Danitsé not quite starving, skinny,
> toughened up, through-and-past despairing,
> more lightly moving, but always failing utterly
> to self-censor fantasy of memories – or memory of
> fantasies; Danitsé, divorced, returned, partly restored
>
> *POSTOJINKSA JAMA*   to favour and employment as
>   official tour-guide in ghostly
>
> whispering grottoes (*UBL* 10)

The harshness of Tito's early rule eased during the late 1950s and early 1960s. After this, Danitsa lives through the ideals and contradictions of 'soft Socialism',

>   ever ready
> for active service in the loyal pursuit of dreamworlds;
> Danitsé, cursed and blest with unrealisable futurities;
> Danitsé of dramatic nostalgias and deep-seated conditionals
> embedded in longings for stable and certain histories (*UBL* 12).

Then, in her own history she embodies various of the contradictory facets in the Serbian experience of the collapse of Yugoslavia. On the one hand, she is a member of the democratic Serbian opposition to Milošević's nationalism:

> *TERAZIJE*   ageless Danitsé, demonstrating,
>   singing and laughing
> nose-to-nose in the front line with students one third
> your own age facing baton-and-water-cannon-bearing
> *SKUPŠTINA*   police backed by tanks and
>   tear gas beneath graceless
> statues to moustachioed sabre-bearing heroes who
> would rather die than surrender to any enemy, ever (*UBL* 13)

---

[11] *Editors' note*: a transliteration of the Serbian spelling 'Danica'.

Yet she is also "mother" to those Serbs from both Bosnia and Serbia who, motivated by that same nationalism, massacred their Moslem neighbours and compatriots at Srebrenica:

> many-times betrayed Danitsé, whose own godforsaken
>   sons have harried, hunted, rooted out,
> *SREBRENICA*   incarcerated, tortured, crippled, mown
> down and, in fields, lanes and woodland ditches left
> grandparents, godparents – whole families – to rot (*UBL* 13)

And, then, in further contrast, she is the victim of the Croatian nationalists' revenge as the breakaway 'Serbian' provinces of Croatia are recaptured by the Croatian army:

> Danice, ousted from your village, whose retaliating
>   grandsons, in spurious names
> *KRAJINA*   of necessity, revenge, honour,
> have shot at, raided, pillaged and re-occupied the house
> you were lucky to get away from (*UBL* 13)

At the end, she fades from view, perhaps "to float off finally / and forever angelic into / a cloudless sky" (*UBL* 15).

The next section, 'By the Banks of the Sava', returns to a *leitmotiv* in this trilogy. This is Berengarten's concern with the extinction of Europe's Jewry in World War II, and with contextualising it in a programme of savagery that was indiscriminate in its victims, Jews and non-Jews alike. This section juxtaposes short epigrams with photos of drowned atrocity victims from the Croatian Fascist death centre at Jasenovac, where many thousands of Jews, Serbs and opponents of the Croatian quisling state in Nazi-occupied Yugoslavia met their fate.

Death, indeed, is a key theme of this book. At times the mood is grim, almost despairing, as with the Sava poems. At times the sense of loss is personal, that of friends and family. Poems and cycles are marked as 'dedicated to the memory' not only of Lalić, but also of other friends: Haša Popa, the wife of the poet Vasko; Ned Goy, former head of Serbo-Croat Studies at Cambridge University; and others. What is sought for, however, is the meaning of death, as life's inevitable other side.

This searching also occurs when the poet considers the dark shifts of history repeating themselves in the Romanian revolution of 1989–1990:

We wanted rest this winter but the world will not let us
pause or sit back an instant. Its borders, like snows, are
shifting, melting, refreezing. The millennium approaches.
Deformed or unformed, living and unborn call Justice
and all our human dead belong to us, all, being human.

(UBL 64)

In *Under Balkan Light*, history and memory are death's thematic counterparts. History, all too often, is unjust death repeated: Jasenovac in the 1940s, Timişoara 1989, Srebrenica 1993. Yet remembering the dead in verse is Berengarten's own attempt to act against oblivion. In this volume, this is not only collective memory of collective slaughter, but also the poet's personal memories of friends who have passed away, as expressed in dedications and footnotes. Memory, in *Under Balkan Light*, both negates death and is ultimately powerless against it. Here, perhaps, Berengarten shows his closest affinity with Lalić – for balancing transience against random survival, loss against fragile memory, is the central theme of Lalić's mature verse. As Berengarten writes in a poem dedicated to the memory of two friends, Serbian poet Jovan Hristić (1933–2002) and South Slavist and poetry translator Bernard Johnson (1933–2003):

> Summer: yes, you could drink it to its uttermost dregs, knowing,
>   so long as consciousness held, this was incorruptible. (*UBL* 89)

As this image suggests, there is also much in this collection that is joyous and tender. Indeed the white angel of the Mileševa Monastery's fresco, that supplies the cover for this book, indicates that the poem in which this angel is addressed is central to the book's interpretation:

> White angel, secret guardian
> of the secret gardens of Yugoslavia,
> you who see through and through
> the tellings of lies and time –
>
> smile on my infant daughter.
> guard her and guide her, white angel. (*UBL* 55)

∽

The Balkans form a central concept, explicit or unspoken, in Berengarten's verse. The region is not only a physical but a personal space, where he and his friends live or have lived, and where his younger daughter partly belongs. It is a space of poetic inspiration, where he found poetic kinship with figures such as Vasko Popa, Miodrag Pavlović, Ivan V. Lalić and Jovan Hrstić and, further south than former Yugoslavia, with George Seferis and Odysseus Elytis. It is a place of memory, both historical and personal, but also a place of vision and epiphany: a place where the blue butterfly of hope can land on the poet's finger at the site of a massacre. As the Bosnian writer Dževad Karahasan has pointed out, stereotypes of the Balkans as a chaotic '*tamni vilajet*' ['dark province'] need not be only negative, for the primordial chaos was the raw material from which the world was created (cited in Jones 2004: 726). Likewise, for Berengarten, the Balkans is a way of seeing and being that incorporates all of these complexities and diversities, and hence is a source of creative power and inspiration.

Berengarten encapsulates this in a poem of *Under Balkan Light* that, to my mind, is the keystone of the whole trilogy, in that it not only gives the title to its collection, but also links the various arcs of Berengarten's poetic thought across all three volumes. This poem, 'On the qualities of light in the Balkans', shows the sense of heightened experience, both harsh and joyful, that this region brings:

> Here is a blue butterfly, arrested on your finger
> at the gate to the site of a massacre. Here is a spider's web
> dewflecked in a morning garden. And here
> a hint of incense suspended among dust
> in a deserted building. Its silence is a song
> launched on the space between separated trays
> of candles lit for the living and the dead.
> And here, the frayed hem fringed around a shadow
> that penetrates deep into it across the porous borders
> drilled into time by ancestors and survivors. (*UBL* 34)

Dizdar, Mak. 1973. *Kameni Spavač* [*Stone Sleeper*]. Mostar: Prva književna komuna [First Literary Commune].

______. 1999. *Kameni Spavač / Stone Sleeper* (trans. F. R. Jones). Sarajevo: Kuča bosanska [Bosnian House].

Jones, Francis R. 2004. 'Ethics, aesthetics and décision: literary translating in the Wars of the Yugoslav Succession', *Meta* 49(4): 711–728. Online at: http://www.erudit.org/revue/meta/2004/v49/n4/009777ar.html. Consulted, 1 February 2016.

Lalić, Ivan V. 1958. *Velika vrata mora* [*The Sea's Great Door*]. Belgrade: Nolit.

______. 1969. *Izabrane i nove pesme* [*Selected and New Poems*]. Belgrade: Srpska književna zadruga [Serbian Literary Association].

______. 1984. *Strasna mera* [*The Passionate Measure*]. Belgrade: Nolit.

______. 1996. *A Rusty Needle* (trans. F. R. Jones). London: Anvil Press Poetry.

Milosavljević, Mila. 2007. 'Nisam Stopostotni Srbin [I'm Not a Hundred-Percent Serb]'. Online at: http://www.novinar.de/2007/05/07/nisam-stopostotni-srbin.html. Consulted, 1 February, 2016.

Popa, Vasko. 1973. *Uspravna zemlja* [*Earth Erect*]. Belgrade: Nolit.

______. 1980. *Vučja so* [*Wolf Salt*]. Belgrade: Nolit.

______. 1997. *Collected Poems* (ed. F. R. Jones, trans. A. Pennington and F. R. Jones). London: Anvil Press Poetry.

Silber, Laura and Little, Allan. 1997. *Yugoslavia: Death of a Nation*. New York, NY: Penguin.

Ujević, Tin. 1990. 'Listen how in this perfumed dark' (trans. RB and Daša Marić), *Celtic Dawn* 5: 52.

Woodward, Susan L. 1995. *Balkan Tragedy: Chaos and Dissolution after the Cold War*. Washington, DC: The Brookings Institution.

Wonderland Through a Cracked Mirror:
An English Poet in Yugoslavia[1]

SVETOZAR IGNJAČEVIĆ

Translated from Serbian by Vera V. Radojević

In prose genres such as the travelogue, the memoir, the short story and the novel, the theme of Yugoslavia has made a considerable mark on modern Anglophone literature. But when it comes to poetry, considerably fewer examples can be found, even though some of these are no less interesting. The crystallisation of an experience into a poem does not necessarily involve a long period of fermentation or detailed research into secondary sources; the recording of a direct impression is often enough. So, among English-speaking poets inspired by Yugoslavia, the majority are those who have been 'passing through', whether as tourists or as participants in literary events; and some of these travellers have recorded hints of their adventures in the Yugoslav Wonderland. Though there are poets of

---

[1] *Translator's note*: This text is an abbreviated and edited version of Svetozar Ignjačević's essay, 'U znaku plavog leptira' [At the Sign of the Blue Butterfly], which appeared as the last chapter in his final book (Ignjačević 2000: 170–186). The book was the second of his two volumes of essays on English-speaking writers influenced by Yugoslav themes. Its ironic title, *Zemlja čuda u izlomjenom pogledalu – ponovo* [*Wonderland through a Cracked Looking Glass – Again*] manages to refer to both of Lewis Carroll's classics in a single phrase. This title has been appropriated for this essay. For publication in this volume, the translator has substantially revised and re-contexualised the original footnotes, in order both to include the kind of explanatory detail that, she believes, the author would have wished to provide, and to bring the information in the essay up to date. Where English and Serbian/Croatian equivalents are provided together, square brackets denote literal meanings and round brackets, actual titles. Acknowledgements to RB for providing some documentary details.

quality among them, it has to be admitted that most of their 'Yugoslav' pieces are marginal within the overall context of their *oeuvres*.[2]

The only real exception to this pattern is Richard Berengarten, one of the most interesting and original of contemporary British poets, whose connections with our country are varied and deep.[3] He writes that, besides London and Cambridge, Belgrade is his "favourite city in the world", because it possesses "a uniquely intimate quality". He adds that the time that he spent here was "happy, intense and full of meaning". As a writer, however, what strikes him as more important is that Belgrade is a place where "sudden, small and unexpected graces can leap into humdrum daily life like firelit epiphanies." In summing up, Berengarten describes Belgrade as a place capable of bestowing "two qualities without which a poet cannot live". These are: "inspiration, and regular contacts with other individuals who recognise that *everybody* is fully blessed with the life of the imagination". He concludes that Belgrade "has a quality I can only describe as *depth*" (RB 1998, 2006).

Berengarten first came to our country in 1982, as a visiting lecturer for the British Council on a summer seminar for teachers. He returned a few months later as a guest at the Belgrade October Writers' Meeting.[4] In the years that followed, he became increasingly involved in literature and education in Yugoslavia – involvements that eventually led to his settling in Belgrade in 1987. He worked as an English language lecturer, first at the Centre for Foreign Languages,[5] and then at the Faculty of Philology. During his three-year stay, in addition to his regular teaching job, he involved himself tirelessly in many aspects of the rich cultural life that existed throughout the country at that time, pioneering his unique bilingual creative poetry workshops for children and as a regular participant in literary events – from Zagreb to Split, Bijelo Polje to Ohrid,

---

[2] For example, English poet Ken Smith, Canadian Barry Callaghan and the Australian Judith Rodriguez.

[3] The phrase "our country" is the exact equivalent of the Serbian expression *naša zemlja*. But the English does not render the historically multi-layered currents made present in the South Slav usage. When Svetozar Ignjačević was writing this essay, Yugoslavia had just broken up. The uncertainty of the time is precisely registered in his ambivalence of linguistic reference. In his case, the usage of *naša zemlja* sometimes denotes the entirety of former Yugoslavia and sometimes Serbia.

[4] An annual international event organised by the Serbian Writers' Association. RB was elected a full member of this Association in 1999, the only British writer to have received this honour.

[5] *Centar za učenje stranih jezika*, a Workers' Co-operative in Vase Pelagića Street, Belgrade.

Kragujevac to Negotin.[6] He was also active in translating Yugoslav poets, for example, Desanka Maksimović, Tin Ujević, Oskar Davičo, Ivan V. Lalić, Vito Marković and Duška Vrhovac.[7]

Of all Berengarten's travels over the length and breadth of our country, the most productive in literary terms was his first visit to Kragujevac, thanks to the 'epiphany' that gave rise to 'The Blue Butterfly'. Several of his descriptions of the inception of this poem appeared in the Serbian press. One day in May 1985, accompanied by his seventeen-year-old daughter Lara, Berengarten visited the Memorial Museum to the victims of the massacre at Šumarice. While they were waiting to enter the museum, suddenly – and wonderfully – a blue butterfly landed on the forefinger of his left hand: "[d]azzling patterned wings, black-speckled, leaf-veined. Scales' iridescent blue tipped with filigree bandings of red and green. Firm-etched, sunlight-catching colours, changing at the slightest tremor." This physical event was elevated in the poet's imagination, so that it acquired a symbolic meaning. "Is this some message from the souls of these dead? A request? A blessing? A command?" (RB 1988b). In a metaphysical sense, the butterfly seemed to Berengarten to represent the souls of the innocent young victims of the Nazi massacre. To Berengarten, the tragedy at Kragujevac was a "universal symbol of suffering". He interpreted the entire event involving the butterfly as a minor miracle: "I understood it as a sign, in the sense of synchronicity according to Jung, that is, as 'meaningful coincidence'" (Jung 1969: 417–531). "…I was struck as a man, as a European, as a Jew, as a poet.[8] Since the butterfly is primarily the symbol of *psyche*, the soul, I interpreted it as a message – and as an injunction: to write." (Ostojić-Pušara 1998).

In response to that call, the first poem that Berengarten wrote was 'The Blue Butterfly' (Vrhovac-Pantović 1988). Within a relatively short period, this short lyric, which was to become the title-poem of the sequence,[9] was published three times in Yugoslavia (RB 1988c).

---

[6] Zagreb and Split are in Croatia; Bijelo Polje, in Montenegro; Ohrid, in Macedonia; Kragujevac and Negotin, in Serbia.

[7] Editions of authors translated by RB include: Petrov (1990), Vrhovac (1991) and Gadjanski (1999). See also Lengold (1990: 53–54) and *OOY*.

[8] These remarks anticipate the line: "I, as human, poet, Jew / am held responsible" (*BB* 14).

[9] Svetozar Ignjačević's essay was written seven years before RB published *The Blue Butterfly*. The Serbian edition (*Plavi leptir*) received the 2007 *Veliki školski čas* [Great School Lesson] award and was performed as an open-air oratorio at Šumarice on 21 October 2007, on the 66th anniversary of the Nazi massacre.

Superficially, the poem is a straightforward record of the event itself, but its deeper theme correlates the tragic fates of the Jewish and Serbian peoples at the time of the Nazi bloodbath. Ostensibly in a leisurely tone and with a mild touch of self-irony, the poet describes his "Jew's hand, born out of ghettos and shtetls, / raised from unmarked graves of my obliterated people", his "pink, educated, ironical left hand / of a parvenu not quite British pseudo gentleman", now stretched "in Serbian spring sunlight" (*BB* 8).[10] Because of the landing of the tiny blue butterfly upon it, this hand is "miraculously blessed" by the fallen martyrs and sufferers of Kragujevac. Through simple association, the basic parallel is developed in a highly effective manner, by being projected into the past – even though, seen from a contemporary perspective, its prophetic implications come across as even more far-reaching and significant. In an ironic sub-tone, the poet remarks on his schooling and education in élite British institutions, and mentions "Latin-reading rugby-playing militarists". To this, all one would need to add would be "button-pressing computer war-game players" and the poem would sound fully and painfully contemporary.[11] Then, by comparing what he describes as the "May blessing", that is, the landing of the butterfly on his hand, to "a virginal / leaf new sprung on the oldest oak in Europe", the author points to the innocence and blamelessness of all the fallen victims. The piece, which is fully realised and effective, embodies an understanding of poetry in which archetypal and visionary qualities come together. The result is multifaceted: adherence and loyalty to tradition combined with colloquial directness and formal innovativeness.

In reflections such as this, the massacre at Kragujevac serves as the starting point for an exploration of perennial human questions. However, the poem variously entitled 'The one who survived' and 'Song of a Survivor' is the direct result of Serbian inspiration (RB 1988d, 1989).[12] Here, a distant echo of a Davičo-like melody can be detected,

---

[10] *Translator's note*: In Ignjačević's Serbian text, quotations from RB's work are provided in translation, by various writers. The author was particularly interested in these translations of RB's writings into Serbian and often consulted them rather than the English. Here, quotations from the original English versions have been restored. As a result of this process, several minor errors of fact and nuance have been corrected.

[11] The main though not sole inference here is to the NATO bombing of Serbia.

[12] Published in English as 'This country weighs so heavy (First statement of a survivor)' (*BB* 53).

transmuted, of course, into the English poet's personal voice.[13] Again the starting point is the tragic experience of war, which has carved terrible scars: "Under each rock, a skull / Under the plough, teeth / In every village graveyard / names of slaughtered brothers / … and in every river, blood." In the second stanza, the author asks how many centuries must pass "to ease the wails of mothers", and for enmities to be forgotten and the thirst for revenge to be quenched. But despite all this, the last verse rises to the heightened level of apotheosis:

> And yet, hard, rugged land
> merciless, wild, ravaged,
> you have showered beauty on me
> to bandage my nightmares
> nourished me, filled my palms
> with your bread and salt
> into my mouth poured
> your wine and kisses
> and, gazing through open eyes
> taught me to fear nothing (*BB* 53)

Berengarten has written a prose piece, 'A Grove of Trees and a Grove of Stones', based on another atrocity, the Kraljevo massacre, which also took place in 1941 (*GTGS*). Interestingly, it deploys the same artistic method as the poems discussed above. The author starts out from the direct registration of concrete details at a specific scene, and then casts a wide net that takes in profound reflections on the eternal issues of life and death, on durability through time, on the links between past, present and future, and on the search for meaning. The text begins with a description of the bridge that leads to the site of the massacre, across which, on the date when Berengarten was visiting this town, "workers from the nearby train-carriage factory" were crossing to the station platform on the other side of it, "on their way home from their day-shifts". From this bridge, the author's gaze shifts to "a massive, stepped semicircle, carved into the facing hillside like an ancient Greek theatre, and below that, a grove of trees and a grove of stones". The contrast is emphasised by the presence of "a young couple … arm in arm" in the park, opposite the "bleak

---

[13] The Yugoslav and Serbian poet and lifelong Communist Oskar Davičo (1909–1989) was a friend of RB in Belgrade. RB dedicated this poem to Davičo, translated some of Davičo's poems (Davičo 1993), and later devoted 'For the Burners of Fires' to Davičo's memory (*ITD* 31–39).

whitened monoliths proffering their silent, brooding commentary on the movement all around" (*GTGS* 408). These truncated stone pillars, the poet points out, in fact "represent felled trees: individual lives brutally cut down". These twin "groves" aptly symbolise what happened in many places in Yugoslavia, "where life and death meet and merge". The significance of Kraljevo, as a warning to the world that such tragedies should never be repeated, is presented simply, both as a challenge and as an urgent attempt to grasp the essence of the atrocity. "Understanding is necessary, crucial. Civilisation depends on it" (*ibid.* 409).

In this effort, the poet first speaks about memory, which "knows no barriers here": on the one hand, memory belongs "to the dead" and, on the other, also "to the living, the sentient". "It is a function of life, continuously in movement – and if it is attributed to the dead this can only be so because the dead live on, in us." Our communication with the dead, which is so warm and intimate, constantly reminds us that "the mysterious stuff we are made of is shared with all other things and beings – wind, flowers, butterflies – and that this intimate connectedness threaded through creation really is the common miracle" (*ibid.* 410).[14]

Here is a personal variation on a pantheistic world-view that can be traced back to the English Romantics. According to Berengarten, the "universal" language of the dead is in fact what constitutes memory. "Memory of the dead, as a constant presence among the living, and memory of the living, unafraid to listen to the voices of the dead, are interconnected links in the chain of being." Hence the author emphasises that the ancient Greek myth of the goddess Mnemosyne "makes all too poignant sense in our own century", for, "as mother of human life and liberty, insisting on honouring her dead", memory relentlessly opposes "all artificial attempts to reduce her children to ciphers". This is exactly what "helps us towards understanding the mentality of those who perpetrated the atrocities in Kraljevo, and so many other places" – and, one might add, that of those liable to repeat such atrocities. The basic elements of such a mentality are expressed not only in the segregation of individuals, "whether according to race, religion, nationality, or whatever other criterion", but also in severing the connections "between the living and the dead" (*ibid.* 410).

Next follows a precise psychological analysis: that such a mentality is "based on a limited and therefore distorted view of the universe". For

---

[14] A self-reference, "the common miracle" being a recurrent theme in RB's work. The phrase provides the title 'Only the Common Miracle' (*BL* 14–15; *FL* 160–161).

"[b]eneath the superficially efficient and cool military exterior...,
such a mentality is frightened, spineless, group-dominated, and easily
organisable to utterly ruthless behaviour; and it finds the silent voices
of the dead either irrelevant or intolerably threatening and disturbing."
Its usual appearances are, not accidentally, "mass round-ups and exe-
cutions – and the burning of books, of libraries". One can scarcely
read this trenchant analysis without finding subtle forewarnings in it.
Nevertheless, Berengarten emphasises that a point in humanity's favour
is that "all the mechanistic and reductionist social experiments conducted
by such mentalities eventually collapse. The dead cannot be wiped out of
us, the living. They refuse to be silenced." For this reason, remembering
the dead is not only the best inoculation against this "emotional plague"[15]
but also "a necessary guardianship of our freedoms" (*ibid.* 411).

Turning back to Yugoslavia, Berengarten points out that our people
"still look each other directly in the eyes when they talk to each other",
with a "frank clear look" in which, still, "a blacker light also shines,"[16]
because "the dead are not only buried all around beneath us, but they
seem very close to the surface." Thus this "grove of stones and grove of
trees" in Kraljevo is a true symbol of memory. This town constantly re-
minds us that we, the living, are "the gatekeepers of memory". And by
maintaining the memory of the dead, Berengarten concludes that "we
are the forest keepers, guardians of the tree of life which gives oxygen to
the born and the unborn, protectors of the future" (*ibid.* 411). For its
inspiration and depth, this essay, which combines aspects of both the
traveller's sketch and the prose-poem, is worthy of comparison with the
best writings of D. H. Lawrence in this interesting hybrid of literary
genres.

During Berengarten's stay in our country, he wrote a number of other
pieces that either focus or touch on Yugoslav motifs. In the poem 'On
the quality of light in the Balkans', the thread with the works discussed
above is maintained by means of spoken rhythms, quick image-shifts
and densely packed metaphor.[17] For example, light is perceived as a
blade, as if it were "honed / on a millstone high above the clouds / to
stab directly down through silver rivers of sky". The reflection of this

---

[15] RB puts this phrase in quotation marks. It derives from Wilhelm Reich, whose work
he studied closely in the 1970s.

[16] Another self-reference to *BL*.

[17] See *UBL* 34–45, where this serves as a title-poem.

light on a windowpane makes it seem as if there were an unknown face there: "neither / living nor dead". This image expands: "[a]nd the smile on this face, which is not exactly a smile / belongs to a white angel, with darkening, blue tipped wings."[18] Here, in the Balkans, are to be found both Berengarten's blue butterfly, "at the gate to the site of a massacre" and "a spider's web / dewflecked in a morning garden". These are explicit contrasts, and their full combined impact, as the poem develops, serves to accomplish an overall sense of balance. The ending is presented in a more elated tone, with an image that basically belongs to the sphere of intimacy and interiors. Here, "the certain chime of light / between eye and eye, as glass clinks against glass",[19] is counterbalanced against an exterior, which is ruled by "the poor death of silence, pierced by nothing more / than a pebble skimmed across water by a casual boy". So the poet ends with a vivid impression, which at once succeeds in lifting the whole to a higher, more universal level.

'New Year Poem 1990'[20] was directly inspired by the overthrow of Nikolae Ceauşescu in Romania. This poem is of a different, more involved nature. It begins with an image of the "fresh dead ... knocking at the windows" of the poet's flat in Georgi Georgiju Deža Street in Zemun.[21] Their hands are "scrabbling vainly with splintery nails of frost". Here occurs yet another variation on the poet's favourite, almost obsessive theme: the constant and continuing relationship between the living and the dead. The poem gives a panoramic view of the contemporary world, with echoes of Yeats's 'The Second Coming'. Here Berengarten says that, although "[w]e wanted rest this winter, ... the world will not let us / pause or sit back an instant" because "its borders, like snows, are / shifting, melting, refreezing." With the coming of the millennium,

---

[18] A reference to the 'White Angel' of Mileševa. See the discussion of the next poem, and note 23 below.

[19] Another passage offers an indirect commentary on this image: "In Yugoslavia, ordinary people still look each other directly in the eyes when they talk to each other. This frank, clear look occurs ritually, for example, whenever two people toast one another, raising their glasses not just with a wish for 'Good Health', as in my country, but for life itself ('Živeli!')." (*GTGS* 411).

[20] An unpublished translation of this poem,'Novogodišnja pesma 1990', was made by Bogdana G. Bobić. It is an early version of "By the Danube, Zemun" (*UBL* 64).

[21] Named after Gheorghe Gheorghiu-Dej, Romanian communist leader, 1948–1965. Since the collapse of Yugoslavia, the street has been renamed *Aleksinačkih rudara* [Aleksinac Miners].

"[d]eformed or unformed, [the] living and unborn call Justice / and all our human dead belong to us, all, being human."

☙

In June 1990, Berengarten's book *Menadžer* (*The Manager*) was launched at the Serbian Writers' Association in Belgrade (*MN*). This event involved moving farewells; it marked his departure from our country, already on the brink of disintegration. Neither then, nor six months earlier, when he wrote his poem about the Romanian Revolution, could Berengarten have had an inkling of the extent to which his words would ring true ten years later. In the following years, although no longer living in Yugoslavia, he took part in public readings and humanitarian support meetings in various parts of the UK, including fund-raising events for refugees from our war-torn country. In winter 1993, as a guest co-editor, he jointly put together *Out of Yugoslavia* (*OOY*), a special issue of the American university journal *North Dakota Quarterly* (*NDQ*) devoted to the literature of former Yugoslavia.[22] Then, when it came to the NATO bombing of Serbia, Berengarten "finally" felt "obliged to speak out", as within the deepest layers of his consciousness he registered the same painful parallel between Serbs and Jews that had initially inspired him to write 'The Blue Butterfly' – one likely to have been all the more deeply etched in his mind by the graphic contrast between the so-called *Merciful Angel* operation (the NATO codename for its 1999 operation against Serbia) and his favourite 'White Angel' of Mileševa.[23] Berengarten's direct response was articulated in two ways: he set up the Cambridge Support Group for Serbia;[24] and he wrote a long analytical piece, very sharply critical of NATO policy in the Balkans and towards Serbia in particular,

[22] *OOY* includes some of RB's translations: from Oskar Davičo, Blaže Koneski, Ivan V. Lalić, Desanka Maksimović, Vito Marković, A. B. Šimic, and Tin Ujević. See also the fragment by one 'Salamon Ruben ben Israel of Salonika, 1668', attributed to Gordana Kuić and "translated by Richard Burns", but in fact written by RB himself. This fragment appears in *UBL*, p. 40.

[23] Medieval fresco, properly entitled "Angel at Christ's Tomb", in the monastery of Mileševa, southern Serbia.

[24] This evolved into Campeace, 'the Cambridge (UK) Campaign for Peace', which still survives. It is described as a group that "started in opposition to NATO's bombing of Yugoslavia". http://mailman-new.greennet.org.uk/cgi-bin/mailman/listinfo/campeace (consulted 22 February 2016).

310

that was widely distributed by email and published in Belgrade (*INR*).[25] At its core lies the same sympathy for our people that has inspired his poems on Yugoslav themes.

One such poem, 'The shadow well', was included in an anthology written in response to the bombing of Serbia (RB 1999a; *BB* 39). Here yet again is a variation on Berengarten's motif of the living and the dead, but presented in a different way. Written from the perspective of a dead soldier, the poem evokes the uselessness and senselessness of war and the cruelty of fate to the ordinary man. The first two quatrains call on both a "Soldier" and a "Deacon" to "ring the bell" and a "Sentry" to shut his telescope. While "the butterfly burns on its flower / Gunner, you will die as well." The next two stanzas address "ribboned Generals / talking in luxurious halls", who are indifferent to the ordinary man rotting "in a common pit". The fifth stanza contains the central message. The poet reaches the top of the social hierarchy by addressing the "Presidents", of whom he asks: "And will the international liars / negotiate to quench these fires?" But as "fierce shadows grope" inwards on the fire "to quench any hope", there is nothing to be done but "pull the rope, ring the bell". This ringing of the bell may be interpreted both as the resigned paying of respect and as a signal of alarm, with the latter meaning all the more evident from the last two lines: "*Like a flickering from hell / light flecks in the shadow well.*" A truly unusual, richly associative, somewhat hermetic, but undoubtedly effective poem.

Once the war was over, in October 1999, Berengarten delivered a keynote speech at the plenary session of the Belgrade Writers' Meetings (*INR*), a shortened version of which was published in the magazine *Književne novine* along with three more poems (*INR*). Here, among other points, the author expresses his conviction that while "[e]very worst, darkest and most inhumane scenario" took real and actual shape in the break-up, the disintegration of former Yugoslavia was by no means a foregone conclusion, and that "for all its faults, the old united Yugoslavia was a far better place than any or all of the smaller units that have replaced it."

---

[25] RB wrote this 5000-word piece in Cambridge between 22 March and the early hours of 24 March 1999, just before the bombing started on 24 March. He immediately sent it out by email to friends, including many in Serbia. One recipient, the poet Ivan Gadjanski, brought it to the attention of the leading Belgrade daily, *Politika*. As a result, RB's piece, the first explicit statement criticising NATO by a non-Serb, was being read in Belgrade as the bombs were falling, in a serialised version published in five consecutive issues of the leading daily newspaper, 28 March–1 April (Vol. 96, Nos. 30683–30687).

To explain why and how the country did fall apart, first of all Berengarten argues that it is necessary to "decode" and "deconstruct" the multiple and complex layerings of linguistic and ideological meaning underlying such terms as *nacionalnost* and *narodnost*,[26] which are, according to him, "constructs". As far as he was concerned, what he found "the best and finest of former Yugoslavia consisted in the multi-ethnicity of its population" and in the "[t]olerance and appreciation of the qualities of the individual". And here we come across a statement that involves both a discovery and a significant claim: that the author's experiences colouring all his writings about Yugoslavia involve "a quality [he] can describe only in terms of *images of light*", that is "a sudden kind of wholly human, and wholly delightful, and always wholly astonishing *clarity and brightness*". Berengarten continues by emphasising the need to re-invoke "that honourable, humane, decent, kind, inclusive vision of the *čovek*" ['man', 'human being', 'person'], with all its implicit recognition and acceptance of cultural, religious and ethnic differences.

Significantly, in each of the three poems published in *Književne novine* (RB 1999b; *UBL* 83, 92, 93), the central symbols to re-emerge are those that epitomise all his poems inspired by Yugoslavia. The first, 'The Voice of Light', is about a voice that is "riverborne or seaborne". It appears while the poet is walking "on the midnight of [his] forty-sixth birthday", from Zemun to the confluence of the Sava with the Danube, all the while remembering his father. At this point, a nightingale, "pouring out his heart / in improbable celebration", expressively embodies "summer peace in the soul and harmony of the world". The sense of an atmosphere of perfect tranquillity, and of perfect accord not only between the living and the dead but also between nature and man, is complete, created by simple but suggestive poetic means.[27] The miniature "Tonight the war ended" again concerns a winged insect, this time not a butterfly but a moth, with a "grey and silver flecked" pattern, which lands on the poet's hand in his bathroom and waits patiently for him "to open the window / and let him out on the street into summer darkness". The contrast between this moth and its far-distant, long-gone harbinger from Kragujevac is clearly

---

[26] Both words mean 'nationality': *nacionalnost* is of Western (Latin) origin and *narodnost* of Slavonic origin. Between them, these words embed such ideas as 'people', 'race', 'kin', 'ethnic group', 'minority ethnic group', 'religious group', etc. Both terms were deployed in complicated ideological ways in the politically correct jargon of Titoist Yugoslavia.

[27] *Translator's note*: I am indebted to RB for pointing out a further layer embedded in this poem: his father, the musician Alexander Berengarten, died on his forty-sixth birthday.

evident, perhaps suggesting the idea that its escape will mark the time for an over-brimming of beauty and joy. The poem 'The face of light' is a variation on the piece 'On the quality of light in the Balkans' discussed above. So much so that, here, in a different context, the line about the smile on the face "that appears on a ray of light" belongs once again to the 'White Angel' of Mileševa. In an eye-to-eye meeting with this "face of light", the poet is required to speak with no more than "the partial but authentic / truthfulness of a witness", because "[a]llowances are made / for sincerity, and even good intentions." His role involves "bearing and remembering / that you, like all made, are parts of this light." If the declaration at the end of the poem about the mercilessness of this light – "eventually [it] will devour you" – seems out of keeping with the poet's previous statements, this discrepancy is no more than superficial, because, at the furthest limit of implication, Berengarten's cohering theme is the divine light that is the beginning and the end of the world.

At any rate, it is clear that this "Balkan light" has illuminated not only the years the poet has spent in Yugoslavia but a significant part of his creativity. In return, Richard Berengarten has become the most consistent of all contemporary English writers in representing the variegated and rich cultural tradition of our country to Western readers.

References[28]

Berengarten, Richard. 1988a. 'Kako je nastala pesma "Plavi leptir" – engleska "Krvava bajka"' ['How the poem "The Blue Butterfly" was made – an English "Bloody Fable"'] (trans. Jadrana Veličković) *Oktobar* XXIII: 15; and *Veliki školski čas* [*The Great School Lesson*] 20: 34–35.

______. 1988b. 'Two Photographs'. Online at: http://www.berengarten.com/site/two-photos.html. Consulted, 1 February 2016.

______. 1988c. 'Na moju ruku' ['On my hand'] (tr. Danilo Kiš and Ivan V. Lalić) *Oktobar* 23: 14; *Veliki školski čas* [*The Great School Lesson*] 19: 32; and *Braničevo* 34(3): 10.

______. 1988d. 'Onaj koje preživeo' ['The one who survived'] (tr. Daša Marić) *Odzivi* 68–69: 56; and *Oktobar* 23: 1.

---

[28] *Editors' note*: The references for this essay include some magazine publications of RB's writings in Serbian translation, which are not included in the Select Bibliography on pp. 404–419 below.

______. 1989. 'Pesma preživelog' ['Song of a Survivor'] (tr. Daša Marić) *Veliki školski čas* [*The Great School Lesson*] 20: 34.

______. 1998. 'A Note on Belgrade' *Serbian Literary Magazine* 1–2 (New series, January–February): 33–34.

______. 1999a. 'Bunar senke' ['The shadow well'] (trans. Srba Mitrović) in *Kletva* [*Curse*] (ed. Moma Dimić). Belgrade: Udruženje književnika Srbije [Association of Serbian Writers].

______. 1999b. 'Glas svetla', 'Večeras je rat završen' and 'Lice svetla' ['The voice of light', 'Tonight the war ended' and 'The face of light'] (tr. Jasna B. Mišić) *Književne novine* [*The Literary Paper*] (15 October): 52/999: 12.

______. 2006. 'A Note on Belgrade' *Serbian Literary Magazine* 1: 95–96.

Davičo, Oskar. 1993. 'Poems from *Hana*' (trans. RB and Jasna B. Mišić), *Out of Yugoslavia, North Dakota Quarterly* 11(1): 55–57. *(OOY)*

Gadjanski, Ivan. 1999. *Balkan Destiny* (trans. RB). Belgrade: RAD.

Ignjačević, Svetozar. 2000. *Zemlja čuda u izlomjenom pogledalu – ponovo* [*Wonderland through a Cracked Looking Glass – Again*]. Belgrade: Filološki Fakultet i Narodna Knjiga [Philological Faculty and National Book].

Jung, C. G. 1969. 'Synchronicity: An Acausal Connecting Principle' in *The Structure and Dynamics of the Psyche* (trans. R. F. C. Hull). London: Routledge and Kegan Paul.

Lengold, Jelena. 1990. 'Passion' (trans. RB) in Wendy Mulford *et al.* (eds.) *The Virago Book of Love Poetry*. London: Virago: 53–54; and note p. 257.

Ostojić-Pušara, Milica. 1998. 'Plavi leptir' ['The Blue Butterfly'], Interview with RB, *NIN* (23 October): 42.

Petrov, Aleksandar. 1990. *Lady in An Empty Dress* (trans. RB). London: Forest Books.

Vrhovac-Pantović, Duška. 1988. 'Povratak duše' ['The Soul's Return'], interview with RB, *Intervju* (4 December): 29–30.

Vrhovac, Duška. 1991. *I Wear My Shadow Inside Me.* (trans. RB and Vera V. Radojević). London: Forest Books.

Poet in the Power of a Butterfly:
An English Poet in the Balkans

Slobodan Rakitić

Translated from Serbian by Vera V. Radojević

In the postscript to his book *In a Time of Drought*, Richard Berengarten says that he read numerous texts "on the history, customs, sociology and folklore of Yugoslavia in particular and the Balkans in general" (*ITD* 75). All of this provided him with a solid basis for the writing of *The Blue Butterfly*.

Among the sources for *In a Time of Drought*, Berengarten discovered a passage in Frazer's *The Golden Bough* which mentioned that, in some areas of the Balkans – Eastern Serbia, Bulgaria and parts of Macedonia – the rain-maiden, *Dodola*, was called *Peperuda*, *Peperudja*, or *Peperuga*, which means 'butterfly' (Frazer 1959: 69–70). In this custom, the *Dodolas* walked across the fields and from house to house, invoking rain, in a kind of procession. Then, always in the same prescribed manner, the householders would pour water over the 'butterfly' and sprinkle flour over her head, while the girls in her train would be presented with gifts of flour, butter and cheese.

In this way, when he was tracing the origin of his poem based on rainmaking ceremonies, Berengarten met the butterfly once again: both as the creature and as the symbol which had already prompted him to embark on writing *The Blue Butterfly*. As a poet totally given to his craft, Berengarten, like the Dodolas themselves, invoked his butterfly and 'fell into' its power. In a way, then, the blue butterfly configures the true meaning of both *In a Time of Drought* (completed in 2001) and, even more so, *The Blue Butterfly* (completed in 2006). His poem 'What power or intelligence' ends with these lines:

... I wish I could hold the moment and be
held by it, just as my blue butterfly captured my hand
and just as that photograph borrowed a moment's light
to catch its imprint for always, allowing the creature
itself, wholly unharmed, to go about its business free. (*BB* 88)

Something paradoxical has happened here, as Berengarten himself notes in his postscript to *In a Time of Drought*; the more the outside world penetrated the poem's structure, by way of a whole range of associations, objects, meanings, references, denotations, sounds, quotations and documentary details, the less there was of *himself* in it, that is to say, of the lyrical subject. It is as if the poet's own identity had merged with that of the blue butterfly. Through the multiple interleavings and layerings of signification in his poems, Berengarten has succeeded in effectively unifying these elements in all their complex allusiveness, though of course we are not dealing here with a poetry whose *raison d'être* is word play or language games, on the one hand, or, on the other, social commentary or satire. Even so, in that sense, both of these books are at one and the same time Serbian, Balkan and English. And as for their handling of their material, they display a veritably encyclopaedic command of poetic forms. In his postscript to *In a Time of Drought*, Berengarten describes this work as "first and foremost an 'English' (and perhaps even ... a *very* English) poem" (*ITD* 77). However, he is clearly also accomplished in his own right as an international (i.e. universal) poet. The same could be said of *The Blue Butterfly*.

As *In a Time of Drought*, *The Blue Butterfly* may be interpreted either as a sequence of poems grouped around a theme, or as a single 'long poem', divided into distinct parts. In what follows, I adopt the latter interpretation, based on my view that the book forms a coherent unity. Accordingly, I deploy the term 'canto' [Serbian *spev*] to denote each of the seven parts of the whole.

In form, *The Blue Butterfly* could be said to derive from *In a Time of Drought*. In the earlier book, Berengarten treated the Serbian cultural and folk customs of the *dodola* rituals and ceremonies in the context both of the Serbian present and recent past.[1] In *The Blue Butterfly* he deals

---

[1] *Translator's note*: 'recent past' refers to the period from 1988 to around 2000, which involved the crumbling of the Yugoslav Federation: the conflicts in Bosnia, Slavonia, the Krajina, Kosovo and Macedonia; the bombing of Serbia by NATO; and the rise and demise of Slobodan Milošević. See pp. 288–289 above, and also *ITD* 73.

with multiple segments of Serbian, Balkan and European history. Hence the titles of particular poems: 'When night covered Europe', 'Unmarked voices from a mass grave', 'From Mauthausen: Man on the Run', and so on. One of the dominant themes, which transcends all the book's cultural, mythical and historical sub-texts, is war, the time that follows war, and the horrific consequences and chaos in the lives of the peoples of the Balkans and Europe that war has left in its wake.

Near the beginning of the first canto, there are two poems based on documents: one an order, delivered in November 1941, and the other a report, made on 30 October 1941. Here, Berengarten establishes the historical, thematic and mythical setting for *The Blue Butterfly*. The German Central Command's 'Standing Orders' stipulate that one hundred Serbs be executed for every German killed and fifty Serbs for every German wounded. The second documentary poem has the form of an administrative report, made to the German general, Commander-in-Chief in Serbia, about the number of prisoners executed in Belgrade, Šabac, Kragujevac and Kraljevo.

ℭ℈

The number seven is built into the basic structure of *The Blue Butterfly*: seven cantos, in each of which there are seven poems. Within this numerically formulated structure, in *The Blue Butterfly*, Berengarten focuses on a particular tragedy: the massacre of schoolchildren in Kragujevac in 1941; and, from that, he creates an arc between the Serbian 'bloody fable'[2] and the genocide of the Jews. A similar structure is found in *In a Time of Drought*, which also has seven cantos: indeed, both these works emerge from the same lyrical matrix.

As Chevalier and Gheerbrant clarify in the long entry in their *Dictionary of Symbols* (1996: 859–866), the number seven has immensely complex and multivalent symbolic resonances. Many of these are either explicit or lie just beneath the surface in *The Blue Butterfly*. Seven symbolises the creation of the world (Chevalier and Gheerbrant: 860, 862), but also the movement and interaction between good and evil and "the end of the world and the fullness of time" (*ibid.* 862). The number seven

---

[2] *Translator's note*: the reference here is to the title of the famous poem by Desanka Maksimović, 'Krvava bajka', written on 23 October 1941, two days after the Kragujevac massacre. See *BB* 135–136.

317

is obtained by "adding the numbers FOUR, symbolizing Earth (with its four points of the compass) and THREE (symbolizing heaven)" (*ibid.* 860). Furthermore, on the evidence of the Talmud, "the Jews also regarded the number seven as a symbol of human wholeness, simultaneously male and female" (*ibid.* 863); and "[t]he Bambara, too, consider seven as the number of perfection since it is the sum of four (female) and three (male)" (*ibid.* 865). This number is the sign of "the universe in its totality, of creation fulfilled and of natural growth. Seven is also the expression of the Perfect Word, and thereby of primal oneness." (*ibid.* 865). The idea of wholeness is best expressed in *The Blue Butterfly* in 'Flight of The Imago', the spellbinding sixth canto, which contains an abundance of symbols, ideas and correspondences belonging to both outer and inner worlds (*BB* 73–102). According to Dante, seven, the number of Heavens, is also the number of the planets, that is to say of the planetary orbs. Indeed, echoes of Dante are directly evident in *The Blue Butterfly*. The sweeping movement in 'Diagonal' (*BB* 70–72), for example, directly implicates the *Divine Comedy* not only in its narrative form, but also in its setting and tone, and in the application of *terza rima*. Dante's visionary descent through the underworld lasted seven days; and Berengarten's journeys in *The Blue Butterfly* are encircled by seven cantos.

Berengarten's blue butterfly is not just a herald but also a messenger. When it settles on the poet's forefinger, it *tells* him something. And if the actual setting where this event happens is borne in mind too – at the memorial to the massacred schoolchildren and citizens of Kragujevac – then the symbolism of this occurrence is, inevitably, capable of taking on many further meanings, some of them metaphysical. I would go so far as to suggest that, in such terms, one interpretation of the landing of the butterfly on the poet's finger at this juncture is to symbolise *resurrection*. That is to say, in *The Blue Butterfly*, the souls of those who died at Šumarice are resurrected.

☙

In addition to the number seven, the title itself, *The Blue Butterfly*, contains its own complex symbolism. In various mythologies, rites and beliefs, both the butterfly and the colour blue possess a wide range of meanings. These are often close and sometimes identical. In Aztec belief, the butterfly was the symbol of solar and daily fire, and also the soul of warriors. Among the Mexicans, it was also "a symbol of the 'Black

Sun' which passed through the Underworlds during its nightly journey."[3]
Ancient Greek and Roman beliefs attribute the shape of a butterfly to
the soul, as it departs from the body of the dead person (Chevalier and
Gheerbrant 141). Similar or identical symbolism relating to the appear-
ance of a butterfly occurs in the beliefs of many European and Balkan
peoples. According to Serbian folk belief, the butterfly "represents a soul
that can move independently of the body. Many peoples ... believe that
the soul leaves the body when a person is asleep and wanders the world."
(Kulišić *et al* 288).

In the very first canto, through the title-poem 'The Blue Butterfly',
Berengarten provides an all-inclusive framework for the overall pattern
and its underlying themes, bringing together Kragujevac and Mauthausen,
Serbian and Jewish histories, present and past, and individual and general
destinies:

>   ...on my
> writing hand, now of a sudden willingly
> stretched before me in Serbian spring sunlight
>
> [...]
>
> a blue butterfly simply fell out of the sky
> and settled on the forefinger
> of my international bloody human hand. (*BB* 8)

The butterfly that alights on the poet's pointing (index) finger at
Šumarice does not emerge from the underworld but from the skies, like a
blessing. In one traditional belief, the index finger is among other things
the finger of life, while the middle finger is the finger of death. In another
belief, the pointing finger is that of the Lord of Words, while the middle
finger is the finger of the word itself (Chevalier and Gheerbrant 378).
In the context of Berengarten's book, the pointing finger combines both
symbolisms: the finger of life is the finger of the word itself, that is, of the
poem itself.

If *The Blue Butterfly* is considered as a single long poem, the entire
work may read as an elegy for innocent victims. Their only gathering
and meeting place is death, as the poet says in the first poem of *The*

---

[3] *Editors' note*: The 'black sun' also figures as a prominent motif elsewhere in RB's work,
especially in his study of Ceri Richards' painting *The Black Apple of Gower* in *Keys to
Transformation* (*KT* 61–106) and throughout the sequence 'Black Light' (*FL* 147–176).

Blue Butterfly. Yet while the poet is writing his verses, it is as if the blue butterfly were still standing on his finger. It directs his heart, his mind and his soul, and eventually his words. And those *over there*, on the other side of the border, those to whom he is speaking through the butterfly, their intermediary, do not feel anything, do not need anything, nor are they in a hurry to go anywhere. In the canto entitled 'Seven Statements of Survivors', the poem 'The Untouchables' (*BB* 54–55) is implicitly addressed to all survivors of atrocities. In this poem, Berengarten emphasises that there is nothing we can do for their sakes and that whatever we do accomplish is merely for our own benefit. It might well be suggested that this idea applies equally and, indeed, even more strongly, to those who did not survive, those who perished. What can we do for them? Nothing.

From the blue butterfly's first entry at the beginning of the book, through its repeated presence in various cantos, to its making (and marking) of the very last movement – on every single one of these occasions, the creature's appearance implies hope and resurrection. The symbolism of the butterfly not only has metaphysical, religious and lyrical meanings, but also a deeply existential one. Its presence leads to *catharsis*. Hence the expressive elegiac tone in *The Blue Butterfly*, particularly in 'Flight of The Imago'.

In the patterning of its cantos and of the poems within them, the structure of *The Blue Butterfly* is gradually manifested as an overarching symbol in its own right: one which invokes the reconciliation and resurrection of human souls. The titles of consecutive cantos provide keys to the gradual unfolding of symbols revealed through and within them: 'The Blue Butterfly', 'The Death of Children', 'Seven Wreaths', 'Seven Songs of The Dead', 'Seven Statements of Survivors', 'Flight of The Imago' and 'Seven Blessings'. Through its coherent gradation of meanings, this patterning conveys a particularly strong dramatic development.

As far as poetic form is concerned, Berengarten's work is dynamic and varied. The poet deploys both free and measured verse: sonnets, tercets, *terza rima*, long free rhythms and lyrical miniatures. *The Blue Butterfly* is dynamic with respect to its meanings too: it is dense, multilayered and associative. As mentioned above, 'Diagonal' is written in Dantesque *terza rima*; and the canto 'The Death of Children' is a sequence of seven villanelles, a form developed in Provençal and French poetry, while 'Seven Wreaths' is a sonnet-sequence, each poem ending with a rhymed couplet in Shakespearean mode.

From the sonnets in 'Seven Wreaths', arching across the canto 'Seven Songs of The Dead', as if one were reading a lyrical novel, one reaches the section 'Flight of The Imago'. This is certainly one of the most ambitiously envisaged and realised cantos, for which Berengarten has chosen the most difficult path: formally long, lyrical poems, in which he writes of historical events that happened in Serbia, not only during the period 1989-2000,[4] but also more than six decades earlier, during the Second World War. Moreover, *The Blue Butterfly* possesses a significance that transcends any such historical time-frames, because – like its companion *In a Time of Drought* – it is a work which intertwines, in a wide variety of poetic forms, numerous themes, toponyms, myths and historical contents. In the long elegies in 'Flight of the Imago', Berengarten has opted for a patterning of poetic forms reminiscent of both Rilke's *Duino Elegies* and Ezra Pound's *Cantos*. His synthesis of various traditional cultural modes with several of the poetic solutions of modernism has resulted in an exceptional poetic opus, which secures for Berengarten a place at the peak of contemporary European poetry.

☙

Berengarten's butterfly is blue. Of all the colours, blue is the deepest and most 'transparent': it symbolises a non-material, metaphysical (meta-real) world. Blue is considered to be the 'coolest' and, in its absolute value, purest of all colours. The symbolism of the colour blue also depends on its foundation values.

The colour blue *dematerialises* objects: it opens and dissolves them, gathers them up, draws them in and gives them its own identity. The colour blue symbolises endlessness, infinity and the higher spiritual spheres, but also emptiness. An emptiness that is not empty. The colour blue is as if not of this world (Chevalier and Gheerbrant: 102–104). That is why it symbolises metaphysical (meta-real) reality, and that is why, like Psyche herself, who is depicted as a beautiful maiden with the wings of a butterfly, it also symbolises the soul's immortality. *The Blue Butterfly* is a poem that intertwines, weaves and amalgamates the voices of the living and the dead ('Seven Songs of the Dead' and 'Seven Statements of Survivors'), so that it almost seems as if some parts of the poem come from the other side. I suggest that that this sense of 'othersidedness' is

---

[4] *Translator's note*: See note 1 above.

321

given to the poem by the colour blue. And while the butterfly and the colour blue each radiate their own full range of symbolic associations, their blending and binding provide Berengarten's poem with an even richer polysemy. If poetry is the deepest expression of metaphysics, these many-faceted qualities of *The Blue Butterfly* confirm it.

The colour blue is also the colour of the bird of luck, the blue bird, which is uncatchable but always close at hand (Chevalier and Ghreebrant 102). One of the most distinguished late European symbolists, the Belgian-born Parisian writer Maurice Maeterlinck, was author of the once-famous drama *The Blue Bird*, which was better known abroad than in France. It was performed at the Hudozhestveni Theatre in Moscow. Maeterlinck's *The Blue Bird* points not only to the mythical and religious meanings of the colour blue but also to its poetic and philosophical ones. Quite independently of each other, *The Blue Butterfly* by Berengarten and *The Blue Bird* by Maeterlinck both show how reality influences meta-reality, and vice-versa. Berengarten's lyrical 'building blocks' are unbearably, painfully real, palpable, even obvious. The 'role' of the blue butterfly within the structure of his poem is to elevate that reality into timelessness and radiance.

In 'Flight of the Imago', the blue butterfly appears more frequently than in previous cantos, both 'in dialogue' with the lyrical subject, and as a complex symbol, within particular poetic contexts, that gives coherent meaning to everything that the poet sings about. The seven elegies that make up 'Flight of The Imago' are full of the most varied images, sounds and associations, embodying both real and imaginary worlds. The opening line of the third elegy has the striking impact of a deep cry: "But the dead do not hear us and we are not Orpheus." Whole stretches consist of lines that, being tightly linked by associations with this world, are striking in their realism; other passages seem to catch glimmers of worlds gone into shadow. However, in his elegy 'Nothing is lost always', the poet also says that things that no longer exist are real too. The elegy 'A twentieth century dream' in the canto 'Seven Statements of Survivors' contains an equally dense range of meanings. Berengarten appears to have accepted Rilke's poetic principle, that lines of poems are not feelings but experiences, and in order to write just one verse it is necessary to travel, watch, remember, suffer and, on every single letter and sound of one's poem, imprint its own image. That is why one should have memories, considers Rilke; but they are not enough by themselves; they become useful only when "they become blood in us, glance and gesture, nameless and no longer to be distinguished from ourselves, only then can it happen that in a very rare hour the first word of a line arises in their midst and strides out of them" (Rilke 2008: 14). This "first word" was initiated by the butterfly appearing in Šumarice and alighting on the poet's finger.

೮৩

Just as it often happens that refugees do not know the language of their own homeland, particularly when exile is connected with expulsion and injustice, so a person's individual suffering may need to be 'relegated' if that person is to 'preserve' his or her own existence. It would be almost impossible to grow up and exist at all if one were permanently submerged in the suffering of the Jewish people – to whom Berengarten belongs. Survival by no means implies a forgetting (oblivion), nor does it mean any denial of empathy. With regard to sensibility, a high degree of stability in personality has been demanded of Berengarten to enable him to come face to face with these depths of suffering while remaining who and what he is. It might even be said that an invisible transformation in Berengarten's soul and unconscious self has occurred through and by means of the emergence of *The Blue Butterfly*, at the locus of suffering of a people, unknown to him, which stopped being unknown to him as from that moment.

The 'weightless pressure'[5] of the blue butterfly was a sufficient and accurate measure to enable the reliving of the human sufferings of the victims at Šumarice. Thus, what would have been *inexpressible* by means of any other 'dimension' or 'weight' *did* become expressible and *was* expressed – and with immeasurable ease. At the moment the blue butterfly sat on his finger, the sufferings of Šumarice were, for Berengaraten, elevated into an image of universal suffering. So it might also be said that the blue butterfly led Berengarten on a journey of spiritual maturation. Berengarten experienced the spiritual union of the *self-he-was* with *his-self-as-descendant* of a sacrificed people. There are even occasions in his poems when the poet Berengarten points to the blue butterfly as their real author.

---

[5] *Translator's note*: This is a reference to 'The telling: Third attempt' (*BB* 14): "I want to tell / – an errant blue butterfly / sat on my finger and *weightlessly pressed* / souls of seven thousand souls at rest / in one thrust through me, and that wound was fatal." (*italics added*.)

The Blue Butterfly is a book against forgetting, against oblivion. For the dead do not hear, do not see, do not speak, do not feel. To forget innocent victims would mean their second death and would be a great sin, even though they truly do not need anything, because they are 'untouchable' (see the poem 'The Untouchables', *BB* 54–55).

REFERENCES

Chevalier, Jean and Gheerbrant, Alain. 1996. *The Penguin Dictionary of Symbols* (trans. John Buchan Brown). London: Penguin.

Frazer, Sir James. 1959 [1922]. *The Golden Bough*, abridged edition. London: Macmillan.

Kulišić, Špiro; Perović, Petar and Pantelić, Nikola. 1998. *Srpski mitološki rečnik* [*Serbian Mythological Dictionary*]. Belgrade: Etnografski institut SANU.

Rilke, Rainer Maria. 2008 [1910]. *The Notebooks of Malte Laurids Brigge* (trans. Burton Pike). Urbana-Champaign, IL: Dalkey Archive Press.

Richard Berengarten:
the Lyrical and the Political

JOHN LUCAS

J. M. Coetzee's novel, *Youth*, published in 2002, takes as its subject a young man, a student in 1950s South Africa, who escapes from his native country to London, where he hopes to breathe the rich cultural air which will nourish his hopes of becoming a poet. The reality is, however, far from enlivening:

> The British magazines are dominated by dismayingly modest little poems about everyday thoughts and experiences, poems that would not have raised an eyebrow half a century ago. What has happened to the ambitions of poets here in Britain? Have they not digested the news that Edward Thomas and his world are gone forever? Have they not learned the lesson of Pound and Eliot, to say nothing of Baudelaire and Rimbaud, the Greek epigrammatists, the Chinese?
>
> (Coetzee 2002: 58)

The date of this reflection is given as 1962, and 1962 happened to be the year of A. Alvarez's famous anthology *The New Poetry*, the introduction to which Coetzee's protagonist uncannily echoes. For Alvarez railed against the "gentility principle" to which he thought most English poets paid obeisance, with dire consequences for the art they held in trust. For gentility, so Alvarez asserts, "is a belief that life is always more or less orderly, people always more or less polite, their emotions and habits more or less decent and more or less controllable; that God, in short, is more or less good" (Alvarez 1962: 21). Alvarez offers as antidote to this gentility the example of such contemporary American poets as Robert Lowell and John Berryman, who between them evince what Alvarez calls "a new seriousness" in trying to confront or at all events engage with a world which cannot be contained within the narrow borders of gentility, quite simply because it is one which has experienced two cataclysmic wars, genocide, and is now faced with the threat of nuclear destruction.

Richard Berengarten – whom I imagine, at the time of Alvarez's challenge, as a young poet consciously reacting against the gentility principle – has refused to be bound by it since.[1] Berengarten's imagination is clearly and strongly fed by European history and politics and, as a consequence, his poetry is properly engaged with them.

There are two obvious dangers to this kind of engagement. One is that it could be deluded. Against Kipling's "What should they know of England who only England know?" (Kipling 1969: 281) there is an obvious riposte, 'They know a damned sight more than those who aren't English'. The other is purely formal. How do you find the poetic means – 'resources' is perhaps a better word – to harness an imagination that may otherwise veer wildly into unmanageable territory? "[L]oad every rift of your subject with ore", Keats famously advised Shelley,[2] by implication rebuking him for brandishing a horn empty of content; and he had the same poet at least partly in mind when he spoke contemptuously of "careless hectorers in proud, bad verse!".[3] "The windiest militant trash", to use Auden's formulation,[4] comes easily to those who take for granted that they are in the right and that the poetry lies in the message. That this produces shoalsful of hopelessly bad verse must be obvious to anyone who has had to endure the vapourings of warm-hearted, ungifted 'poets', convinced that their utterances will save the planet, disarm a dictatorship or ensure the coming of true democracy. I was present at a reading when the late Michael Donaghy invited his audience to join him in applauding itself. We clapped. "There," Donaghy said, "that's all the good that political verse will ever do."

[1] *Editors' note*: A version of Alvarez's article 'Beyond the gentility principle' appeared in *The Observer*, shortly before RB left school and went up to Pembroke College, Cambridge, in September 1961. RB notes that this piece had a huge effect on him. He cut it out and pinned it up on his wall when he was a sixth former. Years later, his own small press published *The Mind Has Mountains* (a.alvarez@lxx), the Festschrift to Alvarez edited by Anthony Holden and Frank Kermode (1999): RB, email, 24 February 2008.

[2] In a letter dated 16 August 1820 (Bernbaum 1948: 851).

[3] 'The Fall of Hyperion', Canto I: l. 208.

[4] 'September 1, 1939': l. 56.

ↄ

Berengarten's two collections, *In a Time of Drought* (2006, 2008) and *The Blue Butterfly* (2006, 2008), are both intensely political – but neither is propagandist.[5] It should therefore come as no great surprise that in the United Kingdom they have been for the most part ignored by poetry reviewers, many of whom are, I fear, incapable of responding adequately to the proper ambitions of the two works. I don't want to spend time in speculating on reasons other than those alluded to above as to why this should be so, though I can't forebear from pointing out that elsewhere in Europe such ambition would be thought natural to poetry, and that in England alone, perhaps, what Donald Davie called "lowered expectations" (Davie 1973: 40) make for an assumption that the ambitious is synonymous with the pretentious.

Nor does Berengarten in any sense present himself as the subject of interest, although he is certainly the carrier of news, in that he writes for English-speaking readers about aspects of European history of which they might otherwise be ignorant, and in doing so he is fulfilling a traditional role: the poet as minstrel, *jongleur*. Having had the chance to hear him give readings from both books, I can attest to how well they work when spoken; and although both books come replete with notes and appendices, all of this material is integral to a genuine and full understanding of the work. The responsibility is all to the poems' subject matter and not at all to the poet's own condition, a point Berengarten himself makes when, in a postscript, he remarks that in trying to keep a watching brief over compositional strategies as he worked on *In a Time of Drought*, he came to realise that he was keen to "eliminate any remnants of 'my own voice'" (*ITD* 77).

ↄ

The setting for *In a Time of Drought*, as for *The Blue Butterfly*, is Southern Europe, more particularly the Balkans, and although the subject matter of the two poems is very different, they have in common a concern with the turbulent, often disastrous history of those states. Moreover, as with classical tragedy, the poems move from immersion in tragic events

[5] *Editors' note*: The first English edition of *In a Time of Drought* was published by John Lucas' Shoestring Press in 2006.

327

towards catharsis, from suffering to wisdom (*To Pathos Mathos*). To say this, however, is not to suggest that the poems offer a blandly optimistic account of history. Rather, their deep rhythms reach for and locate, however tentatively, a kind of *persistence*: an unsubduable force that struggles from darkness into light, which is to be inferred or sensed less in a naturalistic account than in myth, legend, folk tale, ritual – all those human expressions on which anthropology draws in order to study "the science of mankind – in the widest sense", to quote the *Oxford English Dictionary*'s definition of the word *anthropology*. The poems also share a formal structure: both are made up of seven sections, and each section is divided into seven sub-sections. Why seven? It's a number with an almost impossibly rich variety of associations, but here, I will guess, it is especially to be associated with the *menorah* (and its use during the festival of Hanukkah, which commemorates the purification and rededication of the temple of Jerusalem after its pollution by the Syrians). Hanukkah is a celebration of the triumph of good over evil; it greets re-emergent life, welcomes light out of darkness. And I guess that at some level of Berengarten's imagination it is connected to Yggdrasil, the 'World-Tree' of Norse mythology.

In a Time of Drought opens with a section called 'For Dodola (I)', dedicated to the memory of the Serbian and Yugoslav poet Desanka Maksimović. (Each of the poem's seven sections is dedicated to the memory of a particular writer.) In an end-note, Berengarten explains that "in most Serbian songs and ceremonies, *Dodola* is or has become the standardised name for the rain-maiden" (*ITD* 83), and he further explains that in Serbian folk custom the rain-maiden is a kind of fertility goddess, chosen from village and town at a time of drought to go from house to house, dressed from head to toe in grasses, leaves and flowers, singing and dancing and calling on rain to fall:

> Who on the Spring Lord's holiday
> Shall be called out as Queen of the May
>
> Who shall be stripped and dressed in green
> The fairest young woman that ever was seen
>
> Who shall wear shoots of grasses and corn
> The fairest young woman that ever was born
>
> And who shall wear spring flowers in her hair
> The fairest young woman anywhere?

Hey Dodie fetch her away
Peperuda Perperuna
Hey Dodie Dodie Day (*ITD* 3)

This establishes the template followed by the separate poems that make up *In a Time of Drought*: four (for the most part rhyming) couplets followed by a chant. Punctuation is kept to a minimum but spacing is used to denote how the four-stressed lines should be spoken. Or of course, sung. For, as will be at once apparent, we are here in an atmosphere of song and, more especially, of song as *shared* utterance: of skipping, dancing, fluent movement between iamb and anapaest. What may not be apparent, at all events to an Anglophone reader, is that the words "*Peperuda Perperuna*" are variations on one of the Balkan words for butterfly; and although the significance of this fully emerges only in *The Blue Butterfly*, to which in some ways *In a Time of Drought* acts as a prelude or induction, it is worth noting here that Berengarten refers to a passage in Traian Stoianovich's *Balkan Worlds, The First and Last Europe*, which quotes from Frazer's *The Golden Bough* and goes on to explain that

> in Bulgaria, eastern Serbia, and parts of Macedonia, the rain maiden was called Peperuda, Peperudja, or Peperuga, literally 'butterfly'. As the procession of singing and dancing girls moved from house to house, the residents similarly poured water over the 'butterfly', threw flour over her head, and gave flour, butter and cheese to her companions (Stoianovich 1994: 13, quoted in *ITD* 76).

We should also note that the Spring Lord's holiday is the day of St George, traditionally marking the onset of spring in the Slavic Balkans, and that George is traditionally identified with the life and work of the farmer, of "earth-worker" (*ITD* 97–100).

Berengarten's poem engages with history, not so much at the level of actual events, though they are not excluded, but by drawing on resources which compose an enduring history of how people have tried to cope with, understand and outface disaster both natural and man-made: drought and war. Here, a comparison or, more exactly, a contrast suggests itself. In 2005 David Harsent published *Legion*, a book-length poem which sees war in close-up. *Legion* offers an unrelieved, appalled and appalling confrontation with war's brutalities and, by the time it ends, the poem contains – I use that word deliberately, to suggest the work's control as well as its content – an almost post-tragic sense of a world without hope. Harsent himself says that when the poem was beginning to form, he found that the last stanza of Robert Lowell's 'Waking Early Sunday Morning' was at his ear:

> Pity the planet, all joy gone
> From its sweet volcanic cone;
> Peace to our children when they fall
> In small war on the heels of small
> War – until the end of time
> To police the earth, a ghost
> Orbiting forever lost
> In our monotonous sublime. (Lowell 1967: 24)

As it happens I, too, know that stanza by heart, and have done so ever since its plangent, melancholy grandeur entered my consciousness when I read it in America in 1967, at a time when protests against the war in Vietnam were becoming daily more clamorous. I can't be sure whether a starting point for *Legion* was the Rwandan massacres, or whether Harsent had other atrocities in mind, but the overall effect is to make war seem the inescapable human condition, "until the end of time". "Force and violence is alas the ultimate reality", E. M. Forster wrote in 1938, in his great essay 'What I believe' (Forster 1938: 20–21), and both 'Waking Early Sunday morning' and *Legion* seem to concur.

In a Time of Drought, on the other hand, refuses to endorse this fatalistic account of history. The fourth section, 'For the burners of fires', which is dedicated to the memory of Oskar Daviĉo, begins:

> Set aside your guns and knives
> They never served us by saving lives…
>
> > *Blood-red rider upon a green horse*
> > *How far to where the three roads cross* (*ITD* 33)

In Balkan legend St George rides a green horse. Blood drenches the ground to produce new growth. I'm not sure Berengarten quite controls his material at this point, because he wants to conflate so much: ancient sacrificial ritual and modern warfare don't really go together. But this is forgiveable. And the deft weave of custom and lore leads to the book's closing lines, in which repletion is evoked as possibility, a world which is, as the poem itself declares, a "Ringer of harmonies too full for words / Written in fish-scale and plumage of birds":

Antlers of branches   year-rings of trees
Anthems of petals   striped fur of bees

And miracle pigment that patterns and daubs
Butterfly wings with   wands   sceptres   orbs

When will you call for them   teller of spring
Praisesinger raised on this world's suffering?

> *Follow my lead in the dance   one to seven*
> *And I'll climb you a tree that towers to heaven*
>
> *And I'll name you the creatures from millions to one*
> *Alive on this earth under stars moon and sun* (*ITD* 69)

The tree to be climbed could be figured as Yggdrasil or as the tree of life of *Genesis*, the book in which Adam "gave names to all cattle, and to the fowl of the air, and to every beast of the field" (Genesis 2: 20). The praise song with which *In a Time of Drought* concludes both endorses and celebrates a world redeemed from sterility, from "all joy gone". Fullness rather than dearth is what it hymns, and it would clearly be beside the point to say that this utopian vision of a prelapsarian world transcends the here-and-now of contemporary history. *Of course it does*. Just as the *Dodola*, dressed in her fantastic apparel of grass and flowers, expresses a yearning for rain rather than a guarantee that it will fall. She is the glimpsed embodiment of that deep desire for what one of her many variations, Perdita, images as the "quick" of life, a vitality of spirit Berengarten's stanzas both sing and instance. This is what they do and this is what they are.

❧

Though I would never call *In a Time of Drought* a slight work, *The Blue Butterfly* is in all senses built on a larger scale. Not only is it three times as long, but its concern with history requires it to be buttressed by the accretion of details which locate it exactly within a place and a time. It is also formally more various, demanding and in its technical accomplishment alone, a genuine *tour de force*. (One of the things that separates Berengarten from careless hectorers is his care for the craft of poetry. He is neither botcher nor slovenly butcher.) The place is once again Serbia, more specifically the town of Kragujevac and its surroundings, and the time is October 1941, when a massacre of inhabitants was conducted

331

by Nazi invaders, in reprisal for the killing by resistance fighters of a number of German soldiers. In providing a prose summary of the event, Berengarten is careful not to exceed known facts, which means he has to pick his way through the various tellings and re-tellings of the massacre, a difficult matter given, as he notes, that

> Misinformation, lying, spying, cheating and double-crossing were tactics deployed by all sides in the multiple struggles that swept Yugoslavia in the Second World War. The 'facts' turn out to be rigorously knotted in ideologies and, in some cases, to be so inextricable from them as to be deeply resistant to enquiry (*BB* 126).

According to some, as many as 8,000 inhabitants of the town were more or less arbitrarily slaughtered. Others put the figure far lower, at 3,000. But that a massacre took place is beyond doubt. Equally beyond doubt is the fact that at least one of those killed chose to sacrifice himself; and Berengarten provides a section, 'Photographs and Last Messages', in which he documents the images and words of some of the victims, among them a schoolteacher, Miloje Pavlović, who refused to be separated from his pupils when they were led out to be shot. His last recorded words were "Go ahead. Shoot. I am giving my lesson. Now." (*BB* 6). Berengarten transforms these words in an early poem in the book, 'Don't send bread tomorrow' – the last words of another of those whom the Nazis murdered – to "*Go ahead. Shoot. Take a Photograph. Now.*" (*BB* 7). These words are spoken "forty-four years later" by a man visiting the scene of the massacre, a young father, as he carries

> his toddler on his shoulders, chubby arms waving,
> carefully around a flower bed, hoists the child
> to perch astride their grave, while he crouches,
> hidden behind a slab… (*BB* 7)

The lion and the honeycomb, bees building their nest in Mars' cast-aside helmet as he sleeps in the arms of Venus: sweetness out of violence. The familiar *topoi* are here re-cast for modern times, but the weight of the book, its density of reference to what occurred, plus the documentary evidence on show outlaw any suggestion of simple forgiveness. The poem's second, third and fourth sections, in particular, entitled respectively 'The death of children', 'Seven wreaths' and 'Seven songs of the dead', are unsparing in their reckoning of the cost of the massacre. But this reckoning doesn't require the indictment of Nazi Germany and, by implication, exoneration of the rest. That would be too easy. It would also be morally evasive, even despicable. And so at the end of the first of the seven deftly-carried-off villanelles which make up 'The death of children', Berengarten asks:

> Bring comfort then, and courage. Strangers, friends,
> are we not all parents when children die?
> What justice is, nobody comprehends.
> It is the death of children most offends. (*BB* 19)

The villanelle begins and ends, as it must, with this statement, one that reminds us of the terrible fact that through the course of human history, children have repeatedly been sacrificed, murdered, by those in power. Hence the following poem, which Berengarten tells us was a starting point for the entire enterprise.

> In May 1985, I visited Yugoslavia to run a series of poetry workshops for schoolchildren in towns and villages in central Serbia. … After a workshop at a school in Kragujevac on May 25, we were taken to the memorial museum of Šumarice, on the outskirts of the city, which commemorates the massacre by German occupiers…
> It was *Dan mladosti* [Youth Day] in Titoist Yugoslavia, and the place was thronging with children on school outings. While we were queuing to enter the museum, a blue butterfly suddenly came to rest on the forefinger of my left hand – that is, my writing hand. (*BB* 123)

According to Berengarten, the title poem 'The Blue Butterfly' (*BB* 8) was one of two that, he says, "wrote themselves" almost as soon as he was back in England (*BB* 123). This piece very remarkably composes a history that is both personal, racial and, finally, international. And as the poem unspools towards its utterly surprising, but, you then realise, inevitable conclusion, so the self-aware, would-be exculpatory stanzas yield to the implacable recognition of "my … bloody human hand". Such recognition, such knowledge, forbid the poet the luxury of com-mination or judgement on others. Moreover, the bloody human hand, "miraculously blessed" by the blue butterfly is – as it must feel – now empowered to write "*Nada, Elphidha, Nadezhda, Esperanza, Hoffnung*", which is the last line of the other poem, 'Nada: hope or nothing', to have written itself after Berengarten's return from Yugoslavia in 1985 (*BB* 9). In Serbian and Croatian 'Nada' means 'hope'; in Spanish, of course, it means 'nothing'. But Berengarten enlists the words for hope in other languages – Greek, Russian, Spanish and (finally) German – in order to suggest its universality. Even out of death, *always* out of death, voices climb into the air to breathe hope, to seed new life:

> should these dead but awaken, and their tombs
> throw up their burdens, in that timeless time
> when earth harvests redemption, then these blooms
> will rise with scaly wings, like imagos
> of butterflies, blue heralds, cloudy grooms,
> for which, weak angels, harbingers, time shows
> you now, on earth, in blood and crimson rose. (*BB* 32)

"Weak angels": angels, weak or otherwise, are not merely harbingers but links between worlds, and it is notable that in the past few years they have made a comeback in the work of some contemporary poets in the United Kingdom who have refused to settle for 'lowered expectations'. Nor are theirs the "angels of reality" summoned up in the early twentieth century by Stevens and Rilke. Those angels stood guard against metaphysical enquiry. But the angels of Gwyneth Lewis and John Burnside, for example, carry with them intimations if not reports of the numinous,[6] that is, whispers of that which necessarily lies beyond the scope of enquiry of 'gentility'.

This is territory into which, with all due tact, Berengarten's poems reach, and in so doing they testify to a kind of seriousness still not often to be encountered in British poetry, though it is the haunt of such poets as George Seferis and Ivan Lalić.[7] Here, as elsewhere, Berengarten refuses to be bound by the insularity that afflicts so many of his English contemporaries, and this may be one reason for their indifference to his work. Such insular readers would probably find themselves uncomfortable

---

[6] *Editors' note*: The connection pointed out here may be more than coincidental. RB's poem 'Angels' was first published in 1973. In the late 1970s, John Burnside, formerly John Paul Dick, was RB's student at CCAT (Cambridgeshire College of Arts and Technology, now Anglia Ruskin University) and he would have been familiar with this poem. In 1983, as editor of Los Poetry Press, RB published John Paul Dick's early collection, *Homing*, along with Michael Benenson's *Alcman Ape*, and RB's own 'Black Light: in memory of George Seferis, 1900–1971' (*FL* 147–176).

[7] *Editors' note*: The fact that RB has dedicated elaborate sequences of poems to both Seferis and Lalić suggests the strength of their influence on him. See 'Black Light: in memory of George Seferis, 1900–1971' (*FL* 147–176) and 'On the death of Ivan V. Lalić' (*UBL* 97–118).

with *The Blue Butterfly*, and especially its closing section, 'Seven blessings'. The sixth of the 'blessings' is, perhaps not surprisingly, called 'Shalom', and it is very short:

> The unborn and the dead
> gather in the head.
>
> The dead and the unborn
> fill plenty's horn
>
> giving and forgiving
> life for the living. (*BB* 110)

The dedication of *The Blue Butterfly* is 'For the living' and, throughout, the poem is mindful of what in the final blessing, 'Grace', is summoned up as the voices of the dead who "through our own voices" utter a grace that "flows / through everything" (*BB* 111).[8] This is the polar opposite of what is contained in the final quatrain poem, 'Baby Blue', of Harsent's *Legion*:

> She might be singing, 'My buttie, my lolly, my blue-eyed boy'
> as she stoops to take him up in joy,
> then stops on a broken note, her own eyes full
>   as she catches a glimpse of the sky through the skull.
>   (Harsent 2005: 85)

These lines strike me as hard now as when I first experienced them, and it would be absurdly sentimental to suggest that they are in any way capable of being assuaged by the 'Grace' that Berengarten offers. On the other hand, I think it proper to remark that against the horrors of war and of the persistent offences to life dealt by the bloody human hand, *In a Time of Drought* and *The Blue Butterfly* set, between them, poetry's perpetual strength: the power of lyric to praise, to rise repeatedly from death in what Auden called "unlamenting song".[9] Only those who settle for mild lament as poetry's true accomplishment – and I am afraid they are many – will think there is something amiss with the achieved ambition of Berengarten's remarkable poems.

---

[8] *Editors' note: For the Living* was first published in 2004 (Salt Publishing). It was reissued in a second edition in 2008, and then in a third by Shearsman Books in 2011.

[9] 'A Summer Night 1933': line 66.

REFERENCES

Alvarez, A. 1962. 'Beyond the gentility principle'. Introduction to *The New Poetry*. Harmondsworth: Penguin.

Auden, W. H. 1950. *Collected Shorter Poems 1930–1944*. London: Faber and Faber.

Bernbaum, Ernest (ed.). 1948. *Anthology of Romanticism*. New York, NY: The Ronald Press Company.

Coetzee. J. M. 2002. *Youth*. London: Secker.

Davie, Donald. 1973. *Thomas Hardy and British Poetry*. London: Routledge & Kegan Paul.

Forster, E. M. 1938. 'What I believe' in *Two Cheers for Democracy*. London: Arnold.

Harsent, David. 2005. *Legion*. London: Faber and Faber.

Holden, Anthony and Kermode, Frank (eds). 1999. *The Mind Has Mountains* (*a.alvarez@lxx*). Cambridge: Los Poetry Press.

Kipling, Rudyard. 1969. *The Definitive Edition of Rudyard Kipling's Verse*. London: Hodder and Stoughton.

Lowell, Robert. 1967. *Near the Ocean*. New York, NY: Farrar, Straus and Giroux.

Stoianovich, Traian. 1994. *Balkan Worlds, the First and Last Europe*. New York, NY: M. E. Sharpe.

Black Suns on the Scales:
on Richard Berengarten's *The Blue Butterfly*

ANDREW FRISARDI

Richard Berengarten is not as well known as his poetry merits, even in his native England – a situation for which I can think of a couple of reasons. First, his book publications, which go back to the late 1960s, have mostly been with small presses and so have not been widely available or publicised. Salt Publishing has done something about that: *The Blue Butterfly* (2006) is the second volume in an ongoing series of Berengarten's selected writings.[1] Another reason that Berengarten is not as widely discussed and appreciated as he should be is that he is a romantic. Not, of course, in a hokey 'neo-romantic' sense; it's just that, since his earliest publications, he has written about truth and beauty as if they actually matter – not exactly part of the job description in po-biz over the past forty or fifty years. His early collection *Avebury* (1972; and included in *For the Living*, 2004), for example, articulates a foundation myth in terms adapted to the postmodern predicament, a time in which, says Berengarten – responding to Yeats' phrase "the centre will not hold" – the centre is "*every / where*" (to which I would respond, Yeats was talking about a centre that is, precisely, everywhere: within us all) (*FL* 50). Octavio Paz was one of Berengarten's mentors in that sequence of poems, and Berengarten's vision has much in common with that of Paz.

Berengarten has often written on visionary themes without the conceptual distancing, confessional tactics, ironic disclaimers, or aw-

---

[1] *Editors' note*: *For the Living* (2004, 2008), a selection of his longer poems from 1965 to 2000, was the first. Other volumes in the series include *In a Time of Drought* (2006, 2008), *The Blue Butterfly* (2006, 2008) and *Under Balkan Light* (2008), which complete 'The Balkan Trilogy'; as well as *The Manager* (2001, 2008). All five volumes were reissued by Shearsman Books in 2011. Further additions include *Manual* (2013) and *Notness* (2015).

shucks chattiness that so often pass these days for 'contemporary'. This is not at all to say that he has not been writing as a contemporary man speaking to other contemporaries. On the contrary, his poetry is accessible and he grapples with the same cultural uprootedness and metaphysical disorientation as most of us. Berengarten's book-length sequence *The Manager* (first published in 2001) is an extended dramatic monologue of an executive in a multinational corporation, interrupted occasionally by other 'voices'. This fiction gave Berengarten a means for exploring current idioms and jargon – he wrote the sequence in a variable unit he calls a 'verse-paragraph' – and contemporary dissociated mental states. It is the first of Berengarten's books that I read, and I was so impressed by the vitality and inventiveness of the language, and the compassion of the authorial voice, that I had to follow it up with more. What I have learned is that Berengarten is one of the more accomplished English poets currently writing, equally adept at traditional metrical forms, such as sonnets, villanelles, and blank verse, as he is at the free verse lyric or the speech rhythms used so effectively in *The Manager*. One of his virtues, as for any strong poet, is his ability to adapt the form to the poem and the subject matter at hand – and in Berengarten's case the subject is usually serious and far-reaching.

Which brings me to *The Blue Butterfly*. This is another book-length sequence (and the fact that Berengarten has excelled in long poems is another reason for his relative obscurity), this time about a massacre of thousands of Serbians by the Nazis in World War II. Composed between May 1985 and April 2006, the book's conception came about when the author was visiting Šumarice, in the former Yugoslavia (now central-western Serbia), where a museum commemorates the massacre carried out by the Nazis on 19–21 October 1941, six months after the Nazi invasion of Yugoslavia. Šumarice is an area just outside Kragujevac, which is the main city of that part of Serbia. Berengarten explains that, while he and his daughter were waiting to enter the museum, a blue butterfly came to rest on the forefinger of his left hand, which is the hand he writes with (*BB* 123). They each took photographs of the butterfly, one of which is shown on the book's cover.

That this event was deeply meaningful for Berengarten is evidenced by the fact that the title poem and one other poem were written – or wrote themselves, as he says – immediately after his return to England. The title poem, in particular,[2] clearly expresses the moral energy that sustained

---

[2] *Editors' note*: See pp. 357–358 for the full text of this poem.

the poet throughout this twenty-year project. After the writing of this poem and the one that follows it in the collection, entitled 'Nada: hope or nothing' (*BB* 9), Berengarten set out to study the history of World War II in the former Yugoslavia and of the massacre that took place at Šumarice. The fruits of this study are evident in the book's postscript, which documents the historical background, and in the excellent 'Notes' section. From 1987 to 1990 Berengarten lived in Yugoslavia, where he planned the book's structure and composed early drafts of many of its poems.

George Szirtes, in a blurb on the inside front cover of *The Blue Butterfly*, calls it an epic; I would call it an extended meditation on tragedy, on the dead, on beauty and ugliness and good and evil – but not an epic. Epics are narratives in an elevated style and so have been on holiday for a while now in our culture. Berengarten's book is a commemoration, as Szirtes also says; it is a generous, ambitious foray into ritualised grief, dismay, and wonder. It is a richly conceived, integrated sequence, to be sure, beginning in darkness and consternation, undergoing the *katabasis* of existential doubt and despair, and ending with affirmation.

It is clear that Berengarten gave a great deal of thought to the book's design. There are seven sections of seven poems each. Berengarten has often employed number symbolism in his work, one of several ways in which he expresses his affinity with hermetic-kabbalistic thought. For example, he once wrote a long poem called 'Tree' (1980; included in *FL* 117–130), about the kabbalistic tree of life as well as physical trees, which has the same number of lines as a calendar year has days. Berengarten's choice of the number seven for *The Blue Butterfly* would also seem to be related to his Jewish ancestry (his father was an immigrant to London from Warsaw). Seven is a sacred number in many traditions, but I will hazard a guess that Berengarten is using the number seven here as an analogue of the Sabbath, the day of rest that commemorates the seventh day of the creation, on which, Genesis says, God rested because the creation was complete and good. Seven in this sense is the number of the wholeness that blesses – which is how *The Blue Butterfly* ends, with seven 'blessings' of the lives that were desecrated by the massacre.

Very little of the poetry in this book directly recalls the terrible event itself: the documentation at the end, which includes old photographs, serves that function. One poem at the start of the book records the Nazi order to carry out the murder of one hundred Serbs for every German soldier killed by Serbian insurgents, and fifty Serbs for every wounded German. This poem, called 'Two documents', is a dark satire on the officialese whose language it imitates; it expresses the oft-noted dullness of the Nazi mindset, what Hannah Arendt referred to as the banality of evil, of totalitarianism driven by monotonous monomaniacal efficiency (1963). As Berengarten expresses it: "The quick / and ruthless suppression of the Serbian uprising // represents a considerable gain towards the final / German Victory" (*BB* 4). The next poem narrates matter-of-factly the day of the massacre, interspersed with quotations from notes the victims wrote to loved ones just before they were taken to slaughter – a few of the notes are reproduced in the documentary section of the book (*BB* 116–119).

And that is all, in terms of direct, specific reference to the atrocity. The remainder of the book is alternately a commemoration of the victims and a self-reflective exploration of the fact of being a poet-survivor of this and other holocausts (again, Berengarten's ancestry clearly is important here). All of us, as survivors, are left to confront or avoid or gloss over the darkest nadirs of our history, where "lie sentences so deep they are unsayable" (*BB* 54). And yet, as a poet, Berengarten is compelled to try to say the unsayable. In 'The Telling', which is a poem in three 'attempts', as Berengarten calls them, the poet asks: "Is it *language itself* won't do here?" (*BB* 14). His hope is

> to carry a cargo of such immense weight
> of souls from the hold of their burying ground,
> seal pain, refine death, transubstantiate
> blood, to wine, to spirit. This, blue fritillary,
> flight filtered fine in a poem's distillery,
> is how I would ring their memorial sound. (*BB* 13)

And yet, to do this is to confront a paradox: how can the poet craft an aesthetic object based on a tragedy that appears so unredeemable and unspeakable? As the mother of a dead child says in a sequence of seven villanelles called 'The death of children':

> There is no comfort. What comfort can come,
> when neither here below nor up on high
> are love and justice more than martyrdom? (*BB* 20)

Furthermore, what do we, the living, do with the fact of the world's beauty, of our pleasure or happiness on a given day, given the stain on our memory brought about by tragedies like the one in Šumarice?

The mental stench of soil soaked in spilt blood
drowns out even the blueness of this heaven *(BB* 30)

A poem from 'Seven wreaths', a sonnet sequence in this book that takes as its starting point the flowers that have grown where the massacre took place, asks, "Could flowers' quiet voices avenge these fallen?" (*BB* 32). But how can nature heal anything, when, as the father of a dead child puts it, "Bloody in vengeance, red in tooth and claw", nature is so often a force that "snarl[s] at human longing, love and law" (*BB* 21)? On one hand, Berengarten's view of regeneration echoes Shelley in its use of natural imagery to depict an eschatological redemption:

Should ever judgement come to fit this crime,
should these dead but awaken, and their tombs
throw up their burdens, in that timeless time
when earth harvests redemption, then these blooms
will rise with scaly wings, like imagos
of butterflies, blue heralds… (*BB* 32)

and, again echoing Shelley's 'Ode to the West Wind':

Rooted in death, but death's antithesis,
what is this wreath, if not hope's chrysalis? (*BB* 35)

– even if, for now, the flowers the speaker is observing are merely "weak angels, harbingers… / in blood and crimson rose" (*BB* 32). The red of the flowers, lovely to look at, is also a reminder of blood. In this life, the shedding of blood almost always leads to more shedding of blood. Once again, the poet resolves this dilemma by an imaginative leap: "until / red stands for more than … avenging will", and "until revenge'll / take vengeance on itself, take eye for eye / no more" (*BB* 33).

In the above quotations, Berengarten writes in the tradition that stakes a claim for imagination's metaphysical efficacy. But this optimism is tempered in the next sonnet: "Against revenge? No. Just a mass of flowers" (*BB* 34). Similarly, elsewhere he writes that "the dead do not hear us, and we are not Orpheus" (*BB* 78); and "how / can the likes of us claim anywhere anything more / than a handful of smoke and puff or wisp of dust?" (*BB* 81); "I should like to speak with conviction but am condemned / to stammering" (*BB* 81). Further, he asks, can it be that

> everything we have been vanishes
> and consciousness itself of what we have been vanishes
> and all we have imagined, believed, dreamed and aspired to,
> even touched and reached, really consisted of nothing? (*BB* 83)

In such passages, and there are many in this collection and elsewhere in Berengarten's *oeuvre*, we find ourselves in the familiar area of post-modern doubt. Berengarten has been consistent in being a romantic who shares in the existential quandaries of the present. Holding to seemingly contrary opposites – not getting stuck on 'antifoundationalism' and other poststructural gerbil wheels – he practises negative capability in its original, Keatsian sense. Berengarten has elsewhere expressed his debt to the renegade Jungian, James Hillman (*FL* 225, *BB* 146), who has advocated just such an approach, in books such as *The Dream and the Underworld* (1979), which seems directly to inform parts of the longest poem in Berengarten's collection, 'Conversation Between a Blue Butterfly and a Murdered Man at One of the Entrances to the Underworld'. This poem is one of the pieces in 'Flight of the Imago', the most philosophical section in this book, in which the author ruminates in long, metrically loose lines. Hillman has been consistent in his defence of the soul's perspective, which he contrasts with that of the spirit. The spirit, says Hillman, is azure-inclined, arrow-like in its trajectory, ascetic, and detached. The soul, meanwhile, enjoys dark depths, attachments, and polysemy. While the spirit soars, the soul flits – hence its name in Greek, *psyche*, butterfly (see Hillman 1975: 67–70). This is no doubt why the blue butterfly is the muse of this book:

> Teach me, blue butterfly, to open
> these winged words in singing and in dancing. (*BB* 100)

That an actual blue butterfly landed on the author's actual hand does not in the least preclude its being a symbol as well. This is the meaning of synchronicity, which Jung said is the "acausal connecting principle" behind meaningful coincidences (see Jung 1960: 471–531). Elsewhere in Berengarten, this way of thinking is consistent with the hermetic or Orphic worldview, which explains relations between events not in terms of cause and effect but rather in terms of analogy. Synchronicity is the theory of correspondences in practice.

So, in the long dialogue between the blue butterfly and the mur-dered man, the blue butterfly acts as Mercurial psychopomp, or soul-guide, explaining that "Language has gaps and holes and in them lurk / many incomprehensible expanses" (*BB* 91). But for Berengarten, as for Hillman, these gaps are entrances to another kind of consciousness, however disorienting – an underworld consciousness that is totally ungraspable by reason, not just the dead end of *nihil*, as in so much postmodernese. The murdered man asks the butterfly: "*Into or out of what notness do you call me?*" to which the butterfly responds, "Where but under dark. Underneath it. Under / Death" (*BB* 94) – a response that goes back at least to Heraclitus.[3]

Like any contemporary writer, Berengarten has fewer options than the premoderns had for writing about evil and death, which is probably the reason so little poetry these days takes on these enormous themes other than reductively. Dante had all of hell to work with, directed by the moral philosophy of Thomas Aquinas and Aristotle. The Hindus had their pantheon of demons, the Greeks their Furies and fickle gods. We don't have the collective imaginal forms for giving shape to the essences of these experiences, so we are left with existential reflections and private or eclectic symbols. We say, with Berengarten, "What justice is, nobody comprehends":

> Whoever offers arguments pretends
> to read fate's lines. Although we must swear by
> what justice is, nobody comprehends
>
> how destiny of chance weaves. (*BB* 19)[4]

Likewise, in a poem about a woman mourning a loved one, the poet says,

>   She does not believe
> in God, yet to the dead human, god-huge in her head,
> she ferries wordless questions. (*BB* 56)

---

[3] Fragment 42: "You could not discover the limits of soul, even if you travelled by every path in order to do so; such is the depth of its meaning" (Wheelwright 1966: 72). Hillman comments on this fragment: "Soul is not in the surface of things, the superficialities, but reaches down into hidden depths, a region which also refers to Hades and death" (Hillman 1975: 231, note 6).

[4] RB acknowledges that the image of reading "fate's lines" is consciously and explicitly derived from the *I Ching* (RB, personal communication).

And what are we to make of the apparent randomness of fate? "What hand, against the odds, pulled the Warsavian / musician out of the queue from ghetto to gas chamber / … Why him and not another?" (*BB* 85); and "The detached Goddess *Ananke* pours acid on our eyes / and smiles the far-away smile of a lover, thug / or torturer" (*BB* 88). Given this brutal indifference of life, what is the point of poetry – or as one poem title says, 'What then is singing? and what dancing?' (*BB* 99–100). Berengarten's answer is that it is

> an emptying and replenishing
> of the full cup of memory, into now and always
> from the source of always and now (*BB* 99)

by which we

> transform petty purpose into total celebration
> of now in the cup of always, always in the bowl of now (*BB* 99)

Berengarten's response to total death and negation, and ultimately this is no different from the answer that Dante gave, is that despite the unchanging predictable routineness of evil and human stupidity, "we must love" (*BB* 24) – love and courage extend beyond our individual lives or collective present, "to thread… through the fibres of the tree / that outspans and outlasts our histories" (*BB* 24). As another poem puts it:

> I affirm still a man may trace his particular vision
> however vicarious or wavering, like the path
> of a blue butterfly,
>
> [...]
>
> register that, for always, in memory's palpable zone
> for anybody who comes there, everybody who comes there,
> to visit, to be touched by beauty, as one enters a garden.
> (*BB* 101)

One of the most outstanding individual poems in the volume is a dream-vision narrative in *terza rima*. It appears in a section of 'Seven Statements of Survivors' – and, again, it is clear that by 'survivors' Berengarten means all of us. In this poem, the narrator encounters a goddess or *anima* figure by the sea. The sun has just passed beneath the horizon; it is dusk. The feminine figure, whose "silhouetted body might stir love's / unrealised longings in me, yet be bearable" (*BB* 70), comes to the narrator "as if she knew my self-esteem // had sunk so deep, I had lost hope" (*BB* 71). She represents the transformative power of beauty; in this case, given the darkness of the book's subject, beauty that is met on the other side of "the deepest terrors you must face". She is an initiator: "call me keeper of that door // locked fast below fear's last extremity"; "'Your soul is summoned to the secret source of day'", where the sun has gone, below the horizon (*BB* 72). The structure of the book as a whole, it seems, could be seen as an enactment of the sun's journey at night, renewal through descent.[5]

Or, as one of the massacre victim-narrators in 'Seven Songs of the Dead' puts it, addressing his daughter who is mourning him at his grave:

> when your dusk closes
> and your sun fails
> the black suns on my scales
> guide me through mazes
> unthreaded by cock-crow. (*BB* 48)

and in another poem:

> The black light behind the sun
> opens. And on the skies, black stars. (*BB* 107)

This book as a whole is both troubling and consolatory, because the author's response to his difficult subject is complex, sensitive, and unsentimental. Richard Berengarten has already accumulated a distinguished body of work, and *The Blue Butterfly* adds to that resumé.

---

[5] The same motif appears in other writings by RB. See his study of the sun symbolism in Ceri Richards' painting *The Black Apple of Gower* (*KT* 72–73, 74–79) and 'Black Light: In Memory of George Seferis' (*FL* 147–176, especially the two villanelles at *FL* 153 and 173).

REFERENCES

Arendt, Hannah. 1963. *Eichmann in Jerusalem: A Report on the Banality of Evil.* London: Faber & Faber.

Hillman, James. 1975. *Re-Visioning Psychology.* New York, NY: Harper and Row.

______. 1979. *The Dream and the Underworld.* New York, NY: Harper and Row.

Jung, C. G. 1960. 'Synchronicity: an acausal connecting principle' in *The Structure and Dynamics of the Psyche, Collected Works* (Vol. 8), (trans. R. F. C. Hull). London: Routledge & Kegan Paul: 471–531.

Wheelwright, Philip (ed.). 1966. *The Presocratics.* New York, NY: Odyssey Press.

The Blue Butterfly Effect

ALEKSANDAR PETROV

Translated from Serbian by Vera V. Radojević

In the mid-eighties, at the site of the Nazi massacre on the outskirts of Kragujevac in Serbia, a blue butterfly settled on the left hand of the English poet Richard Berengarten. A quarter of a century earlier, Edward Lorenz, an American scientist and meteorologist living in Boston, had discovered a phenomenon that he termed 'the butterfly effect'. Lorenz showed how changes of small proportions in one set of circumstances or conditions are capable of influencing phenomena elsewhere on a much larger scale. Modern chaos theory is based on this observation, because what is conventionally called chaos originates in minute changes that turn out to have unforeseen consequences. Lorenz illustrated his theory with a picturesque example: a butterfly fluttering its wings in Brazil can influence a hurricane in Texas (Lorenz 1963, 1965).

Of course, the concept of chaos in physics is rather different from the usage of the same word, and the notions that go with it, in everyday language. For one thing, the scientific concept highlights how the relationship between cause and effect is considerably more complex than classical physicists believed. For another, it interrogates long-term predictions based on simplistic understandings of the cause–effect relationship.

The fact that, according to the theory, a chaotic system may develop in a manner which is by no means 'chaotic' in any conventional sense but, rather, appears to be 'smooth and harmonious', is outstandingly confirmed by 'the butterfly effect' in the case of Richard Berengarten. The landing of the blue butterfly on the poet's finger brought about unpredictable and far-reaching changes in his own life and work. Readers of the short autobiographical essay 'Arijana's Thread' (*ITD* 73–77) – a piece that might almost be said to have been speckled by the powder of a blue butterfly's wings – will know that this momentary occurrence was the first in a string of events that eventually led to his spending three years in a turbulent Yugoslavia, between July 1987 and June 1990. During that time, he married a Yugoslav woman, Jasna Mišić, and fathered a daughter, Arijana, his third child. In the early years of the twenty-first century, Berengarten also published two volumes of poems on Serbian, Yugoslav and Balkan themes. These are *In a Time of Drought*, published in Serbian in 2004 (*U vreme suše*), two years before its first English publication, and *The Blue Butterfly*, also published in 2006, followed by its Serbian version *Plavi leptir* in 2007.[1] These two books not only confirm Berengarten's reputation as a significant European writer but, in their handling of universal themes, herald his status as a great poet.

So, on a sunny day in May 1985 – 'out of the blue' as the English would say, or 'like a lightning bolt out of a cloudless sky', as the Serbs would have it – a blue butterfly unexpectedly and unpredictably entered Berengarten's life, occupied a central role in it and became an integral image and symbol for much of his subsequent poetry. Berengarten and his first daughter, Lara, who at that time was seventeen years old, caught the butterfly's image for posterity via a camera lens, as the creature perched on the forefinger of the poet's left hand. As soon as he returned to Cambridge, Berengarten wrote a short poem, quickly followed by another. The focus of the first of these, 'The blue butterfly', was this left "writing hand" of his "now of a sudden willingly / stretched before me in Serbian spring sunlight" – which he suddenly saw in an entirely new light: "my Jew's hand, born out of ghettos and shtetls…, / my proud firm hand, / miraculously blessed by … two thousand eight hundred martyred / men, women and children" (*BB* 8). The second poem, 'Nada: hope or nothing', explores how that winged being of indeterminate gender actually landed on his hand (*BB* 9).

In Serbian, the gender of that tiny airborne guest needed to be made explicit. There was a choice between the masculine *leptir* and the feminine *leptirica*, which is also a diminutive. Early co-translators of the first of these pieces were the exceptional poet, Ivan V. Lalić, and Danilo Kiš, a novelist ranking among the finest in Europe. In their version, they

---

[1] *Editors' note*: This essay was written before the appearance of the final volume in RB's 'Balkan Trilogy', *Under Balkan Light* (2008; 2nd edition, 2011).

opted for the masculine variant.[2] Actually, when they did so, they could scarcely have envisaged the sheer force of that blue butterfly's impact – almost that of a blow, I would suggest – let alone how far-reaching its repercussions would be. Still, it is worth mentioning to English-speaking readers that the word for 'soul' or 'psyche' in Serbian [*duša*] is feminine, as are those for 'colour' [*boja*] and 'death' [*smrt*].

The 'arrival' of these two 'core' poems prompted Berengarten to build up a fuller context for them that involved historical, cultural, literary and even entomological information; so that, gradually, an entire superstructure was built up around them. The poet started by studying historical material on the massacre of October 1941 itself. He focused on establishing reliable figures for the number of victims which, he discovered, was just under 2,800, rather than 7,000.[3] He also set out to discover more details about those killed, in terms of age, ethnicity and social background. They included Serbs, Jews and Roma; members of the intelligentsia, workers and peasants; and a large group of schoolboys of high school age (*BB* 132–134). Berengarten also explored information about the perpetrators of the massacre and their own subsequent trials and sentences at Nuremberg, which turned out to be disproportionately lenient (*BB* 126–131 and 141–142). He took pains to find out more about the poets who had already written about the massacre, especially Desanka Maksimović (*BB* 135); and he worked tirelessly to establish the exact species of the fleeting visitant itself (*BB* 124–125). Inevitably, from this research new poems emerged, and these resulted in a sequence of seven poems that included the first two. Six further sequences were developed, each also containing seven poems.

The result of this undertaking is *The Blue Butterfly*. In addition to its forty-nine poems, the book contains poignant photographs, plus several of the victims' last messages (*BB* 113–121), followed by a 'Postscript' and notes which, together, amount to a genuinely scholarly study of the Kragujevac massacre (*BB* 123–137). The book also incorporates a good deal of valuable information about the making of the poems themselves and their historical and biographical backgrounds (*BB* 141-148).

---

[2] *Translator's note*: The first translators of *The Blue Butterfly* into Serbian were Moma Dimić and Ivan Gadjanski.

[3] *Translator's note*: RB came to realise that there had been considerable controversy concerning the number of victims. His major acknowledged source was the historian Staniša Brkić, head of the 21st October Memorial Museum in Šumarice. See *BB* 127-139 and Brkić 2007.

This is an exceptionally complex book in a number of ways. The first section is built around the 'core' of the first two poems mentioned above – 'The blue butterfly' and 'Nada: hope or nothing' – which are still the best known of Berengarten's 'Kragujevac poems'. This part also contains two pieces directly based on documentary material: 'Two documents' (*BB* 4–5) and 'Don't send bread tomorrow' (*BB* 6–7). Even at the slightest assessment, it has to be acknowledged that the long making of this book took considerable poetic stamina, and, as the highest endorsement, it resonates with love for justice and for humanity. The butterfly, in the guise of *psyche*, crowns the whole endeavour as a symbol of rebirth – since the butterfly emerges from its cocoon as from a grave.

In 2007, *The Blue Butterfly* appeared in Serbian in an outstanding translation by Vera V. Radojević. This edition benefited from a pair of essays that served as commentaries and epilogues, by the distinguished poets and essayists Slobodan Rakitić and Srba Ignjatović: the former a one-time President of the Serbian Writers' Association and the latter its incumbent at that time. Both writers praise the book for its high quality and rank Berengarten's work as among the finest in contemporary European poetry. They focus, too, on Berengarten's other 'Balkan' book, *In a Time of Drought* (2006), into which the poet adds detailed commentaries on folklore and mythology. As far as symbolic interpretations are concerned, however – of the butterfly itself, the colour blue, the number seven and aspects such as 'the forefinger' in the culture of the Serbs and other peoples – the poet seems to have left these matters to his critics. This challenge has been taken up most effectively by Slobodan Rakitić (*PL* 151–156).[4]

Among other things, Rakitić points to a key 'butterfly' connection between the two books, partly because one of the names for the girls who take part in the Balkan rainmaking ceremonies is 'butterflies'. This leads him to conclude that, "[i]n a way ... the blue butterfly configures the true meaning" of both books and also that "[i]t is as if the poet's own identity had merged with that of the blue butterfly"; that is to say, the poet "invoked his butterfly and 'fell into' its power".[5] Significantly, Rakitić also notes that their material involves "a whole range of associations, objects,

---

[4] *Editors' note*: The translator, Vera V. Radojević (see 'Poet in the Power of a Butterfly: An English Poet in the Balkans', 'Wonderland Through a Cracked Mirror: An English Poet in Yugoslavia', pp. 315–324 and pp. 302–314 respectively), also translated *The Blue Butterfly* into Serbian as *Plavi leptir* (*PL*).

[5] See p. 315 above.

meanings, references, denotations, sounds, quotations and documentary details", and that in the handling of this material, the poet "display[s] a veritably encyclopaedic command of poetic forms".[6] Critics should also be grateful to Rakitić for comparing *The Blue Butterfly* to the "once famous" symbolist drama, Maeterlinck's *The Blue Bird*, which "points not only to the mythical and religious meanings of the colour blue but also to its poetic and philosophical ones".[7]

It is helpful, too, to compare these books with other literary works. Srba Ignjatović calls *The Blue Butterfly* a "canto" [*spev*] and "a great and impressive memorial" (Ignjatović 157–159). George Szirtes calls it 'epic': "Epic poems are rare. This is one." (*BB* inside front cover).

Among the makers of such contemporary cantos and poems, a special place belongs to the great Serbian poet Vasko Popa. The vast majority of Popa's *oeuvre* has been translated into English (see, for example, 1998); and the epic scope of his books has been extensively explored, especially vis-à-vis their cyclic structure, by critics and commentators such as Miodrag Pavlović (1964: 139–140), Ivan V. Lalić (1971: 7–28), Aleksandar Petrov (2000: 403–417) and Ronelle Alexander (1985: 26–169). Moreover, two of Popa's best known books in this genre, *Sporedno nebo* [*Secondary Heaven*] and *Vučja so* [*Wolf Salt*] have a cyclic structure identical to *In a Time of Drought* and *The Blue Butterfly*: seven cycles of seven poems. Of course, there are both similarities and differences between these two works of Popa's, just as there are between the two by Berengarten; but comparison of all four books would certainly provide a fascinating and worthwhile study. Berengarten himself mentions Popa, who was his personal friend, among the authors who influenced *The Blue Butterfly* (*BB* 'Acknowledgements'). The second cycle of poems of *In a Time of Drought*, 'For the Green Rider', is dedicated to Popa (*ITD* 11–19).

Here, I should like to explore a particular detail in Popa relating to the number seven, that is, the number both of sets of poems and of poems within each set. Between 1962 and 1968, while Popa was working on *Sporedno nebo*, he also compiled an anthology of medieval Serbian poetry, entitled *Jutro misleno* [*Spiritual Morning*] (2008). In 1963, he also published a selection of the writings of Domentijan, an important Serbian poet of the 13th century. In Popa's afterword to Domentijan, I noticed

---

[6] See p. 316 above.

[7] See p. 322 above.

an interesting parallel between his own writing and the "unsilenceable poetry of the medieval Serbian 'goldwinged hymn-writers'", as he called his distant predecessors (Domentijan 1963: 139). As noted by Djordje Trifunović in his preface to a book of Domentijan's writing, one of this Serbian writer's favourite readings was 'Šestodnev' ['The Six Days'], compiled by the eleventh-century Bulgarian scholar John Exarch (*ibid.* 17). This text tells us not only that there are seven heavens in the sky but that these are like "seven circles, over each of which seven stars are distributed ... conjoined in such a way that one [circle] leans against the other" (*ibid.* 25). Popa's *Wayside Heaven* is an absurd comedy, because it depicts the cosmos being devoid of divine presence, despite the fact that, even in our 'secondary' condition, there exists a yearning for the 'primal' paradise, that is to say, for an earthly version of paradise that is anterior to the Fall – or, as it is described in Serbian, 'primal flaw' or 'primal mistake'. And in this version of his own Creation myth, Popa writes that this "mistake" was rather small in the beginning – comparable almost to the light strokes of a butterfly's wings: "Once upon a time there was a mistake / So silly so small / That no one would even have noticed it" (Popa 1977: 68).

Apart from Popa's modern (and hence absurd) vision of the underworld and upper world, contextual and structural comparisons of Berengarten's *The Blue Butterfly* can be pursued in other directions too, especially vis-à-vis Dante. One of Berengarten's poems, 'Diagonal' (*BB* 70–72), adapts the *terza rima* form of the *Divine Comedy*. In this poem, a female figure appears who is comparable to Beatrice. It should also be borne in mind that, besides the numbers three and nine, the number seven is quite significant in Dante's work, particularly in the *Purgatory* – with its seven terraces, and the Angelic guardian at the gate, who writes the letter *P* (standing for *Peccati*, 'Sins') seven times on the poet's forehead, with the point of a sword.[8] Furthermore, one of the many symbolic configurations of the butterfly in Berengarten's long poem is that the creature appears as guardian to "one of the entrances to the Underworld" (*BB* 89–98). Thus, at this point the butterfly takes on the role both of interpreter of the language of the dead and of the Dantesque and Berengartenian "Beyonds" (*BB* 93), that lie on "the Far Side" of silence (*BB* 79).

Of course, the vision of the other world in the work of a modern poet like Berengarten is very different from that of Dante's *Divine*

---

[8] "Sette P nella fronte mi descrisse / col punton della spada" (*Purgatorio*: IX, 111–112).

Comedy – in both 'positive' and 'negative' senses. Berengarten's vision never attains paradise; but neither do we find the warning "Abandon hope all ye who enter here"[9] inscribed over the gates of the hell-on-earth that he explores. Furthermore, Berengarten's blue butterfly is as much the angel and harbinger of death and nothingness as herald of hope and forerunner of love. Berengarten's poetic world is framed within space–time between *hope* and *nothing*. The blue butterfly is a being that inhabits both poles of this world because, in the poet's hand, it paints the most horrifying landscapes of death; but it also takes that hand and "writes / in invisible ink across its page of air / *Nada, Elpidha, Nadezhda, Esperanza, Hoffnung*" (*BB* 9). These words all spell / signify / mean *Hope* – in Serbian and Croatian, Greek, Russian, Spanish and last, and perhaps most significantly of all, German.

❦

I would like to see a future edition of *The Blue Butterfly* published with illustrations from Peter Lubarda's cycle of paintings entitled *Kragujevac 1941*. One of the greatest, if not the greatest of all Yugoslav painters in the second half of the 20th century, Lubarda commenced work on this cycle of twenty-six paintings in 1966 and completed them for his 1968 exhibition in Kragujevac. At that time he had already received several international awards, and distinguished artists, art critics and historians had written in praise of his work. When he donated these paintings to the Memorial Park in Kragujevac, he wrote:

> These paintings are done in various techniques and represent *a single unique set* and *a single indivisible entity*, as can be seen from their titles, starting with *Sećanja na 1941* [*Remembering 1941*] and ending with *Šuplji šlem* [*Hollow Helmet*]. Altogether, they represent a sort of novel in paint, whose subject is the inconceivable suffering caused to a town and its proud citizens.[10]

And in the catalogue for that exhibition, Miodrag B. Protić writes of this set of paintings by Lubarda:

---

[9] "Lasciate ogni speranza, voi ch'intrate" (*Inferno*: III, 9).

[10] Lubarda's 'Letter to the Executive Board of the Kragujevac Memorial Park' was not published, but was included in the exhibition *Lubarda 1907–2007*, held at the Museum of Yugoslav History, Belgrade, 2008.

The 1941 massacre in Kragujevac is a tragic subject that has generated innumerable treatments, both poetic and metaphysical. By confronting a real event, Lubarda pronounces his clear verdict on the gigantic destructive power that evil and terror have wrought throughout history. However, in addition to this verdict, within each painting and throughout the exhibition as a whole we trace secondary and tertiary dimensions; and through these, we are offered the chance to think about even broader and deeper themes: the meaning of life, the peculiar marks that life tracks across eternity, the inevitability of all processes, and cosmic movements and transformations. In this way, his treatment of an event of national significance takes on layers of poetic meaning that are both transcendental and universal. (Protić 1968: 1)

Taken together with the words the great painter himself wrote about *Kragujevac 1941*, this commentary on Lubarda's paintings is highly applicable to Berengarten's poetic treatment of the enormity of evil in the world and condemnation of atrocities throughout history in *The Blue Butterfly*. Indeed, Berengarten submits the multiple layerings and variations of evil and atrocity to identical treatment – in the precise sense that the work's multi-dimensional poetic and metaphysical themes ramify and overarch the poem's primary 'trunk'. And although obviously Berengarten's poems have a good deal to tell us about the poet himself, they at once also involve a "telling" (see *BB* 10–15) of human destiny – and of the sense that humans *make* of destiny within the transformations of earthly and cosmic processes. Moreover, like Lubarda, Berengarten deploys various techniques – poetic ones, in his case, of course – not only in the book's overall design but also within the framework of each of its particular cycles or, rather, circles. The complexity of these techniques and the masterly skill with which they are applied deserve a separate study in itself. One almost has the impression that there is no verse or stanza form, whether classical or modern, that Berengarten does not deploy in *The Blue Butterfly*. All the same, his book works as a unique, indivisible, unrepeatable unity. Its themes widen and intermingle in concentric rings; and, all the while, the blue butterfly seems to flutter over the various *fleurs du mal* sown by human hand across the twentieth century, perching here and there for an instant, not only in Kragujevac, Srebrenica or Kosovo, but in the concentration camp of Mauthausen, in the pit dug out of Manhattan on 9/11, and on the gallows of Rwanda – as well as in places where 'accidents happen', for example, in the Paris tunnel where the 'authors' of one such particular 'accident' were a bunch of paparazzi and a drugged driver (see *BB* 78). Into the air that floats above such sites of accident and evil, the blue butterfly carves words of condemnation and disgust, inscribes question marks and exclamation marks, utters lamentations for victims and intones elegies among those who have somehow, miraculously, survived. The blue butterfly enters into dialogue with those who are dead and those who are sentenced to death; and *that* means with us all in general and each and every one of us in particular. The winged creature weaves metaphorical wreaths above individual graves and mass graves; but it also heralds the mercy of blessing and awakens the hope of resurrection.

The final lines of the book are genuinely symbolic and embed a multitude of meanings: "Red tulip petals / scatter. A blue / butterfly hovers." (*BB* 111). Red and blue. A dead tulip and a blue butterfly hovering above it. Neither hell without hope, nor paradise without suffering and doubt.

References

Alexander, Ronelle. 1985. *The Structure of Vasko Popa's Poetry*. Columbus, OH: Slavica Publishers.

Brkić, Staniša. 2007. *Ime i broj: Kragujevačka tragedija 1941* [*Name and Number: the Kragujevac Tragedy 1941*]. Kragujevac: Spomen park, Kragujevački oktobar [Kragujevac October Memorial Park].

Domentijan. 1963. *Domentijan* (ed. Djordje Trifunović). Belgrade: Nolit.

Ibler, Reinhard (ed.). 2000. *Zyklusdichtung in den slawischen Literaturen.* [*Poetic Cycles in Slavic Literature*]. Frankfurt am Main: Peter Lang.

Ignjatović, Srba. 2007. 'Neuništivi spomenik' ['Indestructible Monument'] in RB *Plavi leptir* (*The Blue Butterfly*) (trans. Vera V. Radojević). Kragujevac and Belgrade: Spomen park Kragujevački Oktobar [Kragujevac October Memorial Park] and Plava Tačka [Blue Spot]: 157–159. *(PL)*

Lalić, Ivan V. 1971. 'Poezija Vaska Pope' ['The Poetry of Vasko Popa'] in V. Popa, *Pesme* [*Poems*], 7–28.

Lorenz, Edward. 1963. 'Deterministic Nonperiodic Flow', *Journal of Atmospheric Science* 20: 131–140.

______. 1965. 'A Study of the Predictability of a 28-Variable Atmospheric Model', *Tellus* 17: 321–333.

Pavlović, Miodrag. 1964. *Osam pesnika* [*Eight Poets*], Belgrade: Prosveta.

Petrov, Aleksandar. 2000. 'Cycles in the Poetry of Vasko Popa', in R. Ibler (ed.), *Zyklusdichtung in den slavischen Literaturen* [*Poetic Cycles in Slavic Literature*]. Frankfurt am Main: Peter Lang: 403–417.

Popa, Vasko. 1968. *Sporedno nebo* [*Secondary Heaven*]. Belgrade: Nolit.

______. 1971. *Pesme* [*Poems*]. Novi Sad and Belgrade: Matica Srpska, Srpska književna zadruga (Serbian Literary Association).

______. 1975. *Vučja so* [*Wolf Salt*]. Belgrade: Nolit.

______. 1977. *Collected Poems 1943–1976* (trans. Anne Pennington, with an introduction by Ted Hughes). Manchester: Carcanet Press.

______. 1998. *Collected Poems* (trans. Anne Pennington and Francis R. Jones). London: Anvil Press Poetry.

______(ed.). 2008. *Jutro misleno* [*Spiritual Morning*]. Novi Sad: Akademska knjiga [Academic Book].

Protić, Miodrag B. 1968. *Petar Lubarda* (catalogue for the exhibition 'Petar Lubarda, *Kragujevac 1941*'). Kragujevac: Spomen park Kragujevački oktobar [Kragujevac October Memorial Park].

Rakitić, Slobodan. 2007. 'Pesnik u vlasti leptira' ['Poet in the Power of a Butterfly'] in RB *Plavi leptir* (*The Blue Butterfly*) (trans. Vera V. Radojević). Kragujevac and Belgrade: Spomen park Kragujevački Oktobar [Kragujevac October Memorial Park] and Plava Tačka [Blue Spot]: 151–156. *(PL)* See also 315–321 above.

Hath Not a Jew Hands?

STEPHEN WILSON

Yes, but in English literature they are not the same as other people's. They have a different anatomy – more often than not, they are disgusting. They favour ducats over daughters. They are murderous paws like those belonging to T. S. Eliot's Rachel *née* Rabinovitch in 'Sweeney Among the Nightingales', or rapacious claws like those of Dickens' Fagin in *Oliver Twist* or Sir Walter Scott's Isaac of York in *Ivanhoe*, whose "hand trembled for joy as he wrapped up the first seventy pieces of gold"; or they are long and dirty like those of Baroness Orczy's Jew of "loathsome appearance" in *The Scarlet Pimpernel*. They have blood on them, like Chaucer's Jews in *The Prioress's Tale*, who cut the throats of innocent Christian children, or they are fat and bejewelled like the fat Jew manager, loathed by Oscar Wilde's Dorian Gray. And they get everywhere, conspire to penetrate every organ of civil society, every nation's political establishment, as in the mind of the poet, Ezra Pound.

From the point of view of a Jew's own canon – *Psalm 137* – the proper functioning of his hands is intimately linked to an unfailing memory of Jerusalem, to the diasporic experience of exile. A Jew's hand will never work properly if he forgets his history, betrays his origins. How shall a Jewish poet sing in a foreign land? What is an Anglo-Jewish poet to make of his hands?

> On my Jew's hand, born out of ghettos and shtetls,
> raised from unmarked graves of my obliterated people
> in Germany, Latvia, Lithuania, Poland, Russia,
>
> on my hand mothered by a refugee's daughter,
> first opened in blitzed London, grown big
> through post-war years safe in suburban England,

on my pink, educated, ironical left hand
of a parvenu not quite British pseudo gentleman
which first learned to scrawl in untutored messages

among Latin-reading rugby-playing militarists
in an élite boarding school on Sussex's green downs
and against the cloister walls of puritan Cambridge,

on my hand, weakened by anomie, on my
writing hand, now of a sudden willingly
stretched before me in Serbian spring sunlight,

on my unique living hand, trembling and troubled
by this May visitation, like a virginal
leaf new sprung on the oldest oak in Europe,

on my proud firm hand, miraculously blessed
by the two thousand eight hundred martyred
men, women and children fallen at Kragujevac,

a blue butterfly simply fell out of the sky
and settled on the forefinger
of my international bloody human hand. (*BB* 8)

Here is a remarkable poem, a beautiful poem which supplies the answer.
What makes the first line so striking is obvious. It is the word "Jew". The
poem could have said: "On my hand, born out of ghettos and shtetls",
then it would have been a quiet poem. Instead it sounds the word "Jew"
loudly, non-pejoratively, as if it were a church bell in a Christian land.
This is clearly a reclamation job. In the Anglophone world the word
"Jew", or "Jew's", is almost universally associated with something nasty
or offensive – to jew someone, to swindle or cheat; Jewy, mingy, tight;
Jewish lightning, deliberate arson for insurance fraud; Jew-boy, The
Jew-Pork Times; Jew's Ear, an ugly rubbery fungus; Jew's Piano, a cash
register; Jew Canoe, used derogatorily to refer to a Jaguar car; a jew nail,
a corrugated or crooked nail used by carpenters (Green 1986: 12, 19,
93, 116). But this poem, written in English, declares itself immediately,
boldly, as the work of a Jew. It is rising from the "unmarked graves" of the
narrator's "obliterated" people in order to make a mark.

The poem harks back to the origin of the hand in "ghettos and
shtetls", in the closed Jewish communities of medieval Christian Europe,
nineteenth-century Eastern Europe, twentieth-century Nazi Europe.

But it is not born *in* these communities it is born *out* of them, *borne* away from them. It has been saved, conveyed across the English Channel by a refugee and her daughter into the safety of "suburban England". The suburbs – places so safe that the ageing Ezra Pound chose to locate his anti-Semitism there, neutralised and scaled down to the form of a "stupid suburban prejudice" (Carpenter 1988: 899). In fact, the lesson many English Jews learned from the genocide of their European brethren was that 'no place is safe', no degree of assimilation a protection against murderous anti-Semitism.

This hand "first opened in blitzed London", with all its connotations of camaraderie, Londoners sleeping in the Underground joined together against a common enemy. But it also first opened at a time when Jews all over Europe were being gassed. English Jews, it became clear, could not rest easy in their liberalised nineteenth-century identity as 'Englishmen of the Mosaic Persuasion'. The consequence of dispersion was, as it had been, that the land of a Jew's birth, a Jew's native language, would always be 'foreign'.

As Jon Silkin puts it in *Making a Republic*:

> You can stay, the Home Office admits.
> What's it like, Alien? In
> Japan, my agit was for, not England – it was: for
> a suburb's mildness in bronchial evenings;
> but I missed English, being my speech,
> what else for a Jew, but another's language? (2002: 72)

The advantage of dispersion (pitifully costly) was that a Diaspora Jew was immunised against the excesses of nationalism.

The third, fourth and fifth stanzas of 'The blue butterfly' deliver their explicitly ironised message concerning the status of the narrator's hand, as if it were being seen through the cultural spectacles of 'the other' or the 'internalised other'. It is undoubtedly an 'Anglo-Jewish hand'. It is a "pink" hand, at first a baby's hand, maybe a little piggy, a pinkie, a feeble hand. Certainly not a rough hand or heavy hand; but it grows into a left hand, perhaps a sinister hand; an élite, educated hand which is the "writing hand" of the author, but an upstart hand, an out-of-place-hand, a pseudo-gentleman's hand. It feels itself to be anomic, unaffiliated. It is non-militaristic in a society in which militarism is a sign of superior status and self-confidence, where it is *de rigueur* for kings, queens and princes to be in the armed forces. It is not the hand of a forward in the rugby scrum.[1] It is cloistered in Cambridge rather than immured in Warsaw, yet it does not feel comfortable.

But then something unexpected happens, something uplifting, and it seems that the hand has to be in Serbia, in Eastern Europe rather than England, for this to happen. Suddenly it is spring and the hand is enlivened, bathed in sunlight. It recovers its will, it stretches "willingly" before the narrator, it almost stretches forth Biblically, it is "firm" rather than attenuated, "virginal", unsullied, and appears to have recovered from some deep diasporic malaise.

This hand is no longer defined by others. It is no longer enervated by negative group stereotyping. It has emerged from the stigmatised generality to become "unique". It belongs to its owner, not to the name-callers. It belongs to the person in the poem who has a history of which he is proud, it has become itself. And it has been "blessed" by the victims of a Nazi massacre, one might say enjoined by them to memorialise and celebrate their lives – and life itself. So in my reading, this is a profoundly humanistic life-affirming poem.

The oak tree is often used as a narrowly nationalist symbol of England connoting steadfastness, integrity, courage – "Heart of oak are our ships, / Heart of oak are our men" (Garrick 1759: online), but in Berengarten's poem the revitalised hand gains strength from its rootedness on "the oldest oak in *Europe*". It could not have acquired these characteristics in England because in English usage, heavily inflected with centuries of Christian anti-Semitism, the word 'Jew' connotes the opposite – rootlessness, untrustworthiness, cowardice. Arguably the same (or worse) could be said of other European languages. But it seems to me that from the point of view of the voice in the poem, liberation from the constrictions of English nationalism is an essential condition of its freedom. And this is experienced by virtue of returning to Eastern Europe, a home of sorts, albeit the home of a destroyed people.

To become a scion of the oldest oak in Europe is to throw off the spoiled identity of an English Diaspora Jew, a non-English Englishman, and transform it via supranational identifications into a positive universal form of being, a fully human being. The process is inspired by the experience of having the blue butterfly settle on the forefinger of the poet's hand. It is an honour, a privilege, rather like D. H. Lawrence's encounter with a

---

[1] But outside the poem RB played rugby throughout his schooldays. He obtained colours and was prop forward in the First XV at Mill Hill School (personal communication).

snake at his water-trough – "Was it humility, to feel so honoured? / I felt so honoured" (Lawrence 1957: 77). Or Jon Silkin's:

> blue flies, before the weight of summer gets pushed
> by spring to melt into winter, come
>   one day, and die that same one.
>   Which means snow soon,
>   suffocating all smells
>   but its own scent.
> 'I was honoured by their coming upon me,' your
> son, his maiden companions. (2002: 72)

The blue butterfly alights on the poet's finger like a sword placed upon the shoulder by a reigning monarch, like manna falling from heaven, like the quality of mercy. It ennobles him, it ordains him and he becomes a spiritual aristocrat. I am reminded of Disraeli's alleged rejoinder to Daniel O'Connell, who had referred disparagingly to his Jewish ancestry in the House of Commons: "Yes, I am a Jew, and when the ancestors of the right honourable gentleman were brutal savages in an unknown island, mine were priests in the temple of Solomon" (Aberbach: 142).

Constant repetition of the words "on my" in Berengarten's poem has the anaphoric character of a chant or prayer which builds up a tension, an expectation concerning the next "on my", reaching a climax in the penultimate stanza. Then in the final one we are released. In place of the expected "on my" we have an explosion of rhyme – butterfly, sky. It is as if an identity slowly grows through the deposition of qualities, one layer after another; and then undergoes a sudden change, an epiphany sparked by the landing of the blue butterfly. Berengarten has succeeded in crafting a form which exactly matches the content of his poem.

I want to compare Berengarten's butterfly with the butterflies of another Anglo-Jewish poet, the late Michael Hamburger:

> WHEN THE sun breaks through,
> From hiding-places unnoticed
> Comes a flutter, a spreading of wings,
> The small blue butterflies
>
> Out again, reprieved,
> On the apple-mint flowers
> Together with copper, meadow brown
> And grey-buff mottled day-moth.

A redolence rises, phlox,
Offers to waft me back
Into a childhood garden,
Tenderness outlived,
Hopes fulfilled, discarded.
And I refuse the offer,
Let a fir's harsher breath
Propose to take me farther,
Beyond birth, beyond
Any garden I have known,

Played in, laboured in, lost;
To the wilderness rather
In which the grand fir grew
Before those whose guest I was
Made it theirs, called it theirs,
The continent never mine. (Hamburger 1997: 42)

Hamburger's long elegiac poem 'Late', from which this section is taken, is clearly the work of an older man preparing himself for death. He "refuses" the offer of "redolence" conveyed by the blue butterflies and chooses instead a "harsher" more stringent experience that will carry him beyond anything he has known, beyond life itself. Like the opening of Berengarten's 'The blue butterfly', 'Late' gives poignant expression to a refugee status, which is written into the sensibility of all English Jews, whether or not they were born, like Hamburger, in another land:

IF NOW, a guest, I go back
To my native city,
What I see is not what I know
Who from certain death in childhood
Was removed for a second birth
In another city, another country. (*ibid.* 25)

Here the Jewish experience of exile – of being at best a guest, at worst a reviled alien – is universalised into the human condition. We are all existentially transient, all passing guests in the natural world, all Jews who must look beyond the false comforts provided by national allegiance. To face this stark reality without the comforts of group solidarity, without the temptations offered by the strength of the 'fasces', the gratifications of social bonding, is a difficult thing to do.

In a now famous interview published in *The Paris Review*, Ted Hughes says: "Maybe all poetry, insofar as it moves us and connects with us, is a revealing of something that the writer doesn't actually want to say, but desperately needs to communicate, to be delivered of" (Hughes 1995: 1). Consider the final stanza of 'The blue butterfly' with its deceptively simple content but highly complicated prosody – rhymes, half-rhymes, visual rhymes, suggested rhymes, imperfect rhymes, weaving an intricate pattern of associative links, a wonderful structure of poetic ambiguity. Is the blue butterfly actually a Jew-butterfly? The colour blue, with its association to Heaven, is a symbolic reminder of the presence of God in Jewish tradition. The Hebrew Bible commands Jews to make fringes in the corners of their garments in which a thread of blue should be present, "that ye may look upon it, and remember all the commandments of the LORD, and do them" (Numbers 15: 39).

That a blue butterfly is a suitable metaphor for God is nicely confirmed in Rodney Pybus's poem, 'Holly Blues', written in memory of the Tienanmen Square dead, June 1989. Here, in the beginning of the poem, the absence of the butterfly is equivalent to the loss of hope, the loss of peace, the loss of life:

> Look friends, when ever-
> green lustrous leaves turn brown
> and fall on dying soil
>
> you know there can be
> no transformations,
> no unfurling of amazement –
>
> you are not going to see, after all,
> hope's double parings of sky
> become shy, pacific

but as in Berengarten's poem, there is a development. The Holly Blue reappears and the metaphor is extended in a brilliant poetic coup. Now the oscillations of the butterfly's wings presenting blue when open, grey when closed, are made to represent the constant intermingling of life and death, once more in similar vein to Berengarten. But this seems to me a peculiarly Christian expression of the idea, especially since the butterfly is "Holly" and putting her "Sunday / morning" wings together in obvious reference to a church service:

the year's earlier young
are tolled and gone.
Watch how that Holly Blue –
there in front of
your eyes – puts her Sunday
morning wings together.

Let us praise her!
They close, and she turns to
the world not blue, but almost

colourless grey,
its sheen lightly
spotted with full-stops. (Pybus 1994: 31)

To return to Berengarten's work, the Greek word for butterfly, *psyche*, also means soul, and the metamorphosis characteristic of a butterfly's development corresponds to the soul's condition, its immortality. According to *Bulfinch's Mythology*, "Psyche, then, is the human soul, which is purified by sufferings and misfortunes, and is thus prepared for the enjoyment of true and pure happiness" (online). So, in this case, we could see the Hebrew 'blue', fused with the Greek 'butterfly', in the central image of the poem.

This fits well with the poem's transcendental movement, its revelation. I remarked earlier that the poet sang out "Jew" like a church bell. And it seems to me that further evidence for the unconscious rhetorical fusion of Jewish self with Christian homeland, England, mediated via the image of the butterfly, is to be found in line three of the second stanza of Berengarten's poem 'The shadow well', where he introduces his own name (Burns) in close juxtaposition to the insect:

Climb up, Deacon, to the tower,
pull the rope and ring the bell.
The butterfly burns on its flower.
Gunner, you will die as well. (*BB* 39)

'The blue butterfly' processes deep diasporic emotions in a transformative sequence of images – a weak hand becomes a proud firm hand. In this way feelings of persecution associated with membership of a reviled minority are magicked into feelings of security associated with membership of a privileged oligarchy. This is what the poet "doesn't actually want to say". "Sussex's green downs", the precious stone set in the silver sea, from

which the poet feels unwillingly estranged, are superseded by the blue
butterfly's landing in Serbia. It creates perhaps a precious European Jew-el,
perhaps a ring on the finger in which the 'Jew' himself is linguistically
set, a place where he can feel at home. Berengarten's visionary Blakeian
poem, 'The Rose of Sharon', reinforces the point:

> Moses on the mountain saw
> jewels blazing at his throat,
> ornaments without a flaw
> and upon the tablets wrote: (*FL* 94)

Is the "international bloody human hand", by virtue of its association
with the blue butterfly, a blue-blooded hand, an international aristocrat
rather than an international conspirator? Has it been dignified by royalty,
as were the Jews of Denmark when, in legend, their King donned a
yellow star? A hand raised high rather than "lower than the wharf rat
dives"?[2] (Eliot 1971: 119). Is it "bloody" because its blood has been spilt?
Is it "bloody" because it has been subject to a centuries old 'blood-libel'?
Is it "bloody" because it is burdensome? Is it "human" because it has
participated in the spilling of others' blood? It is all of these things.

But to focus on the hidden psychological metabolism of 'The blue
butterfly' is to do a disservice to its immensely generous spirit, to what
the poet *does* actually want to say and succeeds so well in saying. In the
decades immediately following World War II, critics such as Theodor
Adorno and George Steiner expressed the view that 'silence' was the only
appropriate response to the Holocaust, that it was somehow obscene for
it to be incorporated into the domain of art (Adorno *et al.* 1980, Steiner
1967); "I have no wish to soften the saying that to write lyric poetry after
Auschwitz is barbaric", Adorno wrote (1980: 188).

Berengarten's poem, 'The Telling', takes a different view:

> Numb silence, though, is no answer to evil.
> To remain tacit, to call up no speech on its
> repeated occurrences, is to grovel
> before it, as to some pre-ordained essence
> demanding just as complete acquiescence
> as the rotations of seasons and planets,

---

[2] See *New York Review of Books*, 29 March and 27 September 1990.

> and that won't do. Fail or not, I must try
> this telling: like a treadmill, mangle, wringer,
> or spinning drum squeezing spongy death dry,
> let me crush thought, sacrifice-soaked, to drain
> oil from slaughter, juice from the fruit of pain
> into my blood, along my writing finger (*BB* 12)

He is offering himself as a conduit for meaning, an interpreter for the dead. Poets must write poems, and have to morph their human experience, whatever it may be, into the best form that language allows. If the strict forms and end rhymes of pre-modern poems often seem 'forced' and likely to trivialise, they may also be employed in a post-modern context to powerful effect. As Robert Lowell said in a *Paris Review* interview in 1961: "we [Lowell and the poet Allen Tate] wanted our formal patterns to seem a hardship" (10). It is as if the very need for the poem to conform to a pattern creates a precarious membrane for the unspeakable emotions, the unspeakable horrors which are all the time threatening to burst out. Berengarten puts it this way in 'The corners of the mouth':

> a black ring to bind speech, carved
> in jet or onyx, to contain
> the unsayable (*BB* 106)

Take his harrowing villanelle, 'The death of children':

> It is the death of children most offends
> nature and justice. No use asking why.
> What justice is, nobody comprehends.
>
> What punishment can ever make amends?
> There's no pretext, excuse or alibi.
> It is the death of children most offends.
>
> Whoever offers arguments pretends
> to read fate's lines. Although we must swear by
> what justice is, nobody comprehends
>
> how destiny or chance weaves. Who defends
> their motives with fair reasons tells a lie.
> It is the death of children most offends.

Death can't deserve to reap such dividends
from these, who scarcely lived, their parents cry.
What justice is, nobody comprehends.

Bring comfort then, and courage. Strangers, friends,
are we not all parents when children die?
What justice is, nobody comprehends.
It is the death of children most offends. (*BB* 19)

To paraphrase Adorno, one might almost say, "After Auschwitz there can be only lyric poetry." Berengarten's work is, above all, a testament to two things: just as he doesn't flinch from the record of human depravity, so he never fails to preserve the spirit of human hope. And it is inclusive – we are *all* made parents when children die. We are brought together not by the iron bonds of totalitarianism but the compassion inspired by tragedy. 'The blue butterfly' has to be read in conjunction with its companion poem, 'Nada: hope or nothing', printed on the opposite page. It is:

like a rainbow without rain, like the invisible
hand of a god stretching out of nowhere
to shower joy brimful from Plenty's horn (*BB* 9)

and the butterfly takes the poet's hand and writes, "in invisible ink across its page of air / *Nada, Elpidha, Nadezhda, Esperanza, Hoffnung*" (*BB* 9). Here is poetry's synecdochic reply to Robert Frost's mischievous question:

Why make so much of fragmentary blue
In here and there a bird, or butterfly,
Or flower, or wearing-stone or open eye,
When heaven presents in sheets the solid hue? (Frost 2001: 220)

I suggest that Berengarten's *The Blue Butterfly* is a quintessentially Anglo-Jewish work; more than anything a twenty-first century Book of Psalms, conveying in modern English idiom traditional Messianic trust, the triumph of hope over despair, enduring faith in the goodness of life.

Acknowledgments

I should like to thank Kate Wilson and Matthew Francis for comments, and Claire Crowther for allowing me sight of Chapter 4, 'Blue Horizon' in her MPhil thesis, *Blue*, 2004, Glamorgan University.

References

Aberbach, David. 2013. *The European Jews, Patriotism and the Liberal State 1739-1939*. Abingdon: Routledge.

Adorno, Theodor. 1980. 'Commitment' in T. Adorno *et al.* (eds), *Aesthetic and Politics: The Key Texts of the Classic Debate with German Marxism*. London: Verso, pp. 177–195.

Bulfinch's Mythology. 'Vertumnus and Pomona, Cupid and Psyche' (Chapter 6). Online at: http://www.online-literature.com/bulfinch/mythology_fable/6/. Consulted, 1 February 2016.

Carpenter, Humphrey. 1988. *A Serious Character: The Life of Ezra Pound*. Boston, MA: Houghton Mifflin.

Eliot, T. S. 1971. *The Waste Land: A Facsimile and Transcript of the Original Drafts Including the Annotations of Ezra Pound*. (ed. Valerie Eliot). London: Faber and Faber.

Frost, Robert. 2001. *The Poetry of Robert Frost* (ed. Edward Connery Lathem). London: Vintage.

Garrick, David. 1759. *Heart of Oak*. Online at: http://www.contemplator.com/england/heartoak.html. Consulted,1 February 2016.

Green, Jonathon. 1986. *The Slang Thesaurus*. London: Hamish Hamilton.

Hamburger, Michael. 1997. *Late*. London: Anvil Press Poetry.

Hughes, Ted. 1995. 'The art of poetry No. 71', *The Paris Review* 134 (Spring): 54–94. Online at: http://www.theparisreview.org/interviews/1669/the-art-of-poetry-no-71-ted-hughes. Consulted, 22 February 2016.

Lawrence, D. H. 1957. *The Complete Poems* (Vol. 2). London: Heinemann.

Lowell, Robert. 1961. 'The art of poetry No. 3', *The Paris Review* 25 (Winter-Spring): 1–41. Online at: http://www.theparisreview.org/interviews/4664/the-art-of-poetry-no-3-robert-lowell. Consulted, 22 February, 2016.

Pybus, Rodney. 1994. *Flying Blues*. Manchester: Carcanet Press.

Silkin, Jon. 2002. *Making a Republic*. Manchester: Carcanet Press.

Steiner, George. 1967. *Language and Silence: Essays on language, literature and the inhuman*. New York, NY: Atheneum.

'Do vidjenja Danitsé':
the Beauty of Complexity

Andrija Matić

'Do vidjenja Danitsé' is a long poem of more than 400 lines. It is strategically positioned as the opening piece in *Under Balkan Light* (2008, pp. 1–15), the final volume in Richard Berengarten's *Balkan Trilogy*. An authorial note tells the reader that the Serbian title means 'Goodbye Danitsa'. An English subtitle provides the gloss: 'Goodbye Balkan Belle' (*UBL* 1). Then comes an epigraph in Serbian, which, as a further authorial note explains, refers to a song popular in former Yugoslavia, a country that has fallen – or, rather, been torn – apart. So from the outset, the entire linguistic and historical context locates the poem firmly outside normative Anglo-American experience and far from any easily recognisable Anglophone poetic zone. Thus, it might be said that this poem belongs in both a Balkan and an English time-and-space zone, a rare if not unique combination.

Apart from title and context, the first aspects to strike the reader are the poem's structure and layout. Gradually the reader discovers that the entire piece consists of a single sentence, which might possibly even merit it a place in the *Guinness Book of Records* as the longest sentence ever written in Anglo-American poetry. The poem is also modelled around a large number of Balkan toponyms, all from former Yugoslavia. These names are inserted into the text, in capitals, almost as though they had strayed, or been pushed, into it – or even invaded it – from the left hand margin. The lines against which they have been juxtaposed appear to have been halved in length:

Danitsé with your bitter black cherries and heavenly
lilac abundant on hillsides and your nightingales
VOŽDOVAC pouring song all spring long
over sprawling city gardens
through throats purged of every mortal impurity
as if by the translucent flame of *rakija*, insidiously
ZLATIBOR steeping unsuspecting hillsides
in a longing for immortality (*UBL* 3)

The text is accompanied by voluminous notes, most of which explain the places and historical events mentioned in the poem. However, this overall structure is in no sense experimental or ornamental but provides a closely-fitting functional framework for the poem's idiosyncratic symbolism.

This symbolism operates on three levels. First, the form of the poem's single constituent sentence is a series of direct addresses to a person or personage named 'Danitsé', and this name is repeated during each call *to* her or invocation *of* her. As the authorial notes explain, 'Danitsé' is the vocative case of 'Danitsa', which is an English transliteration of 'Danica', a Serbian woman's name, and mythological epithet for the morning star: hence, the Slavonic equivalent of the planet Venus, goddess of love and harbinger of daylight [> Srb. *dan*, 'day'] (Skok 1971: 380; Kulišić 1989: 143–144). This combination suggests several thematic groupings that are crucial for an understanding of the poem: femininity and nature; the present and the past; the realistic and the symbolic; and the individual and elemental (or personal and archetypal). Second, throughout the poem, this multivalent symbol is broadened and amplified. Each passage is mapped onto a toponym, and not only does each of these embody the unique features of a particular place, but taken together, they carry a wide range of meanings, since they all refer to Balkan history and culture, scenes of ordinary life, literary allusions, music, art, and so on. Finally, by uniting the introductory meanings with all the layers that have been accreted throughout the poem, Danitsa is transformed into a new, complex symbol, and, as a result, reflects an imaginative force that is quite rare in contemporary European poetry. Furthermore, each of these three levels comprises numerous 'secondary' meanings which, in context, expand into additional poetic perspectives, thereby ramifying interpretative possibilities.

'Do vidjenja Danitsé' celebrates multiple aspects of femininity, from the perspective of a male speaker/persona. 'Danitsa' herself is protean: she unites almost all possible female characteristics – including both carnal and spiritual attributes. Thus, "wearing a thousand faces and expressions inside a minute", she is at the same time "moody", "contradictory", "tolerant", "spontaneous", "opinionated", "unpredictable", "nobody's and everybody's", "dangerous", etc. She commands a varied and powerful sex appeal that spans age: the mischievousness of a young girl, the vigour of a teenager and the combined sensitivity and common sense of a mature woman, as well as an infinitely seductive 'come-and-get-me-if-you-dare' demeanour. Her composite character is deepened by being both rural and urban, housewife and businesswoman, idealist and pragmatist. She has also been single, married and divorced. Danitsa often evokes female archetypes such as daughter, mother, wife, goddess, harlot, harridan and crone, all of which strengthen her symbolic nature. Yet she is equally firmly situated in realistic Balkan contexts: by turns an innocent child, "playing with imported Barbies", a martyr, suffering in a communist political prison, and an impoverished cancer sufferer who sweeps church floors.

Finally, she is closely connected with particular places in former Yugoslavia. These include regions, cities, towns, suburbs, villages, streets, markets, monasteries and islands – as well as several cafés, a prison, a park and a mountain or two. Since she is pictured directly against these places, each of them forms another backdrop that highlights her complexity. Furthermore, the smooth transitions within the text, from the references and associations of one toponym to another, in which the end of the previous one blends seamlessly into the beginning of the next, transform these *topoi* into complementary poetic elements; these attain their full meanings only by virtue of their interaction with all other elements in the poem. And if this seamlessness applies to the place-names, it is all the more relevant to Danitsa herself, whose distinctly portrayed features also overlap, blur and merge, and draw their strengths from all other components. This is to say: the full meanings of Danitsa's complex femininity cannot be understood by the reader unless this strange process of overlapping and merging is realised.

As has already been mentioned, nature is one of the most important motifs in the poem. It provides Danitsa with the characteristics that elevate her above – and deepen her, as it were, 'elementally' beneath – the condition of a simple human being. Danitsa takes from nature its untamed powers, its perfect order, its hidden causes and effects, and its indifference to any human tragedy. Thus, she ceases to be any 'mere' individual woman and becomes a universal symbol containing and expressing those aspects of the world that ordinary mortals will never quite be able to attain.

'Do vidjenja Danitsé' sometimes offers a harsh contrast between urban and natural environments. There are passages in which the city – as in the works of Gottfried Benn, for example[1] – functions as a supreme symbol of dehumanisation. At times, the city evokes horrors that human beings have perpetrated upon one another for thousands of years; at others, it emphasises a meaningless and often neurotic or absurd way of living. On the other hand, when nature is presented in a pristine condition, it usually signifies purity, immortality and perfection. And since Danitsa is linked with both city and nature, she reveals both sides of her beauty: she is "jolie-laide" – ugly and beautiful – embodying the Baudelairian dichotomy without which beauty can never be complete. However, this is not the only meaning that the urban environment carries in Berengarten's poem. The city also has its 'positive' features. For instance, it frequently comes alive both *for* Danitsa and *because of* Danitsa, as the site of compassion, civility, nourishment and music, especially in passages focused on communal space and shared activities, such as parks, markets and restaurants. So, the city in this poem should be considered in the same way as Danitsa – it is multidimensional, often contradictory, and resistant to any kind of generalisation.

Apart from being the embodiment of femininity and nature, Danitsa is deeply imbued with the past, or rather, with multiple pasts. First, she echoes ancient empires, Roman, Turkish and Serbian, along with their rulers, their soldiers and enemies, their brigands ("hajduks" and "uskoks"), not to mention their "song festivals" and distinctive architectures, their fortresses, amphitheatres, mosques and monasteries. At times the imagery is similar to that found in the poems of W. B. Yeats and Ivan V. Lalić on Byzantium, and perhaps such passages even suggest deliberate echoes:[2]

---

[1] See Gottfried Benn's 'Mann und Frau gehen durch die Krebsbaracke' [Man and Woman Go through the Cancer Ward], 'Nachtcafé' [Night Café], 'Karyatide' [Caryatid] and 'Die Gitter' [The Bars] (Benn 1956: 24–25, 28–29, 55, 279).

[2] See W. B. Yeats, 'Byzantium', and also Ivan V. Lalić, 'From The Works of Love, or Byzantium' (Lalić 1981: 49–61).

                                                  Danitsé
among punch-drunk butterflies mating in the rubble
                                          of fortresses where ghosts
SMEDEREVO
                                          of solitary sentinels
tonight as forever will patrol their starry vigil, over
moonbathed ramparts floodlit by rippling waters (*UBL* 3)

…impoverished monasteries with peeling stucco walls,
crumbling arched colonnades, and cool interiors blessed
                                          by tall gazes of saints,
SOPOĆANI, MORAČA
                                          presiding glances of angels,
undamaged lords and ladies of distant imagined heavens
watching down the centuries (*UBL* 8)

Later, Danitsa rekindles memories of the most severe atrocities that have
occurred in former Yugoslavia during the twentieth century. But she is
also the more-or-less indiscriminate carrier into the modern world of
the 'effects' of these various pasts. She bears mobsters and their henchmen,
football and basketball players, pensioners arguing about chess, and poli-
ticians and their followers who are fully prepared to put their tribal and
nationalistic beliefs 'into practice', as they did at Srebrenica (Bosnia)
and in the Krajina (Croatia) during the break-up of former Yugoslavia.
It might even be said that, at one time or another, Danitsa opens up
within herself an entire compendium of permutations generated by the
inherently Balkan 'warrior' archetype. However, on a higher plane, she
is also an actualised embodiment of the Eliotic interaction between past
and present. Such a perspective implies that, on the one hand, every
human being in the present is pervaded by the entirety of the world's
heritage, which can be detected in every individual thought or action;
but that, on the other, each person living in the present brings his or
her own specific flavour to the past (Eliot 1967: 49). Thus, encumbered
by the entire heritage and all the characteristics acquired in the present,
each individual makes the meanings of the past fluid and, accordingly,
difficult to understand.

   In order to depict such 'spirits' of the past more vividly, Berengarten
sometimes deploys local references, such as the Balkan musical genre
of *starogradske pesme* ['Old Town Songs']. In the passage dedicated to
the Petrovaradin fortress near the town of Novi Sad and to Skadarlija,
Belgrade's bohemian quarter, readers, especially those familiar with
Serbia, will be likely almost to hear 'the soundtrack' of the past overlaying,
penetrating and infusing the present.

The past in Berengarten's poem can be considered from yet another viewpoint. Its cultural, religious and aesthetic richness is often directly contrasted with brutally simple and unimaginative features of the modern world. Thus, ancient amphitheatres and fortresses are set against forbidding Socialist-Realist tower blocks that loom over "wheely bins where the poor rummage for stale bread, newspapers, cardboard". Similarly, the spiritual aesthetics of medieval monasteries, that contain frescoes by unknown painters prefiguring the murals of Giotto, are juxtaposed against a "two-roomed apartment / in a block where the lifts don't work, on the shabbier / side of town at the end of the shambling tramline"; and, in the same way "Diocletian's palatial alleys" are offset by "unrepaired pitted motorways" and traffic lights at which

crippled

gypsy children hawk newspapers

SREMSKA packed with handfuls of wan roses

and plead for the privilege of cleaning your dusty

windscreen (*UBL* 7)

Presented in this way, the past often functions as a foil for ironic contrast, since readers are forced to keep in mind the unpleasant images of the modern world and, as the splendour of the past remains evident in the background, the contrast makes images of the present even drearier. Of course, this does not imply that the past is invariably regarded as being on a 'higher' plane, and hence more valued, than the present: rather, it indicates Berengarten's multidimensional perspectives vis-à-vis the interflow between present and past. Just like the urban environment in this poem, the present can be the locus not only of suffering but also celebration, not only ugliness but poignant beauty, not only deprivation but also epiphany:

Danitsé treading precarious foam-washed rocky promontories

bordering a blue more intense

ZADAR, TROGIR than cobalt glass, whose gulls wheel

over white-stoned palaces tucked into curling bays and

harbours decked out like watery gardens (*UBL* 3)

❧

Humour is another important aspect of this poem, and its functions are manifold. In the passage referring to the fortress of Kalemegdan, Danitsa walks in the park

                                         while grandads play chess,
    KALEMEGDAN   surrounded by gangs
    of neighbours, all commentating, analysing, cussing,
    all experts, all specialists, all Kasparovs, all Karpovs (*UBL* 4)

In Zvezdara and at the Slavija, two neighbourhoods of Belgrade, she argues politics with

                          brilliant impoverished
    internationally informed taxi-drivers who steer
    SLAVIJA   battered Fords and Mercedes in
                      bedroom slippers (*UBL* 9)

Anyone who has been to Belgrade, and has been exposed to the conspiracy-theory-ridden monologues and idiosyncratic dress-sense of local taxi-drivers, is likely to be overwhelmed by the affectionately comic and ironic implications carried by this image. Danitsa is also forced to live among provincial snobs and backbiting spinsters, "who would drink pure acid / rather than reveal their own personal secrets to a single / stranger". And to make such humorous scenes more vivid, Berengarten offsets relatively formal diction against a strongly vernacular register, as in the following passage:

    Danitsé delivering your firstborn in the local maternity
    clinic, sworn at by underpaid sadists masquerading
    as uniformed midwives, possessed of the vilest and
    most colourful proficiency in the art of rhetorical
    abuse – *didn't you scream loud and long enough*
    when he stuffed you senseless bitch so stuff
    your moaning screaming whining bitching now (*UBL* 8)

Such passages are not, of course, inserted merely as doses of well-polished purple to sweeten or spice up the taste-buds of the common reader so that he or she can 'swallow' more demanding passages. They are, rather, additional ways in which Danitsa's polymorphic character is constellated, since they add attributes at once individualised and commonplace – more earthy and earthly – and so insulate her from two-dimensionality or abstraction. They also help to constitute the ambivalent character of the world she inhabits. Since these humorous passages are introduced side by side with various tragic episodes of Balkan history and gloomy scenes of modern life, they establish a counterbalance, whose function is twofold. First, it provides the horrifying passages with their opposite qualities. For evil is never perfect or absolute. It always has its 'good side', which is the main reason it is so often hard to recognise as evil. Second, the juxtaposition of tragic and comic features, of images of horror and their humorous or absurd counterparts, means that the world is depicted as a terrifying place, since it cannot be boiled down to a simple set of proverbial rules and injunctions which can easily be adhered to, in order to enable one to make the right choices between good and evil. On the other hand, the humour also demonstrates that, even in such a world, there are gleams of goodness and delight. Once these have been discovered, they will never allow terror to reign absolute.

Ⴍ

'Do vidjenja Danitsé' also builds up an extraordinarily thorough panorama of social and political events and implications across the entire temporal and spatial zone of 'former Yugoslavia'. The poem highlights numerous similarities among the various territorial, ethnic and national Balkan entities that, together, constituted it and, separately, survived it, not only in terms of such factors as culture, architecture and natural environment but also, and above all, in mentality – including blind spots, communally maintained fallacies and charmingly untypical idiosyncrasies. The poem also alludes to a wide range of dramatic historical events that have occurred in the Balkans, mostly during the twentieth century. So, Danitsa's "three / second cousins" were taken to Staro Sajmište, the Nazi concentration camp in Belgrade during the Second World War, where they "smoothly vanished overnight, never to be recovered, / never heard of, never mentioned again". Danitsa finds herself incarcerated on Goli Otok (*aka* Naked Island), the prison that Josip Broz Tito established after 1948 for his political opponents. Later, in Srebrenica, Bosnia (1995), Danitsa's "godforsaken / sons" kill hundreds of people; and she too becomes a refugee, having been forced to leave her village in Krajina, Croatia (1995).

It may well be argued that events such as these, combined with all the previously mentioned similarities among the people and peoples of the Balkan region, point towards connections that are so engrained as to be ineradicable, despite whatever temporary enmities politicians may try to impose. All of which suggests that Richard Berengarten may have succeeded in discovering considerably deeper layers in the Balkans than any foreign politician, journalist or political analyst has ever done. His long poem provides a remarkable example of the superiority of poetic thinking and perception to any kind of political analysis. It demonstrates that poetry – provided that it is constituted into a work of art and not political propaganda in verse – tends to dig more deeply and search out more hidden substrata than politics, which focuses on temporary and, usually, less important elements.

∾

Overall, the polysemic and multilayered complexity of Danitsa's symbolism is best approached through the final passage in the poem. After the male speaker/persona has been drawn in by so many of Danitsa's attributes, and after he has pointed to so many associations triggered by them, at the peak of his poetic elation he seems to stumble – or tumble – into the question: "these days – why is it you look and sound like / everybody else…?" This utterance may look simple, but we shall see that, at a conceptual level, in keeping with the poem's richly polysemic complexity, it offers several overlapping interpretations.

One reading hinges initially on the phrase "these days": that is, if the 'communal space' of Yugoslavia no longer exists, then the unique, complex individuality of Danitsa may well have 'disappeared' along with it; for, as the toponyms scattered throughout the poem indicate, Danitsa *is* the zones that she inhabits, no more and no less. Her very character consists of them. And if her identity is 'spatially' coterminous with them, then why not 'temporally' too? However, whether the phrase "these days" implies 'temporarily' or 'permanently' is a moot question.

Added to this, a complementary interpretation may be developed: that Danitsa's uniqueness and complexity can be detected only by means of a specifically *poetic* way of perceiving the world. And, more precisely, that this mode of perception involves deconstruction of the 'real' world. Otherwise, if Danitsa is to be approached according to modes of 'ordinary' thinking and feeling (which may well mean *lack* of thought or feeling), she will inevitably appear both mundane and banal, and bear no more than superficial and stereotypical resemblances to other people and things. Thus, Danitsa's very ambiguity not only functions as the precise marker of the chasm between poetic (i.e., deep, individualised, particular) and non-poetic (i.e., superficial, generalised, bland) perception, but also enables us to realise that, embedded within 'simple' 'everyday' significations, there resides 'another' emotional, spiritual and intellectual field, in which the beauty of life is constantly evident and accessible.[3] Moreover, the liminality that is a defining characteristic of this ambiguity means that such a symbol can never be quite understood. It will always bear meanings that will resist any attempt to exhaust its symbolic power. In other words, *Danitsa can never be fully explained.* She is approachable – or 'describable', as Richard Rorty would say (Rorty 1989: 5)[4] – only within a *poetic* framework, in which some of her features will be visible and some associations will be hinted at, while the rest will have to be left to the reader's imagination. And to imagine her, with 'all conceivable hues', one will have to use one's entire imagination. Hence, the speaker/persona, at the very end of the poem, is aware that a 'rupture' or 'failure' of imagination has led to Danitsa's disappearance:

> I at least can't trace
> you at home or anywhere and currently no longer
> have an inkling how to find you in the morning (*UBL* 15)

At this point, it is left unexplained whether the rupture or failure in imagination to perceive and recognise Danitsa is individual or social, or both. At any rate, it may be suggested that Danitsa will appear again only when the necessary imaginative leap into 'poetic perception' has been made, whatever may be the conditions for that leap to occur.

Within the openness of this possibility, and inherent in the impermanence of the word 'currently' and of the phrase "these days", these overlapping interpretations cohere and coalesce. For now the single long sentence that has gradually been spinning itself throughout the poem – in fact, the single sentence that *itself constitutes the poem* – has finally reached its term, but in the unexpected tonality of *a question*:

---

[3] RB has coined a term for this 'epiphanic' field in previous poems. He calls it "the common miracle". See 'Only the Common Miracle' (*FL* 160–161), and 'The Voice in the Garden' and 'In the mirror' (*UBL* 71–74 and 75).

[4] In the book entitled *Contingency, Irony, and Solidarity*, Rorty argues that the truth about the world cannot be found out. One can only strive for more appropriate descriptions of the world. And in order to provide such description, one has to redescribe old vocabularies – philosophies, literary works etc. (Rorty 1989: 8, 27, 75–76, 78).

"why is it…?" And, significantly, in this question, the first-person speaker identifies himself explicitly for the first time – "I at least…". So the speaker's attainment of first-person identity coincides with his uncertainty whether Danitsa's disappearance is temporary or permanent: a question that is also left wide open. While the possibility that Danitsa has gone "down river" might suggest the end of an era and the beginning of a new one, that of her floating "off, finally / and forever angelic, into / a cloudless sky" might equally well imply the ultimate ascension of the merely mortal woman and her victorious transformation into the celestial goddess of the morning. In the margin, at this point, the final toponym that occurs is a non-toponym: *NEBESNA* means 'heavenly'. And here, we are brought full circle, back to the Serbian title, and are reminded that 'Do vidjenja' does not mean a final and absolute *Goodbye*, but rather *Au revoir*: '*Till the seeing-again*'.

§

So, in the last resort, 'Do vidjenja Danitsé' indicates that one of the primary goals of Richard Berengarten's work is to depict complexity. The appreciation of complexity is intricately bound up in awareness of beauty, each being dependent on the other. In poetry, beauty has never been a simple matter. It has always been complex: syncretic, polysemic, multidimensional. Even readers who are not inclined to seek 'big themes' in literature are likely to respond to the beauty of complexity in Berengarten's poem, especially those familiar with the Balkans, because 'Do vidjenja Danitsé', to paraphrase T. S. Eliot, will keep their minds diverted while doing its work upon them (Eliot 1933: 151).

REFERENCES

Benn, Gottfried. 1956. *Gesammelte Gedichte.* (*Collected Poems*) Wiesbaden: Limes Verlag.

Eliot, T. S. 1933. *The Use of Poetry and the Use of Criticism*. London: Faber and Faber.

______. 1967. *The Sacred Wood,* London: Methuen and Co.

Kulišić, Špiro; Petrović, Petar and Pantelić, Nikola (eds). 1998. *Srpski Mitoloski Rečnik* [*Serbian Mythological Dictionary*]. Belgrade: Interprint.

Lalić, Ivan V. 1981. *The Works of Love*, Section III (trans. Francis R. Jones). London: Anvil Press Poetry.

Rorty, Richard. 1989. *Contingency, Irony, and Solidarity*. Cambridge: Cambridge University Press.

Skok, Petar. 1971. *Etimološki rječnik hrvatskoga ili srpskoga jezika* [*Etymological Dictionary of the Croatian or Serbian Language*] (Vol. 1). Zagreb: Jugoslovenska akademija znanosti i umjetnosti [Yugoslav Academy of Science and Fine Arts].

PART IV

Richard Berengarten and the Cambridge Poetry Festival: A Vision of Community

Mick Gowar

Inspiration, according to Auden, came to Luther in the privy, but to Richard Berengarten it came somewhat later on in preparations for a new day – on the bus to work:

> I was sitting on top of the 103 bus from Great Shelford to Cambridge one cold February morning in 1973, as I was going in to work to teach at CCAT [Cambridgeshire College of Arts and Technology]. I met my friend Roger Dykes at the bus stop, and on the bus we had a desultory early morning conversation about how in the UK a mediocre poetry establishment was getting more than its own way and far more than its deserved share of attention. I found myself saying something like "What we really need is a poetry festival in this damn town." I was speaking in a casual off-the-cuff kind of way. But even as I said this, I caught myself surprising myself: I realised that there was no reason why the idea couldn't be put into action, and why this shouldn't be done by me.[1]

Like many apparently sudden or inspired ideas, Berengarten's notion of starting an international poetry festival looks in hindsight to be anything but the spontaneous impulse that his recollection of the conversation with Roger Dykes might suggest.

The idea of the Festival was, as Berengarten has said many times, founded on an "underlying vision of community" (Kelleher 1975). This

---

[1] Correspondence between author and RB, March 2008. Further references to this source are listed as 'Correspondence 2008'.

"vision" of a community of poets, thinkers and readers was – and still is – central to Berengarten's particular sense of himself as a poet. Moreover, this "vision" has continued to inform his poetics at a fundamental level: "Ancient laws of reciprocity, hospitality and magnanimity are necessary to the poetry of this time and this place too. Anything else or less is not good enough and will not serve adequately. A poet without such qualities can only be second-rate, however clever, skilled and cunning" (*ALF1*, 8). As John Kelleher observed in March 1975, just before the first Cambridge Poetry Festival: "Community is a word that recurs constantly as Richard discusses the festival – an event that has deep significance both for himself personally and for his continuing work as a poet."

Berengarten himself dates his commitment to this idea of community back to his schooldays:

> The origins of my belief in the integral connection between poetry and community reside in my own inner experience of poetry. The theoretical underpinnings of this belief flow through/are to be found in my readings, both as a schoolboy and as a student at Cambridge University, of Aristotle's *Poetics*, various of Plato's dialogues, Sidney's *Apologie for Poetrie*, Wordsworth's 'Preface to Lyrical Ballads' and Shelley's *Defence of Poetry*. (Correspondence 2008)

But until that morning on the Shelford to Cambridge bus, Berengarten's vision of community must have seemed to him to be frustratingly unrealisable. Despite the presence of lecturers of international reputation, and in their very different ways, of internationalist sympathies – such as Raymond Williams and George Steiner – Berengarten had failed to find an internationally-minded community of poets at Cambridge University. As an undergraduate from 1961 to 1964, he tried to establish a sense of community among young poets at Oxford and Cambridge universities by co-founding the joint Oxbridge magazine *Carcanet*, but this initiative failed due to precisely the sort of factionalism and petty squabbling that *Carcanet* magazine was set up to combat. In 1963, the year before Berengarten's graduation, a leading barrister could still feel confident in asking an Old Bailey jury if *Lady Chatterley's Lover* was a book "you would wish your wife or servants to read".[2] Britain in 1963 must have seemed, to Berengarten and many others, to be hopelessly

---

[2] Mervyn Griffith-Jones, prosecuting counsel, quoted on http://news.bbc.co.uk/on-this-day

trapped not only in post-wartime habits of petty-minded bureaucracy and austerity, but also in pre-war class prejudices and snobberies. If, as Berengarten strongly believed, "poetry depends on hospitality, generosity, magnanimity" (Correspondence 2008), England in 1963 must indeed have seemed to be *Das Land ohne Poesie*.[3] Berengarten recalls:

> I was an internationalist with a strong sense of European culture … I had been reading Eliot avidly and Pound to some extent too, as well as the Beat poets and many contemporary European poets in translation, especially Greek poets such as Seferis.
>
> I was also in strong opposition to all the tendencies in contemporary English poetry, especially The Movement and The Group, all of whose work I found drab, uninspiring, insipid and depressing. (Their heirs today fill me with the same gloom and dread.) Nor was I particularly enamoured of Ted Hughes and Thom Gunn, whose work was being advocated by the London establishment at the time as new and exciting. I was more interested in the entire tradition of English (and American) expatriates from Byron, Keats and Shelley to Henry Miller, Durrell and Robert Graves.
>
> Abroad was the best place to go. (Correspondence 2008)

From 1964 to 1966, Berengarten lived in Italy. In 1965, he and Kim Landers, his student contemporary at Cambridge and then his wife, moved into the flat of the English poet and Poundian, Peter Russell, in Venice. From 1967 to 1968, they lived in Greece, first in Thebes, then in Athens. They taught English, and Berengarten also began to translate poetry from Italian and Greek into English. The difficulties and delights of translation have remained a vital part of his work, strongly informing his own poetry and poetics.

However, Berengarten's mother's terminal illness meant the couple had to return to England in 1968. In 1969, following her death, they moved back to Cambridge; but now they were to join a very different community from the one they had left in 1964. Berengarten had been taken on to teach English and Liberal Studies at what was then the Cambridgeshire College of Arts and Technology, which at that time was slowly transforming itself from a combined technical college and art school into an institution of higher as well as further education, a process

---

[3] *Editors' note*: This phrase is a variation of a well-known slur by Richard Strauss that England was "Das Land ohne Musik" [the land without music].

which would eventually result in its being granted university status as Anglia Ruskin University. In the peculiar local parlance of Cambridge, Berengarten had made the decisive move from 'Gown' to 'Town' – that is, from the exclusivity of one of the oldest and most prestigious universities in the world to the rough and tumble of teaching not only English Literature but also English as a Foreign Language (EFL) and Liberal Studies to the always unpredictable and occasionally violent "Meat One".[4] Across the green parkland of Parker's Piece, it was a journey of less than half a mile to CCAT from Downing College, where F. R. Leavis had been a Fellow – and, by a curious quirk, Berengarten is now himself a Bye-Fellow. But in the middle of Parker's Piece, painted on the Victorian lamppost that marked the half-way point between the two colleges, was the warning sign: "You Are Now Passing Reality Checkpoint." In the view of many, Berengarten had not only gone into the reality of town life, he had also gone beyond the pale.

At CCAT, Berengarten found himself working among other writers and poets. Sidney Bolt, the Head of Department of English and Liberal Studies, and brother of the playwright and screen writer Robert, had recruited a number of writers to his staff, many with international interests and connections. A key figure was John James, who was then gaining a reputation as one of the group of poets that included J. H. Prynne, Andrew Crozier and Douglas Oliver – who later, along with other younger poets like Nigel Wheale and John Wilkinson, were collectively to be nicknamed the 'Cambridge Leisure Centre' (Duncan 2002). James had an interest in the Black Mountain poets – Charles Olson, Edward Dorn, Robert Duncan, Robert Creeley, etc. – which he passed on to Berengarten. Also teaching at CCAT in 1969 was Elaine Feinstein, who had already published her first collection, *In a Green Eye* (1966), and was deeply immersed in Russian poetry, especially that of Marina Tsvetayeva, whom she was translating. Omar Pound, Ezra Pound's son, was working on the translations that were soon to be published as *Arabic and Persian Poems in English* (1970), while also teaching part-time at CCAT, and the poet and medic Miles Burrows had a full-time post teaching Liberal Studies. This heterogeneous group of colleagues, as Berengarten has recognised, provided him with a good deal of information, not least in

---

[4] *Editors' note*: a reference to the hilarious fictional designation of a class of part-time students (apprentice butchers) in Tom Sharpe's comic novel *Wilt* (1976), about a lecturer in further education. RB was a colleague of Tom Sharpe at CCAT, from which the latter obtained much of his satirical material.

helping him catch up on what had been happening in British poetry while he'd been living in Europe, as well as, to some extent, in sharing connections.

An even stronger influence was Octavio Paz, the Mexican Nobel Laureate, who was spending a year in Cambridge as Simón Bolívar Fellow at Churchill College. In 1972, Berengarten would dedicate his long poem 'Avebury' to Paz (*FL* 23–50). Berengarten recalls a reading in the CCAT auditorium, later called the Mumford Theatre, by the writers named above, in 1971:

> Paz came to that Auditorium opening reading at CCAT and sat in the front row. He commented afterwards to the effect that the poets in Cambridge were to be found "at the Tech, not in the University". This was the generous if inaccurate view of a visitor, although it did highlight two further facts: first, that the University had no monopoly over interesting poetry; and second, that there didn't appear to be much interest in internationalism among poets on the English Faculty at that time, except in directions narrowly focused on the USA. (Correspondence 2008)

Berengarten had returned as something of an outsider as far as the Cambridge poetry scene of the time was concerned, but nonetheless, by the early 1970s he was extremely well-informed on many of the latest developments in British, European and American poetry. But much of what he saw he disliked intensely. As he stated to Roger Dykes in 1973, it was his firm belief that "a mediocre poetry establishment was getting more than its own way and far more than its deserved share of attention" (Correspondence 2008). Berengarten would then have described himself, as he does now, as "a European poet who writes in English" (*TM1* inside back cover), but he was living in an England in which, as Tom Paulin despairingly remarked on an edition of *The Late Show* on BBC 2 TV, "the national poet sleeps every night with his teddy bear."

If many of the constituent elements that would enable Berengarten to found the first Cambridge Poetry Festival were already in place, as in some chemical reactions a catalyst was required. And that catalyst was the death of Ezra Pound. As Berengarten now recognises: "Pound's death was in itself a turning point, that I now see in retrospect as a strong subliminal factor in influencing me to want to 'do something' – to move or change the situation" (Correspondence 2008). Berengarten had of course read Pound with close attention while living in Peter Russell's apartment in

Venice (*PRV*) but, more significantly, Pound had also been someone outside the contemporary mainstream as far as his interests, reading and vision of what poetry could achieve were concerned. And like Pound, Berengarten looked to the Mediterranean to inspire and nourish his own work. But above all, Pound was an example of a poet who not only had a vision of an artistic community, but also had the strength of belief in that idea and the energy to attempt to create such a community, in London and Paris in the early years of the twentieth century.

☙

Once Berengarten had articulated the idea of a Cambridge Poetry Festival, albeit in a throwaway manner, it wouldn't lie still:

> I realised that there was no reason why the idea couldn't be put into action, and why this shouldn't be done by me. But I immediately dismissed the idea, realising too that it would involve an enormous amount of work.
>
> But the idea kept coming back. It refused to go away. It haunted me. I'd wake up in the middle of the night thinking about it. It became an obsession.
>
> So I decided to run with it. (Correspondence 2008)

But *why* a festival? Why such a large and, by Berengarten's admission, daunting public event?

It is probable that the idea of a festival was to a great extent shaped and informed by the times. If 1963, to many creative people, seemed like the last year of the drab and austere 1950s, then they might have also thought of 1973 as the last year of the exuberant and optimistic 1960s. In 1973, Woodstock – and the dream of the 'Woodstock Nation' – was only four years in the past. In 1970, the Isle of Wight Music Festival had easily surpassed both the popularity and squalor of Woodstock by attracting 600,000 people. Funding for large literary and cultural events was available from the Arts Council of Great Britain and Regional Arts Associations. Festivals in general seemed the most appropriate way to both celebrate and consolidate radical changes that had apparently been achieved against what appeared to be a defeated and rapidly retreating Establishment.

Of more immediate relevance as precedents – or possibly warnings – were the *Poetry International* readings at the South Bank in London,

390

which had been founded by Ted Hughes in the late 1960s and continued through the 1970s under the direction of Charles Osborne; the poetry conferences organised by Roger Guedella and Chris Brookeman between 1973 and 1974 at the Polytechnic of Central London; and, of course, the notorious Horovitz/Ginsberg *International Poetry Incarnation* at the Royal Albert Hall in 1965.

What Berengarten imagined, however, was not just a series of readings by star poets or a platform for a single school or group of poets, or a particular theory of poetics or any one specific critical theory or ideology. He visualised instead an inclusive event that would bring together a much more varied community – or maybe it would be better to describe it as a series of concentric communities, each containing different characteristics and different constituencies, rather like the concentric walls of the city he describes in 'Ys', the unfinished poem he was working on at the time he conceived the idea for the Festival.[5] Starting with the core community of the city of Cambridge, the Festival would embrace local poets, then poets from different parts of England, Wales, Scotland and Ireland, with strong emphasis on regional and localised energy bases, English language poets from the USA and other English-speaking countries and finally foreign language poets with substantial reputations in their own countries and internationally.

Here in summarised form are some of the founding principles of the Festival that Berengarten established for members of the original Festival committee and to guide future Festival co-ordinators and administrators:

The atmosphere should be welcoming, convivial and open.

It should be eclectic, and should definitely not favour any single group or school. The organisers should be aware of tendencies in the poetry world to jostlings for power and influence, and be canny in dealing with them, opposing all attempts to capture favourite or hegemonic positions.

The festival should at all times emphasise variety, diversity, inclusiveness, polyculturalism.

It should be democratic, with no kowtowing to 'stars' or 'big names' – i.e. well known and famous poets would be treated in the same way as the lesser known. (Correspondence 2008)

---

[5] What has survived from that sequence is published in *FL* (97–104).

As well as readings, there would be seminars, discussions under the title of 'Poetry Forums', and lectures. Various distinct schools of poetry and shades of opinion would be represented in a series of small press and magazine readings, each chaired and organised by the editor/proprietor. Although the emphasis was to be on community and communality, disagreement and controversy were not to be avoided. Nor were academic communities in Cambridge and elsewhere to be ignored. In subsequent Festivals, the 'Poetry Forums' developed into distinct one-day conferences on particular poets, including Mandelstam (1981),[6] Seferis (1983) and Pound (1985). There was also a programme of events for children and schools, which amounted virtually to a festival in itself. And surrounding the Festival – both figuratively and literally – was a programme of related film shows, dance and drama performances, as well as exhibitions of paintings, illustrations, sculptures and other art works.

But it was never the intention for the Cambridge Poetry Festival to develop into a general arts festival. One belief that Berengarten and succeeding co-ordinators of the Festival shared – perhaps the only belief they did all share – was in the primacy, the uniqueness of poetry.

> All literate societies (cultures) possess poetry. Thus it may be said that poetry, the existence of a poetry, is one of the defining features of a literate society. Similarly, if the notion of 'poetry' is extended / expanded to include song and storytelling (an inclusion that in some languages is unnecessary being self-evident),[7] then it may be argued that poetry is one of the defining features of all human societies, and hence of culture itself. (Correspondence 2008)

❧

There were five more Cambridge Poetry Festivals over the next twelve years, until 1987.[8] As he had always intended, Berengarten stepped down as co-ordinator after the first Festival in 1975, although he remained

---

[6] *Editors' note*: RB co-edited and published (with George Gömöri) the anthology *Homage to Mandelstam* for the 1981 Festival.

[7] "In some of the Slavonic languages of the Balkans, the word for 'song' and 'lyric poem' is the same: for example, Croatian *pjesma* and Serbian *pesma*." (footnote from RB's own text).

[8] The coordinators of the festival have been: RB (1975); Paul Johnstone (1977); Peter Robinson (1979); Mick Gowar (1981); Alison Rimmer (later Alison Blair-Underwood) and Anne Grubb (1983); and John Alexander (1985).

a committed and supportive member of the Festival's co-ordinating committee. At its peak, in 1981, the Festival lasted for a full week and involved 200 participants. Eventually, I think, the Cambridge Poetry Festival became a victim of its own success. It outgrew the human resources available to continue organising and administering it. It was a major international event that, year after year, was forced to draw on the same tiny pool of volunteers who, like Berengarten, were able to straddle the crucial 'Town/Gown' divide.

However, the vision which shaped the first Festival has, in Berengarten's case at least, continued to provide the energy for a range of projects and poems.

> I have always been interested in 'the long poem'. There were many moments during the time I was organising the CPF when it struck me that the process of creating a poetry festival out of nothing was not entirely dissimilar to writing a long poem. I also think that the experience of 'writing the Festival' fed into the making of my long poem *The Manager*. And in retrospect, I can now see that the entire concept of the Cambridge Poetry Festival, as well as the way that it was structured and organised in practice, was based on my belief in community and connects with my involvement in what I am now calling *Universal Poetics*, a project in the first stages of development. (Correspondence 2008)

It is clear, then, that the 'vision of community' that motivated and was carried into the 1975 Cambridge Poetry Festival is not only integral to an understanding of Berengarten's poetry and poetics, but remains just as relevant now as it was then. As Eliot Weinberger writes of the work of Octavio Paz, Berengarten's friend and mentor: 'The revolution of the word is the revolution of the world, and ... both cannot exist without the revolution of the body: life as art, a return to the mythic lost unity of thought and body, man and nature, I and the other" (Weinberger, 1990).

References

Duncan, Andrew. 2002. 'Such that commonly each: a various art and the Cambridge Leisure Centre', *Jacket* 20 (December). http:// jacketmagazine. com/20/dunc-camb.html. Consulted, 1 February 2016.

Feinstein, Elaine. 1966. *In a Green Eye: Poems by Elaine Feinstein*. London: Goliard Press.

Kelleher, John. 1975. 'Poet's personal vision now a festival reality', *Cambridge Evening News* (21 March 1975): 4.

Pound, Omar (ed.) 1970. *Arabic and Persian Poems in English*. London: Fulcrum Press.

Weinberger, Eliot. 1990. 'Biography of Octavio Paz'. Online at: http://nobelprize.org/nobel_prizes/literature/laureates/1990/paz-bio.html. Consulted, 1 February 2016.

Language Teaching and Poetry through the Iron Curtain: Richard Berengarten in Czechoslovakia / The Czech Republic

ZDENĚK KŘIVSKÝ

Richard Berengarten's contribution to the changes in my country has been considerably broader, and has had a stronger impact, than simply running poetry-writing workshops or teaching English. We began our co-operation and friendship in the 1980s, when any direct contacts with the West, and books and journals from that source, were a rarity, like isolated candles in darkness. Our first projects were language courses for scientists who were critical of the establishment. These were formally organised by the Czechoslovak Scientific and Technological Society. The name we gave to these week-long intensives, 'English Terminology for Research Workers', may not have made much sense, but it sounded plausible enough to enable us to obtain official approval to organise the event and invite foreign lecturers in.

At the first event, the trainer was Peter Mansfield; at the second, Peter Mansfield came with Richard; and at those that followed, Richard brought his colleague Anita Debska. These courses were located in small mountain hostels operated by Czech companies as holiday facilities for their employees. Richard and his friends received some support from the British Council, but I am sure they covered some of the costs out of their own pockets. I remember how, on forest walks, we first discussed the entire project. Our goal was clear: to help the younger generation by training them in English, and so enable them to access information. To broaden the programme's impact, we also decided to invite some locally-based teachers of English; and two of these young language teachers were later awarded scholarships by Peter Mansfield to his language school in Stratford-upon-Avon.

The atmosphere at these events was extraordinarily friendly and relaxed. We were not used to having such fun, either in training sessions or at work, from breakfast until midnight. Red-hatted Richard, acting and reading his poems and cajoling the audience to do the same, charmed and impressed everyone, especially the Czech women. I remember a late-night presentation on how to make a marriage proposal. A lot of wining, dining and singing helped to break down language and culture barriers. There was even a rumour that Richard and Peter found a particular strong-smelling local cheese so delicious that they took some home and had to throw away their luggage as a result. Their hosts in Moravia liked them so much that, on a visit to the city of Brno after the course, they were taken to see the famous *Venus of Dolní Věstonice* in the local museum. As this figurine is probably one of the oldest known ceramic statuettes in the world, and the most valuable archaeological artefact in the country, it is hardly ever accessible to the public. But the original was brought into the Museum Director's office specially for them to see.[1]

I also remember our first training session after the Velvet Revolution, when many former participants on our courses came back for more. By this time, among them were university rectors and professors, managers of government institutions and Members of Parliament.

☙

On the shelves of my bookcase, there are several small books that have been worn out by the hands of many readers. They were smuggled through the Iron Curtain into Czechoslovakia by Richard and his friends. At a time when satellite TV was not available, radio broadcasts were jammed and the import of literature strictly forbidden, you can imagine how hungry readers welcomed imported foreign books and journals. The border patrols were especially sensitive to books and journals that might refer to events and people in a way that reflected domestic and Eastern Bloc politics.

Looking at my collection of such books, I have to admire the good taste of the person who chose the titles – for example, amongst the editors

---

[1] *Editors' note*: RB's photograph of the statuette and the palm of his left hand was taken at that time. This photograph, which serves as the cover design to his *Manual 4* (2008) is the source of the first poem in that chapbook.

396

of *Voices of Czechoslovak Socialists* (Merlin Press, 1977), is Jan Kavan who, in the nineties, became Foreign Minister of the Czech Republic and Chairman of the General Assembly of the UN. Among the authors is Václav Havel, at that time a dissident, but later the President (and symbol) of a free Czechoslovakia. There is also *Homage to Mandelstam,* edited by Berengarten and George Gömöri (Los Poetry Press, 1983). At that time, few Czechs were familiar with the name of Mandelstam but, thanks to Richard's book, the tragic story of the St. Petersburg poet, who perished in an icy Stalinist gulag in the Vladivostok region, found a wider audience.

ↄ

Richard had many friends among poets in different countries, and Czechoslovakia was no exception. For example, he was in contact with the immunologist and poet Miroslav Holub. Holub had taken an active part in the reformist movement in Czechoslovakia in the 1960s but, after the Russian invasion in 1968, was sacked from the Microbiological Institute in 1970 and suffered a publication ban – nor was he allowed to travel abroad or appear in public. Much of his writing was translated into English, however, as well as into more than thirty other languages, and he received a number of awards. Richard had managed to invite him to the first international Cambridge Poetry Festival, which he had founded and organised, in 1975. I was glad to be present at a cordial meeting between Richard and Holub, in Prague's Park Hotel, in 1989. The Ambassador of the Republic of Yugoslavia in 1996, Djoko Stojičić, was also a poet, and one of the friends Richard met up with in Prague. Richard has translated some of his poems into English.

ↄ

In the wake of the Velvet Revolution, there was an urgent need to bring about huge changes in politics, economics, environmental protection and culture, and a corresponding demand for experts capable of managing these transformations. However, there was a lack not only of teachers with the right skills and experience, but also of teacher trainers, not to mention suitable educational texts in the Czech language. Our poor foreign language skills even led to a bottleneck when it came to our ability actually to achieve any benefit from the offers we were receiving from foreign consultants. So it was that, in spring 1990, we held urgent discussions with our British friends on the subject of when and how to set up English language programmes. There were all too few Czech teachers of English, and those who had been trained by English native speakers were all but non-existent. We were strongly advised to train teachers as a first priority, so that, progressively, they could cascade their knowledge into wider programmes. However, this would mean several years of delay, and time was short.

Richard had just set up his company English Plus International, which offered tailor-made language and management training to industrial organisations in Eastern Europe. In the Czech Republic, through the recently established North Bohemian Economic Association, these programmes were taken up by several large chemical and glass enterprises. The courses took place both in the Czech Republic and in the UK; an experienced professional usually delivered the managerial side of the training. An important part of the UK-based training consisted of meetings with, and visits to, British institutions and industrial companies. At this early stage of the project, these courses in the UK provided many participants with their very first exposure to any country with a market economy and, hardly surprisingly, the trainees were particularly lacking in confidence. Richard had to explain many trivial facts to them: some of these would sound like a joke nowadays but, at that time, this was a great help. Both sides learned a lot from working together – not only about their partners, but also about themselves. I am pretty sure that these projects helped to inspire Richard's poem *The Manager* (2001).

You can lead a horse to water, but you can't make it drink. We also tried to help politicians by providing them with English communication skills training but, in contrast to their colleagues in industry, this scheme met with no success. Many Czechs who were elected to the European Parliament or to top positions in the European Commission did not understand English at all. The worst examples were our candidates for posts as Commissioners. In the 1990s, Richard conducted similar projects in many places across the collapsed Soviet empire, from Yakutia in Siberia and Moscow, to various locations in Poland, Latvia and the Czech Republic. He also co-organised several exciting projects at Tbilisi University in Georgia.

At the same time, many volunteers, mostly young students from the USA and UK, came to help us in language training. Richard offered them a helping hand as both supervisor and consultant. Our young volunteers enjoyed seeing Richard teaching, and were proud to work on the same project as a well-known English poet.

With more and more enthusiastic Czechs being trained in English and as English teachers, Richard's undisputed professionalism began to produce results. Local teachers, who had at first felt threatened by native-speaking trainers, started to take part in the common effort. For example, Richard gave the opening speech for an English training project at the Glaverbel Czech glass company. This programme went on for several years and involved 300 people. Although we joked that this would shut down the company's operations altogether, in fact it turned out to be one of the most successful projects of its kind in the whole of Czech industry.

Sometimes, Richard helped to transfer expertise in fields that were outside his specialist competence. For example, in December 1997, the proprietors of a leading Czech spa appointed him to conduct an in-depth week-long in-house investigation into all aspects of its services – ranging from baths and beds to the local drink, Becherovka. On completing his anonymously-conducted inspection, he submitted a confidential report. We were told that the proprietors, unlike the locally-based staff, were pleased and amused by the details of the report and many of its recommendations have been followed.

Richard also helped build bridges by enabling young Czechs to study in England. He provided academic support and guardianship services to students who had received Glaverbel scholarships for full-time university degree courses in the UK, and recommended summer language schools for Czech students.

❧

The Holocaust, and the expulsion of Germans after World War II, transformed the multicultural pre-war Czechoslovakia into a country practically devoid of minorities. Moreover, during the Nazi and Communist eras, separation from the outside world further eroded the ability of Czechs to live and co-operate with other nationalities. North Bohemia is well known as a region in which tension exists between its majority population and its fast-growing settlements of Roma in certain areas. It has often been argued that the most common reason for the difficulties experienced by members of the Roma community in integrating into society is the fact that education is of low priority in their value-system. So it was something of a surprise when Richard offered to run a bilingual

Czech-English poetry-writing workshop in a school mainly attended by Roma, in Předlice, a district of Ústí nad Labem. The head teacher will-ingly found funding for the event from his budget; and the day-long workshop, which took place during the spring school holidays, was attended by more than forty Roma children and teenagers. This unusual event received a good deal of attention, and was attended and closely observed by a Member of the Czech Senate for the region. Contrary to expectation, the event was a great success. The children wrote interesting small poems, mainly about their families, pleasures and dreams. The workshop was described in an article by Jitka Stuchlíková in a highly favourable double-page spread in *Top víkend magazín*, a well-known Czech magazine.[2]

❧

It is amazing just how many lives, in so many distant countries, have been influenced by one man of talent and vision from Cambridge. It was a pleasure to work with him in difficult, but exciting times. My thanks go to Richard for what he has done for my country.

---

[2] Jitka Stuchlíková (1998), 'Básníkovi z Cambridge se v romské 'kole líbilo' ['Cambridge poet enjoyed visit to Romany school'], *Top víkend magazín* (27 March), pp. 12–13.

Richard Berengarten in School:
A Teacher's Perspective

Margaret Setchell

As the years have passed and teaching methods have changed, it would not be an exaggeration to say that Richard has rescued me on more than one occasion from disillusionment in the face of modern educational strategies. He does this simply by sharing the process of making a poem, getting to the heart of writing.

In a typical workshop, at both primary and secondary level, Richard will engage with a large audience of perhaps two year-groups at a time. Pupils are seated in the school hall and equipped with pen and paper. Richard, armed with briefcase and one or two of his own books, is introduced as a respected poet and guest speaker, but soon transforms into 'Hatman' the performer, with an array of reward hats handed out to surprised and delighted children, those brave individuals who make the first contributions. In rapid delivery style, Richard employs an overhead projector, transparencies and coloured pens to record lines of poetry as they come into being. A word pattern is established as a starting point for the imagination: "My poem leaps into the surf, / My poem taps its foot impatiently, / My poem sips green tea from a china cup…". Richard demonstrates how words may work together. Pupils and teachers catch on to the game, turning over different words, different sounds, different associations in their minds, experiencing various stages of cliché, blankness and, in time, pleasure at choosing words which best convey their ideas. Yet the challenge is issued always within a manageable framework, building on personification, probing a simile or hunting down a vividly precise verb, adjective, adverb.

Meanwhile, Richard circulates, praising certain word choices, showing individuals how to redraft a first effort. Hats are passed on as more children find the courage to share their lines. Of course, many pupils get to their feet and speak shyly before such a large audience, so Richard sometimes tapes their words on his dictaphone, then turns up the volume for all to appreciate. But more often, he becomes their voice, repeating and relishing their line, placing a value on the individual's choice of expression, imbuing the words with a resonance that casts an immediate, powerful spell. In the school hall, the contrast with day-to-day announcements and a teacher's voice is marked. This sound is of an entirely different quality. Words are now astonishing.

This ability to present us with the word as an entity, bringing it into such sharp focus for pupils, is linked to Richard's facility with languages. He sometimes slips quietly into a different language, perhaps in response to an individual child for whom English is the second language. But such powers are used sparingly, leaving us to wonder at a foreign word which, holding no meaning for us, denies us that casual, instant access of familiar communication and reminds us, almost incidentally, of the gap between word and world. We relax into non-comprehension, freed from the tyranny of fixed meanings. And from this point we can begin to see our own words afresh, as we test the effect we can create by reordering and juxtaposing two words, in a search for clarity and truth to perceptions.

With such a wide frame of reference and knowledge of languages, this is a powerful intellect guiding us. But, more than this, Richard is a passionate poet and man. The response and the respect he gains from pupils and teachers spring equally from this source of shared humanity. The reading glasses are characteristically cast off by Richard and left dangling on their chain as he darts around the hall. With a light touch, he gives us access to the world of feeling. In swift strokes he shows us the man who has been angered, irritated, moved, overjoyed, tormented by toothache, scared, victorious, aroused by love, consumed by jealousy. Across the hall, a thoroughly disaffected Year 6 boy realises that he is permitted to write down intense negative feelings. A glum, silent Year 5 girl is stirred into choosing an adjective which, in turn, deepens her own understanding of an experience. Another pupil writes: "My happiness is like / A new-born chick, / A slave breaking free." Children become excited; pupils and their teachers feel empowered. It is this glimpse of man's emotional complexity and vulnerability which draws us so powerfully into the shared act of creative endeavour.

When Richard enters a school for a day, he generates a hugely positive and exciting force. His role entails creative risk, the kind of risk which is essentially missing from today's planning machine, transcripts of lessons and set objectives; the kind of risk or creative *frisson* which keeps us all awake, interested, intrigued and challenged, raising awareness and understanding of how the language of poetry works for both pupils and teachers alike.

Richard Berengarten:
Select Bibliography and References

This bibliography has been updated to June 2016. Works dated 2007 and earlier were published under the name Richard Burns; works dated 2008 and later were published under the name Richard Berengarten. Titles of works below are given acronyms, each of which is listed in brackets at the end of the entry. For the full list of acronyms, see *Abbreviations*, pp. xi–xiii. This bibliography includes online references but excludes the following: poems and translations by RB in periodicals and anthologies; posters, pamphlets and prints; book reviews, obituaries and short stories by RB; and essays and reviews of RB's work in journals.

Poetry Books and Chapbooks

1969   *The Easter Rising 1967*. Brighton: Restif Press. (pseudonym: Agnostos Nomolos)

1971   *The Return of Lazarus*. Cambridge: Bragora Press. (*RL*)

1972   *Double Flute*. London: Enitharmon Press. (*DF*)

1972   *Avebury*. London: Anvil Press Poetry with Routledge and Kegan Paul. (*AVE*)

1976   *Inhabitable Space*. Groningen: John Morann. (*IS*)

1977   *Some Poems, Illuminated by Frances Richards*. London: Enitharmon Press.

1980   *Learning to Talk*. London: Enitharmon Press. (*LT*)

1980   *Tree*. London: Menard Press.

1982   *Roots/Routes* (with seven monotypes by Douglas Kinsey). Cleveland, OH: Cleveland State University Poetry Center. (*RR*)

1983   *Black Light*. Cambridge: Los Poetry Press. 1995. Norwich: King of Hearts. (*BL*)

1998   *Half of Nowhere: riddles and spells for children*. Cambridge: Cambridge University Press. Reprinted 2006. Cambridge: Hatman Books.

1999   *Croft Woods*. Cambridge: Los Poetry Press. (*CW*)

1999   *Against Perfection*. Norwich: King of Hearts. (*AP*)

2001   *The Manager*. London and Bath: Elliott and Thompson. (*TM1*)

2003   *Book With No Back Cover*. London: David Paul Press. (*BWNBC*)

2004   *For the Living: Selected Longer Poems 1965–2000*. Cambridge: Salt Publishing. (*FL1*)

2005   *In a Time of Drought*. Nottingham: Shoestring Press. (*ITD1*)

2005   *Breath (the poem without end)*. With Casimiro de Brito, Kata Kulavkova and Hyam Yared. Ohrid: PEN International.

2006   *The Blue Butterfly*. Cambridge: Salt Publishing. (*BB1*)

2006   *Manual, the first 20*. Paekakariki, New Zealand: Earl of Seacliffe.

2007   *Holding the Darkness: Manual, the second 20*. Paekakariki, New Zealand: Earl of Seacliffe.

2008   *For the Living: Selected Longer Poems 1965–2000* (second revised edition). Selected Writings, Vol. 1. Cambridge: Salt Publishing. (*FL*)

2008   *The Manager* (second revised edition). Selected Writings, Vol. 2. Cambridge: Salt Publishing. (*TM*)

2008   *The Blue Butterfly* (second revised edition). Selected Writings, Vol. 3 (*The Balkan Trilogy: Part 1*). Cambridge: Salt Publishing. (*BB*)

2008   *In a Time of Drought* (second revised edition). Selected Writings, Vol. 4 (*The Balkan Trilogy: Part 2*). Cambridge: Salt Publishing. (*ITD*)

2008   *Under Balkan Light*. Selected Writings, Vol. 5 (*The Balkan Trilogy: Part 3*). Cambridge: Salt Publishing. (*UBL*)

2008   *Holding the Sea: Manual, the third 20*. Paekakariki, New Zealand: Earl of Seacliffe.

2009   *Manual, the fourth 20*. Paekakariki, New Zealand: Earl of Seacliffe.

2011   *For the Living*, Selected Writings, Vol. 1 (3rd edition); *The Manager*, Selected Writings, Vol. 2 (3rd edition); *The Blue Butterfly*, Selected Writings, Vol. 3 (3rd edition); *In a Time of Drought*,

Selected Writings, Vol. 4 (3rd edition); *Under Balkan Light,*
Selected Writings, Vol. 5 (2nd edition). All volumes Bristol:
Shearsman Books.

2014 *Manual,* Selected Writings, Vol. 6. Bristol: Shearsman Books

2015 *Notness – Metaphysical Sonnets,* Selected Writings, Vol. 7. Bristol:
Shearsman Books.

2016 *Changing,* Selected Writings, Vol. 8. Bristol: Shearsman Books.

Prose Books and Chapbooks

1981 *Ceri Richards and Dylan Thomas: Keys to Transformation.*
London: Enitharmon Press. (*KT*)

1985 *Anthony Rudolf and the Menard Press.* Cambridge: Los Poetry
Press.

1999 *Address to the Plenary Session of the 36th International Meeting of
Writers, organised by the Association of Serbian Writers, Belgrade,
October 1999.* Bilingual edition: Serbian tr. Jasna Levinger-Goy.
Cambridge: Los Poetry Press. (*IMW*)

2012 *Imagems 1.* Bristol: Shearsman Books.

2017 *Richard Berengarten: A Portrait in Inter-Views,* Selected Writings,
Vol. 9. Eds Paschalis Nikolaou and John Z. Dillon. Bristol:
Shearsman Books (forthcoming). (*API*)

Books by RB in Translation

1976 *Avebury* (Italian tr. Roberto Sanesi). Macerata: La Nuova Foglio.
(*AVI*)

1984 *Crna Svetlost* (*Black Light*). (Serbo-Croat tr. Bogdana G. Bobić).
Gornji Milanovac: Dečje Novine.

1986 *Arbol / Tree* (bilingual edition: Spanish tr. Clara Janés). Madrid:
Papeles de invierno.

1989 *Baum* (*Tree*) (German tr. Theo Breuer). Kall-Sistig: private
printing.

1990 *Menadžer* (*The Manager*) (Serbian trs. Vladimir Sekulić and Jasna B. Mišić). Titograd and Nikšić: Udruženje Književnika Crne Gore with Univerzitetska riječ [Association of Writers of Montenegro with University Word]. (*MEN*)

1996 *Schwarzes Licht* (*Black Light*) (German tr. Theo Breuer). Lintig-Meckelstedt: Bunte Raben Verlag.

2004 *U vreme suše* (*In a Time of Drought*). (Serbian tr. Vera Radojević.) Belgrade: RAD. (*UVS*)

2004 *Črna svetloba / Black Light* (bilingual edition: Slovenian tr. Ana Jelnikar). Ljubljana: Aleph Publishing.

2005 *Μαύρο φως* [Mavro fos] / *Black Light* (Greek trs. Nasos Vayenas and Ilias Lagios). Athens: Typothito. (*MF*)

2007 *Plavi leptir* (*The Blue Butterfly*) (Serbian tr. Vera. V. Radojević). Kragujevac and Belgrade: Spomen park Kragujevački octobar with Plava tačka [Kragujevac October Memorial Park with Blue Spot]. (*PL*)

2007 *Las manos y la luz* [Hands and Light] (bilingual edition: Spanish trs. Miguel Teruel and Paul Scott Derrick). València: Universitat de València, Aula de Poesía (24)

2012 *Do vidjenja Danice: Goodbye Balkan Belle* (bilingual edition: Serbian tr. Vera V. Radojević). Belgrade and Kragujevac: Srpska književna zadruga i grad Kragujevac [Serbian Literary Association and the City of Kragujevac].

2013 *Во бреме на суша* [*Vo vreme na suša*] (*In a Time of Drought*) (Macedonian tr. Lidija Nikolova). Skopje: Diversity collection of PEN International.

2013 *Crna svetlost* (*Black Light*) (Serbian tr. Vera V. Radojević). Vršac: KOV.

2015 *O voar da bolboreta azul* [The Flight of the Blue Butterfly] (bilingual edition: Galician trs. Loreto Riveiro Álvarez and F. R. Lavandeira). Culleredo, A Coruña: Espiral Maior Auliga.

2016 《改变》 [*Gai Bian*] (*Changing*): a selection of 20 poems (bilingual edition: Chinese tr. Wang Bang 王梆. Hangzhou City: 泼先生 [Pulsasir] (forthcoming).

2016–17 Béatrice Bonhomme (ed.). *L'œuvre de Richard Berengarten*: including poems in French, Breton, Chiac and Occitan. *Nu(e)*, special edition (forthcoming).

2017–18 《易》 [*Yi*] (*Changing*): (Chinese trs. Chen Shangzhen 陈尚真, Xiao Xiaojun 肖小军 and Wang Fei 王飞) (forthcoming).

Poetry books translated by RB

1968 Aldo Vianello. *Time of a Flower* (tr. from Italian). London: Anvil Press Poetry.

1978 Nasos Vayenas. *Biography* (tr. from Greek). Cambridge: Lobby Press. Reprinted 1980, *Journal of the Hellenic Diaspora* 7(1) (Spring).

1990 Aleksandar Petrov. *Lady in an Empty Dress* (tr. from Serbian). London: Forest Books.

1991 Duška Vrhovac. *I Wear My Shadow Inside Me* (tr. from Serbian with Vera V. Radojević). London: Forest Books.

1999 Ivan Gadjanski. *Balkan Destiny* (quadrilingual edition, tr. from Serbian). Belgrade: RAD.

2008 Aldo Vianello. *Selected Poems* (tr. from Italian with Peter Jay and Linda Lappin). London: Anvil Press Poetry.

2013 *Twelve Poems by Tin Ujević* (bilingual edition: tr. from Croatian with Daša Marić). Bristol: Shearsman Books.

2015 *12 Greek Poems After Cavafy* (bilingual edition: tr. from Greek with Paschalis Nikolaou). Bristol: Shearsman Books.

Prose books translated by RB

1969–70 Antonis Samarakis. *The Flaw* (tr. from Greek with Peter Mansfield). London: Hutchinson; and New York, NY: Weybright and Talley.

1972 Roberto Sanesi. *The Graphic Works of Ceri Richards* (tr. from Italian). Milan: Cerastico.

1972 Alberico Sala. *Michele Cascella, Objects in Their Ecstasy* (tr. from Italian). Milan: Edizioni d'arte Levi.

1973 Guido Ballo. *Mario Radice* (tr. from Italian with Joan Hall). Turin: ILTE.

1977   Roberto Sanesi. *On the Organic Language of Henry Moore* (tr.
        from Italian). Macerata: La Nuova Foglio.

Edited by RB (selected)

1971   *Peter Russell: Paysages Legendaires.* London: Enitharmon Press.

1972   *An Octave for Octavio Paz.* Rushden and London: Sceptre Press
        and Menard Press. With Anthony Rudolf.

1975   *Poster-Poems Series.* Cambridge Poetry Festival, Cambridge.

1980   *Ceri Richards: Drawings to Poems by Dylan Thomas.* London:
        Enitharmon Press. (*CRDT*)

1980   *Rivers of Life: a Gravesham Anthology.* Gravesend: Victoria Press.

1981   *Homage to Mandelstam.* Cambridge: Los Poetry Press. With
        George Gömöri.

1982   *Roberto Sanesi: In Visible Ink, Selected Shorter Poems, 1955–1979.*
        Prospice 13. (*IVI*)

1986–87 *Margin* 1 and 2: Winter and Spring. With W. Perrie and R.
        Magowan.

1993   *Out of Yugoslavia: North Dakota Quarterly* (*NDQ*) 61/1: Winter.
        (ed. with Stephen C. Markovich). (*OOY*)

2009   *For Angus: Poems, Prose, Sketches and Music.* With Gideon
        Calder. Cambridge: Los Poetry Press.

2010   *Nasos Vayenas. The Perfect Order: Selected Poems 1974–2010* (tr.
        from Greek). With Paschalis Nikolaou. London: Anvil Press
        Poetry.

2015   *The Xu Zhimo Festival 2015: Poems.* With Alan MacFarlane and
        Wang Zilan. Cambridge: King's College with Cambridge Rivers
        Press (August).

2015   *A Festschrift for Tony Frazer.* With Martin Anderson *et al.* Online
        at: http://tonyfrazer.weebly.com/

Essays and Introductions (Selected)

1971   'A Poet in Cambridge: Richard Burns on the achievement of
        Octavio Paz', *Times Educational Supplement* (1 January).

1971   'Introduction' to Peter Russell, *Paysages Légendaires*. London: Enitharmon Press.

1979   Untitled tribute to John Riley, in *For John Riley*: 114-116. Pensnett: Grosseteste Press.

1980   'Editor's Preface' to *Rivers of Life: A Gravesham Anthology*: 3-8. Gravesend: Victoria Press.

1980   'Introduction' to *Ceri Richards: Drawings to Poems by Dylan Thomas*: vii-xvi. London: Enitharmon Press. (*CRDT*)

1981   'Editors' Preface' to *Homage to Mandelstam*: 7-8. With George Gömöri. Cambridge: Los Poetry Press.

1981   'Roberto Sanesi: An Italian Among Welshmen', *Poetry Wales* 17(2) (Autumn). Reprinted 2004, in Giuseppe Langella (ed.), *L'interrogazione infinita, Roberto Sanesi, Poeta*: 219-226. Novara: Interlinea Edizioni. (*RS*)

1982   'Introduction' to Roberto Sanesi, *In Visible Ink: Selected Shorter Poems, 1955–1979*. Prospice 13. Skye: Aquila. (*RSI*)

1989   'Anthony Dorrell, Notes for a Memoir', in *Anthony Michael Dorrell, 1920–1987: Paintings, Drawings, Prints*. St. Michael's Mount, Cambridge: privately printed.

1989–90 'A Grove of Trees and a Grove of Stones', *Tel Aviv Review* 2. (*GTGS*) Reprinted 1993, *Out of Yugoslavia: North Dakota Quarterly* 61/1 (Winter). (*OOY*)

1990   'Introduction' to Aleksandar Petrov, *Lady in an Empty Dress* (tr. from Serbian): v-vi. London: Forest Books.

1991   'Introduction' to Duška Vrhovac, *I Wear My Shadow Inside Me* (tr. from Serbian with Vera V. Radojević): 1. London: Forest Books.

1992   'Bare Ruined Choirs', *Times Educational Supplement* (6 March). Reprinted 1993, as 'A Living Embroidery: English teaching and cultural contacts in Yugoslavia', *Out of Yugoslavia, North Dakota Quarterly* 61/1. (*OOY*)

1996   'With Peter Russell in Venice 1965–1966', in James Hogg (ed.), *The Road to Parnassus: Homage to Peter Russell on his Seventy-Fifth Birthday*. Salzburg: University of Salzburg: 107-123. Reprinted 1997, *Notre Dame Review* 4 (Summer). (*PRV*)

2002   'A Single Composite and Mysterious Reality' (on W. S. Graham), *Aquarius* 25/26.

2002   'Pour toi (Frayed Strands)'. Keynote paper for conference, *Une poétique mondiale de la poésie?* Paris: La Bibliothèque Nationale de France (13 May). Reprinted 2004, *CCCP* (Cambridge Conference of Contemporary Poetry).

2003   'Pour toi / Per te'. *Chorus (rivista letteraria europea)* 1/1.

2004   'Pour la Joie', *Chapman* 105. Reprinted 2004, *The Paper* 8.

2005   'The Art of Unthinking', in Ban'ya Natsuishi (ed.), *Collected Speeches for the World Haiku Association Conference*. World Haiku Association, Sofia, Bulgaria. Reprinted 2006, *Writing in Education* 39.

2006   'Dodola and Peperuda: Balkan rainmaking customs', *Poetry Review* 96(1).

2006–7 'A Little Further?' plus Spanish version (tr. Miguel Teruel Pozas and Paul S. Derrick, '¿Un poco más lejos?') *SERTA, Revista Iberorománica de Poesía y Pensamiento Poético* 9. (*ALF1*)

2007   'Getting Unknotted', *Writing in Education* 40. Reply to Mike Harris's critique of 'The Art of Unthinking' entitled 'The Art of Thinking', *Writing in Education* 39.

2007   'Il mio ultimo incontro con Peter Russell' ('My last meeting with Peter Russell') (Italian tr. Claudia Azzola). *Chorus (rivista letteraria europea)* 4/4.

2008   'Un poco più lontano' ('A Little Further?'). *Chorus (rivista letteraria europea)* 5/5.

2008–9 'Rain and Dust'. *Studia Mythologica Slavica* 11.

2009   'Editors' Preface' to *For Angus: Poems, Prose, Sketches and Music*. With Gideon Calder. Cambridge: Los Poetry Press: xvii-xviii.

2009   'On Poetry and Sound – the Ontogenesis of Poetry: Twelve Propositions'. Conference paper: Lahti International Writers Reunion, Finland (June).

2009   'The Cambridge Poetry Festival: 35 years after', *The Cambridge Literary Quarterly* 1.

2014   'Thinking of Sebastian'. (On Sebastian Barker). *Agenda* 48/1-2.

2014   'The *Dictio* Interview: Richard Berengarten' (interviewed by Paschalis Nikolaou), in *Dictio, the Ionian University Yearbook*: 75-103.

2015   'Introduction' to *The Xu Zhimo Festival 2015 Poems*: 9.
       Cambridge: King's College with the Cambridge Rivers Press
       (August).

2015   'Octavio Paz en Cambridge, 1970: reflejos e iteraciones'
       ('Octavio Paz in Cambridge: Reflections and Iterations', tr.
       Alejandro González Ormerod), in *Octavio Paz y el Reino Unido*
       [*Octavio Paz and the United Kingdom*]. Mexico, D.F.: Consejo
       Nacional para la Cultura e las Artes [National Council for
       Culture and the Arts].

2016   'Universalism and Particularism; or Looking at Flowers Again',
       in *Whirlwind of Words Across the Daliangshan Highlands*.
       Xichang: Xichang-Qinghai Silk Road International Poetry
       Week.

Poetry and Translations on the Web (selected)
Dates indicate publication

2003   *Avebury*: A Shearsman Ebook. Online at: http://www.shearsman.
       com/ws-public/uploads/223_avebury.pdf

2005   Hyam Yared Shoucair, from *The Wounds of Water* (tr. from
       French with Melanie Rein). *Shearsman* 61. Online at: http://
       www.shearsman.com/ws-public/uploads/223_shearsman_61.pdf

2006   Poems from *Book With No Back Cover* (bilingual text: Chinese tr.
       Chee Lay Tan). *Poetry Sky* 5. Online at: http://www.poetrysky.
       com/quarterly/quarterly-5-richardburns.html. (*PS*)

2006   Poems by Guillaume Apollinaire (tr. from French) and by Tin
       Ujević (tr. from Croatian with Daša Marić), Brindin Press.
       Online at: http://www.brindin.com.

2008   'Goodbye Balkan Belle' ('Do vidjenja Danitsé'), *Sibila*. Online
       publication. No longer available. (*DVD*)

2009   'Volta: A Multilingual Anthology (one poem: 93 languages)',
       The International Literary Quarterly 9. Online at: http://interlitq.
       org/ issue9/volta/job.php

2013   'Like dew upon the morning', six poems, *Spokes Magazine* 9.
       Online at: http://www.simegen.com/writers/spokes/Spokes%20
       2012/spokes_page_03.html

2013 《地球之树》 ['Di qiu zhi shu'; 'Tree Planted in the Earth']: extract from 'Tree' (Chinese tr. 王莹 Wang Ying), 人民网 [*Renmin Ribao*] (*The People's Daily*): November 5. (Pseudonym, 李道 Li Dao) Online at: http://paper.people.com.cn/rmrbhwb/html/2013-11/05/content_1320175.htm

2014 'Μια Σεβάσμια Κυρία' ['Mia Sevasmia Kyria'] ('A respected lady') and 'Οι Αγαπημένοι' ['I Agapimeni'] ('The loved ones'), (Greek tr. Paschalis Nikolaou), *Poeticanet*. Online at: http://www.poeticanet.gr/dyo-poiimata-a-1474.html

2014 'Poems from 'Changing', *Fortnightly Review* (June). Online at: http://fortnightlyreview.co.uk/2014/06/richard-berengarten/

2014 'For you', *No Rules Magazine*. Online at: http://norulesmagazine.com/2014/dec/richard-berengarten

2014 'Дерево' ['Derevo'] ('Tree', Russian tr. Aleskandar Makarov-Krotkov). *Дети Ра* [*Deti Ra*] 9(119) Online at: http://magazines.russ.ru/ra/2014/9/14b.html

2014 《树》 ['Shu']. ('Tree'). (Chinese tr. 王莹 Wang Ying), 今天 *Jintian* [*Today*] (11 November). RB's Chinese name: 李 道 Li Dao. Online at: http://www.jintian.net/today/html/74/n-46974.html

2015 'Poems from *Manual* (Italian tr. Silvia Pio), *Margutte*. Online at: http:// www.margutte.com/?p=8357⟨ and http://www.margutte.com/?p=8357&lang=en

2015 'From *Notness: Metaphysical Sonnets*', *The Bow-Wow Shop*. Online at: http://www.bowwowshop.org.uk/page16.htm

2015 'From *Changing*, *Contrapasso* 8 (April). Online at: https://contrappassomag.wordpress.com/2015/08/20/from-issue-8-poetry-by-richard-berengarten-%E6%9D%8E%E9%81%93/

2015 'Darkening', from *Changing*, *Molly Bloom* 7 (Spring). Online at: http://mollybloompoetry.weebly.com/richard-berengarten1.html

2015 'Dwelling ~ for the Shekhinah': ten sonnets from *Notness*, *International Literary Quarterly: English Writers 1*. Online at: http://www.interlitq.org/englishwriters1/richard-berengarten/job.php

2015 'Falling (in a pit)', from *Changing*, *Molly Bloom* 8 (Autumn). Online at: http://mollybloompoetry.weebly.com/richard-berengarten2.html

2017   'Tree', with translations into six other languages: Greek
        ('Δέντρο' ['Dentro'], tr. Paschalis Nikolaou); German ('Baum',
        tr. Theo Breuer); Irish ('Crann', tr. Gabriel Rosenstock); Italian
        ('Albero', tr. Silvia Pio); Spanish ('Arbol', tr. Clara Janés); and
        Swedish ('Träd', tr. Jan Östergren) Online, *Margutte* website
        (forthcoming).

Prose on the Web (selected)

1981   'Roberto Sanesi: an Italian among Welshmen'. Online at: http://
        www.berengarten.com/site/Sanesi.html

1988   'A Grove of Trees and a Grove of Stones'. Online at: http://www.
        berengarten.com/site/Grove-of-trees.html (*GTGS1*)

1999   'Is NATO Right to Bomb Yugoslavia? A Personal View'. Online
        at: http://www.europe.com/kosovo/articles/ Richard_Burns.htm
        (*INR*)

2001–2 '*The Manager*: Eliot's "influence"'. Online at: http://www.
        berengarten.com /site/Eliot-influence.html

2002   'Pour toi: frayed strands'. Online at: http://www.berengarten.
        com/site/Pour-toi.html

2003   'Pour la joie'. Online at: http://www.berengarten.com/site/Pour-
        la-joie.html

2003   'Peter Russell: The Poet Odyssified'. Online at: http://epc.
        buffalo.edu/authors/misc/russell.htm

2005   'A Little Further? Twelve propositions'. Online at:
        www. berengarten.com/A-little-further.html (*ALF*)

2009   'Border/Lines: An Introduction' (to *The Volta Project*). *The
        International Literary Quarterly* (9). Online at: http://interlitq.
        org/issue9/berengarten/job.php

2010   'The dialectics of oxygen: twelve propositions', *Jacket* 40. Online
        at: http://jacketmagazine.com/40/berengarten-dialectics.shtml

2011   'A Nimble Footing on the Coals: Tin Ujević, Lyricist: some
        English perspectives', [*sic*] – *a journal of literature, culture and
        literary translation* 2. Online at: http://www.sic-journal.org/
        ArticleView.aspx?aid=117

2015 'Octavio Paz in Cambridge: reflections and iterations',
      Fortnightly Review (July). Online at: http://fortnightlyreview.
      co.uk/2015/07/octavio-paz/2015

2015 'On Poetry and Sound: the ontogenesis of poetry', *International
      Literary Quarterly: English Writers 2*. Online at: http://www.
      interlitq.org/englishwriters2/richard-berengarten-1/job.php

2015 'On Writing and inner speech', *International Literary Quarterly:
      English Writers 2*. Online at: http://www.interlitq.org/
      englishwriters2/richard-berengarten-1/job.php

2015 'Tony Frazer, In Non-Standard Territory: a sort of editorial'.
      Introduction to *A Festschrift for Tony Frazer*. Online at: http://
      tonyfrazer.weebly.com/editorial.html

Interviews on the Web
(Dates indicate publication)

2014 Richard Berengarten and Paschalis Nikolaou, 'Under Greek
      Light', *The International Literary Quarterly* 21. Online at:
      http://www.interlitq.org/issue21/paschalis-nikolaou/job1.php

2014 Richard Berengarten and Paschalis Nikolaou, 'Following Black
      Light', *The International Literary Quarterly* 21. Online at:
      http://www.interlitq.org/issue21/paschalis-nikolaou/job2.php

2014 Richard Berengarten and Sean Rys, 'I Must Try This Telling',
      The International Literary Quarterly 21. Online at: http://www.
      interlitq.org/issue21/sean-rys/job.php

2016 Richard Berengarten and John Z. Dillon, 'The Interview as Text
      and Performance', *Fortnightly Review* (September). Online at:
      http://fortnightlyreview.co.uk/2016/02/interview-text-
      performance/

2016 Richard Berengarten and Ruth Halkon, 'Aspects of the Work',
      International Literary Quarterly: English Writers 3. Online at:
      http://www.interlitq.org/englishwriters3/ruth-halkon/job.php

2016 Richard Berengarten and Joanne Limburg, 'Managing the Art',
      International Literary Quarterly: English Writers 3. Online at:
      http://interlitq.org/englishwriters3/joanne-limburg/job.php

Video and sound recordings on the Web (selected)
(Dates indicate publication)

2001   Video reading from *In a Time of Drought*. Vilenica: International Literary Festival (September). Online at: http://videolectures. net/mlfv01_burns_pore/

2005   Video reading from *Manual*. Tokyo: First Tokyo Poetry Festival. Online at: https://www.youtube.com/watch?v=KXUrUI9fAB4

2006   Audio recording, James Gordon singing 'Man on the Run', RB's translation of 'Ο δραπέτης' [O Drapetis]: song by Mikis Theodorakis, based on poem by Yakovos Kampanellis (November). Online at: http://www.berengarten.com/assets/rbu01/ img/01%20Man%20On%20The%20Run.mp3

2007   Video reading from 'Do Vidjenja Danice', and interview in Serbian (tr. Vera V. Radojević). TV Kragujevac. Online at: https://www.youtube.com/watch?v=gUM2f8Kfe_Q

2012   Audio readings, six poems. Bowdoin: *From the Fishouse* (April). Online at: http://www.fishousepoems.org/category/richard-berengarten/

2012   Video reading, 'Do vidjenja Danitsé: Goodbye Balkan Belle'. Berkeley: *Lunch Poems* series (12 April). Online at: https://www. youtube.com/watch?v=vPpNqvU4xiI

2015   Video interview by Alan Macfarlane: *Ancestors* (March). Online at: https://www.youtube.com/watch?v=j6Xsq4pVk5s; and http://www.alanmacfarlane.com/ancestors/audiovisual.html

Other critical writing on RB since 2014 (selected)

2014   Clegg, John. '"Translating" Folklore: Richard Berengarten's *In a Time of Drought*', in *The Eastern European Context of Poetry in English after 1950*: Chapter 4. University of Durham: PhD dissertation. Online at: http://etheses.dur.ac.uk/9507/. Consulted, June 15, 2016.

2014   Lawson, Peter. '*Manual*, aesthetic and heartfelt', *Jewish Chronicle* 38 (14 August). Online at: http://www.thejc.com/arts/books/ 121253/manual-aesthetic-and-heartfelt

2014 Tabios, Eileen. 'MANUAL and IMAGEMS 1', *Galatea Resurrects* (December). Online at: http://galatearesurrection23.blogspot.co.uk/

2015 Derrick, Paul Scott. 'An Unexpected European Voice', 'A Poet for a Time of Need' (reprinted from this book) and '*Manual*: All Hands Clapping', in *Lines of Thought 1983–2015*: 153–187. València: Universitat de València, Biblioteca Javier Coy d'estudis nord-americans.

2015 Lawson, Peter. 'Notness: sonnets by Richard Berengarten', *Jewish Quarterly* 62(2): 79.

2015 Álvarez, Loreto Riveiro and Lavandeira, F. R. 'Introdución: Un intento de tradución de Richard Berengarten' [Introduction: an attempt to translate Richard Berengarten], in *O voar da bolboreta azul* [*The Flight of the Blue Butterfly*]. Culleredo, A Coruña: Espiral Maior Auliga.

2016 Gorza, Marisa. 'La via del molteplice' ['The Manifold Path']. *Ticino Sette* 12 (18 March): 8–9.

2016 Daly, Dennis. 'Review of *Manual*', *Weights and Measures* (March 23). Online at: http://dennisfdaly.blogspot.co.uk/2016/03/review-of-manual-by-richard-berengarten.html

2016 Ng, Catherine (ed.). *Richard Berengarten*. Cambridge: Los Poetry Press.

2016–17 Bonhomme, Béatrice (ed.). *L'œuvre de Richard Berengarten*. Including essays in French by Paul Scott Derrick, Sabine Huynh, A. Robert Lee and Anthony Rudolf, and an interview by Paschalis Nikolaou (trs. Marie Chabbert and Margaret Rigaud). *Nu(e)*, special edition (forthcoming).

2017 Pio, Silvia. 'La voce straordinaria e multiforme di un poeta universale' ['The Extraordinary Composite Voice of a Universal Poet'], *Poesía* (forthcoming).

2017 Derrick, Paul Scott and Rys, Sean (eds). *Managing the Manager*. Critical essays on RB's *The Manager* by Robert Archambeau, Mike Barrett, Paul Scott Derrick, Manana Gelashvili, A. Robert Lee, Sean Rys, Anthony Walton, Tyrone Williams and Kay Young (forthcoming).

Other published material referred to in this book

1981   Roberto Sanesi. 'Elegy for Vernon Watkins' (tr. from Italian),
       Poetry Wales 17(2). (*EVW*)

1988   'Gaj kamena i gaj drveča' ('A Grove of Trees and a Grove of
       Stones': Serbian tr. Jadrana Veličković), *Oktobar* XXIII. (*GTGS1*)

1993   In *Out of Yugoslavia: North Dakota Quarterly* 61(1): (1) Ivan
       V. Lalić, 'Some Notes on Yugoslav Literature: A Historical
       Approach' (tr. from Serbo-Croat with Jadrana Veličković); (2)
       Oskar Davičo, 'Poems from Hana' (tr. from Serbian with Jasna
       B. Mišić); (3) Blaže Koneski, 'Prayer' (tr. from Macedonian with
       Dragana Marinković); (4) Desanka Maksimović, four poems
       (tr. from Serbian with Jasna B. Mišić); (5) Vito Marković,
       extracts from *Analects* (tr. from Serbian with Vera V. Radojević);
       (6) A. B. Šimić, 'Poets' (tr. from Croatian with Daša Marić);
       (7) Aleksandar Petrov, three poems (tr. from Serbian with the
       author); (8) Tin Ujević, six poems (tr. from Croatian with Daša
       Marić); (9) Duška Vrhovac, five poems (tr. from Serbian with
       Vera V. Radojević. (*OOY*)

Unpublished material referred to in this book

2002–3 'Statement for *Love and Justice*'. (*SLJ*)
2007   '"My" Anne Frank, a memoir'. (*MAF*)
2008   'Ten Drachmas for a Pound'. (*TDP*)
2008   'Notes on *Avebury*'. (*NA*)

Awards, etc. (selected)

1972   Eric Gregory Award for Poetry.
1973   Arts Council of Great Britain: Writer's Grant.
1974   Keats Memorial Prize for Poetry.
1979–81 Arts Council of Great Britain Writer's Fellowship: Victoria
       Centre for Adult Education, Gravesend, Kent.
1982   Arvon Poetry Competition: Duncan Lawrie Award.
1990   Yeats Club: First Prize for translation.
1992   H. H. Wingate–*Jewish Quarterly* Award for Poetry.

1994 CELJ (Council of Learned Journals of America): Runner-up for
      'Best Special Issue 1994' (for *Out of Yugoslavia, North Dakota
      Quarterly*).
2003–5 Royal Literary Fund Fellowship: Newnham College,
      Cambridge.
2005 Morava Charter International Award for Poetry, Serbia.
2005–6 Royal Literary Fund Project Fellowship.
2007 *Veliki školski čas* [*The Great School Lesson*]: oratorio commem-
      orating the 1941 massacre at Šumarice, based on *Plavi leptir*
      (*The Blue Butterfly*), Kragujevac, Serbia.
2011 *Manada* Prize, Tetovo, Macedonia.
2012 Honorary citizenship of Kragujevac, Serbia.
2012 Fellow of the English Association.

Compiled by the editors and RB, May 2010
Revised and updated by Catherine E. Byfield and RB, June 2016

Notes on Contributors

Angus Calder (1942–2008), historian, poet, literary critic and editor, did his first degree in English at Cambridge, where he edited *Granta*, followed by a doctorate in History at Sussex. His book *The People's War* (1969) is a seminal work of social history. Subsequent books include *Russia Discovered*, on nineteenth-century Russian fiction (1976); *Revolutionary Empire* (1981); *The Myth of the Blitz* (1991); and *Gods, Mongrels and Demons* (2003). After teaching for three years at the University of Nairobi, in 1971 he, his first wife Jenni and their three children made their home in Edinburgh, where he taught for the Open University until 1993, becoming a notable figure in Scottish cultural life. In the early 1980s, Angus Calder helped set up the Scottish Poetry Library, having won a Gregory Award in 1967. His five volumes of poetry include *Waking in Waikato* (1997) and *Sun Behind the Castle* (2004).

Stefano Maria Casella is a university lecturer in English and Anglo-American literature, a literary critic, and poet. He has published essays on T. S. Eliot, Ezra Pound, Modernism, and comparative literature in editions such as *The International Reception of T. S. Eliot* (eds. S. Bagchee and E. Daümer, 2007), *The Ezra Pound Encyclopaedia* (eds. D. P. Tryphonopoulos and S. J. Adams, 2005), and *Ezra Pound and Poetic Influence* (ed. H. M. Dennis, 2000). Several other writings have also appeared in journals such as *Italian Americana, Ricerca Research Recherche, Paideuma* and *Lingua e Letteratura*. A life member of Clare Hall, Cambridge, he was a Visiting Fellow there (1996) and a Fellow in Literature at the Bogliasco Foundation-Liguria Study Centre for the Arts and Humanities (Genoa/New York, 2000). He is a regular speaker at literary conferences and symposia, and an active member of international literary organisations and cultural foundations, such as The Ezra Pound International Conference, the T. S. Eliot Society, A.I.S.N.A., the Bogliasco Foundation (Genoa) and the Romualdo Del Bianco Foundation (Florence). His poems have been published under the pseudonym D.M.M. in literary journals and in two anthologies: *Altramarea, Poesia come cosa viva* [*Altramarea. Poetry as a living thing*] (ed. Angelo Tonelli, 2006) and *Le Avventure della Bellezza* [*The Adventures of Beauty*] (ed. Tomaso Kemeny, 2008).

PAUL SCOTT DERRICK is a Senior Lecturer in American literature at the University of Valencia. His main fields of interest are Romanticism and American Transcendentalism and their manifestations in subsequent American literature and art. He has published two collections of essays in English and has co-authored a number of bilingual, critical editions of works by Ralph Waldo Emerson, Emily Dickinson and Henry Adams. He is co-editor of *Modernism Revisited: Transgressing Boundaries and Strategies of Renewal in American Poetry* (Rodopi, 2007). His most recent book-length publication is *La tierra de los abetos puntiagudos* (Biblioteca Javier Coy, 2008), a translation and critical study of Sarah Orne Jewett's *The Country of the Pointed Firs*. He has published translations into English of poems by Jorge Luis Borges, Luis Cernuda and Pablo Neruda and, with Miguel Teruel, co-translations of RB's poems into Spanish (*Las manos y la luz*, València, 2008).

MARIA FILIPPAKOPOULOU was born in Kalamata, Greece in 1968 and did her first degree in philosophy (Athens) and translation studies (Ionian University, Corfu). After completing her PhD at the University of Edinburgh, on 'Reflective operations in Edgar Allan Poe's transatlantic reception' (2003), she became Associate Director of the British Centre for Literary Translation at the University of East Anglia. In 2008, she became Research Fellow at the Institute for Advanced Studies in the Humanities at the University of Edinburgh. Besides translations into Greek (such as Richard Wolin's *The Seduction of Unreason. The Intellectual Romance with Fascism from Nietzsche to Postmodernism*, 2007), she writes and publishes on theoretical issues of translation and the reception of literary works. A recent paper is 'Translation drafts and the translating self', in *Translating Selves: Experience and Identity between Languages and Literatures*, eds. P. Nikolaou and M.-V. Kyritsi (Continuum, 2008).

ANDREW FRISARDI was born in Boston, Massachusetts. He graduated from Syracuse University with a Master of Fine Arts in 1996, and since 1999 has lived in Orvieto, Italy, where he teaches periodically at Gordon College. He has also trained as a psychotherapist, with a special emphasis on Jungian ideas and methods. He has published two books of poetry in translation. His *Giuseppe Ungaretti: Selected Poems* obtained the 2003 Raiziss/de Palchi Prize (Farrar, Straus and Giroux, 2002, 2004; and Carcanet, 2003). His selections from the Milanese poet Franco Loi, *Air and Memory*, appeared in 2007 (Counterpath Press, Denver). His translation and commentary of Dante's *Vita Nova* was published by Northwestern University Press in 2012. His poems, articles, reviews, and translations have appeared in *Atlantic Monthly, Hudson Review, Kenyon Review, New Republic, New Yorker, Poetry*, and other magazines and webzines.

Manana Gelashvili is a Professor of English at Tbilisi State University. She obtained her PhD for her dissertation on Coleridge, Wordsworth and the Romantic Imagination. She writes on many aspects of English and American literature, including James Joyce, Virginia Woolf, William Faulkner and Ezra Pound, as well as on translations from English into Georgian, and vice versa. Her latest book, *Drois Problema Modenistul Literaturasi* [*The Problem of Time in Modernist Literature*] (2005), focuses on the poetics of Modernist movements. Her critical studies on modern poetry include articles on Carmen Bugan, and Georgian poetry in English translation. She has also edited scholarly books on, *inter alia*, James Joyce and Somerset Maugham. Her translations from English and French include works by Paul Verlaine, Thomas Wolfe and T. S. Eliot. She is currently preparing, as a co-editor (with David Chandler), *Collected Essays on English Literature Today.*

John Gery is a poet and critic of modern and contemporary poetry. Among his books of poetry are *Charlemagne: A Song of Gestures* (1983), *The Enemies of Leisure* (1995), *American Ghost: Selected Poems* (English-Serbian, translated by Biljana Obradović, 1999), *Davenport's Version* (2003), and *A Gallery of Ghosts* (2008). Other books include *Nuclear Annihilation and Contemporary American Poetry: Ways of Nothingness* (1996), (with others) *In Venice and in the Veneto with Ezra Pound* (2007), and (with Vahe Baladouni) *Hmayeak Shems: Armenian Poet of Pure Spirit* (2010). A Research Professor of English at the University of New Orleans, John Gery directs the Ezra Pound Center for Literature, Brunnenburg, Italy, and is Secretary of the Ezra Pound International Conference. In 2006, he was a Research Fellow at the University of Minnesota, and in 2007 a Fulbright Fellow at the University of Belgrade.

Mick Gowar is a writer, poet, performer and workshop leader. Since 1980, he has written or edited more than 120 books for children and young people, and has visited schools, libraries, colleges and festivals in the UK and other countries to give readings and performances and to lead workshops. A part-time lecturer at the Cambridge School of Art at Anglia Ruskin University, he has taught courses in creative writing both at Anglia Ruskin and at the University of Northumbria. He has contributed regularly to courses at the Arvon Foundation and the National Centre for Writers in Wales, and undertaken educational projects for the Philharmonia Orchestra, Scottish Chamber Orchestra, Sinfonia 21, Fitzwilliam Museum and Kettle's Yard Gallery, Cambridge. A member of the Cambridge Poetry Festival Society from 1975 to 1986, he was Co-ordinator of the 1981 Cambridge Poetry Festival.

Jeremy Hooker, Emeritus Professor at Glamorgan University, was born near Southampton in 1941, and educated at Southampton University. He has taught English and creative writing at universities in England, the Netherlands, the USA, and Wales, retiring as Professor of English at the University of Glamorgan in 2008. *The Cut of the Light: Poems 1965–2005* (Enitharmon, 2006) is a substantial selection from his ten volumes of poetry. His other books include: *Welsh Journal* (Seren, 2001); *Upstate: A North American Journal* (Shearsman Books, 2007); *Writers in a Landscape* (University of Wales Press, 1996) and *Imagining Wales: A View of Modern Welsh Writing in English* (University of Wales Press, 2001). He has edited selections of writings by Frances Bellerby, Richard Jefferies, Alun Lewis, Wilfred Owen and Edward Thomas. His features for BBC Radio 3 include *A Map of David Jones*, first broadcast in 1995.

Svetozar Ignjačević (1938–2002) was a professor of English, literary critic and translator. After taking his MA and then his PhD at the Philological Faculty in Belgrade, with a thesis on the English novel between the two World Wars, he taught English Literature at higher schools and universities in Prizren, Priština and Niš, returning to Belgrade to become a Professor of English at the Philological Faculty in 1981. An active member of the Serbian Writers' Association, he translated fiction, criticism and works on literary, art and film theory from English, including books by Irwin Panofsky (1975), Philip Roth (1979, 1982), Murray Krieger (1982) and D. H. Lawrence (1988). He published many essays, studies and articles in leading Yugoslav scholarly and literary periodicals, and wrote two books of critical essays on Anglophone writers in Yugoslavia, under the title *Wonderland Through a Cracked Mirror* (1994 and 2000). His essay in this volume is taken from the second of these volumes.

Simon Jenner was born in Cuckfield, Sussex in 1959. Failing everything at school except art, he learnt to fly instead, but discovering poetry forestalled a career in airframes. He was belatedly educated at Leeds, then Cambridge, where his PhD topic was 'Oxford Poetry of the 1940s'. He undertook poetry tours in Germany (1996, 1997) and published two volumes there in the same years, with parallel texts in English and German. He received a South East Arts Bursary (1999) and Royal Literary Fund grants (2003, 2006). His first British collection, *About Bloody Time*, was published by Waterloo Press (2007). He has directed Survivors' Poetry since 2003 and has been a Royal Literary Fund Fellow, first at the University of East London (2008–2009), and then at Chichester University (2009–2010).

Francis R. Jones studied modern languages at Cambridge and Yugoslav poetry at Sarajevo University. He has an MA from Reading and a PhD from Newcastle, both in applied linguistics, and he teaches translation studies at Newcastle University. He translates poetry from Bosnian-Croatian-Serbian and Dutch, plus Hungarian, Russian and Dutch creoles, into English, Yorkshire and Northumbrian. His fifteen book-length poetry translations have won eleven prizes in Europe and the USA. He has been the only person to win the UK's European Poetry Translation Prize twice: in 1991 and (jointly) in 1997, for translations from the works of the Serbian poet Ivan V. Lalić. His translations from the Croatian poet Drago Štambuk, Bosnian poets Mak Dizdar and Skender Kulenović, and Dutch poet Hans Faverey have also won awards. He has written extensively about poetry and translation, especially from ex-Yugoslavia. A collection of his travel essays and articles, *Prevoditeljev put* [*Translator's Road*], appeared in 2004 from Buybook, Sarajevo.

Norman Jope has published four books of poems: *For The Wedding-Guest* (Stride Publications, 1997); *The Book of Bells and Candles* (Waterloo Press, 2009), *Dreams of the Caucasus* (Shearsman Books, 2010) and *Aphinar* (Waterloo Press, 2011). With the late Ian Robinson, he co-edited the anthology *In the Presence of Sharks: New Poetry from Plymouth* (Phlebas, 2006) and he has edited the literary/cultural magazine *Memes*. His poetry and criticism have appeared in many magazines, webzines and anthologies, including *Tears in the Fence, Poetry Salzburg Review* and *Terrible Work*, and his poems are currently being translated into Romanian. Born in Plymouth, Norman Jope has lived in other UK cities, most recently Swindon and Bristol, and in Budapest. He currently works as an administrator at University College Plymouth St Mark and St John.

TEMUR KOBAKHIDZE is Chair of the Department of English at Metekhi National University, Tbilisi, Georgia. His research and academic interests focus on twentieth-century British and American modernist literature and the literary aesthetics of Modernism, with special attention to the structural functions of myth in modernist poetry, prose and drama. His publications include *Myth and the Literary Aesthetics of Modernism* (1998), *T. S. Eliot: Poetry and Mythos* (1991) and *Hereditary Poetics: John Donne, W. B. Yeats, T. S. Eliot* (1984), as well as numerous articles and chapters in books. He is a member of various learned and professional societies, including the International T. S. Eliot Society, the T. S. Eliot Society of the United Kingdom, and the International Association of University Professors of English (IAUPE). He is presently writing a book on modernist literature and the culture of Italy.

ZDENÉK KŘIVSKÝ graduated from the Prague Institute of Chemical Technology (ICT), received a Fellowship from the Technological Institute in Leningrad, earned his doctoral degree from the Czechoslovak Academy of Science, and was a Visiting Professor at the Catholic University of Leuven (1990). He has co-authored 40 scientific papers and has been granted several international patents on gas absorption. After the Prague student protests of May 1962, he was expelled from the ICT and sent to work on the construction of a petrochemical plant. During the Prague Spring of 1968, he was a member of the regional leadership of the non-communist movement, for which he was banned from university teaching and had his passport seized for several years. After the 1989 Velvet Revolution, he was co-opted as an MP. In the 1990s he directed the North Bohemian Economic Association, an NGO assisting transformation of regional industry. He presently directs a consulting company and lives in North Bohemia.

PHILIP KUHN Poet, historian, designer, book-binder, photographer, archivist and audio artist, philip kuhn currently lives on Dartmoor from where he also co-hosts the 'occasional readings series'. His historical articles have appeared in psychoanalytic journals in England, America and Germany. He founded *itinerant press* in July 2007 and has produced and published six limited edition hand-bound books. Three of his own book-length poems have been published: *at maimonides' table* (Shearsman Books 2009), *paradoxes becoming* and *how to make radical leaflets* (itinerant press 2009 and 2011, respectively). With Ruth von Zimmermann he has also translated some late poems by Gertrud Kolmar (1894-1943), published as *Worlds* (Shearsman Books, 2012). He is also an occasional contributor to *Tremblestone* and *Shearsman*. Other recent projects include *cracking texts* (exploring relationships between images and words) and *a walk along the leat*, a sectional mapping (in sound and image) of the leat from which he and his partner Rosie draw their water.

Dídac Llorens Cubedo is a researcher at the Universitat Jaume I, in Castelló, Spain, where he also teaches English literature. He has taught Spanish in Northern Ireland, and Spanish and Catalan at Fitzwilliam College and the Faculty of Modern and Medieval Languages of the University of Cambridge. He has recently completed a comparative study of the poetic imagination of T. S. Eliot and the Catalan poet Salvador Espriu, and co-edited *New Literatures of Old: Dialogues of Tradition and Innovation in Anglophone Literature* (2008).

John Lucas, Professor Emeritus of English at the Universities of Loughborough and Nottingham Trent, is a poet, writer, publisher, jazz musician and former enthusiastic cricketer. His eight books of poems include *About Nottingham* (Byron Press, 1971), *A World Perhaps, New and Selected Poems* (Sow's Ear Press, 2002), *Field Music* (2006) and, most recently, *Flute Music*. His many critical works include *The Radical Twenties: Writing, Politics, Culture* (Five Leaves, 1997) and *Starting to Explain: Essays on 20th Century British and Irish Poetry* (2003). His translation of the poems of *Egils Saga* is an Everyman Modern Classic (Dent, 1985), and his book about Greece, *92 Acharnon Street*, won the Author's Club Dolman Award for Best Travel Book of 2007. He also runs Shoestring Press.

Andrija Matić is a literary critic and writer. His primary critical fields are Anglo-American Modernism and European twentieth-century literature. He has published essays on James Thomson ('B.V.'), James Joyce, T. S. Eliot, Gottfried Benn, George Orwell, Dylan Thomas, Paul Auster, Ian McEwan and William Trevor. He is the author of the first Serbian study of Eliot, entitled *T. S. Eliot: Poet, Critic, Playwright* (2007). Besides literary criticism, he writes fiction. His novels include *The Disappearance of Zdenko Kupresanin* (2006) and *Manhole* (2009). He lives in Belgrade, Serbia.

Neli Moody is a poet and a lecturer at San Jose State University, where she teaches composition and creative writing. She received her M.F.A. in Creative Writing from SJSU. She has received numerous awards for her work, including the Phelan Award and the Virginia Araujo Award sponsored by the American Academy of Poetry. *After Altamira*, published by Ishmael Reed Publishing Company in 2006, was nominated for a National Book Award. Her work has appeared in such publications as *Brick and Mortar Review, Konch Magazine, Art Times, Appalachian Heritage,* and *Reed Magazine.* Her multicultural background and lifelong studies in dance, music, and art have informed her poetry and scholarly work, and formed the foundation of her unique multidisciplinary approach to her classes.

Antoinette Moses is a playwright and author. She has published prize-winning educational novellas for Cambridge University Press and her plays have received rehearsed readings and performances in Norwich, Cambridge, London and Paris. Her stage plays include: *Autumn* (2001); *The Colours In Between,* 2002); *Soutine* (2005); *Interval* (2007); and the work-in-progress *Cuts,* extracts from which were short-listed for the Samuel Beckett Theatre Trust Award (2008). A former journalist and editor, Antoinette Moses has written and presented two television series for Channel 4 on film animation, and she directed the Cambridge Animation Festival from 1979 to 1984. She has recently completed a creative/critical PhD on authorship and ownership in contemporary verbatim theatre, entitled *Constructing the Real,* at the University of East Anglia, where she teaches creative writing. She lives in Norwich.

Mario Nicolao is a poet, essayist and classical scholar who lives in Genoa, where, since 2003, he has published and co-edited the international journal of poetry, poetics, art and aesthetics, *Chorus,* in collaboration with his son, the philosopher and translator from French, Federico Nicolao. Mario Nicolao's books include *La maschera di Rossini* [*The Mask of Rossini*] (Rizzoli, 1990); *Il viaggio di Odisseo* [*The Voyage of Odysseus*], with Vincenzo Consolo (Bompiani, 1999); and a selection of poems *Carte Perse* [*Lost Pages*] (Edizione San Lorenzo, 2001). His essays appear regularly in *Chorus.*

Paschalis Nikolaou completed his doctoral studies at the University of East Anglia, supported by an Alexander S. Onassis Foundation scholarship, with a thesis entitled 'The Translating Self: Literary Translations and Life-Writing'. He currently teaches literary translation at the Ionian University in Corfu, Greece. He is the co-editor of *Translating Selves: Experience and Identity between Languages and Literatures* (Continuum, 2008). His reviews, translations and poetry have appeared in *The London Magazine*, *MPT*, *Etchings*, *The Wolf* and other periodicals. His essays have been published in edited volumes, such as *Translating and Interpreting Conflict* (Rodopi, 2007). With RB, he has edited *Nasos Vayenas. The Perfect Order: Selected Poems 1974–2010* (Anvil Press Poetry, 2010).

Aleksandar Petrov writes in Serbian and Russian and has published over 25 books, including poetry, fiction, criticism, literary theory and history. He has lectured at many universities in the USA and other countries and, since 1993, has been affiliated with the University of Pittsburgh. Among his most recent publications are three novels: *Zlato u vatri* [*Like Gold in Fire*] (1998), *Turski Beč* [*Turkish Vienna*] (2000) and *Lavlja pećina* [*The Lion's Cave*] (2004). His poems have been translated into 28 languages and his books have appeared in former Yugoslavia, China, Hong Kong, Israel, Japan, Poland, Romania, Spain, Sweden, Taiwan, the UK, and the USA. In 2004, he received the Lucian Blaga Major Poetry Award in Romania, and in 2008 an award in Moscow as the best Russian-language poet writing in the Russian diaspora.

Mark Pirie is an internationally known New Zealand poet, fiction writer, editor and small press publisher (HeadworX). He has published twenty-one books of poetry, including the selection *Gallery* (Salt, 2003), as well as a book of short stories and a book of song lyrics. His critical writings have appeared in more than ten countries, and an early essay of his appeared in the *Journal of Commonwealth Literature* while he was a postgraduate student at the University of Otago, Dunedin. He contributed an 8,000-word introduction to his anthology of 'Generation X' New Zealand writing, *The NeXt Wave* (University of Otago Press, 1998) and he has written poetry reviews and articles for *brief* (NZ), *Jacket* (Australia), *JAAM* (NZ), *New Zealand Books*, *Poetry NZ* and *Southern Ocean Review* (NZ).

Gabriele Poole was born in Naples, Italy in 1963. His father is North-American and his mother Italian, and he spent part of his childhood in the US before moving back to Italy. He studied English and Swedish literature at the Istituto Universitario Orientale in Naples and holds a PhD in English from the University of Notre Dame, where his dissertation was on Byron. He currently teaches English Language and Translation at the University of Cassino. He has written on English literature, theatre, and language theory, and he has edited and translated into Italian a selection of poems by John Matthias, *Nuotando a Mezzanotte / Swimming at Midnight* (Dante and Descartes, Naples, 2008). He has translated most of the Italian section of www.poetryinternational.org.

PATRICK QUERY is an Assistant Professor of English at the United States Military Academy at West Point, New York. He has published articles and chapters on T. S. Eliot, W. B. Yeats, Evelyn Waugh, Graham Greene, and W. H. Auden, and he is an Associate Editor of the *Evelyn Waugh Newsletter and Studies*. His recently completed book manuscript, *The Idea of Europe in Ritual and Writing, 1919–1939*, deals with how British and Irish writers of the interwar years used verse drama, bullfighting, and Catholic ritual to explore ideas of European identity. He is currently working on a project exploring RB's poetic response to T. S. Eliot.

VERA RADOJEVIĆ has translated the first two parts of RB's *Balkan Trilogy* into Serbian (*The Blue Butterfly* and *In a Time of Drought*) and she has recently finished working on the third part (*Under Balkan Light*). Her translation of *In a Time of Drought* (*U vreme suše*, RAD, Belgrade, 2004) was awarded the international *Morava Charter* prize. Her translation of *The Blue Butterfly* (*Plavi leptir*, Plava tačka, Belgrade, 2008) received the *Veliki školski čas* [*Great School Lesson*] award in Kragujevac, and extracts from the Serbian text were performed as an open-air oratorio at Šumarice on 21 October 2008, in commemoration of victims of the 1941 Nazi massacre there. She has also translated RB's *Do vidjenje Danice: Goodbye Balkan Belle* and *Black Light*, both of which have appeared in bilingual editions, the former from Srpska književna zadruga, Belgrade, 2012; and the latter from KOV, Vršac, 2013. With RB she has co-translated a book of poems by Duška Vrhovac, *I Wear My Shadow Inside Me* (Forest Books, 1991) and a collection of epigrams by Vito Marković.

SLOBODAN RAKITIĆ (1940-2013) was born in Raška, Southern Serbia in 1940, and went to secondary school in Novi Pazar. He studied at the Faculty of Medicine in Belgrade before graduating from the Philological Faculty. He edited several leading literary journals, including *Knjizevna reč* [*Literary Word*] and *Savremenik* [*Contemporary*]. As author of more than twenty books of poems, his *Selected Works* appeared in an edition of five volumes (Belgrade, 1994). He received more than a dozen major literary prizes in Serbia, and his poems have been translated into fourteen languages, including *L'Age d'Homme* (Lausanne, 1990), and bilingual collections in Romanian and Czech. Slobodan Rakitić was President of the Writers' Association of Serbia (1994–2004), and at the time of his death was President of the Serbian Literary Cooperative.

TESSA RANSFORD (1938-2015) published more than seventeen poetry collections and contributed essays, reviews, poems and articles to many anthologies and journals. An established poet, translator and literary editor, she was a cultural activist on many fronts. She was president of Scottish PEN (2003–2006), founder and director of the Scottish Poetry Library (1984–1999), and editor of *Lines Review* (1988–1998). She initiated the annual Callum Macdonald Memorial Award for publishers of pamphlet poetry in Scotland, with the attendant fairs and online sales (website: www.scottish-pamphlet-poetry.com), and she held Royal Literary Fund fellowships at the Centre for Human Ecology and Queen Margaret University.

MARGARET SETCHELL has a degree in English Literature from the University of Exeter and an HND in Fine Art (Contemporary Practice) from Anglia Polytechnic University. She has woven an alternative career path for herself as a teacher, in pursuit of a creative, cross-curricular education for children. From large comprehensive to small primary, she now stays on the edge of the system, teaching part-time in school, while leading freelance workshops for the Wildlife Trust and in country parks. She is married to a musician and has two sons.

P. S. SRI is a Professor of Comparative Literature in the Department of English at the Royal Military College, Kingston, Ontario. His research includes East-West literary and philosophical ideosynthesis, post-colonial, multicultural, Commonwealth literature, Arabic and Persian literature, and Sanskrit and Tamil literature. His academic publications include *T. S. Eliot, Vedanta and Buddhism* (University of British Columbia, 1985) – now translated into Korean – and articles on Margaret Laurence, Bharati Mukherjee, Yeats, Shaw, Eliot, Forster and Rumi, and Sanskrit and Tamil literature. He has also published a novel, *The Temple Elephant* (New Horizon Media Pvt. Ltd., 2007) and his trans-*creation* in English of a modern Tamil historical romance, Kalki's *Sivakamiyin Sabadam* [*Sivakami's Vow*] (Sahitya Akademi, 2008), running to 853 pages. He has received many awards and won literary prizes.

CHEE LAY TAN's books of poems include: *Chi Chu Cheng Xing* [*Walking Alone*], 1997; *Chen Zhi Rui Shi Xuan* [*Tan Chee Lay's Poetry Collection*], 1999; and *Zao Jian Di* [*Where Swords are Forged*], 2002. His prose publications include: *Si Shu* [*The Four Books*], 1999, co-authored with J. F. Pan, D. C. Zhou and Y. B. Ke; *Ge An Guan Wo* [*Gazing At Myself from the Opposite Shore*], critical works and essays, 2000; *Lao Shi de Zuo Ye Ben* [*Sir's Homework*], prose and short stories, 2004; *Huang Se de Yu Yi* [*The Yellow Raincoat*], 2006; and *Chu Ren Yi Liao, Ru Wen Yi Zhong* [*The Unexpectedness of Literature*], 2009. Born in Singapore in 1973, Chee Lay Tan took his PhD at Cambridge University. His thesis was on Chinese poetry with particular focus on poets of exile. He is currently Assistant Professor in Chinese at Nanyang Technological University (NTU), Singapore, and Deputy Executive Director of the Singapore Centre for Chinese Language, NTU.

NASOS VAYENAS was born in the city of Drama, Greece in 1945. His volumes of poetry include *Field of Mars* (1974), *Biography* (1978), *Roxane's Knees* (1981), *Travels of a Stay-at-Home* (1986), *Flyer's Fall* (1989), *Barbarous Odes* (1992), *Dark Ballads and Other Poems* (2001) and *Garland* (2004). Currently a Professor at the University of Athens, he is author of a number of critical books and works on literary theory, including: *Poetry and Translation* (1989), *The Language of Irony* (1993), *Notes from the End of the Century* (1999) and *Postmodernism and Literature* (2002). He has edited the anthology *Conversing with Cavafy* (2000). He is the recipient of many literary awards, including the Greek National Prize for Poetry (2005), the Attilio Bertolucci poetry prize (Italy, 2007), and the Branko Radičević Prize (Serbia, 2007). His books have been translated into Bulgarian, German, Italian, Romanian, Serbian and English, the most recent being *Nasos Vayenas. The Perfect Order: Selected Poems 1974–2010* (eds. RB and Paschalis Nikolaou, London: Anvil Press Poetry, 2010).

RĂZVAN VONCU is a Lecturer in the Department of Romanian Literature in the Faculty of Letters at Bucharest University. He teaches medieval and contemporary Romanian literature, as well as courses in cultural studies. He has published eight books of literary history and criticism, two books of journalism, and a diary. He is a regular contributor to some of the most important cultural reviews of Romania and Serbia; and he has received several prestigious literary prizes, including the Romanian Academy Prize for Literary Criticism (2003). He is a member of the Writers' Union of Serbia and a founder member of the Association of Literary Critics of Romania. Together with Simona Drăgan, he is currently preparing the first translation of RB's work into Romanian, a version of *In a Time of Drought*.

STEPHEN WILSON is a Fellow of the Royal College of Psychiatrists and was formerly Consultant and Honorary Senior Clinical Lecturer in the Department of Psychiatry, University of Oxford. Having retired from a professional career in medicine, he now devotes himself entirely to work as a poet and literary critic. His first collection, *Fluttering Hands*, was published in 2008. He is also the author of *The Bloomsbury Book of the Mind* (2003), *Introducing the Freud Wars* (2003), *Sigmund Freud, A Pocket Biography* (1997), *The Cradle of Violence: Essays on Psychiatry, Psychoanalysis and Literature* (1995) and a synoptic biography of Isaac Rosenberg (2010). In 2013 he published a major study of Anglo-Jewish poetry, *Poetics of the Diaspora*, and a second collection of poems, *Things Hard for Thought*. He has also translated two early works by Irène Némirovsky: *Le Pion sur l'échiquier* (*The Pawn on the Chessboard*) and *L'enfant génial* (*The Child Prodigy*).

CRAIG WOELFEL is an Assistant Professor in English at Flagler College, Florida. He earned his PhD from the University of Notre Dame, with specialisations in British and American literature and the history of aesthetics. His dissertation focused on varieties of aesthetic and religious experience and literary modernism, and his current research interests continue to combine literature, aesthetic theory, and religious and cultural studies. He has published essays on T. S. Eliot and E. M. Forster.

Wyatt, Thomas, 39, 221, 223

Yakutia (Siberia), 398
Yates, Francis,
    *Giordano Bruno and the Hermetic
        Tradition*, 232
Yeats, William Butler, 32, 48, 49, 51, 69,
    88, 138, 144, 169, 309, 337, 373
'Second Coming, The', 138, 169, 309
Yggdrasil, 169, 328, 331
Young, Julian, 101
Yu, Pauline, 268
Yugoslav Federation, 286, 288, 316
Yugoslavia, 2, 4, 6, 36, 46, 51, 64, 76, 88,
    105, 183–6, 234, 285–6, 288–90, 293,
    296–7, 299–300, 302–5, 307, 308–13,
    315, 332–3, 338–9, 348, 350, 370,
    372, 374, 377–8, 399

Zagreb, 288, 303
Zemun, 309, 312
Zeno, 92, 160
Zeus, 99
Zhou, Zhuang, 46
Zion, 57, 103, 111, 112
Zukofsky, Louis, 260